THE SHORT PROSE READER

FOURTH EDITION

Gilbert H. Muller

Harvey S. Wiener

*The City University of New York,
LaGuardia*

McGRAW-HILL BOOK COMPANY

*New York   St. Louis   San Francisco   Auckland
Bogotá   Hamburg   Johannesburg   London   Madrid
Mexico   Milan   Montreal   New Delhi   Panama   Paris
São Paulo   Singapore   Sydney   Tokyo   Toronto*

THE SHORT PROSE READER

1234567890 BKPBKP 89432109876

ISBN 0-07-044021-2

This book was set in Century Schoolbook
by Monotype Composition Company, Inc.
The editors were Emily G. Barrosse and David Dunham;
the cover designer was Joan E. O'Connor;
the production supervisor was Leroy A. Young.
The Book Press, Inc., was printer and binder.
Cover painting: *Girl Reading* by Jean Auguste Renior
(Three Lions).

Library of Congress Cataloging-in-Publication Data

The Short prose reader.

  Bibliography: p.
  1. College readers.   2. English language—Rhetoric.
I. Muller, Gilbert H., date.   II. Weiner,
Harvey S.
PE1417.S446 1987   808'.0427   86-10408
ISBN 0-07-044021-2

See Acknowledgments on page 422.
Copyrights included on this page by reference.

ABOUT THE AUTHORS

Gilbert H. Muller, who received a Ph.D. in English and American Literature from Stanford University, is currently professor of English at LaGuardia Community College of the City University of New York. He has also taught at Stanford, Vassar, and several universities overseas. Dr. Muller is the author of the award-winning study *Nightmares and Visions: Flannery O'Connor and the Catholic Grostesque* and other critical texts. His essays and reviews have appeared in *The New York Times, The New Republic, The Nation,* the *Sewanee Review,* the *Georgia Review,* and elsewhere. He is also a noted author and editor of textbooks in English and composition, including *The McGraw-Hill Reader,* and, with John Williams, *The McGraw-Hill Introduction to Literature.* Among Dr. Muller's awards are a National Endowment for the Humanities Fellowship, a Fulbright Fellowship, and a Mellon Fellowship.

Harvey S. Wiener, professor of English at LaGuardia Community College of the City University of New York, codirects the National Testing Network in Writing (NTNW) and College Assessment Program Evaluation (CAPE). He was founding president of the Council of Writing Program Administrators. Dr. Wiener is the author of many books on reading and writing for college students and their teachers, including *The Writing Room* (Oxford, 1981). He is coauthor with Richard Marius of *The McGraw-Hill College Handbook,* a reference grammar and rhetoric text. Dr. Wiener is a member of the Standing Committee on Assessment for the National Council of Teachers of English, and he is chair of the Teaching of Writing Division of the Modern Language Association (1987). He has taught writing at every level of education from elementary school to graduate school. A Phi Beta Kappa graduate of Brooklyn College, he holds a Ph.D. in Renaissance literature from Fordham University. Dr. Wiener has won grants from the National Endowment for the Humanities, the Fund for the Improvement of Postsecondary Education, and the Exxon Education Foundation.

CONTENTS

Preface   xix

1 ON WRITING   1

Eudora Welty ONE WRITER'S BEGINNINGS   5
Beginnings are mysterious. An award-winning,
internationally renowned writer tells us of the childhood
perceptions that helped shape her life and career.

Dan Greenburg HOW I OVERHAULED MY
MECHANIC'S NOVEL   12
According to author Dan Greenburg, writers can be just
as unscrupulous as car mechanics—if they set their
minds to it.

Norman Cousins WHY JOHNNY CAN'T WRITE   20
The "intricate and highly demanding art" of good
writing is not *flourishing in America's schools, according*
to this well-known writer, editor, and social analyst.

William Zinsser SIMPLICITY   28
According to this writer-teacher, "clutter is the disease
of American writing." We must simplify. In this essay,
Zinsser connects clear writing to clear thinking, which,
he declares, doesn't appear nearly enough these days.

2 DESCRIPTION   40

Truman Capote   LOUIS ARMSTRONG   42
*From descriptions of the "pleasure steamer that paddled
between New Orleans and St. Louis" to an unashamed
declaration of love, we learn of "The Satch's" far-
reaching and long-lasting effects on one of America's
most controversial writers.*

Jade Snow Wong   UNCLE KWOK   47
*The curious routine of an unusual man arouses feelings
of both love and fear in this childhood reminiscence.*

William Least Heat Moon   ARIZONA 87   53
*Drive with this writer through the Arizona desert and
into its mountains: The landscape is sometimes,
"reminiscent of old Chinese woodblock prints," but the
towns have "no center, no focus for the eye and soul."*

Richard Selzer   THE DISCUS THROWER   61
*A surgeon and an author offers a chilling, yet moving
and dignified, description of a patient's last day.*

3 NARRATION   69

Elizabeth Wong   THE STRUGGLE TO BE AN ALL-
AMERICAN GIRL   71
*In a narrative of her youth, a writer remembers her
efforts to obtain "a cultural divorce" from the heritage
into which she was born.*

Langston Hughes   SALVATION   79
*One of America's foremost poets tells of his childhood
disillusionment as he struggles desperately to see Jesus.*

Al Young   JAVA JIVE   86
*A fact of nature, which occurs perhaps millions of times
each day, is the basis for this childhood memoir that
leads us to the author's understanding of "the cosmic
drama."*

Goerge Orwell   A HANGING   97
*The renowned author of 1984 discovers how precious
human life is as he tells of witnessing an execution in*

*Burma. "It is curious," he recalls, "but till that moment, I
had never realized what it meant to destroy a healthy,
conscious man."*

4 ILLUSTRATION 109

Edwin Newman   BAYBUH, BAYBUH . . . 111
*A popular television and radio commentator tells of a
term he seems to hear too much and understand
too little.*

Randall Williams   DADDY TUCKED THE BLANKET 118
*A contemporary journalist shows what it means to be
poor and how the environment of poverty can
destroy families.*

Ray Bradbury   TRICKS! TREATS! GANGWAY! 127
*Here from the noted science fiction writer is the wonder
of Halloween, 1928, with all its gorilla fangs, pumpkin
pies, creaking stairs, black confetti, banshee trains, and
much more.*

Lewis Thomas   DEATH IN THE OPEN 138
*This biologist and popular writer says that death "is a
natural marvel" throughout the universe of animals and
plants; and that humans, sharing a kinship with other
life forms, will have to stop seeing death as a catastrophe.*

5 COMPARISON AND CONTRAST 147

Rachel Carson   A FABLE FOR TOMORROW 149
*One of America's most celebrated naturalists warns us
of the future in a grim contrast between a flourishing
environment and a destroyed landscape plagued by a
mysterious curse.*

Russell Baker   THE TWO ISMO'S 156
*The ammunition in this columnist's "urban war zone"
includes quiche, kiwi fruit, zippered plastic briefcases,
and gourmet Swedish toothpaste as he explores two
social doctrines:* machismo *and* quichismo.

Bruno Bettelheim FAIRY TALES AND
MODERN STORIES   164
One of the world's foremost child psychologists explains
that traditional fairy tales give solace to children, but
that modern tales "fail to provide the escape and
consolation that children need."

Roger D. McGrath THE MYTH OF FRONTIER
VIOLENCE   172
A history professor believes that our own society may
indeed be more "shoot-'em-up" than that
of the Old West.

6 DEFINITION   181

Ellen Goodman AN UNDERSTANDING WOMAN   183
Is the capacity for "sympathetic comprehension" awesome
or awful? According to Ellen Goodman, it's a little of
each, and its personal effects may be a mixed blessing
as well.

Suzanne Britt Jordan FUN, OH BOY. FUN.
YOU COULD DIE FROM IT.   191
If you've ever felt that you should have been having fun
but that somehow you weren't, this essay proves that
you're not alone.

Gregg Easterbrook ESCAPE VALVE   199
One of the results of modern living, according to this
writer, is the "automatic-out," a means for avoiding long-
term commitments. Here, he explains this trend toward
escaping responsibilities, a trend that produces serious
results in the way we develop relationships.

Elizabeth Janeway SOAPS, CYNICISM,
AND MIND CONTROL   207
Randomness as a way of life may work out just fine on
television, but real life isn't the same as TV. Are we, a
nation of video addicts, in danger of mind control by the
Media Establishment?

7 CLASSIFICATION 217

Judith Viorst FRIENDS, GOOD FRIENDS—AND
SUCH GOOD FRIENDS 219
*This popular writer believes that friendships "are
conducted at many levels of intensity" and "meet different
needs." Here she categorizes eight types of friends,
including Convenience friends, Historical friends, and
Crossroads friends.*

E. B. White THE THREE NEW YORKS 229
*Natives, commuters, and those who come searching:
These are the inhabitants of E. B. White's three cities in
one in this fascinating look at the world's most talked
about city.*

Noel Perrin COUNTRY CODES 236
*How do "town-bred people who live in rural areas" cope
with the strange rules of country living? A Vermonter
shows how to talk, act, and get things done far from the
urban scene.*

James T. Baker HOW DO WE FIND THE STUDENT
IN A WORLD OF ACADEMIC GYMNASTS AND
WORKER ANTS? 247
*This gently cynical essay introduces twelve types of
students everyone knows and loves—including among
others, the Performer, the Jock, the Lost Soul, the Worker
Ant, and finally,* the Student.

8 PROCESS ANALYSIS 256

Sam Negri LOAFING MADE EASY 258
*Here are all the do's and don'ts of "America's most
treasured art form": the art of simply doing nothing.*

Leo Rosten HOW TO TELL A JOKE 265
*Did you ever tell a joke that nobody laughed at? Then,
you'd better learn this joke-teller's "three simple rules"
and "six basic tips."*

Grace Lichtenstein   COORS BEER   273
Investigating the most famous beer in the West, this
reporter unlocks the secret to "the Coors mystique."

Ernest Hemingway   CAMPING OUT   280
Avoiding insects. Getting a good rest. Cooking trout just
right. This essay can make anyone's next camping trip
a success.

9   CAUSE-AND-EFFECT ANALYSIS   288

Anne Roiphe   WHY MARRIAGES FAIL   291
In the United States, new marriages have a 50 percent
chance of succeeding—or failing, depending on your
outlook. A contemporary novelist explains in this essay
why "happily ever after" may become an extinct phrase.

Boyce Rensberger   WHY YOU LIKE SOME FOODS
AND HATE OTHERS   302
"There is no accounting for taste," the old saying goes,
but this essay tells what genetic, cultural, and sensory
factors help determine what will and what will not
taste good.

Linda Bird Francke   THE AMBIVALENCE
OF ABORTION   312
Political convictions and personal experience make an
unforgettable mix in this haunting essay about abortion.

Susan Jacoby   WHEN BRIGHT GIRLS DECIDE THAT
MATH IS "A WASTE OF TIME"   323
A one-time straight-A algebra student explains why
math and science are a no-woman's land for promising
young scholars.

10   ARGUMENTATION AND
     PERSUASION   333

Howard Scott   VEGETABLE GARDENS ARE
FOR THE BIRDS   336
An "earth widower" argues in favor of cellophane-
wrapped, pale dry store-bought vegetables and against
those that are too crispy or tangy for his tastes.

Joseph Wood Krutch   THE VANDAL AND
THE SPORTSMAN   343
*Sports hunters are evil and their joy lies in the
destruction of God's creatures. So argues a lifelong
naturalist in this emotionally charged essay.*

Judy Syfers   I WANT A WIFE   351
*Author, wife, and mother, Judy Syfers ironically argues
that men often take wives for granted. "My God," she
concludes, "who wouldn't want a wife?"*

Rachel L. Jones   WHAT'S WRONG WITH
BLACK ENGLISH   358
*"Y'all crazy if you ain't gon vote for me." No voter would
choose a top politician who spoke that way, says a black
college student in this argument against black English
as a viable language in its own right.*

11   PROSE FOR FURTHER READING   366

Lillian Hellman   MEMOIR OF A NEW ORLEANS
BOARDING HOUSE   367
*The famous playwright fondly remembers an American
way of life "completely replaced now by the ugly,
cold motel."*

Akira Kurosawa   BABYHOOD   371
*Babyhood memories are "a form resembling out-of-focus
bits of film footage," says a modern cinematographer in
this essay about his own infancy.*

Maya Angelou   THE FIGHT   374
*When Joe Louis defeated Max Schmeling for the
heavyweight championship in 1936, more than just a
boxing title was at stake.*

Garrison Keillor   A RETURN TO BASICS:
MEALTIME WITHOUT GUILT   378
*Do you prefer a meal to be "a joyous, life-affirming
experience" or "a truly unique dining experience"? This
writer-radio commentator longs for unsophisticated
meals and offers guidelines for getting "back to basics
in the food line."*

Richard M. Restak   THE OTHER DIFFERENCE
BETWEEN BOYS AND GIRLS   382
*A neurologist and writer leaps into a provocative
controversy over the ways that males and females think.*

Judy Klemesrud   SPORTORIAL SPLENDOR   387
*When you visit a friend and wear your "sweats" are you:
announcing your love of sports? dressed for comfort?
worried about "social-connectedness"? seeking status?
What really does lie behind the $650 million annual
sales in sweatsuits alone, not counting the layers of other
sports clothes?*

Nora Ephron   LIVING WITH MY VCR   390
*Confessions of "a compulsive videotaper"! Simultaneously
addicted to and hateful of her VCR, Ephron nevertheless
goes on taping, hoping she'll live long enough to be able
to watch everything she's recorded.*

John Slote   THE SOCIAL SPORT   395
*Though "Softball is the game of baseball made less
challenging," the writer gives us a play-by-play trip
around the bases of this exciting "social sport."*

Richard Rodriguez   COMPLEXION   401
A man labeled feo *as a child (*feo *means "ugly" in
Spanish) remembers how his dark skin set him apart
from those around him.*

George Steiner   THE FUTURE OF READING   405
*George Steiner worries that in America where nearly a
quarter of the population is illiterate or semi-literate, and
where microchips and video images may soon become
more recognizable than the printed page, "the renewed
miracle that is the encounter with a book" may soon
become ancient history.*

Glossary   409
Acknowledgments   422

ALTERNATE
THEMATIC
CONTENTS

CHILDHOOD AND FAMILY

Eudora Welty	ONE WRITER'S BEGINNINGS	5
Truman Capote	LOUIS ARMSTRONG	42
Jade Snow Wong	UNCLE KWOK	47
Elizabeth Wong	THE STRUGGLE TO BE AN ALL-AMERICAN GIRL	71
Langston Hughes	SALVATION	79
Al Young	JAVA JIVE	86
Randall Williams	DADDY TUCKED THE BLANKET	118
Ray Bradbury	TRICKS! TREATS! GANGWAY!	127
Bruno Bettelheim	FAIRY TALES AND MODERN STORIES	164
Lillian Hellman	MEMOIR OF A NEW ORLEANS BOARDING HOUSE	367
Akira Kurosawa	BABYHOOD	371
Maya Angelou	THE FIGHT	374
Richard Rodriguez	COMPLEXION	401

SOCIAL PROBLEMS AND ISSUES

Norman Cousins	WHY JOHNNY CAN'T WRITE	20
Richard Selzer	THE DISCUS THROWER	61
Elizabeth Wong	THE STRUGGLE TO BE AN ALL-AMERICAN GIRL	71
Al Young	JAVA JIVE	86
George Orwell	A HANGING	97
Edwin Newman	BAYBUH, BAYBUH . . .	111
Randall Williams	DADDY TUCKED THE BLANKET	118
Rachel Carson	A FABLE FOR TOMORROW	149
Roger D. McGrath	THE MYTH OF FRONTIER VIOLENCE	172
Ellen Goodman	AN UNDERSTANDING WOMAN	183
Gregg Easterbrook	ESCAPE VALVE	199
Elizabeth Janeway	SOAPS, CYNICISM, AND MIND CONTROL	207
Anne Roiphe	WHY MARRIAGES FAIL	291
Linda Bird Francke	THE AMBIVALENCE OF ABORTION	312
Judy Syfers	I WANT A WIFE	351
Richard Rodriguez	COMPLEXION	401
George Steiner	THE FUTURE OF READING	405

MEN AND WOMEN TODAY

Ellen Goodman	AN UNDERSTANDING WOMAN	183
Elizabeth Janeway	SOAPS, CYNICISM, AND MIND CONTROL	207
Judith Viorst	FRIENDS, GOOD FRIENDS—AND SUCH GOOD FRIENDS	219
Anne Roiphe	WHY MARRIAGES FAIL	291

Linda Bird Francke	THE AMBIVALENCE OF ABORTION	312
Susan Jacoby	WHEN BRIGHT GIRLS DECIDE THAT MATH IS "A WASTE OF TIME"	323
Judy Syfers	I WANT A WIFE	351
Richard M. Restak	THE OTHER DIFFERENCE BETWEEN BOYS AND GIRLS	382
Judy Klemesrud	SPORTORIAL SPLENDOR	387

THE MINORITY EXPERIENCE

Jade Snow Wong	UNCLE KWOK	47
Elizabeth Wong	THE STRUGGLE TO BE AN ALL-AMERICAN GIRL	71
Al Young	JAVA JIVE	86
George Orwell	A HANGING	97
Rachel L. Jones	WHAT'S WRONG WITH BLACK ENGLISH	358
Maya Angelou	THE FIGHT	374
Richard Rodriguez	COMPLEXION	401

CITY AND COUNTRY

William Least Heat Moon	ARIZONA 87	53
Lewis Thomas	DEATH IN THE OPEN	138
Rachel Carson	A FABLE FOR TOMORROW	149
Russell Baker	THE TWO ISMO'S	156
E. B. White	THE THREE NEW YORKS	229
Noel Perrin	COUNTRY CODES	236
Ernest Hemingway	CAMPING OUT	280
Howard Scott	VEGETABLE GARDENS ARE FOR THE BIRDS	336
Garrison Keillor	A RETURN TO BASICS: MEALTIME WITHOUT GUILT	378

SPORTS, TRAVEL, AND LEISURE

William Least Heat Moon	ARIZONA 87	53
Sam Negri	LOAFING MADE EASY	258
Grace Lichtenstein	COORS BEER	273
Ernest Hemingway	CAMPING OUT	280
Howard Scott	VEGETABLE GARDENS ARE FOR THE BIRDS	336
Joseph Wood Krutch	THE VANDAL AND THE SPORTSMAN	343
John Slote	THE SOCIAL SPORT	395
Garrison Keillor	A RETURN TO BASICS: MEALTIME WITHOUT GUILT	378
Judy Klemesrud	SPORTORIAL SPLENDOR	387
Nora Ephron	LIVING WITH MY VCR	390

PSYCHOLOGY AND BEHAVIOR

Dan Greenburg	HOW I OVERHAULED MY MECHANIC'S NOVEL	12
Lewis Thomas	DEATH IN THE OPEN	138
Russell Baker	THE TWO ISMO'S	156
Bruno Bettelheim	FAIRY TALES AND MODERN STORIES	164
Ellen Goodman	AN UNDERSTANDING WOMAN	183
Suzanne Britt Jordan	FUN, OH BOY. FUN. YOU COULD DIE FROM IT.	191
Gregg Easterbrook	ESCAPE VALVE	199
Elizabeth Janeway	SOAPS, CYNICISM, AND MIND CONTROL	207
Judith Viorst	FRIENDS, GOOD FRIENDS—AND SUCH GOOD FRIENDS	219
Sam Negri	LOAFING MADE EASY	258

| Richard M. Restak | THE OTHER DIFFERENCE BETWEEN BOYS AND GIRLS | 382 |
| Nora Ephron | LIVING WITH MY VCR | 390 |

SCIENCE, TECHNOLOGY, AND MEDICINE

Richard Selzer	THE DISCUS THROWER	61
Lewis Thomas	DEATH IN THE OPEN	138
Rachel Carson	A FABLE FOR TOMORROW	149
Grace Lichtenstein	COORS BEER	273

LANGUAGE AND THOUGHT

Eudora Welty	ONE WRITER'S BEGINNINGS	5
Dan Greenburg	HOW I OVERHAULED MY MECHANIC'S NOVEL	12
Norman Cousins	WHY JOHNNY CAN'T WRITE	20
William Zinsser	SIMPLICITY	28
Edwin Newman	BAYBUH, BAYBUH ...	111
Bruno Bettelheim	FAIRY TALES AND MODERN STORIES	164
Leo Rosten	HOW TO TELL A JOKE	265
Rachel Jones	WHAT'S WRONG WITH BLACK ENGLISH	358
Richard M. Restak	THE OTHER DIFFERENCE BETWEEN BOYS AND GIRLS	382
George Steiner	THE FUTURE OF READING	405

HUMOR AND SATIRE

| Dan Greenburg | HOW I OVERHAULED MY MECHANIC'S NOVEL | 12 |

Langston Hughes	SALVATION	79
Edwin Newman	BAYBUH, BAYBUH . . .	111
Russell Baker	THE TWO ISMO'S	156
Suzanne Britt Jordan	FUN, OH BOY. FUN. YOU COULD DIE FROM IT.	191
James T. Baker	HOW DO WE FIND THE STUDENT IN A WORLD OF ACADEMIC GYMNASTS AND WORKER ANTS?	247
Sam Negri	LOAFING MADE EASY	258
Leo Rosten	HOW TO TELL A JOKE	265
Howard Scott	VEGETABLE GARDENS ARE FOR THE BIRDS	336
Judy Syfers	I WANT A WIFE	351
Garrison Keillor	A RETURN TO BASICS: MEALTIME WITHOUT GUILT	378

PREFACE

Now in its fourth edition, *The Short Prose Reader* continues to offer lively reading selections for college composition courses. Its eleven chapters cover all important patterns of writing, offering students concise and lively prose models for analysis, discussion, and imitation. Designed as a practical text, it addresses the challenge that faces today's college students in reading and writing short essays.

The organization of *The Short Prose Reader* is one of its major strengths. In this edition we offer a new first chapter to focus attention on the importance of writing in our culture. Chapter 1 offers four unique views of the craft of writing by well-known authors. Each of the following nine chapters contains four short essays that illustrate clearly a specific pattern or technique—description, narration, illustration, comparison and contrast, definition, classification, process analysis, causal analysis, or argumentation. For this edition we offer new selections in every chapter. We organize the text by starting with the forms of prose mastered most readily by college students, and by then moving carefully to more difficult types of analytical and argumentative writing. Students learn to build upon earlier techniques and patterns as they progress through the book. The last chapter, consisting of ten essays, offers students the opportunity to read and to discuss short prose pieces that reflect the various rhetorical strategies.

Teachers and students will discover that the essays appeal to a broad audience. Readers will be excited by William Least Heat Moon's "Arizona 87," Langston Hughes's "Salvation," Al Young's "Java Jive," Ernest Hemingway's "Camping Out," Judy Syfer's "I Want a Wife," and the many other timely or controversial pieces included in the text. This is a readable text, and one that has ample representation by many different types of writers. Moreover, the essays, which range typically between 300 to 1,200 words, achieve their goals succinctly and clearly and are easy to read and to understand. The essays will alert students both to the *types* of college writing expected of them and to the *length* of essay required frequently by teachers.

Finally, the exercises we have included for each essay are comprehensive and integrated—designed to develop and reinforce the key skills required in college writing. We have included two vocabulary exercises for each selection; the Words to Watch exercise alerts students to words they will read in context, and the Building Vocabulary exercise uses other effective methods (prefix/suffix, context clues, synonym/antonym, abstract/concrete) of teaching vocabulary. A section called Understanding the Writer's Ideas reinforces reading comprehension. Sections entitled Understanding the Writer's Techniques and Exploring the Writer's Ideas provide an excellent basis for class discussion and independent reading and analysis. The last exercise for each essay involves a dynamic approach to writing projects. Guided writing activities—a novel feature of *The Short Prose Reader*—tie the writing projects to the reading selections. Instead of simply being told to write an essay on a certain topic, students through Guided Writing will be able to move from step to step in the process of composition.

The Short Prose Reader can be used flexibly and effectively by students and teachers alike. The text is simple yet sophisticated, presenting essays and exercises that are easy to follow but never are condescending. Weighing the needs and expectations of today's college freshmen, we have designed a rhetoric-reader that can serve as the major text for the composition course.

We wish to thank our friend and aide, Don Linder, for the invaluable assistance he gave us in developing the text. Next, we wish to thank our colleagues over the country for their support and are especially grateful to those who read the manuscript for this and previous editions and offered helpful suggestions: Professors Harry Crosby, Boston University; Mary Daly, College of DuPage; Robert Esch, University of Texas, El Paso; Rowena Flanagan, Kansas City Kansas Community College; Doug Fossek, Santa Barbara City College; Albert Geritz, Ft. Hays State College; Owen W. Gilman, Jr., St. Joseph's University; Wallace Goldstein, Westfield State College; Wilma H. Hasse, Mitchell College; Roland Holmes, University of Illinois, Champaign-Urbana; Sharon Katz, Iona College; Isabel Kidder, Holyoke Community College; Elizabeth Latosi-Sawin, Missouri Western State College; Robert Reising, Pembroke State University; Michael H. Riley, West Virginia Northern Community College; J. C. Searles, Pennsylvania State University; and Ann N. Weisner, New York Institute of Technology.

Gilbert H. Muller
Harvey S. Wiener

1

On Writing

Writing is not an isolated act. It is a definitive and integral part of daily human communication.

Writing is historic. Whether we try to imagine the "meanings" of prehistoric cave drawings or we plow through a satellite-transmitted newspaper each Sunday morning, we are participating in the same human impulse to communicate ideas to other people.

Writing is a product—whether that product is Thoreau's *Walden* or a student's essay calling for a ban on smoking in the college cafeteria.

And, perhaps most crucially, writing is a process—a process of transferring ideas from head to hand. Certainly that process is not absolute; the steps in producing a written piece vary from writer to writer and follow no exact order. Still, considering some of the common elements in this process is instructive for anyone embarking on a study of writing.

Few writers begin without some warmup activity. Generally called prewriting, the steps they take before producing a draft almost always start with thinking about their topic. They talk to friends and colleagues; they browse in libraries and rifle through reference books; they read newspaper and magazine articles. Sometimes they jot down notes and lists in order to put on paper some of their thoughts in very rough form. Some writers use free-association: they record as thoroughly as possible their random, unedited ideas about the topic. Using the raw, often disorganized materials produced in this preliminary stage, many writers try to group related thoughts with a scratch outline or some other effort to bring order to their written notes.

In these early stages serious writers consider their *purpose* and their *audience*. Purpose means "intent," and all writers must know clearly what they intend to accomplish in a particular piece. Often the purpose evolves as the writer continues to think and write about the topic. The issue of audience is important too. Whom does the writer want to read the work? A clear sense of what readers may know and what they may expect helps a writer identify essential issues and choose appropriate language that can win the audience's support.

Prewriting efforts lead to a first draft. Like all works in progress, drafts are generally messy affairs—words crossed out or erased, loops and arrows drawn from one phrase to another, sentences scrawled in the margin.

As they read over their drafts, writers check for clarity of ideas and expression. Are thoughts *unified:* do they relate to an obvious main point? Are thoughts *coherent:* do they follow a logical plan, one idea flowing smoothly into the next? Which ideas require expansion with details? Which ideas should be eliminated? Which thoughts and words are vague or imprecise? In attempting to answer these questions, writers often try to find a friendly reader to look over the draft and to give advice. Whatever else they may look for at this stage, they do not pay much attention to spelling or other matters of correctness. Scissors and paste help in the transfer of one part of the text to another. A good word-processing program that can move blocks of sentences around on a computer screen saves time and simplifies revision.

One draft invariably leads to another. Of course, no one can predict how many drafts a piece of writing will require, but not many writers get by with fewer than two or three attempts. It's always necessary to produce a final copy—the manuscript that a writer will allow others to read and perhaps evaluate. At this point careful attention to sentence structure, grammar, and spelling are very important. The final copy is the writer's best, cleanest effort.

With this brief overview, we've tried to sketch in some of the important elements in the writing process. But we don't want to lose the idea that writing is both a process of inspiration and of craft. Many writers have tried to explain how the two connect in their own particular efforts to create. The novelist and short story writer Katherine Anne Porter, for example, tells how inspiration becomes communication in her writing: "Now and again thousands of memories converge, harmonize, and arrange themselves around a central idea in a coherent form, and I write. . . ." Jean Cocteau, the playwright, asserts the need to shape inspiration into language for a page of writing: "To write, to conquer ink and paper, accumulate letters and paragraphs, divide them with periods and commas, is a different matter from carrying around the dream of a play or a book." The point made by Porter and Cocteau is that writing emerges from both creativity and skill, instruction and technique, talent and effort. As we said, writing is a process of inspiration *and* craft.

Why do people write?

We all (and we *all* can consider ourselves writers) attempt to explain things—what we see, what we feel, what we understand, what we experience, what we dream—so that we and others may better know the world and each other. We all—whether we are writing essays, poems, or stories, whether we are second graders attempting to describe a snowfall or philosophers attempting to explain the meaning of life—have an impulse, as James Baldwin states, "to examine attitudes, to go beneath the surface, to tap the source."

Because communication involves an audience, we need to be aware of a certain communal responsibility as writers. This is a responsibility to both form and content. As for content, we must be accurate—truthful, faithful to facts and details. As for form, we must carefully shape our words and sentences so that they represent what we perceive in our unique, exact, and precise way of viewing things.

It is no wonder that the four writers included in this chapter—four writers who represent a broad spectrum of personal histories, stylistic methods, and intellectual concerns—are all dedicated to exactitude and precision. Whether it's Eudora Welty's account of a critic's advice to "Always get your moon in the right part of the sky" or William Zinsser's pleas for the preciseness that comes only with simplicity, all are minutely concerned with the nuts and bolts of the process of shaping what Baldwin terms the "explicit medium of language."

The four writers represented here also run the gamut of expository techniques discussed in subsequent chapters. None of their essays is simply a "set piece." For example, Norman Cousins combines causal analysis with illustration and argumentation, while Dan Greenburg blends satire with comparison and narration. It can even be suggested that for some of the most successful writers, the process of writing may be even more important than the product.

Finally, although later on in this book you will find George Steiner lamenting a society where illiteracy is on a frightening upsurge and a floppy disk may become more easily recognizable than a printed page, the basic medium of communication is still words. And, in order for these words to survive from generation to generation, there must be writing. It will always be true, in the words of Henry Miller, that "Writing, like life itself, is a voyage of discovery."

Eudora Welty

ONE WRITER'S BEGINNINGS

Eudora Welty was born in 1909 in Jackson, Mississippi, where she still lives in the house her father built. She has won the Pulitzer Prize, the American Book Award for Fiction, and the Gold Medal for the Novel given by the American Academy and Institute of Arts and Letters for her entire body of fiction. The following selection comes from her book *One Writer's Beginnings,* published in 1984, an autobiographical work in which she traces the "continuous thread of revelation" that has characterized Welty's work as a writer. In this short selection, she tells of the need for exactness in the writer's craft. Eudora Welty's other works include *The Ponder Heart* (1954), *The Optimist's Daughter* (1972), and her collected stories, published in 1980.

Words to Watch

stamps (par. 1): imprints; leaves an impression
pulse (par. 1): rhythmical beating or vibration
whiffs (par. 2): slight gusts of air or odor
horizon (par. 3): the imaginary line between earth and sky
chalky (par. 3): having an off-whitish, dull color
respectively (par. 4): in the order presented
constellation (par. 5): a configuration of stars, often named for mythological figures
myths (par. 5): age-old stories made up to explain natural or social phenomena
eclipses (par. 5): the obscurings of celestial bodies by others

Learning stamps you with its moments. Childhood's 1
learning is made up of moments. It isn't steady. It's a pulse.

In a children's art class, we sat in a ring on kinder- 2
garten chairs and drew three daffodils that had just been
picked out of the yard; and while I was drawing, my
sharpened yellow pencil and the cup of the yellow daffodil
gave off whiffs just alike. That the pencil doing the drawing
should give off the same smell as the flower it drew seemed
part of the art lesson—as shouldn't it be? Children, like
animals, use all their senses to discover the world. Then
artists come along and discover it the same way, all over
again. Here and there, it's the same world. Or now and then
we'll hear from an artist who's never lost it.

In my sensory education I include my physical 3
awareness of the *word*. Of a certain word that is; the
connection it has with what it stands for. At around age
six, perhaps, I was standing by myself in our front yard
waiting for supper, just at that hour in a late summer day
when the sun is already below the horizon and the risen
full moon in the visible sky stops being chalky and begins
to take on light. There comes the moment, and I saw it
then, when the moon goes from flat to round. For the first
time it met my eyes as a globe. The word "moon" came into
my mouth as though fed to me out of a silver spoon. Held
in my mouth the moon became a word. It had the roundness
of a Concord grape Grandpa took off his vine and gave me
to suck out of its skin and swallow whole, in Ohio.

This love did not prevent me from living for years 4
in foolish error about the moon. The new moon just appearing
in the west was the rising moon to me. The new should be
rising. And in early childhood the sun and moon, those
opposite reigning powers, I just as easily assumed rose in
east and west respectively in their opposite sides of the sky,
and like partners in a reel they advanced, sun from the
east, moon from the west, crossed over (when I wasn't
looking) and went down on the other side. My father couldn't
have known I believed that when, bending behind me and
guiding my shoulder, he positioned me at our telescope in

the front yard and, with careful adjustment of the focus, brought the moon close to me.

The night sky over my childhood Jackson was velvety 5 black. I could see the full constellations in it and call their names; when I could read, I knew their myths. Though I was always waked for eclipses, and indeed carried to the window as an infant in arms and shown Halley's Comet in my sleep, and though I'd been taught at our diningroom table about the solar system and knew the earth revolved around the sun, and our moon around us, I never found out the moon didn't come up in the west until I was a writer and Herschel Brickell, the literary critic, told me after I misplaced it in a story. He said valuable words to me about my new profession: "Always be sure you get your moon in the right part of the sky."

BUILDING VOCABULARY

1. Welty is extremely precise in her descriptions of things. For example, she writes "kindergarten chairs" instead of simply *small chairs,* "my sharpened yellow pencil" rather than *my pencil.* Select five other such instances of precise description.

2. Explain the following adjective-noun combination descriptions in your own words:

  a. sensory education (par. 3)
  b. physical awareness (par. 3)
  c. risen full moon (par. 3)
  d. visible sky (par. 3)
  e. foolish error (par. 4)
  f. velvety black (par 5)

UNDERSTANDING THE WRITER'S IDEAS

1. What would you say is Welty's overall message or theme in this essay? Does she ever state it directly? How do you know what it is?

2. What is Welty's opinion of the nature of childhood learning?

3. What, according to the author, is the similarity between the ways in which children and animals learn things? What is the relation between the perceptions of artists and of children? How broadly do you think Welty is using the term "artists"? Give examples of the types of artists she probably includes.

4. Describe in your own words how Welty developed her understanding of the word *moon*. At what age did this awareness develop? Where was she? What "moment" is she actually describing when she writes, "There comes the moment, and I saw it then, when the moon goes from flat to round" (par. 3)? How does she misinterpret that moment? What is her "foolish error about the moon"?

5. What is "This love" to which the author refers at the beginning of paragraph 4? How is it related to her misconceptions about the moon?

6. Why does she call the sun and the moon "those opposite reigning powers"? What is the meaning of that description? What does she mean by referring to the sun and moon "like partners in a reel"? What is a reel?

7. What is Halley's Comet? When did Welty first see it? Under what conditions? Name all the ways in which her parents made her aware of concepts and events of astronomy. How could she later refine that awareness?

8. Who is Herschel Brickell? What effect did he have on Welty? What was Brickell's exact message to Welty? Why did he say it to her? What implied, more general, message to all writers is included in Brickell's advice?

UNDERSTANDING THE WRITER'S TECHNIQUES

1. Why does Welty use two very short sentences at the end of paragraph 1? What is the effect of following with a long flowing sentence to begin paragraph 2?

2. Perhaps you have always been told that pronouns

must have clear *antecedents* (previous words to which they refer). What is the antecedent, or meaning, for the pronoun *it* in the following sentences from paragraph 2: "Then artists come along and discover *it* the same way, all over again" and "Or now and then we'll hear from an artist who's never lost *it*"? How are the two uses different, not only in meaning but in effect as well?

3. In paragraph 2, Welty uses two familiar and general expressions: "Here and there" and "now and then." Evaluate their use in that paragraph.

4. The first sentence of paragraph 3 is a general statement, a topic sentence that the writer then supports in the body of the paragraph. How does the second sentence qualify or limit the scope of the first? What sort of support material does Welty use to support the topic sentence?

5. Narration (see Chapter Three) is storytelling, and writers often use personal narratives about their childhood or adult lives as a part of a more general essay. How does Welty use narration in paragraphs 2, 3, and 5? Which is the most fully developed of these narrations? Why do you think that's so?

6. At the end of paragraph 3, Welty seems to add the abrupt tag phrase, "in Ohio." Why does she add this information? Why does she place it where she does? What is the effect of the information and its placement on the reader's understanding? Does it in any way make the story seem "more normal"? How?

7. In the final paragraph, how does the author make a transition (connection) between her childhood and adult perceptions?

8. An *understatement* is a deliberately low-key presentation of an an important idea in order to achieve greater effect. How might you characterize Welty's use of Brickell's advice to her as understatement? Why does she end the essay with it?

9. What kind of overall feeling or mood did you get from reading this essay? Explain, with specific references to elements of Welty's writing, why you felt this way.

EXPLORING THE WRITER'S IDEAS

1. Eudora Welty obviously loves her work as a writer and uses this essay, in part, to convey her sense of the necessity of exactitude in writing. Is there something you like to do on a basis comparable to Welty's love of writing? How important is precision or exactitude to that activity? In general, how careful are you in the things you do? What are the advantages of carefulness and precision? What are some disadvantages?

2. Welty's piece suggests that she knew at age six that she'd grow up to be a writer. Did you or any of your friends know what you wanted to be when you were very young? What most influenced your decisions?

3. Welty begins this essay with a short discussion of the nature of childhood's learning. How are children's learning patterns and techniques different from those of adults? Compare some of your own most significant learning experiences from your childhood and your adulthood.

4. How do childhood learning patterns and experiences set the stage for adult knowledge of things? Child psychologist Jean Piaget suggests that young children actually reason differently from adults and are often incapable of comprehending logical reasoning. Do you agree or disagree with Piaget's opinion? Explain.

5. In general, do you learn things better through self-taught experiences, by being instructed by an expert or teacher, or by reading about them? Explain with specific examples.

IDEAS FOR WRITING

Guided Writing

Write a brief essay about how you "discovered" or became aware of a particular word or concept. Try to explain the power of that word—its ability to affect you deeply then and now.

1. Begin with a brief statement of your notion of how children learn.

2. Follow with a short, personal example of how you learned a word or concept as a child and how your learning conforms to your belief in how children learn in general.

3. Write a short narration that explains how you learned, on your own, the particular significant concept.

4. Relate your learning experience to the attitudes and actions of those closest to you—parents, grandparents, other close relatives.

5. Explain your initial understanding of the concept.

6. Be as precise as possible in your description throughout the essay.

7. At the end of your essay, explain the significance of that word for you today.

8. End the paper with a statement—your own or someone else's—that embodies your message and purpose in writing the essay.

More Writing Projects

1. Write an essay in which you discuss how you began doing something that is now very important to you.

2. Write an essay about a word that you misunderstood or used incorrectly or inappropriately as a child but understand more clearly today.

3. Write a description of how you recently learned to do something: drive, swim, lift weights, type, and so on.

Dan Greenburg

HOW I OVERHAULED MY MECHANIC'S NOVEL

In Dan Greenburg's take-off on repair service ethics, notice how humor can help carry a discussion of what ultimately can be a serious problem. Also note how Greenburg tells a story which, while relating to all our experiences, includes a great deal of information about the craft and skills of writing.

Words to Watch

handy (par. 5): clever in doing things, especially with the hands
defective (par. 18): not in proper working order
queasy (par. 29): ill-at-ease; causing nausea
superficial (par. 29): shallow in thought; concerned only with obvious meanings
customizing (par. 33): making over specially for a particular purpose
cannibalize (par. 35): to take apart something for parts to be used for something else

My mechanic was having trouble with his novel. 1 Knowing I am an author, he asked if I could help. I hold him I'd have a look. He told me he needed it back pretty soon. I told him it was my busy season, but I'd see what I could do. A couple days later my mechanic came by to see what I had found. "Well," I said, "I opened her up and took a look, and I'm afraid you've got a little trouble there."

"Serious trouble?" he asked. 2

"Probably not too serious. The timing's off on four 3 of your six characters, and two of the others ought to be replaced."

"Do you think I might be able to do the work myself?" 4 he asked.

I shrugged. "Don't know how handy you are," I said, 5 "or what tools you got. You own a thesaurus?"

"A what?" he asked. 6

"That's what I thought," I said. "No, I don't think 7 you ought to do the work yourself. You get it all apart, you might not be able to put the pieces back together again."

"Maybe you could help me," he said. "I'd pay you, 8 of course."

"I'm not cheap—$37.50 an hour. Plus parts." 9

"Parts?" 10

"You know—typing bond, carbon paper, typewriter 11 ribbon, correction fluid, transparent tape—that kind of thing." I scribbled an estimate on an index card. He looked at it and whistled.

"Remember, that doesn't include syntax either," I 12 said.

"Don't you think this is a little high?" he asked. I 13 gave him the names of a couple of my novelist friends and suggested he get competitive bids. He said he didn't really know their work and guessed he'd stick with me.

"When do you think I could pick the manuscript 14 up?" he asked. I told him to check with me in about a week.

One week later to the day, he dropped by. "Is it 15 ready?" he asked.

"Afraid not," I said. "Once I opened her up and really 16 took a hard look, I discovered a few more problems."

"Like what?" he asked. 17

"Well, for one thing," I said, "there's a lot of cheap 18 imagery in there that ought to come out—similes, metaphors, personifications—they're just clogging up the action.

You also have some defective aphorisms. Then there's a hole in your plot about a mile wide that needs to be filled up. Plus which your superstructure is rusty and falling apart."

He seemed really upset. "What about those two 19 characters you said ought to be replaced?"

"I'm afraid it's worse than that," I said. "If it was 20 me, I'd replace all six of them. They're really shot. It's not just their timing that's off, it's their motivations—you left out their motivations when you hooked them up, and now I can't even get them to turn over, much less speak."

"I can't afford to replace all six of them." 21

"Well, then, maybe they can be rebuilt," I said. "But 22 you definitely need to replace your protagonist."

"My protagonist?" he asked. 23

"I'm afraid so." 24

He smiled sheepishly. "Look," he said. "I'm not even 25 sure I know what a protagonist *is*."

I pointed. "It's this guy right here, see?" 26

"But why does he need to be replaced?" 27

"He's weak. He's not going to be able to go the 28 distance. He's going to give out in mid-plot, and when he does he's going to tear the hell out of the whole thing—it'll be a real mess."

My mechanic looked a little queasy. I almost felt 29 sorry for him. "Listen," I said, "I hate to have to be the bearer of such bad news, but I figured you'd want to know the truth. Another novelist might give you a different story, tell you all you needed was a superficial tune-up—wider margins, a retype job, stuff like that—and just forget about your protagonist. But that's not the way I operate."

He nodded miserably. "How long before my protag- 30 onist gives out?" he asked.

I shrugged. "Hard to say. Could be he'd last you all 31 the way up to the climax in the twelfth chapter. Could be he'd give out in the first thirty pages. You just can't tell with a weak protagonist. If it was me, I'd pick up a new one, slap it in there and be done with it."

"How hard would it be to find one?" he asked. "A 32 used one, I mean. I don't know if I can afford a new one."

"Well," I said, "a novelist I know has just scrapped 33

a trilogy he's been working on. You could maybe make a deal with him on *his* protagonist. In a piece that long, even a *minor* character could work as a protagonist for you—after a little customizing."

"Could you give this guy a call and see if he'd be 34 willing to sell me a minor character? A protagonist from a work that size has got to be out of my price range."

"I'll call him," I said. "Of course, I don't know how 35 eager he's going to be to cannibalize a whole trilogy to sell you just one minor character."

"Look," he said, a pasty smile on his face, "maybe 36 you could ask for a special favor."

"I could," I said. "Unless . . ." 37

"Unless what?" 38

"Well," I said, "unless you've ever done any work 39 on his car."

BUILDING VOCABULARY

1. In this essay, Greenburg uses a number of words connected with the skills and processes of writing—both for fiction and non-fiction. Look up and write definitions for the following words:

syntax (par. 12)
manuscript (par. 14)
imagery (par. 18)
similes (par. 18)
metaphors (par. 18)
personifications (par. 18)
aphorisms (par. 18)
plot (par. 18)
characters (par. 19)
motivations (par. 20)
protagonist (par. 23)
climax (par. 31)
trilogy (par. 33)

2. In relating the dialogue with his mechanic, Greenburg uses descriptions of actions to indicate each man's attitudes. For each of the following phrases, explain what attitude the italicized words express:

a. I *shrugged* (pars. 5 and 31)
b. I *scribbled* an estimate (par. 11)
c. He looked at it and *whistled* (par. 11)
d. He *smiled sheepishly* (par. 25)
e. He *nodded miserably* (par. 30)

UNDERSTANDING THE WRITER'S IDEAS

1. What is the mechanic's problem in this essay? Why does he approach Greenburg for assistance? How does Greenburg propose to solve the problem?

2. Briefly outline the story of this essay. Do the events seem as if they actually could have happened in this way? Why? What really *is* Greenburg's purpose in writing this essay? At what is he poking fun? What ideas is he really trying to convey to the reader?

3. What is a *thesaurus*? Why does Greenburg ask the mechanic if he owns one? Why, when the mechanic indicates that he doesn't know what a thesaurus is, does Greenburg say, "That's what I thought"?

4. In general, what is Greenburg's attitude towards his mechanic's literary skills? What does he think of the novel on first reading? How does that opinion change with a closer second reading? Cite a few examples to support your responses.

5. What is wrong with the mechanic's protagonist? What does Greenburg suggest he do to rectify his problems?

6. What does Greenburg suggest that another novelist might do if the mechanic took the novel elsewhere? Do you feel he is being completely honest on this point? Why?

7. What general part of the writing process is Greenburg actually describing in this essay? What specific writing skills does he mention?

UNDERSTANDING THE WRITER'S TECHNIQUES

1. How does Greenburg use *humor* in this essay? How does humor affect your reaction to the essay? Give examples of what you consider the most humorous sections.

2. Throughout the essay, Greenburg is actually comparing one professional relationship to another. What are they? How does Greenburg present a "new twist" on the old relationship? Identify examples of how the author sustains the comparison.

3. Greenburg relies heavily upon dialogue to record the events in this essay. Why doesn't he simply tell us what happened? How does his technique make the essay more effective?

4. What is Greenburg's underlying attitude toward his mechanic as a professional and as a person (not just as a novelist)? Explain your answers with specific examples from the essay. How does the last line of the essay especially indicate that attitude? Explain the underlying meaning of the last line.

5. Greenburg uses quite a bit of informal language in this essay. For example, in paragraph 13 he writes, "He said he didn't really know their work and *guessed* he'd *stick* with me." Why is the author so informal throughout the essay? Find other examples of such informality and explain their meanings.

6. What kinds of readers do you think would be most interested in Greenburg's essay? Why? How does Greenburg's style reflect the tastes and interests of such readers? Support your answer with specific references to the essay.

EXPLORING THE WRITER'S IDEAS

1. We have all had "interesting" experiences with auto mechanics (or know of someone who has) in which we've felt helplessly at the mechanic's mercy and whim. Describe such an experience and its results.

2. Have you, or has anyone you have known, ever had the feeling of being cheated or "conned" by someone? How did you feel about it at the time? Did you try to get even? If so, how successful were you? If not, why not? What is your general method of dealing with feeling cheated? Is there any technique that you admire more than your own? Why?

3. Discuss how Greenburg takes a serious subject and deals with it in a funny way. How does "looking on the light side" help us deal with difficult situations?

IDEAS FOR WRITING

Guided Writing

Write an essay about how you once helped someone even though you felt that person hadn't previously been kind or fair to you.

1. Begin with a direct statement of what the person's problem was and why he or she chose to come to you for assistance.

2. Make sure you specify your relationship with the other person.

3. Describe what you did at first and what your initial reaction was. How did the other person respond in turn?

4. Early in the essay, begin to report what you and the other person actually said to each other, and try to use the dialogue as a technique for developing the essay.

5. Indicate what you felt you could do for the other person's problem; also, indicate the other person's reactions.

6. Don't be too serious in your essay. Make it somewhat funny for your readers, even though you may be dealing with a fairly serious situation.

7. Where possible, use descriptions of how the two of you behaved around each other.

8. Close your essay by saying something to the other person, which subtly indicates your real feeling about that person's previous treatment of you.

More Writing Projects

    1. Write about a time that you turned to someone for help with your own writing. Why did you need help? Did you get what you wanted? Or, perhaps you can write about a time someone turned to you for help in writing. Were you able to provide assistance? How?

    2. Tell about a time you needed to ask a favor from someone to whom you really didn't want to be obligated, but had no choice.

    3. Write a conversation between two people in which the first is trying to convince the second to do something which he or she really doesn't want to do.

Norman Cousins

WHY JOHNNY CAN'T WRITE

Norman Cousins is a writer, past editor of the *Saturday Review,* social activist, and critic—and he's concerned about deteriorating writing skills in this country. This article appeared just at the beginning of what many social commentators have termed "the writing crisis" in America's education system. In the essay, Cousins traces the causes and effects of this crisis with insights that remain remarkably perceptive today.

Words to Watch

sanctioning (par. 3): giving permission or approval to do something
valid (par. 3): acceptable; effective; correct
reflective (par. 3): meditative; purposefully considered
medium (par. 5): a channel or means for doing something
painstakingly (par. 6): with great care
fashioning (par. 6): designing; giving particular shape to something
heinous (par. 7): hatefully or shockingly evil; outrageous
integrated (par. 8): formed into a whole unit
enabling (par. 9): allowing or making possible to happen

One of the first questions in the final examination 1
of a California high-school English class asked the student
to write a 500-word essay describing a character in a play
by Shakespeare. Another question asked him to reconstruct
a vivid conversation from a recent novel he had read. There

were at least four other questions involving skill in English composition. All this was to be done in two hours.

An examination in a Midwest college asked the 2 student to write a short essay on the subject: "The status symbols today are those other than money can buy." The paper was to be completed in an hour.

These tests reveal little except the unfortunate role 3 of schools in fostering and sanctioning bad writing habits. If Johnny can't write, one of the reasons may be a conditioning based on speed rather than respect for the creative process. Speed is neither a valid test of nor a proper preparation for competence in writing. It makes for murkiness, glibness, disorganization. It takes the beauty out of the language. It rules out respect for the reflective thought that should precede expression. It runs counter to the word-by-word and line-by-line reworking that enables a piece to be finely knit.

This is not to minimize the value of genuine facility. 4 With years of practice a man may be able to put down words swiftly and expertly. But it is the same kind of swiftness that enables a cellist, after having invested years of effort, to negotiate an intricate passage from Haydn. Speed writing is for stenographers and court reporters, not for anyone who wants to use language with precision and distinction.

Thomas Mann was not ashamed to admit that he 5 would often take a full day to write 500 words, and another day to edit them, out of respect for the most difficult art in the world. Flaubert would ponder a paragraph for hours. Did it say what he wanted it to say—not approximately but exactly? Did the words turn into one another with proper rhythm and grace? Were they artistically and securely fitted together? Were they briskly alive, or were they full of fuzz and ragged edges? Were they likely to make things happen inside the mind of the reader, igniting the imagination and touching off all sorts of new anticipations? These questions are relevant not only for the established novelist but for anyone who attaches value to words as a medium of expression and communication.

E. B. White, whose respect for the environment of 6

good writing is exceeded by no other word artist of our time, would rather have his fingers cut off than to be guilty of handling words lightly. No sculptor chipping away at the granite block in order to produce a delicate curve or feature has labored more painstakingly than White in fashioning a short paragraph. Obviously, we can't expect our schools to make every Johnny into a White or a Flaubert or a Mann, but it is not unreasonable to expect more of them to provide the conditions that promote clear, careful, competent expression. Certainly the cumulative effort of the school experience should not have to be undone in later years.

7 Speed is not the only demon. Neatness is often valued above style. A composition paper full of corrections and crossed-out lines may be far more valuable to the teacher in appraising a student's awareness of the preciousness of the right word or phrase than an immaculately typed essay. Writing is one subject in which the student ought to be encouraged to ramble around and even be messy, if need be, in search of his answers. Nor is there anything particularly heinous about the use of a dictionary during an English examination or even a test in spelling. Not everyone can spell, even with the most conscientious study; but everyone can develop the habit of using a good dictionary effectively and consistently.

8 It would be a mistake to blame it all on the English teacher. Poor writing habits are developed in a wide range of courses. Homework assignments aren't always integrated. It is not unusual for a child to be given three overnight writing assignments, any one of which requires several full days' work to be done properly. Moreover, the teacher doesn't always have complete authority in the preparation of examinations, especially those of a year-end or state-wide nature. The root of the problem is that not much thought has been given to the requirements of good writing. The concept of expression as an intricate and highly demanding art has never fully been accepted.

9 The area in which a poor education shows up first is in self-expression, oral or written. It makes little difference how many university courses or degrees a man may own. If

he cannot use words to move an idea from one point to another, his education is incomplete. Taking in a fact is only part of the educational process. The ability to pass it along with reasonable clarity and even distinction is another. The business of assembling the right words, putting them down in proper sequence, enabling each one to pull its full weight in the conveyance of meaning—these are the essentials. A school is where these essentials should feel at home.

BUILDING VOCABULARY

1. In paragraph 3, Cousins writes that too much emphasis on speed as part of the writing process makes for "murkiness, glibness, disorganization." What does he mean by each of those terms as they relate to writing?

Read through the essay and select other words that describe both positive and negative qualities of writing. Explain each.

2. Cousins refers to a number of artists throughout history. Identify each of the following: William Shakespeare (paragraph 1); Franz Joseph Haydn (paragraph 4); Thomas Mann (paragraph 5); Gustave Flaubert (paragraph 5); E. B. White (paragraph 6). Why does Cousins refer to these people on an essay about writing and education today?

3. Explain in your own words the meanings of these expressions drawn from Cousins' essay:

   a. runs counter to (par. 3)
   b. finely knit (par. 3)
   c. This is not to minimize the value of (par. 4)
   d. genuine facility (par. 4)
   e. briskly alive (par. 5)
   f. ragged edges (par. 5)
   g. medium of expression (par. 5)
   h. cumulative effort (par. 6)
   i. the preciousness of the right word (par. 7)
   j. the most conscientious study (par. 7)

UNDERSTANDING THE WRITER'S IDEAS

1. Who is "Johnny" in this essay? Is he a real person?

2. What examples of typical English class exams does Cousins provide in paragraphs 1 and 2? When he ends the first paragraph with the sentence, "All this was to be done in two hours," what purpose other than simply providing information do you think he has in mind? Explain.

3. According to the author, how does writing under the pressures of time limits affect the quality of students' writing? What are some of the negative results of writing for speed? What other causes for poor writing ability—other than time pressures—does Cousins identify in this essay? Which seems to be the most important, most general cause of students' poor writing abilities?

4. In paragraph 3, Cousins writes about "respect for the creative process." In your own words, what does he mean by "the creative process"?

5. What elements of "good writing" does Cousins allude to in paragraph 3? Which of these elements are part of the *process* and which are part of the *results* of careful writing?

6. What does Cousins mean by "facility" in the first sentence of paragraph 4? For what good is the facility of writing quickly? For what is it especially *not* useful?

7. What is "the most difficult art in the world" (paragraph 5)? What examples of the difficulties of this art does Cousins offer?

8. What is Cousins' opinion of the writer E. B. White? On what does he base this opinion? (White is represented in this book by his essay "The Three New Yorks," pages 230–231.) To what other type of artist does Cousins compare White? Why?

9. What is the author's opinion about sloppy essay papers? What does he think about using dictionaries during in-class writing? Why? How are the two opinions related?

10. According to Cousins, what should be expected from schools when it comes to teaching students about writing? What is the most obvious result of an education

that has not sufficiently stressed techniques of good communication? What examples does he offer in support of his opinion?

UNDERSTANDING THE WRITER'S TECHNIQUES

1. What is Cousins' major purpose in this essay? Does he want to warn people? To convince people? To make people take certain actions in the future? Explain your answer with specific references to the article. What is the relation in purpose and idea between paragraphs 1 and 2? Why does Cousins begin the essay in this way?

2. What is the effect of all the questions in paragraph 5? Does Cousins really expect answers to these questions? Does he ever answer them, either directly or indirectly? Explain your answer.

3. In paragraph 7, Cousins mentions "neatness" as another cause of poor writing skills. How does he provide a link between speed and neatness as causes of the problem?

4. What is the meaning of the expression "The root of the problem" in paragraph 8? How is it important to the development of Cousins' ideas in this essay? How does its placement in the essay signify the importance Cousins attaches to this cause of poor student writing?

5. How does Cousins' description of writing as "an intricate and highly demanding art" in paragraph 8 serve as a means to *unify* the essay? (To *unify* means to bring various parts of the essay together.) How does it compare with a previous description in this essay? How are they similar? How are they different?

6. Discuss Cousins' use of specific examples of things to stand for larger concepts throughout this essay.

7. Up through the end of paragraph 8, Cousins stresses *causes* of poor writing abilities. Yet, in the last paragraph, he shifts to discussing its effects. Why does he do this? How does this change make the essay more complete than if he had ended it with the dramatic and summary last sentence of paragraph 8?

8. Read through the essay once again and list all the elements of the writing process that Cousins mentions.

EXPLORING THE WRITER'S IDEAS

1. Cousins complains in this essay about the emphasis on writing for speed rather than beauty, and about the fact that students may have too many writing assignments at one time to do justice to any one. What are some of your experiences with writing under time pressures? Do you work well under pressure as some people do? Why or why not? In general, do you leave writing assignments for the last minute, or do you try to work on them gradually? Have you found any differences in quality between writing on which you have spent considerable time and writing you started and finished the night before it was due? Explain.

2. Do you agree with Cousins that writing is "the most difficult art in the world"? Explain, comparing writing with other art forms.

3. Cousins writes about precision in writing. Compare his ideas about exactness with Eudora Welty's in her essay "One Writer's Beginnings" (pages 5–7). How are they similar? How different? What do their ideas tell you about writers' attitudes towards the processes and results of their work?

4. In the last line of the essay, Cousins states: "A school is where these essentials should feel at home." What do you think are "the essentials" of a college education? What is your opinion about the importance of "essentials" in a university's or college's curriculum? Should they be stressed more than they are now? Explain your answer.

5. Do you believe that there is a "crisis in writing" among America's college students? If so, what are its causes? How important are good writing skills to being successful after college? How would you evaluate the communications skills of your fellow students? How would you evaluate your own skills?

IDEAS FOR WRITING

Guided Writing

Write an essay that you title "Why Johnny (or any other appropriate man's or woman's name) Can't _____ ."

Fill in the blank with an educational skill that you consider essential to a successful life. Such choices as "write," "read," "speak," "listen," "think," and "compute" would be appropriate.

1. Begin your essay with examples of how a common activity of growing up or going to school inhibits the development of the skill.

2. Discuss one of the main causes for lack of development of the skill. Give examples of what will result if this cause is allowed to become too important.

3. Use examples of famous people who have become successful in their fields because they mastered the skill. Tell what you know about how they approached the process of enacting the skill.

4. Discuss two or three other causes for problems people have with the skill. Try to identify clearly the *main* cause of the problem.

5. Point out the ultimate importance of mastering this skill.

6. In your final paragraph, discuss the most important effects on an individual of his or her lack of facility with the skill.

7. Try to identify a person whom you consider a leading contemporary master of the skill.

More Writing Projects

1. Write a short essay in which you discuss what you consider the essentials of communications skills. What are they? How and where are they best learned?

2. Write a 500-word essay in which you respond to one of the topics named in paragraph 1 of Cousins' essay. Try to complete the essay in forty-five minutes. Then, write a short evaluation about how you felt writing so much in so little time.

3. Look through newspaper and magazine articles to find examples of "murkiness, glibness, disorganization" in writing (see paragraph 3 of this essay). In a short essay, explain why they fall into these categories.

William Zinsser

SIMPLICITY

In this chapter from *On Writing Well,* William Zinsser begins with a fairly pessimistic analysis of the clutter that pervades and degrades American writing, and he offers many examples to prove his point. Zinsser deals with almost all major aspects of the writing process—thinking, composing, awareness of the reader, self-discipline, rewriting, and editing—and concludes that simplification is the key to them all.

Words to Watch

decipher (par. 2):   to make out the meaning of something obscure
adulterants (par. 3):   added substances which make something impure or inferior
mollify (par. 4):   to appease; to soothe
spell (par. 4):   a short period of time
assailed (par. 8):   to attack with words or physical violence
spruce (par. 8):   neat or smart in appearance
rune (par. 11):   character in an ancient alphabet
surfeit (par. 14):   an overabundant supply
superfluous (par. 15):   wasteful; extravagant
enumerate (par. 16):   to count or list in order

Clutter is the disease of American writing. We are 1
a society strangling in unnecessary words, circular constructions, pompous frills and meaningless jargon.

Who really knows what the average businessman is 2
trying to say in the average business letter? What member

of an insurance or medical plan can decipher the brochure that tells him what his costs and benefits are? What father or mother can put together a child's toy—on Christmas Eve or any other eve—from the instructions on the box? Our national tendency is to inflate and thereby sound important. The airline pilot who wakes us to announce that he is presently anticipating experiencing considerable weather wouldn't dream of saying that there's a storm ahead and it may get bumpy. The sentence is too simple—there must be something wrong with it.

But the secret of good writing is to strip every 3 sentence to its cleanest components. Every word that serves no function, every long word that could be a short word, every adverb which carries the same meaning that is already in the verb, every passive construction that leaves the reader unsure of who is doing what—these are the thousand and one adulterants that weaken the strength of a sentence. And they usually occur, ironically, in proportion to education and rank.

During the late 1960's the president of Princeton 4 University wrote a letter to mollify the alumni after a spell of campus unrest. "You are probably aware," he began, "that we have been experiencing very considerable potentially explosive expressions of dissatisfaction on issues only partially related." He meant that the students had been hassling them about different things. As an alumnus I was far more upset by the president's syntax than by the students' potentially explosive expressions of dissatisfaction. I would have preferred the presidential approach taken by Franklin D. Roosevelt when he tried to convert into English his own government's memos, such as this blackout order of 1942:

> Such preparations shall be made as will completely obscure all Federal buildings and non-Federal buildings occupied by the Federal government during an air raid for any period of time from visibility by reason of internal or external illumination.

"Tell them," Roosevelt said, "that in buildings where 5 they have to keep the work going to put something across the windows."

Simplify, simplify. Thoreau said it, as we are so 6
often reminded, and no American writer more consistently
practiced what he preached. Open *Walden* to any page and
you will find a man saying in a plain and orderly way what
is on his mind.:

> I love to be alone. I never found the companion that was so
> companionable as solitude. We are for the most part more lonely
> when we go abroad among men than when we stay in our
> chambers. A man thinking or working is always alone, let him
> be where he will. Solitude is not measured by the miles of space
> that intervene between a man and his fellows. The really diligent
> student in one of the crowded hives of Cambridge College is as
> solitary as a dervish in the desert.

How can the rest of us achieve such enviable freedom 7
from clutter? The answer is to clear our heads of clutter.
Clear thinking becomes clear writing: one can't exist without
the other. It is impossible for a muddy thinker to write good
English. He may get away with it for a paragraph or two,
but soon the reader will be lost, and there is no sin so grave,
for he will not easily be lured back.

Who is this elusive creature, the reader? He is a 8
person with an attention span of about twenty seconds. He
is assailed on every side by forces competing for his time:
by newspapers and magazines, by television and radio and
stereo, by his wife and children and pets, by his house and
his yard and all the gadgets that he has bought to keep
them spruce, and by that most potent of competitors, sleep.
The man snoozing in his chair with an unfinished magazine
open on his lap is a man who is being given too much
unnecessary trouble by the writer.

It won't do to say that the snoozing reader is too 9
dumb or too lazy to keep pace with the train of thought. My
sympathies are with him. If a reader is lost, it is generally
because the writer has not been careful enough to keep him
on the path.

This carelessness can take any number of forms. 10
Perhaps a sentence is so excessively cluttered that the
reader, hacking his way through the verbiage, simply doesn't

know what it means. Perhaps a sentence has been so shoddily constructed that the reader could read it in any of several ways. Perhaps the writer has switched pronouns in mid-sentence, or has switched tenses, so the reader loses track of who is talking or when the action took place. Perhaps Sentence B is not a logical sequel to Sentence A—the writer, in whose head the connection is clear, has not bothered to provide the missing link. Perhaps the writer has used an important word incorrectly by not taking the trouble to look it up. He may think that "sanguine" and "sanguinary" mean the same thing, but the difference is a bloody big one. The reader can only infer (speaking of big differences) what the writer is trying to imply.

Faced with these obstacles, the reader is at first a 11 remarkably tenacious bird. He blames himself—he obviously missed something, and he goes back over the mystifying sentence, or over the whole paragraph, piecing it out like an ancient rune, making guesses and moving on. But he won't do this for long. The writer is making him work too hard, and the reader will look for one who is better at his craft.

The writer must therefore constantly ask himself: 12 What am I trying to say? Surprisingly often, he doesn't know. Then he must look at what he has written and ask: Have I said it? Is it clear to someone encountering the subject for the first time? If it's not, it is because some fuzz has worked its way into the machinery. The clear writer is a person clear-headed enough to see this stuff for what it is: fuzz.

I don't mean that some people are born clear-headed 13 and are therefore natural writers, whereas others are naturally fuzzy and will never write well. Thinking clearly is a conscious act that the writer must force upon himself, just as if he were embarking on any other project that requires logic: adding up a laundry list or doing an algebra problem. Good writing doesn't come naturally, though most people obviously think it does. The professional writer is forever being bearded by strangers who say that they'd like to "try a little writing some time" when they retire from their real profession. Good writing takes self-discipline and, very often, self-knowledge.

Many writers, for instance, can't stand to throw 14 anything away. Their sentences are littered with words that mean essentially the same thing and with phrases which make a point that is implicit in what they have already said. When students give me these littered sentences I beg them to select from the surfeit of words the few that most precisely fit what they want to say. Choose one, I plead, from among the three almost identical adjectives. Get rid of the unnecessary adverbs. Eliminate "in a funny sort of way" and other such qualifiers—they do no useful work.

The students look stricken—I am taking all their 15 wonderful words away. I am only taking their superfluous words away, leaving what is organic and strong.

"But," one of my worst offenders confessed, "I never 16 can get rid of anything—you should see my room." (I didn't take him up on the offer.) "I have two lamps where I only need one, but I can't decide which one I like better, so I keep them both." He went on to enumerate his duplicated or unnecessary objects, and over the weeks ahead I went on throwing away his duplicated and unnecessary words. By the end of the term—a term that he found acutely painful— his sentences were clean.

"I've had to change my whole approach to writing," 17 he told me. "Now I have to *think* before I start every sentence and I have to *think* about every word." The very idea amazed him. Whether his room also looked better I never found out. I suspect that it did.

Two pages of the final manuscript of this chapter. Although they look like a first draft, they have already been rewritten and retyped—like almost every other page—four or five times. With each rewrite I try to make what I have written tighter, stronger and more precise, eliminating every element that is not doing useful work, until at last I have a clean copy for the printer. Then I go over it once more, reading it aloud, and am always amazed at how much clutter can still be profitably cut.

is too dumb or too lazy to keep pace with the ~~writer's~~ train of thought. My sympathies are ~~entirely~~ with him. ~~He's not so dumb.~~ If the reader is lost, it is generally because the writer ~~of the article~~ has not been careful enough to keep him on the ~~proper~~ path.

This carelessness can take any number of ~~different~~ forms. Perhaps a sentence is so excessively ~~long and~~ cluttered that the reader, hacking his way through ~~all~~ the verbiage, simply doesn't know what *it* ~~the writer~~ means. Perhaps a sentence has been so shoddily constructed that the reader could read it in any of *several* ~~two or three different~~ ways. ~~He thinks he knows what the writer is trying to say, but he's not sure.~~ Perhaps the writer has switched pronouns in mid-sentence, or ~~perhaps he~~ has switched tenses, so the reader loses track of who is talking ~~to whom,~~ or ~~exactly~~ when the action took place. Perhaps Sentence B is not a logical sequel to Sentence A — the writer, in whose head the connection is ~~perfectly~~ clear, has not *bothered to provide* ~~given enough thought to providing~~ the missing link. Perhaps the writer has used an important word incorrectly by not taking the trouble to look it up ~~and make sure.~~ He may think that "sanguine" and "sanguinary" mean the same thing, but ~~I can assure you that~~ the difference is a bloody big one ~~to the~~

~~reader~~. *The reader* ~~He~~ can only ~~try to~~ infer **xhxt** (speaking of big differences) what the writer is trying to imply.

Faced with ~~such a variety of~~ *these* obstacles, the reader is at first a remarkably tenacious bird. He ~~tends to~~ blames himself. ~~H~~He obviously missed something, ~~he thinks,~~ and he goes back over the mystifying sentence, or over the whole paragraph, piecing it out like an ancient rune, making guesses and moving on. But he won't do this for long. ~~He will soon run out of patience.~~ The writer is making him work too hard, ~~harder than he should have to work~~ and the reader will look for ~~a writer~~ *one* who is better at his craft.

The writer must therefore constantly ask himself: What am I trying to say? ~~in this sentence?~~ Surprisingly often, he doesn't know. ~~And~~ Then he must look at what he has ~~just~~ written and ask: Have I said it? Is it clear to someone *encountering* ~~who is coming upon~~ the subject for the first time? If it's not, ~~clear,~~ it is because some fuzz has worked its way into the machinery. The clear writer is a person ~~who is~~ clear-headed enough to see this stuff for what it is: fuzz.

I don't mean ~~to suggest~~ that some people are born clear-headed and are therefore natural writers, whereas *others* ~~other people~~ are naturally fuzzy and will ~~therefore~~ never write well. Thinking clearly is *a* ~~an entirely~~ conscious act that the writer must *force* ~~keep forcing~~ upon himself, just as if he were *embarking* ~~starting out~~ on any other ~~kind of~~ project that *requires* ~~calls for~~ logic: adding up a laundry list or doing an algebra problem ~~or playing chess.~~ Good writing doeesn't ~~just~~ come naturally, though most people obviously think *it does.* ~~it's as easy as walking.~~ The professional

BUILDING VOCABULARY

1. Zinsser uses a number of words and expressions drawn from areas other than writing; he uses them to make interesting combinations or comparisons in such expressions as *elusive creature* (par. 8), *hacking his way through the verbiage* (par. 10), and *a remarkably tenacious bird* (par. 11). Find other such expressions in this essay. Write simple explanations for the three above and the others that you find.

2. List all words or phrases in this essay that pertain to writing—the process, the results, the faults, the successes. Explain any with which you were unfamiliar.

3. Identify any other words in this essay which were new to you. Write their dictionary definitions.

UNDERSTANDING THE WRITER'S IDEAS

1. State simply Zinsser's meaning in the opening paragraph. What faults of "bad writing" does he mention in this paragraph?

2. To what is Zinsser objecting in paragraph 2?

3. What, according to the author, is the "secret of good writing"? Explain this "secret" in a few simple words of your own. What does Zinsser say detracts from good writing? What is the meaning of the word *ironically?* Why does Zinsser write that the incidence of these writing faults "occur, *ironically,* in proportion to education and rank"?

4. What was the "message" in the letter from the president of Princeton to the alumni? Why does Zinsser object to it? Was it more objectionable in form or content?

5. Who was Thoreau? What is *Walden?* Why are references to the two especially appropriate to Zinsser's essay?

6. What, according to Zinsser, is the relation between clear thinking and good writing? Can you have one without the other? What is meant by a "muddy thinker" (par. 7)? Why is it "impossible for a muddy thinker to write good English"?

7. Why does the author think most people fall asleep while reading? What is his attitude towards such people?

8. Look up and explain the "big differences" between the words *sanguine* and *sanguinary; infer* and *imply.* What is Zinsser's point in calling attention to these differences?

9. In paragraph 12, Zinsser writes about a writer's necessary awareness of the composing process. What elements of the *process* of writing are included in that paragraph? In that discussion, Zinsser speaks of *fuzz* in writing—so does Norman Cousins in his essay, "Why Johnny Can't Write" (pages 20–23). What do they mean by that word as it relates to the writing process? To what does Zinsser compare the writer's thinking process? Why does he use such simple comparisons?

10. Explain the meaning of the last sentence. What does it indicate about Zinsser's attitude towards his work?

UNDERSTANDING THE WRITER'S TECHNIQUES

1. Explain the use of the words *disease* and *strangling* in par. 1. Why does Zinsser use these words in any essay about writing?

2. For what purpose does Zinsser use a series of questions in paragraph 2? Compare his use of questions to Cousins' use of them in paragraph 5 of the essay on pages 20–23.

3. Throughout this essay, Zinsser makes extensive use of examples to support general opinions and attitudes. What attitude or opinion is he supporting in paragraphs 2, 3, 4, 5, and 10? How does he use examples in each of those paragraphs?

4. Analyze the specific structure and organization of paragraph 3:

    a. What general idea about writing does he propose?

    b. Where does he place that idea in the paragraph?

c. What examples does he offer to support his general idea?

d. With what new idea does he conclude the paragraph? How is it related to the beginning idea?

5. Why does Zinsser reproduce exactly portions of the writings of a past president of Princeton University, President Franklin D. Roosevelt, and Henry David Thoreau? How do these sections makes Zinsser's writing clearer, more understandable, or more important?

6. What is the effect on the reader of the words, "Simplify. Simplify," which begin paragraph 6? Why does Zinsser use them at that particular point in the essay? What do they indicate about his attitude towards his subject? Explain.

7. Why does the author begin so many sentences in paragraph 10 with the word *Perhaps?* How does that technique help to *unify* (see page 25) that paragraph?

8. For what reasons does Zinsser include the two pages of "rough" manuscript as a part of the finished essay? What is he trying to show the reader in this way? How does seeing these pages help you to understand better what he is writing about in the completed essay?

9. Overall, how would you describe Zinsser's attitude toward the process and craft of writing? What would you say is his overall attitude toward the future of American writing? Is he generally optimistic or pessimistic? On what does his attitude depend? Refer to specifics in the essay to support your answer.

10. Do you think Zinsser expected other writers, or budding writers, to be the main readers of this essay? Why or why not? If so, what main idea do you think he would like them to come away from the essay with? Do you think readers who were not somehow involved in the writing process would benefit equally from this essay? Why?

EXPLORING THE WRITER'S IDEAS

1. Do you think that Zinsser is ever guilty in this essay of the very "sins" against writing about which he is

upset? Could he have simplified any of his points? Select one of Zinsser's paragraphs in the finished essay and explain how you might rewrite it more simply.

2. In the reading that you do most often, have you noticed overly cluttered writing? Or, do you feel that the writing is at its clearest level of presentation and understanding for its audience? Bring to class some examples of this writing and be prepared to discuss it. In general, what do you consider the relation between the simplicity or complexity of a piece of writing and its intended readership?

3. In the note to the two rough manuscript pages included with this essay, Zinsser implies that the process of rewriting and simplifying may be endless. How do you know when to stop trying to rewrite an essay, story, or poem? Do you ever really feel satisfied that you've reached the end of the rewriting process?

4. Choose one of the rough manuscript paragraphs and compare it to the finished essay. Which do you feel is better? Why? Is there anything Zinsser deleted from the rough copy that you feel he should have retained? Why?

5. Comment on Zinsser's assertion that "Thinking clearly is a conscious act that the writer must force upon himself" (par. 13). How does this opinion compare with the opinions of the three other writers in this chapter?

IDEAS FOR WRITING

Guided Writing

In a 500 to 750-word essay, write about what you feel are some of the problems that you face as a writer.

1. In the first paragraph, identify the problems that you plan to discuss.

2. In the course of your essay, relate your problems more generally to the society-at-large.

3. Identify what, in your opinion, is the "secret" of good writing. Give specific examples of what measures to

take to achieve that secret process and thereby to eliminate some of your problem.

4. Try to include one or two accurate reproductions of your writing to illustrate your composing techniques.

5. Point out what you believe were the major causes of your difficulties as a writer.

6. Toward the end of your essay, explain the type of writer that you would like to be in order to succeed in college.

More Writing Projects

1. Reread an essay that you wrote recently. Even if you've already received it back with a grade and comments from your instructor, rewrite the essay, simplifying where appropriate.

2. Compare the need to "simplify" in writing to the desirability of simplifying some other process or activity, such as making an omelet, buying an automobile, or learning to play tennis, for example.

3. Over a course of a few days, listen to the same news reporter or talk-show host on television or radio and make a list of at least ten examples that indicate the use of "unnecessary words, circular constructions, pompous frills and meaningless jargon." Or, compile such a list from an article in a newspaper or magazine you read regularly. Then write an essay presenting and commenting on these examples.

2

Description

Since a writer's main purpose is to explain things clearly, description is an important aid to good writing. To add liveliness to an essay, descriptive details are necessary to create a visual impression of an object or a scene. As a technique in writing, description matches the sort of details we see in vivid and effective photographs. Good descriptive writers help the reader to "see" objects, scenes, and even moods by means of language.

The essays in this section reflect key qualities in all good descriptive writing. First, description relies on a basic talent that we all have—the ability to see, touch, taste, hear, or smell various elements in the world. Talented descriptive writers refine the power of their five senses in order to recreate people, places, things, emotions, and ideas. Second, in descriptive writing, the author must select details carefully. There might be thousands of details in any given scene, but clearly a writer cannot present all of them. Instead, the writer must choose only those details most useful in painting a picture for the reader. Third, writers must organize their descriptions carefully. With description, the writer must decide on a perspective (for instance, top to bottom, left to right, front to back) and then move carefully from detail to detail. The descriptive writer has a "camera eye" that ranges over its subject in a careful, consistent way. Fourth, descriptive writing creates a "dominant impression" of its subject. This main impression arises from the author's focus on a single subject, and from the feelings that the writer brings to that subject. Finally, descriptive writing offers a thesis or main idea concerning its subject, as does all sound writing. In short, description makes a point.

Writing good descriptive papers is a challenge, because we (like the authors in this section) have to look at our world anew, to remember, to search for meaningful details, to recreate the images around us. As we write descriptive paragraphs and essays, we should keep a basic goal in mind—to permit the reader to see the world that we describe in a fresh, vivid, and concrete way. As descriptive writers, we have to be willing to look at the world, perhaps for the first time, close up.

Truman Capote

LOUIS ARMSTRONG

In this selection from *The Dogs Bark,* Capote uses a unique blend of sensual and realistic description to convey to us his fondness for one of jazz's all-time greats. Though a short remembrance, this selection has a tremendous range of descriptive elements, which help create an entire world around Capote and Armstrong.

Words to Watch

belligerently: assertively, even warlike
steamer: a ship propelled by steam energy
mulatto: a person of mixed black and white parentage
talcum: a usually-perfumed powder applied to the body
vaudeville: a stage entertainment made up of a series of unrelated acts
boater: a type of stiff straw hat
vain: having excessive pride in one's appearance or accomplishments
benefactor: a person who makes a gift to, or confers benefit on, another

Surely the Satch has forgotten, still, he was one of 1
this writer's first friends. I met him when I was four, that
would be around 1928, and he, a hard-plump and belliger-

ently happy brown Buddha, was playing aboard a pleasure steamer that paddled between New Orleans and St. Louis. Never mind why, but I had occasion to take the trip very often, and for me the sweet anger of Armstrong's trumpet, the froggy exuberance of his come-to-me-baby mouthings, are a piece of Proust's madeleine cake: they make Mississippi moons rise again, summon the muddy lights of river towns, the sound, like an alligator's yawn, of river horns—I hear the rush of the mulatto river pushing by, hear, always, stomp! stomp! the beat of the grinning Buddha's foot as he shouts his way into "Sunny Side of the Street" and the honeymooning dancers, dazed with bootleg brew and sweating through their talcum, bunny-hug around the ship's saloony ballroom. The Satch, he was good to me, he told me I had talent, that I ought to be in vaudeville, he gave me a bamboo cane and a straw boater with a peppermint head-band; and every night from the stand announced; "Ladies and gentlemen, now we're going to present you one of America's nice kids, he's going to do a little tap dance." Afterward I passed among the passengers, collecting in my hat nickels and dimes. This went on all summer, I grew rich and vain; but in October the river roughened, the moon whitened, the customers lessened, the boatrides ended, and with them my career. Six years later, while living at a boarding school from which I wanted to run away, I wrote my former, now famous, benefactor, and said if I came to New York couldn't he get me a job at the Cotton Club or somewhere? There was no reply, maybe he never got the letter, it doesn't matter, I still loved him, still do.

BUILDING VOCABULARY

1. In his attempt to capture the noises and rhythms of life on the Mississippi riverboat, Capote employs many words that suggest action and sound. For instance, he writes, "I *hear* the *rush* of the mulatto river *pushing* by." Find five other action and sound words in the essay. Explain what the writer meant for each of them, why he chose them, and if you think they were effective.

Capote puts together some words in this essay to create original adjectival or verbal descriptions. Explain in your own words the meanings of the following italicized words as well as the full expressions in which they appear:

a. a *hard-plump* and belligerently happy brown Buddha

b. his *come-to-me-baby* mouthings

c. dazed with *bootleg brew*

d. *bunny-hug* around the ship's *saloony ballroom*

e. a *peppermint headband*

UNDERSTANDING THE WRITER'S IDEAS

1. Who was "the Satch?" What did he do?

2. What was the relation between Armstrong and Capote almost fifty years ago? What did Armstrong do for Capote? How had that relation changed years later? What was Capote's attitude toward Armstrong at the time he wrote this essay?

3. What *specific* effects of hearing Armstrong play does Capote describe? What *general* meaning can be derived from those specific effects?

4. What did Capote do on the riverboat trips? How did he like this activity? What were its personal effects for Capote?

5. Summarize briefly the difference between summer and autumn on the Mississippi riverboat.

6. What is the Cotton Club? Why would Capote want to work there?

7. What does the following description tell you about Capote's attitude towards Armstrong's music: "the sweet anger of Armstrong's trumpet, the froggy exuberance"?

UNDERSTANDING THE WRITER'S TECHNIQUES

1. What is the tone of this essay? (*Tone* means the writer's attitude towards his or her material.) In other words, what is Capote's overall attitude towards Armstrong

in this essay? Give specific details from the essay to support your idea.

2. Louis Armstrong died in 1971. How does the use of verb tense in the first sentence indicate whether this article was written before or after Armstrong's death?

3. What is the effect of Capote's referring to himself as "this writer" in the first sentence?

4. Why does Capote refer to Armstrong as a "happy brown Buddha" and "the grinning Buddha"? How do these descriptions influence our attitude towards Armstrong?

5. What is the effect of Capote's use of the phrase, "Never mind why"? What feeling is he trying to produce for his audience?

6. What is the meaning of the common expression, "It's a piece of cake"? Who was Proust? What is a madeleine cake? What, then, is the meaning of Capote's description ". . . a piece of Proust's madeleine cake"?

7. How does Capote combine both common language with more formal language in this essay? Give examples. Why does he do so?

EXPLORING THE WRITER'S IDEAS

1. This article perhaps seems rather short for a remembrance of a person about whom Capote writes, "I still loved him, still do." Do you feel Capote has sufficiently described Armstrong and his attitude about him? Do you feel he needed further character development? Why? How much of the reader's enjoyment of this piece depends on a previous knowledge of Louis Armstrong? Explain.

2. Why do you think Capote writes that he wasn't bothered that he never received a reply to the letter he wrote Armstrong? Do you think he's being one hundred percent truthful when he writes, "it doesn't matter"? Why or why not?

3. Based on your reading of this essay, in what ways do you think the passage of so many years influenced Capote's memories of Armstrong? How have time and separation affected your memories of people who were important in your life?

4. Try to listen to recordings of Armstrong's music. Has Capote, in your opinion, characterized it well? Explain your answer.

IDEAS FOR WRITING

Guided Writing

Write a short remembrance of someone older (other than a relative) who influenced you greatly in your childhood or adolescence.

1. Establish the time, place, and circumstances of your earliest interactions with the person.
2. Use original descriptive phrases to indicate the person's effects on you.
3. Try to capture the nature of the most important activities in your relation through vivid descriptions of the actions, sounds, and rhythms of your interactions.
4. Indicate some reference to others around you.
5. Describe at least one specific thing the person did for you.
6. Use a combination of common and more formal language.
7. End with a short description of how your relation changed over the years. Explain at what point it now stands.

More Writing Projects

1. Choose a music, film, or television celebrity whose performance you recently saw. Write a description of how the person looked and acted during the performance. Try to include your reactions to the performance.
2. Bring to class at least five photographs that portray the stages of a person's life or career. This person can either be someone you know or someone who is famous. Be prepared to analyze the details in these photographs and what they reveal about the person. Then write a descriptive essay based on the images in the photographs.

Jade Snow Wong

UNCLE KWOK

In this selection from *Fifth Chinese Daughter,* an autobiography of her childhood in San Francisco's Chinatown,
Jade Snow Wong creates a unique portrait of her Uncle
Kwok. As you read this short essay, try to picture Uncle
Kwok—his dress, features, and behavior. How does the
description the author provides show that, from the moment that he enters the Wong Factory (which also serves
as the family's home), Uncle Kwok is a decidedly unusual
man?

Words to Watch

ambled (par. 1): walked in a leisurely manner
satchel (par. 1): a small bag for carrying clothes, books, or articles
deviation (par. 3): a turning aside from a normal pattern of
        behavior
sauntered (par. 4): walked carelessly or idly
meticulousness (par. 4): extreme care about details
fastidious (par. 5): not easy to please; excessively refined

Among the workers in Daddy's factory, Uncle Kwok   1
was one of the strangest—a large-framed, awkward, unshaven man whose worn clothes hung on him as if they did

not belong to him. Each afternoon around three-thirty, as some of the workers were about to go home to prepare their early dinners, Uncle Kwok slowly and deliberately ambled in through the Wong front door, dragging his feet heavily, and gripping in one hand the small black satchel from which he was never separated.

Going to his own place at the sewing machine, he 2 took off his battered hat and ragged coat, hung both up carefully, and then sat down. At first Jade Snow was rather afraid of this extraordinary person, and unseen, watched his actions from a safe distance. After Uncle Kwok was settled in his chair, he took off his black, slipperlike shoes. Then, taking a piece of stout cardboard from a miscellaneous pile which he kept in a box near his sewing machine, he traced the outline of his shoes on the cardboard. Having closely examined the blades of his scissors and tested their sharpness, he would cut out a pair of cardboard soles, squinting critically through his inaccurate glasses. Next he removed from both shoes the cardboard soles he had made the day before and inserted the new pair. Satisfied with his inspection of his renewed footwear, he got up, went to the waste can some seventy-five feet away, disposed of the old soles, and returned to his machine. He had not yet said a word to anyone.

Daily this process was repeated without deviation. 3

The next thing Uncle Kwok always did was to put 4 on his own special apron, homemade from double thicknesses of heavy burlap and fastened at the waist by strong denim ties. This long apron covered his thin, patched trousers and protected him from dirt and draft. After a half hour had been consumed by these chores, Uncle Kwok was ready to wash his hands. He sauntered into the Wong kitchen, stationed himself at the one sink which served both family and factory, and with characteristic meticulousness, now proceeded to clean his hands and fingernails.

It was Mama's custom to begin cooking the evening 5 meal at this hour so that the children could have their dinner before they went to the Chinese school, but every day she had to delay her preparations at the sink until slow-moving Uncle Kwok's last clean fingernail passed his fastidious inspection. One day, however, the inconvenience tried her patience to its final limit.

Trying to sound pleasantly persuasive, she said, 6 "Uncle Kwok, please don't be so slow and awkward. Why don't you wash your hands at a different time, or else wash them faster?"

Uncle Kwok loudly protested the injustice of her 7 comment. "Mama, I am not awkward. The only awkward thing about my life is that it has not yet prospered!" And he strode off, too hurt even to dry his hands finger by finger, as was his custom.

BUILDING VOCABULARY

1. You can sometimes determine what words mean if you look at smaller words which make them up. What are definitions for the words below? First write down words within them, or based on them, that you may be able to recognize; then write your definition.

    a. deliberately (par. 1)
    b. ragged (par. 2)
    c. inaccurate (par. 2)
    d. thicknesses (par. 4)
    e. characteristic (par. 4)

2. In several of her sentences, Jade Snow Wong uses two or three descriptive words in a series. For example, in the first sentence she describes Uncle Kwok as a "large-framed, awkward, unshaven man." Write similar sentences, using a series of descriptive words for the following subjects.

    a. woman
    b. factory
    c. subway
    d. storm
    e. highway

UNDERSTANDING THE WRITER'S IDEAS

1. What is the main point that Jade Snow Wong wants to make about Uncle Kwok? In which sentence in the selection is the point clearly established?

2. Describe in your own words the specific details we learn about Uncle Kwok.

3. Describe Uncle Kwok's daily routine.

4. What do we learn about Jade Snow Wong's attitude toward Uncle Kwok and about her mother's attitude toward him?

UNDERSTANDING THE WRITER'S TECHNIQUES

1. Descriptive writing relies on words that create pictures (images) that the reader can see. These words create images because they appeal to our sense of sight (through color and action), sound, smell, touch, and taste. In this essay, the writer concentrates on the sense of sight because she wants to create a visual impression of her uncle. What are some details about Uncle Kwok's features and his clothing? How do these descriptive details help to create a dominant impression of him?

2. We also see Uncle Kwok in motion. Describe the way he moves. Find five words in the essay that capture the quality of his motion.

3. Writers often provide a *thesis sentence* to express the main idea of a composition. The thesis sentence establishes the subject, limits it, expresses the writer's attitude toward it, and when well expressed, captures the reader's interest. Is there a thesis sentence in this essay? Which one is it?

4. Why does the thesis sentence appear in the place that it does? Which functions of a good thesis sentence does it reflect? Does it capture your interest?

5. Wong arranges details carefully; the essay progresses from one stage in the description to another until we have a sound impression of Uncle Kwok. At what point do we meet Uncle Kwok? What are the stages in his

activities? How do these stages correspond to the paragraphs in the essay? How do the individual paragraphs help us understand the pattern of Uncle Kwok's activity?

6. What is the purpose in selecting a short one-sentence paragraph (par. 3)?

EXPLORING THE WRITER'S IDEAS

1. The author suggests that people (like Jade Snow's mother) become upset by those who follow set routines. Do you agree? Describe someone you know who annoys you because he or she follows set patterns.

2. Why do we fall back on set routines or repeat the same pattern of behavior from day to day?

3. What makes an individual "strange"? Is the word ever misleading? Should we fear "strange" individuals?

4. What does Uncle Kwok's statement in paragraph 7 explain about his behavior?

IDEAS FOR WRITING

Guided Writing

Write an extended paragraph or a short essay describing someone you found strange, frightening, delightful, amusing, or eccentric when you were a child.

1. Establish a strong thesis sentence and place it near the start of your composition.

2. Concentrate on images of sight (color, outline, appearance, and action) to describe the individual.

3. Try to use a series of descriptive terms in several sentences. See paragraph 4 in Wong's essay, for example.

4. Fill in the details of your character in a carefully organized manner. Place the character in a particular setting at a given point in time. Try to use a "camera eye" movement that follows the character from detail to detail in the description.

5. Try to create a "dominant impression" of the character, one that conforms to the main idea expressed in your thesis sentence.

More Writing Projects

     1.   Write a vivid description of one of your teachers or of someone in your class.

     2.   Cut out a photograph of someone from a newspaper or magazine and then write a clear description of that individual.

     3.   Describe one of your favorite television or movie personalities.

William Least Heat Moon

ARIZONA 87

In this chapter from his 1982 book, *Blue Highways,* William Least Heat Moon presents us with a bittersweet, richly detailed description of the landscape he sees while driving his truck called *Ghost Dancing* through the Southwestern United States. As he drives through central Arizona, his careful eye photographs both the natural and the human landscape around him. In converting these snapshots to language, Least Heat Moon relies upon rich sensory detail and especially vivid and original comparisons.

Words to Watch

friable (par. 1): easily crushed or pulverized
persnickety (par. 1): fussy about small details
pollinate (par. 3): to carry pollen to fertilize plant seeds
kamikaze (par. 3): a member of a corps of Japanese pilots assigned to make a suicidal crash at a target
aerial (par. 3): occurring in the air
cache (par. 4): something hidden
marauding (par. 6): roaming about in search of plunder
Apaches (par. 6): a tribe of Native Americans of the southwestern United States
rodeo (par. 4): a performance featuring cowboy stunts
badger (par. 7): a burrowing animal with long claws
diabolic (par. 7): devilish
unobtrusively (par. 9): not very obviously
escarpment (par. 9): a long cliff
coalesced (par. 12): came together

I don't suppose that saguaros mean to give comic 1
relief to the otherwise solemn face of the desert, but they
do. Standing on the friable slopes they are quite persnickety
about, saguaros mimic men as they salute, bow, dance, raise
arms to wave, and grin with faces carved in by woodpeckers.
Older plants, having survived odds against their reaching
maturity of sixty million to one, have every right to smile.

The saguaro is ninety percent water, and a big, two- 2
hundred-year-old cactus may hold a ton of it—a two-year
supply. With this weight, a plant that begins to lean is soon
on the ground; one theory now says that the arms, which
begin sprouting only after forty or fifty years when the
cactus has some height, are counterweights to keep the
plant erect.

The Monday I drove northeast out of Phoenix, sa- 3
guaros were in bloom—comparatively small, greenish-white
blossoms perched on top of the trunks like undersized Easter
bonnets; at night, long-nosed bats came to pollinate them.
But by day, cactus wrens, birds of daring aerial skill, put
on the show as they made kamikaze dives between toothpick-
size thorns into nest cavities, where they were safe from
everything except the incredible ascents over the spines by
black racers in search of eggs the snakes would swallow
whole.

It was hot. The only shade along Arizona 87 lay 4
under the bottomsides of rocks; the desert gives space then
closes it up with heat. To the east, in profile, rose the
Superstition Mountains, an evil place, Pima and Maricopa
Indians say, which brings on diabolic possession to those
who enter. Somewhere among the granite and greasewood
was the Lost Dutchman gold mine, important not for whatever cache it might hide as for providing a white dream.

North of the Sycamore River, saguaro, ocotillo, 5
paloverde, and cholla surrendered the hills to pads of prickly
pear the size of a man's head. The road climbed and the
temperature dropped. At Payson, a mile high on the northern
slope of the Mazatzal Mountains, I had to pull on a jacket.

Settlers once ran into Payson for protection from 6
marauding Apaches; after the Apache let things calm down,

citizens tried to liven them up again by holding rodeos in the main street. Now, streets paved, Payson lay quiet but for the whine of sawmills releasing the sweet scent of cut timber.

I stopped at an old log hotel to quench a desert 7 thirst. A sign on the door: NO LIVE ANIMALS ALLOWED. I guess you could bring in all the dead ones you wanted. A woman shouted, "Ain't servin' now." Her unmoving eyes, heavy as if cast from lead, watched suspiciously for a live badger under my jacket or a weasel up my pantleg.

"This is a fine old hotel," I said. She ignored me. 8 "Do you mind if I look at your big map?" She shrugged and moved away, safe from any live animal attack. I was hunting a place to go next. Someone had marked the Hopi Reservation to the north in red. Why not? As I left, I asked where I could water my lizard. She ignored that too.

Highway 260, winding through the pine forests of 9 central Arizona, let the mountains be boss as it followed whatever avenues they left open, crossing ridges only when necessary, slipping unobtrusively on narrow spans over streams of rounded boulders. But when 260 reached the massive escarpment called the Mogollon Rim, it had to challenge geography and climb the face.

I shifted to low, and Ghost Dancing pulled hard. A 10 man with a dusty, leathery face creased like an old boot strained on a bicycle—the old style with fat tires. I called a hello, he said nothing. At the summit, I waited to see whether he would make the ascent. Far below lay two cars, crumpled wads. Through the clear air I could count nine ranges of mountains, each successively grayer in a way reminiscent of old Chinese woodblock prints. The Mogollon was a spectacular place; the more so because I had not been anesthetized to it by endless Kodachromes. When the cyclist passed, I called out, "Bravo!" but he acknowledged nothing. I would have liked to talk to a man who, while his contemporaries were consolidating their little empires, rides up the Mogollon Rim on a child's toy. Surely he knew something about desperate men.

The top of the great scarp, elevation sixty-five hundred 11

feet, lay flat and covered with big ponderosas standing between dirty snowdrifts and black pools of snowmelt. I began anticipating Heber, the next town. One of the best moments of any day on the road was, toward sunset, looking forward to the last stop. At Heber I hoped for an old hotel with a little bar off to the side where they would serve A-1 on draft under a stuffed moosehead; or maybe I'd find a grill dishing up steak and eggs on blue-rimmed platters. I hoped for people who had good stories, people who sometimes took you home to see their collection of carved peach pits.

That was the hope. But Heber was box houses and 12 a dingy sawmill, a couple of motels and filling stations, a glass-and-Formica cafe. Heber had no center, no focus for the eye and soul: neither a courthouse, nor high church steeple, nor hotel. Nothing has done more to take a sense of civic identity, a feeling of community, from small-town America than the loss of old hotels to the motel business. The hotel was once where things coalesced, where you could meet both townspeople and travelers. Not so in a motel. No matter how you build it, the motel remains a haunt of the quick and dirty, where the only locals are Chamber of Commerce boys every fourth Thursday. Who ever heard the returning traveler exclaim over one of the great motels of the world he stayed in? Motels can be big, but never grand.

BUILDING VOCABULARY

1. *Compound words* are made up of two separate words joined together. They help intensify description by focusing on the connection between two words. Some compounds are formed by joining two nouns (*photograph, chairperson*); others combine nouns with nonnoun prefixes, suffixes, or combining forms (*childlike, self-pity*). Some compounds use hyphens between the two words, although the general current trend is to omit the hyphens. For example, such words as *today* or *tomorrow* were regularly hyphenated just 100 years ago. However, many compound words are still acceptable in all three steps of development: two separate words, a single hyphenated word, a single nonhyphenated word (*war monger, war-monger, warmonger*).

Locate at least ten compound words that in Least Heat Moon's essay are formed by joining two nouns. Use each in a sentence of your own.

2. *Denotation* refers to the dictionary definition of a word; *connotation* refers to the various shades of meaning and feeling readers bring to a word or phrase. Look up and write dictionary definitions for each of the words in italics. Then, explain in your own words the connotative meaning of each sentence or phrase.

    a. "the otherwise *solemn* face of the desert" (par. 1)
    b. "to *quench* a desert thirst" (par. 7)
    c. "it had to *challenge* geography (par. 9)
    d. "I had not been *anesthetized* by endless *Koda-chromes*" (par. 10)
    e. "glass-and-*Formica* cafe" (par. 12)

3. Least Heat Moon is a careful observer of the plants, rocks, and wildlife of the Arizona landscape. List six of the words drawn from this landscape and write dictionary definitions of them.

UNDERSTANDING THE WRITER'S IDEAS

1. What are the saguaros? What are the odds of their reaching full growth? How old may saguaros become? At what age do they begin to sprout arms?

2. For what purpose do the cactus wrens use the saguaros? What is the major danger to these birds?

3. Explain the sentence: "The only shade along Arizona 87 lay under the bottom sides of rocks." (par. 4)

4. What is the American Indian legend about Superstition Mountains? Explain the "diabolic possession." What is supposedly hidden in these mountains and what is its importance? What is meant by "a white dream"?

5. How was the weather in Payson different from the weather when the writer started driving through the desert? What used to be the atmosphere in Payson? What is it like now?

6. Paragraph 9 describes the route of Highway 260.

In your own words, how does the highway relate to the environment that surrounds it?

7. What is Moon's attitude toward the man on the bicycle? What do we learn about the man's appearance? How does the man react to Moon? What does Moon describe as "a child's toy"? Why?

8. How do we know that some cars fell off the Mogollon Rim?

UNDERSTANDING THE WRITER'S TECHNIQUES

1. Writers often sharpen descriptions by making unusual comparisons. In this essay Least Heat Moon makes many such comparisons. Locate and explain the meaning of what each of the following things is compared to:

a. The shape and look of the saguaros
b. The saguaro blossoms
c. The dives of the cactus wrens
d. The appearance of the nine mountain ranges

Locate and explain other comparisons in the essay.

2. How does Moon use elements of space and time to order details in this description? Why is this method effective? Why does he introduce himself ("I drove") in paragraph 3? Why does he wait until then to introduce himself?

3. What is the effect of the short sentence "It was hot" (par. 4) coming as it does after a number of much longer sentences in preceding paragraphs?

4. *Imagery* refers to clear, vivid description rooted in sensory detail. List several images of vivid details that employ the senses: sight (color and action), sound, smell, touch, and taste.

5. In describing the old log hotel in paragraphs 7 and 8, Moon uses *dialogue,* or accurate recordings of actual conversations (see Glossary). What is the effect of dialogue on that descriptive scene?

6. Least Heat Moon makes use of humor to make

biting observations about the hotel in Payson. Explain what he means by "I guess you could bring in all the dead ones you wanted" (par. 7) and "As I left, I asked where I could water my lizard" (par. 8). Why does the woman ignore him? Why does he use biting humor in this way?

7. Least Heat Moon does not simply present factual details of the Arizona desert. Instead, his descriptions are highly subjective, colored with personal emotions. Locate five sentences of highly subjective description. Why is he so subjective? What impression does he give you of the scenes he describes? How does his subjectivity help create the *tone* of this essay? What is that tone?

8. Do you find the ending suitable? Is it too abrupt or is it consistent with the rest of the selection? Explain. Remember, this selection is a complete chapter of a book by the author.

EXPLORING THE WRITER'S IDEAS

1. In the final paragraph Least Heat Moon writes about the disappearance of "civic identity" or "a feeling of community" from small-town America. He blames this loss on the replacement of once-bustling hotels with impersonal motels. Do you think the writer believes this is the only reason for the change? In your experience, how else have American small towns lost their unique flavors or identities?

2. In paragraph 10, in discussing the bicyclist, the author writes, "Surely he knew something about desperate men." Why do you think he feels this way about the cyclist?

IDEAS FOR WRITING

Guided Writing

Write a short essay describing a landscape you traveled through at one time. This can be a city, suburban, or countryside landscape.

1. Begin by concentrating on a particular or dominant element of the landscape.

2. Focus on the environmental conditions and the weather. Note any changes of the climate.

3. Arrange your description as you travel in time from place to place in the landscape.

4. Include at least one interaction with another person who helped you to formulate your feelings about the place.

5. Use concrete sensory detail as you write images of color, action, sound, smell, touch, and taste.

6. Use vivid and varied comparisons to describe what you saw.

7. Conclude your essay with a description and explanation of something that either greatly disappointed or excited you about your travels through this place.

More Writing Projects

1. Concentrating on both the setting and the person, write a short description of a chance encounter with someone, as Least Heat Moon does with the bicyclist on the Mongollon Rim. End by coming to a conclusion about this person's personality.

2. Describe a particular place that you feel has been changed very much by modernization. Include descriptions of both the old and the new ways the place looks and feels. Also include your reactions to both the old and the new.

Richard Selzer

THE DISCUS THROWER

Richard Selzer, a surgeon, gives his readers vivid insights into the excitement as well as the pathos of the world of medicine. His books include *Rituals of Surgery* (1974) and *Mortal Lesions* (1977). His essays are widely published in magazines, including *Esquire, Harper's,* and *Redbook*. In this essay, Selzer dramatically describes a patient's final day.

Words to Watch

furtive (par. 1): sly
pruned (par. 2): cut back; trimmed
facsimile (par. 2): an exact copy
shard (par. 20): a broken piece; fragment
forceps (par. 20): an instrument used in operations for holding or pulling
athwart (par. 21): leaning across
probes (par. 33): investigates thoroughly
hefts (par. 33): tosses; heaves

I spy on my patients. Ought not a doctor to observe 1 his patients by any means and from any stance, that he might the more fully assemble evidence? So I stand in the doorways of hospital rooms and gaze. Oh, it is not all that furtive an act. Those in bed need only look up to discover me. But they never do.

From the doorway of Room 542 the man in the bed ²
seems deeply tanned. Blue eyes and close-cropped white hair give him the appearance of vigor and good health. But I know that his skin is not brown from the sun. It is rusted, rather, in the last stage of containing the vile repose within. And the blue eyes are frosted, looking inward like the windows of a snowbound cottage. This man is blind. This man is also legless—the right leg missing from midthigh down, the left from just below the knee. It gives him the look of a bonsai, roots and branches pruned into the dwarfed facsimile of a great tree.

Propped on pillows, he cups his right thigh in both ³
hands. Now and then he shakes his head as though acknowledging the intensity of his suffering. In all of this he makes no sound. Is he mute as well as blind?

The room in which he dwells is empty of all posses- ⁴
sions—no get-well cards, small, private caches of food, day-old flowers, slippers, all the usual kick-shaws of the sickroom. There is only the bed, a chair, a nightstand, and a tray on wheels that can be swung across his lap for meals.

"What time is it?" he asks. ⁵

"Three o'clock." ⁶

"Morning or afternoon?" ⁷

"Afternoon." ⁸

He is silent. There is nothing else he wants to know. ⁹

"How are you?" I say. ¹⁰

"Who is it?" he asks. ¹¹

"It's the doctor. How do you feel?" ¹²

He does not answer right away. ¹³

"Feel?" he says. ¹⁴

"I hope you feel better," I say. ¹⁵

I press the button at the side of the bed. ¹⁶

"Down you go," I say. ¹⁷

"Yes, down, " he says. ¹⁸

He falls back upon the bed awkwardly. His stumps, ¹⁹
unweighted by legs and feet, rise in the air, presenting themselves. I unwrap the bandages from the stumps, and begin to cut away the black scabs and the dead, glazed fat

with scissors and forceps. A shard of white bone comes loose. I pick it away. I wash the wounds with disinfectant and redress the stumps. All this while, he does not speak. What is he thinking behind those lids that do not blink? Is he remembering a time when he was whole? Does he dream of feet? Of when his body was not a rotting log?

He lies solid and inert. In spite of everything, he 20 remains impressive, as though he were a sailor standing athwart a slanting deck.

"Anything more I can do for you?" I ask. 21

For a long moment he is silent. 22

"Yes," he says at last and without the least irony. 23 "You can bring me a pair of shoes."

In the corridor, the head nurse is waiting for me. 24

"We have to do something about him," she says. 25 "Every morning he orders scrambled eggs for breakfast, and, instead of eating them, he picks up the plate and throws it against the wall."

"Throws his plate?" 26

"Nasty. That's what he is. No wonder his family 27 doesn't come to visit. They probably can't stand him any more than we can."

She is waiting for me to do something. 28

"Well?" 29

"We'll see," I say. 30

The next morning I am waiting in the corridor when 31 the kitchen delivers his breakfast. I watch the aide place the tray on the stand and swing it across his lap. She presses the button to raise the head of the bed. Then she leaves.

In time the man reaches to find the rim of the tray, 32 then on to find the dome of the covered dish. He lifts off the cover and places it on the stand. He fingers across the plate until he probes the eggs. He lifts the plate in both hands, sets it on the palm of his right hand, centers it, balances it. He hefts it up and down slightly, getting the feel of it. Abruptly, he draws back his right arm as far as he can.

There is the crack of the plate breaking against the 33 wall at the foot of his bed and the small wet sound of the scrambled eggs dropping to the floor.

And then he laughs. It is a sound you have never 34

heard. It is something new under the sun. It could cure cancer.

Out in the corridor, the eyes of the head nurse 35 narrow.

"Laughed, did he?" 36

She writes something down on her clipboard. 37

A second aide arrives, brings a second breakfast 38 tray, puts it on the nightstand, out of his reach. She looks over at me shaking her head and making her mouth go. I see that we are to be accomplices.

"I've got to feed you," she says to the man. 39

"Oh, no you don't," the man says. 40

"Oh, yes I do," the aide says, "after the way you just 41 did. Nurse says so."

"Get me my shoes," the man says. 42

"Here's oatmeal," the aide says. "Open." And she 43 touches the spoon to his lower lip.

"I ordered scrambled eggs," says the man. 44

"That's right," the aide says. 45

I step forward. 46

"Is there anything I can do?" I say. 47

"Who are you?" the man asks. 48

In the evening I go once more to that ward to make 49 my rounds. The head nurse reports to me that Room 542 is deceased. She has discovered this quite by accident, she says. No, there had been no sound. Nothing. It's a blessing, she says.

I go into his room, a spy looking for secrets. He is 50 still there in his bed. His face is relaxed, grave, dignified. After a while, I turn to leave. My gaze sweeps the wall at the foot of the bed, and I see the place where it has been repeatedly washed, where the wall looks very clean and very white.

BUILDING VOCABULARY

1. In this essay, Selzer uses a few words that derive from languages other than English. Look up the following

words and tell what language they come from. Then, write a definition for each:

 a. *bonsai*
 b. *kick-shaws*
 c. *caches*

 2. Use these words from the essay in complete sentences of your own: *vile, repose, dwarfed, glazed, inert, accomplices*.

UNDERSTANDING THE WRITER'S IDEAS

 1. What reason does Selzer give for a doctor's spying on his patients?

 2. What does the man in Room 542 look like? Why is his skin brown? How does Selzer know he is blind? Why does Selzer think the patient may be mute? When do we know that he is not mute?

 3. What is the author's meaning of the phrase "vile repose"?

 4. How do we know that this patient does not receive many visitors?

 5. Aside from wanting to know the time of day, what is the patient's one request? Do you think he is serious about his request? Why?

 6. Why does the patient hurl his food tray against the wall?

 7. For what reason does the head nurse complain about the patient?

 8. What does Selzer feel and think about the patient? How do you know?

UNDERSTANDING THE WRITER'S TECHNIQUES

 1. Throughout the essay, Selzer asks a number of questions. Locate at least three of these questions that are not a part of the dialogue. To whom do you think they are addressed? What is their effect on the reader?

 2. Like William Least Heat Moon, Selzer heightens

the description by making vivid and unusual comparisons. Locate and explain in your own words three comparisons that you feel are especially descriptive and intriguing.

3. Selzer uses some very short sentences interspersed among longer ones. Locate at least four very short sentences. How do they draw your attention to the description?

4. Locate in Selzer's essay at least five examples of vivid description (imagery) relating to illness. What is their emotional effect on the reader?

5. How does Selzer use *dialogue* to reveal the personality of the patient? of the doctor? of the head nurse?

6. In paragraph 24, Selzer states that the patient delivers his request "without the least irony." *Irony* (see Glossary) is saying what is opposite to what one means. Why might Selzer have expected irony from the patient? Why might someone in the sick man's condition use irony? What do you think the man means by his request "You can bring me a pair of shoes"—if, in fact, the remark is not an ironical one?

7. What does the title of the essay mean? What is a discus thrower? Why has Selzer chosen an ancient image of an athlete as the title of this essay? In what way is the title ironic?

8. Why does Selzer use such an unusual word as *kick-shaws* (par. 4)?

9. *Double entendre* (see Glossary) is a French expression that indicates that something has a double meaning, each equally valid. What might be the two meanings of the nurse's words "It's a blessing"?

10. In this essay, the author uses a *framing* device: that is, he opens and closes the essay with a similar image or idea. What is that idea? Why is it effective? What are the differences in the use of this idea in the opening and closing paragraphs?

11. The heart of this essay is the patient's insistence upon throwing his breakfast plate at the wall, and yet Selzer does not attempt to explain the man's reasons for such an act. Why do you think the man hurls his breakfast across

the room each morning—and why does he laugh? Why does Selzer not provide an analysis of the action? How does the title help us see Selzer's attitude toward the man's act?

EXPLORING THE WRITER'S IDEAS

1. In the beginning of the essay Selzer asks, "Ought not a doctor to observe his patients by any means from any stance, that he might more fully assemble evidence?" Do you feel that a doctor should have this right? Why? What rights do you believe patients should have in a hospital?

2. The head nurse in Selzer's description seems fed up with the patient in Room 542. Why do you think she feels this way? Do you think that a person in her position has the right to express this feeling on his or her job? Why or why not?

3. The patient's attitude is influenced by his physical state and his nearness to death. How have physical ailments or handicaps changed the attitudes of people you have known? How has an illness influenced your thoughts at any time?

IDEAS FOR WRITING

Guided Writing

Describe a person you have observed who was seriously ill, in danger, or under great stress.

1. Base your description upon close observation of the person during a short but concentrated span of time: a morning or afternoon, an hour or two, even a few minutes.

2. Begin with a short, direct paragraph in which you introduce the person and the critical situation he or she faces.

3. Include yourself ("I") in the description.

4. Describe the vantage point from which you are "spying" or observing, and focus on the particular subject of the scene.

RICHARD SELZER 67

5. Throughout your essay, ask key questions.

6. Use imagery and original comparisons to highlight the description of your subject.

7. Include some dialogue with either the subject or another person.

8. Describe at least one very intense action performed by your subject.

9. Tell how the subject and scene had changed when you next saw them.

More Writing Projects

1. Describe a hospital room in which you stayed or visited some other person. Focus on your sensory perceptions of the place.

2. Describe an interaction you had with a person who was blind or deaf or was disabled in some other way. In your description, focus closely on the person's features. Write about your reactions during and after the interaction.

3

Narration

Narration is the telling of a story. As a technique in essay writing, it normally involves a discussion of events that are "true" or real, events that take place over a period of time. Narration helps a writer explain things and, as such, it is an important skill for the kind of writing often required of you.

Writers who use narration usually rely on descriptive details to advance their stories. Moreover, in the narrative essay, there always must be some purpose in the telling, a purpose that goes beyond mere enjoyment of the story itself. Consequently, narration in an essay advances a thesis, or main idea. For example, if you had to write an essay on the happiest event in your life, you might choose to narrate the day your team won the state championship. You would establish your thesis—your main point—quickly, and then go on to tell about the event itself. In short, you would use narration as a means to an end—to make a significant statement about an important moment in your life.

The manner in which you relate this event depends on the simplicity or complexity of the story that you want to tell. If the season before the winning game was itself filled with excitement, you certainly would want to explain that and to trace the exciting events over a period of time. If the championship itself provided most of the thrills, you would want to concentrate on a much shorter period of time, breaking your narration down to days, hours, even minutes, instead of months. Learning to present time—whether in a single personal event, a series of related events, a historical occurrence, or an aging process—is one of the key elements in narrative prose.

Normally in a narrative essay you would start at the beginning and move to the end, or from past to present, or from old to new, but there are many other ways to relate events in the narrative essay. For instance, you could begin an essay on the death of someone important to you by detailing the day of the funeral, and then moving backward in time to flesh out the events leading up to the funeral. For beginners this "flashback" technique often causes very confused writing; but skilled writers know how to "jump around" in time without confusing the reader, blurring the thesis, or destroying the progression of the essay.

As with descriptive writing, the narrative essay requires a careful selection of details. Certain moments within any time order are more important than others, and these crucial moments will be emphasized and developed fully by a good writer. Other moments, significant but less important than the main moments, will take up less space, while unimportant items will be eliminated entirely. However, the writer must connect each event in the time span to other events that come before or after. Here, transitions of time—words like "afterwards," "soon," "a day later," "suddenly"—serve as bridges to connect the various moments in the narrative pattern.

There are other aspects of narration that appear in this chapter. For example, you must select a point of view for your story—whether presenting events through your own eyes or from a more objective or detached position. You must also decide on the value of dialogue (recording of conversations). Finally, you must be aware that other techniques of prose writing (like description) can reinforce your narrative pattern. Fortunately, most individuals have a basic storytelling ability and know how to develop stories that make a point. Once you master narration as a writing pattern, you will be able to use it in a variety of situations.

Elizabeth Wong

THE STRUGGLE TO BE AN ALL-AMERICAN GIRL

In this poignant remembrance, Elizabeth Wong tells of the hurts and sorrows of her bicultural upbringing. Wong effectively blends concrete description and imaginative comparisons to give a vivid look into the life of a child who felt she had a Chinese exterior but an American interior.

Words to Watch

stoically (par. 1): without showing emotion
dissuade (par. 2): to talk out of doing something
ideographs (par. 7): Chinese picture symbols used to form words
disassociate (par. 8): to detach from association
vendors (par. 8): sellers of goods
gibberish (par. 9): confused, unintelligible speech or language
pidgin (par. 10): simplified speech that is usually a mixture of two or more languages

It's still there, the Chinese school on Yale Street 1 where my brother and I used to go. Despite the new coat of paint and the high wire fence, the school I knew 10 years ago remains remarkably, stoically the same.

Every day at 5 P.M., instead of playing with our 2
fourth- and fifth-grade friends or sneaking out to the empty
lot to hunt ghosts and animal bones, my brother and I had
to go to Chinese school. No amount of kicking, screaming,
or pleading could dissuade my mother, who was solidly
determined to have us learn the language of our heritage.

Forcibly, she walked us the seven long, hilly blocks 3
from our home to school, depositing our defiant tearful
faces before the stern principal. My only memory of him is
that he swayed on his heels like a palm tree, and he
always clasped his impatient twitching hands behind his
back. I recognized him as a repressed maniacal child killer,
and knew that if we ever saw his hands we'd be in big
trouble.

We all sat in little chairs in an empty auditorium. 4
The room smelled like Chinese medicine, an imported
faraway mustiness. Like ancient mothballs or dirty closets.
I hated that smell. I favored crisp new scents. Like the soft
French perfume that my American teacher wore in public
school.

There was a stage far to the right, flanked by an 5
American flag and the flag of the Nationalist Republic of
China, which was also red, white and blue but not as pretty.

Although the emphasis at the school was mainly 6
language—speaking, reading, writing—the lessons always
began with an exercise in politeness. With the entrance of
the teacher, the best student would tap a bell and everyone
would get up, kowtow, and chant, "Sing san ho," the phonetic
for "How are you, teacher?"

Being ten years old, I had better things to learn 7
than ideographs copied painstakingly in lines that ran right
to left from the tip of a *moc but,* a real ink pen that had to
be held in an awkward way if blotches were to be avoided.
After all, I could do the multiplication tables, name the
satellites of Mars, and write reports on "Little Women" and
"Black Beauty." Nancy Drew, my favorite book heroine,
never spoke Chinese.

The language was a source of embarrassment. More 8
times than not, I had tried to disassociate myself from the

nagging loud voice that followed me wherever I wandered in the nearby American supermarket outside Chinatown. The voice belonged to my grandmother, a fragile woman in her seventies who could outshout the best of the street vendors. Her humor was raunchy, her Chinese rhythmless, patternless. It was quick, it was loud, it was unbeautiful. It was not like the quiet, lilting romance of French or the gentle refinement of the American South. Chinese sounded pedestrian. Public.

In Chinatown, the comings and goings of hundreds 9 of Chinese on their daily tasks sounded chaotic and frenzied. I did not want to be thought of as mad, as talking gibberish. When I spoke English, people nodded at me, smiled sweetly, said encouraging words. Even the people in my culture would cluck and say that I'd do well in life. "My, doesn't she move her lips fast," they would say, meaning that I'd be able to keep up with the world outside Chinatown.

My brother was even more fanatical than I about 10 speaking English. He was especially hard on my mother, criticizing her, often cruelly, for her pidgin speech—smatterings of Chinese scattered like chop suey in her conversation. "It's not 'What it is,' Mom," he'd say in exasperation. "It's 'What *is* it, what *is* it, what *is* it!" Sometimes Mom might leave out an occasional "the" or "a," or perhaps a verb of being. He would stop her in mid-sentence: "Say it again, Mom. Say it right." When he tripped over his own tongue, he'd blame it on her: "See, Mom, it's all your fault. You set a bad example."

What infuriated my mother most was when my 11 brother cornered her on her consonants, especially "r." My father had played a cruel joke on Mom by assigning her an American name that her tongue wouldn't allow her to say. No matter how hard she tried, "Ruth" always ended up "Luth" or "Roof."

After two years of writing with a *moc but* and 12 reciting words with multiples of meanings, I finally was granted a cultural divorce. I was permitted to stop Chinese school.

I thought of myself as multicultural. I preferred 13

tacos to egg rolls; I enjoyed Cinco de Mayo more than Chinese New Year.

At last, I was one of you; I wasn't one of them. 14

Sadly, I still am. 15

BUILDING VOCABULARY

For each of the words in italics, choose the letter of the word or expression that most closely matches its meaning.

1. the *stern* principal (par. 3)
a. military   b. very old
c. immoral   d. strict

2. *repressed* maniacal child killer (par. 3)
a. quiet   b. ugly
c. held back   d. retired

3. an imported faraway *mustiness* (par. 4)
a. country   b. moth balls
c. chair   d. staleness

4. a *fragile* woman (par. 8)
a. elderly   b. frail
c. tall   d. inconsistent

5. her humor was *raunchy* (par. 8)
a. obscene   b. unclear
c. childish   d. very funny

6. thought of as *mad* (par. 9)
a. foreign   b. angry
c. stupid   d. crazy

7. quiet *lilting* romance of French (par. 8)
a. musical   b. tilting
c. loving   d. complicated

8. what *infuriated* my mother most (par. 11)
a. angered   b. humiliated
c. made laugh   d. typified

UNDERSTANDING THE WRITER'S IDEAS

1. What did Elizabeth Wong and her brother do every day after school? How did that make them different

from their friends? What was their attitude toward what they did? How do you know?

2. What does Wong mean when she says of the principal "I recognized him as a repressed child killer"? Why were she and her brother afraid to see his hands?

3. What was the main purpose of going to Chinese school? What did Wong feel she had learned at "regular" American school? Which did she feel was more important? What are *Little Women, Black Beauty,* and *Nancy Drew*?

4. In the first sentence of paragraph 8, what language is "the language"?

5. What was Wong's grandmother like? What was Wong's attitude toward her? Why?

6. When Wong spoke English in Chinatown, why did the others think it was good that she moved her lips quickly?

7. What was her brother's attitude toward speaking English? How did he treat their mother when she tried to speak English? Why was it unfortunate that the mother had the American name *Ruth*? Who gave her that name? Why?

8. Explain the expression "he tripped over his own tongue" (par. 10).

9. In paragraph 13, Wong states, "I thought of myself as multicultural." What does that mean? What are tacos, egg rolls, and Cinco de Mayo? Why is it surprising that Wong includes those items as examples of her multiculturalism?

10. Who are the "you" and "them" of paragraph 14? Explain the significance of the last sentence. What does it indicate about Wong's attitude toward Chinese school from the vantage point of being an adult?

UNDERSTANDING THE WRITER'S TECHNIQUES

1. What is the author's purpose in writing this narrative? Is the technique of narration an appropriate one to her purpose? Why or why not?

2. Wong does not state a thesis directly in a thesis

sentence. How does her title imply a thesis? If you were writing a thesis sentence of your own for this essay, what would it be?

3. This narrative contains several stories really. The first one ends after paragraph 7 and tells about Wong's routine after 5:00 P.M. on school days. Paragraphs 8 and 9, 10 and 11, and 12 and 13 offer other related narratives. Summarize each of these briefly. How does Wong help the reader shift from story to story?

4. The writer of narration will present *time* in a way that best fulfills the purpose of the narration. This presentation may take many forms: a single, personal event; a series of related events; a historical occurrence; an aging process. Obviously Wong chose a series of related events. Why does she use such a narrative structure to make her point? Could she have chosen an alternative plan, do you think? Why or why not?

5. Writers of narration often rely upon descriptive details to flesh out their stories. Find examples of sensory language here that makes the scene come alive for the reader.

6. Writers often use figurative comparisons to enliven their writing and to make it more distinctive. A *simile* is an imaginative form of figurative comparison using "like" or "as" to connect two items. One thing is similar to another in this figure. A *metaphor* is a figure of speech in which the writer compares two items not normally thought of as similar, but unlike in a simile, the comparison is direct— that is, it does not use "like" or "as." In other words, one thing is said to be the other thing, not merely to be like it. For example, if you wanted to compare love to a rose, you might use these two comparisons:

(simile)   My love is *like* a red, red rose.
(metaphor) My love *is* a red, red rose.

In Wong's essay, find the similes and metaphors in paragraphs 2, 3, 4, 10, and 12. For each, name the two items compared and explain the comparison in your own words.

7. Narratives often include lines of spoken lan-

guage, that is, one person in the narrative talking alone or to another. Wong uses quoted detail sparsely here. Why did she choose to limit the dialogue? How effective is the dialogue that appears here? Where do you think she might have used more dialogue to advance the narrative?

8. The last two paragraphs are only one sentence each. Why do you think the author chose this technique?

9. What is the irony in the last sentence of the essay? (See Glossary). How would the meaning of the last sentence change if you eliminated the word *sadly*? What is the irony in the title of the essay?

10. What is the tone (see Glossary) of this essay? How does the tone here compare with the tone in Jade Snow Wong's description of Uncle Kwok?

EXPLORING THE WRITER'S IDEAS

1. Wong and her brother deeply resented being forced to attend Chinese school. When children very clearly express displeasure or unhappiness, should parents force them to do things anyway? Why or why not?

2. On one level this essay is about a clash of cultures, here the ancient Chinese culture of Wong's ancestry and the culture of the twentieth-century United States. Is it possible for someone to maintain connections to his or her ethnic or cultural backgrounds and at the same time to become an "all American" girl or boy? What do people of foreign backgrounds gain when they become completely Americanized? What do they lose?

3. Because of their foreign ways, the mother and grandmother clearly embarrassed the Wong children. Under what other conditions that you can think of do parents embarrass children? Children, parents?

IDEAS FOR WRITING

Guided Writing

Write a narration in which you tell about some difficult moment that took place in grade school or high school, a moment that taught you something about yourself, your needs, or your cultural background.

1. Provide a concrete description of the school.
2. Tell in correct sequence about the event.
3. Identify people who play a part in this moment.
4. Use concrete, sensory description throughout your essay.
5. Use original similes and metaphors to make your narrative clearer and more dramatic.
6. Use dialogue (or spoken conversation) appropriately in order to advance the narrative.
7. In your conclusion, indicate what your attitude toward this moment is now that you are an adult.
8. Write a title that implies your thesis.

More Writing Projects

1. In an essay, tell about your happiest childhood memory and explain why it made you so happy.
2. Write a short narration about an experience you had with a person of another culture.

Langston Hughes

SALVATION

For more than forty years, Langston Hughes (1902–1967) was a major figure in American literature. In poetry, essays, drama, and fiction he attempted, as he said himself, "to explain and illuminate the Negro condition in America." This selection from his autobiography, *The Big Sea* (1940), tells the story of his "conversion" to Christ. Salvation was a key event in the life of his community, but Hughes tells comically how he bowed to pressure by permitting himself to be "saved from sin."

Words to Watch

dire (par. 3): terrible; disastrous
gnarled (par. 4): knotty; twisted
rounder (par. 6): watchman; policeman
deacons (par. 6): clergymen or laymen appointed to help the minister
serenely (par. 7): calmly; tranquilly
knickerbockered (par. 11): dressed in short, loose trousers that are gathered below the knees

I was saved from sin when I was going on thirteen. 1
But not really saved. It happened like this. There was a big revival at my Auntie Reed's church. Every night for weeks

there had been much preaching, singing, praying, and shouting, and some very hardened sinners had been brought to Christ, and the membership of the church had grown by leaps and bounds. Then just before the revival ended, they held a special meeting for children, "to bring the young lambs to the fold." My aunt spoke of it for days ahead. That night I was escorted to the front row and placed on the mourners' bench with all the other young sinners, who had not yet been brought to Jesus.

My aunt told me that when you were saved you saw 2 a light, and something happened to you inside! And Jesus came into your life! And God was with you from then on! She said you could see and hear and feel Jesus in your soul. I believed her. I had heard a great many old people say the same thing and it seemed to me they ought to know. So I sat there calmly in the hot, crowded church, waiting for Jesus to come to me.

The preacher preached a wonderful rhythmical ser- 3 mon, all moans and shouts and lonely cries and dire pictures of hell, and then he sang a song about the ninety and nine safe in the fold, but one little lamb was left out in the cold. Then he said: "Won't you come? Won't you come to Jesus? Young lambs, won't you come?" And he held out his arms to all us young sinners there on the mourners' bench. And the little girls cried. And some of them jumped up and went to Jesus right away. But most of us just sat there.

A great many old people came and knelt around us 4 and prayed, old women with jet-black faces and braided hair, old men with work-gnarled hands. And the church sang a song about the lower lights are burning, some poor sinners to be saved. And the whole building rocked with prayer and song.

Still I kept waiting to *see* Jesus. 5

Finally all the young people had gone to the altar 6 and were saved, but one boy and me. He was a rounder's son named Westley. Westley and I were surrounded by sisters and deacons praying. It was very hot in the church, and getting late now. Finally Westley said to me in a whisper: "God damn! I'm tired o' sitting here. Let's get up and be saved." So he got up and was saved.

Then I was left all alone on the mourners' bench. 7
My aunt came and knelt at my knees and cried, while
prayers and songs swirled all around me in the little church.
The whole congregation prayed for me alone, in a mighty
wail of moans and voices. And I kept waiting serenely for
Jesus, waiting, waiting—but he didn't come. I wanted to see
him, but nothing happened to me. Nothing! I wanted something to happen to me, but nothing happened.

I heard the songs and the minister saying: "Why 8
don't you come? My dear child, why don't you come to Jesus?
Jesus is waiting for you. He wants you. Why don't you come?
Sister Reed, what is this child's name?"

"Langston," my aunt sobbed. 9

"Langston, why don't you come? Why don't you come 10
and be saved? Oh, Lamb of God! Why don't you come?"

Now it was really getting late. I began to be ashamed 11
of myself, holding everything up so long. I began to wonder
what God thought about Westley, who certainly hadn't seen
Jesus either, but who was now sitting proudly on the
platform, swinging his knickerbockered legs and grinning
down at me, surrounded by deacons and old women on their
knees praying. God had not struck Westley dead for taking
his name in vain or for lying in the temple. So I decided that
maybe to save further trouble, I'd better lie, too, and say
that Jesus had come, and get up and be saved.

So I got up. 12

Suddenly the whole room broke into a sea of shouting, 13
as they saw me rise. Waves of rejoicing swept the place.
Women leaped in the air. My aunt threw her arms around
me. The minister took me by the hand and led me to the
platform.

When things quieted down, in a hushed silence, 14
punctuated by a few ecstatic "Amens," all the new young
lambs were blessed in the name of God. Then joyous singing
filled the room.

That night, for the last time in my life but one—for 15
I was a big boy twelve years old—I cried. I cried, in bed
alone, and couldn't stop. I buried my head under the quilts,
but my aunt heard me. She woke up and told my uncle I was
crying because the Holy Ghost had come into my life, and

because I had seen Jesus. But I was really crying because I couldn't bear to tell her that I had lied, that I had deceived everybody in the church, that I hadn't seen Jesus, and that now I didn't believe there was a Jesus any more, since he didn't come to help me.

BUILDING VOCABULARY

1. Throughout this essay, Hughes selects words dealing with religion to emphasize his ideas. Look these words up in a dictionary. Then tell what *connotations* the following words have for you. (See Glossary).

     a. sin (par. 1)
     b. mourner (par. 1)
     c. lamb (par. 3)
     d. salvation (title)

2. Locate additional words that deal with religion.

3. When Hughes talks about lambs in the fold—and lambs in general—he is using a figure of speech, a comparison. What is being compared? How does religion enter into the comparison? Why is it useful as a figure of speech?

UNDERSTANDING THE WRITER'S IDEAS

1. According to Hughes' description, what is a revival meeting like? What is the effect of the "preaching, singing, praying, and shouting" on the "sinners" and the "young lambs"?

2. Why does Westley "see" Jesus? Why does Langston Hughes come to Jesus?

3. How does the author feel after his salvation? Does Hughes finally believe in Christ after his experience? How do you know?

UNDERSTANDING THE WRITER'S TECHNIQUES

1. Is there a thesis statement in the essay? Where is it located?

2. How does the first paragraph serve as an introduction to the narrative?

3. What is the value of description in this essay? List several instances of vivid description that contribute to the narrative.

4. Where does the main narration begin? How much time passes in the course of the action?

5. In narration, it is especially important to have effective *transitions*—or word bridges—from stage to stage in the action. Transitions help the reader shift easily from idea to idea, event to event. List several transition words that Hughes uses.

6. A piece of writing has *coherence* if all its parts relate clearly and logically to each other. Each sentence grows naturally from the sentence before it; each paragraph grows naturally from the paragraph before it. Is Hughes' essay coherent? Which transitions help advance the action and relate the parts of a single paragraph to each other? Which transitions help connect paragraphs together? How does the way Hughes organized this essay help establish coherence?

7. A story (whether it is true or fiction) has to be told from the first-person ("I, we"), second-person ("you"), or third-person ("he, she, it, they") *point of view*. Point of view in narration sets up the author's position in regard to the action, making him either a part of the action or an observer of it.

a. What is the point of view in "Salvation"—is it first, second, or third person?

b. Why has Hughes chosen this point of view instead of any other? Can you think of any advantages to this point of view?

8. What is your opinion about the last paragraph, the conclusion of this selection? What does it suggest about the mind of a twelve-year-old boy? What does it say about adults' misunderstanding of the activities of children?

9. What does the word "conversion" mean? What conversion really takes place in this piece? How does that

compare to what people usually mean when they use "conversion" in a religious sense?

EXPLORING THE WRITER'S IDEAS

1. Hughes seems to suggest that we are forced to do things because of social pressures. Do you agree with his suggestion? Do people do things because their friends or families expect them to? To what extent are we part of the "herd"? Is it possible for a person to retain individuality under pressure from a group? When did you bow to group pressures? When did you resist?

2. Do you find the religious experience in Hughes' essay unusual or extreme? Why or why not? How do *you* define religion?

3. Under what circumstances might a person lie in order to satisfy others? Try to recall a specific episode in which you or someone you know was forced to lie in order to please others.

IDEAS FOR WRITING

Guided Writing

Narrate an event in your life where you (or someone you know) gave in to group pressure or were forced to lie in order to please those around you.

1. Start with a thesis statement.

2. Set the stage for your narrative in the opening paragraph by telling where and when the incident took place. Use specific names for places.

3. Try to keep the action within as brief a time period as possible. If you can write about an event that took no more than a few minutes, so much the better.

4. Use description to sketch in the characters around you. Use colors, actions, sounds, smells, sensations of touch to fill in details of the scene.

5. Use effective transitions of time to link sentences and paragraphs.

6. Use the last paragraph to explain how you felt immediately after the incident.

More Writing Projects

1. Explain an abstract word like "salvation," "sin," "love," or "hatred" by narrating an event that reveals the meaning of the word to you.
2. Narrate an important event that affected your relationship to family, friends, or your community during your childhood.
3. Tell about an important religious experience you remember. You might want to narrate an event about your own "conversion."

Al Young

JAVA JIVE

"Java Jive" comes from Al Young's unique collection of autobiographical essays entitled *Kinds of Blue*. The collection is unique because each of its memoirs is inspired by a song. In this particular memoir, Young recalls how a collection of specific incidents added up to an understanding of the universal design of things. Pay close attention to his use of description and his ability to weave in and out of a simple chronological narrative line.

Words to Watch

glimpsing (par. 2): looking at very briefly
luminous (par. 3): glowing with light
oleomargarined (par. 4): covered with oleomargarine, more commonly referred to today as "margarine"
linoleum (par. 4): a stiff, yet flexible floor covering
quiescent (par. 7): inactive; untroublesome
pried (par. 7): opened with difficulty
blurt (par. 8): to say or shout suddenly
aviator (par. 9): a flier or pilot
tentative (par. 10): unsure; uncertain
sprawled (par. 11): spread out comfortably
fickle (par. 13): easily changing attitude or direction
abetting (par. 13): assisting or encouraging in the achievement of a purpose

For several mornings at the age of three I stood quietly by the living-room window in our little one-story house in Ocean Springs, Mississippi, and studied the way a spider trapped a fly in his web and carefully devoured her. Why I thought the fly was a she and the spider a he would be tough to explain, but that was the way it played in my literal head of dream pictures, whose images, now that I think about it, were clearly made up of tiny quivering dots the way magazine or newspaper photos look when you subject them to intensive magnification.

Words didn't come easily for what I was seeing, yet somehow I knew deep beneath or beyond what little mind I must've had by then that I was glimpsing a mystery of some kind; some important, worldly essence was being vividly played out before my unblinking eyes.

Then, finally, it all fell into place. The sun—like a hot, luminous magnet—happened to be shining powerfully that antique afternoon. My father was busy being his auto mechanic self, and I could see him through the dusty window screen out there in the grass and dirt and clay of the side-yard driveway, fixing on our dark blue Chevy coupe, grease all over his face and forearms; black on black. Pious as a minister or metaphysician, he was bent on fixing that car.

My mother was in the next room, the kitchen, fixing red beans and rice. My very intestines were tingling with gladness, for red beans and rice as far as I was concerned, had no parallel; there simply wasn't anything like it anywhere in the world, whatever the world was. To dine every day on red beans and rice—or to breakfast, lunch, or snack on them—would've suited me just fine. Lifetimes from my spider-and-fly moment, just before nightfall, I knew we children would be gobbling our portions of dinner—complete with chopped onions and oleomargarined slices of white Bond bread—on the linoleum down under the kitchen table with newspaper for placemats. And I'd be spoiling to tell everybody about the spider and how he'd stuck it to the fly with his web, even though it was going to be years—and I seem to have glimpsed this too—before I'd be able to make heads or tails of any of it, in words anyway.

From the big Zenith radio console, the wood case 5
shining with furniture oil, probably lemon, the Ink Spots
were singing "Java Jive." Except for "I like coffee/I like
tea," the words made no sense to me, but I liked the way
the tune kept winding around and around to make its point,
and I loved the way they came out of it all with: "A cup/a
cup/a cup/a cup, ahhhhhhh!" That sigh at the tag
meant everything, said it all: it signaled my Aunt Ethel,
the big coffee addict in the family, who, even then, always
came to mind with her lips cradling the edge of some hot
cup, breathing and exhaling steam and steaminess; big fogs
of warmth in which sugar and sweetmilk or Pet Milk played
some part. Watching her I could not fail to get the idea that
something glad was going on between Aunt Ethel and that
coffee of hers. If you or anyone else had taken time out to
explain that the coffee bean and its narcotizing effect on
people everywhere was an industry that involved colored
peoples doing the picking all over the world, I wouldn't have
connected with what you were saying any more than I
would've understood the meaning of the Man in the Moon,
but I might've had a notion. Around the same time, you see,
the Andrews Sisters were drawing checks off something
called "They've Got an Awful Lot of Coffee in Brazil."

Being three, you see, isn't that much different from 6
being a hundred and three, particularly when you begin to
understand it's all a matter of putting two and two together.

July seeped into the room, quiescent with harmony 7
and heat, the beat; the beating of the fly's wings as the
spider ingested her from head to toe, boodie and sole. I stood
there. I stood still. Time stood still and the whole of
Mississippi, maybe the whole world, stood there soaking up
this three-year old's vision of how the world really works
whether you realize it or not. It was as if, for me at least at
that moment, my father had pried open the engine of life
itself and motioned me over to have a look at how it worked
and then, without so much as a seventh-grade shop class
explanation, snapped the lid back on, leaving me the idea
that there was something, some mechanism or cause, that
lay behind any and everything I would ever experience in

this ever-shifting, not-to-be-believed existence that mystics—when you boil what they say down to a simmering, low gravy—say is only a movie, the acting out of something vaster than ourselves; the cosmic drama, if you will.

I wanted to taste this java, sample this coffee, this 8 tea they were rhythmizing so invitingly. Feeling my insides beginning to gladden, I rushed out into the yard to hear my father say, "Hey, Skippy! C'mere, boy, and gimme some sugar!"—meaning: *Let me kiss you smack on the jaw.* I liked that. I liked it so much, I got confused. I wanted to race over and blurt out to him everything I'd just figured out about the spider and the world and the mystery and the tingling I felt inside, even though I didn't feel ready yet to pull the words together. There were no words, really; there was only this soundless understanding puffing up with feeling like a rainbow-colored balloon filling up all too fast with smooth summer air.

Just then, just as I was about to make my move 9 toward Daddy, I saw a bright aquaplane zoom in close overhead, low enough for me to see the pilot, a white man, making me think at once of a crisp, airborne Nabisco saltine. He was wearing one of those old-time aviator helmets with earflaps and goggles. He waved at me. He waved and smiled and now, millions of mind-hours later, I can draw a wayward cloud of comic strip balloon over his head that shows him thinking: "Long as I'm up here foolin around, lemme just wave at that lil ole colored boy on the ground down there and give him a thrill!"

This bubbling moment and all that led up to it— 10 like the family's first tentative move to Detroit and the unbelievable coldness of ice and snow and the tight light of what my folks kept calling "movin upnorth to the city"— are etched into me like the lines of some play; a kind of play that's had to settle for being sliced up over the years into what I eventually learned to call poetry or prose.

We lived close enough to the Gulf of Mexico for low- 11 flying aquaplanes to be a commonplace, but that was the very first time I'd ever seen a pilot up close. It was entirely different from those blackout nights when coastal air raid alerts were up, when Ella Mae Morse would be on the Zenith singing "The House of Blue Lights," and there we'd be, me and my brothers, sprawled on the floor or blanketed down in bed, listening and remembering, with those blue emergency lightbulbs screwed into the lamp and ceiling sockets, their cooling glow softening the edge that was forever cutting a line between the seeable and the hearable worlds.

I rushed into my father's arms, gave him that sugar, 12 wondering why we called those people crackers and why kids weren't supposed to fool with coffee.

As for the spider and the fly and my insights into 13 the mystery of that spectacle, all I can say is that the craziness of my excitement has thickened over the years. Now I'm given to believing that the web is only the world, the spider desire, and the fly the fickle, innocent, and positively neutral nature of existence. Beyond that stands some youthful presence, more consciousness than thing, taking it all in with astonishment and, as a matter of fact, aiding and abetting and allowing it all to happen as if— like the web—it were either staged or created by design.

BUILDING VOCABULARY

1. Young creates a number of original and interesting adjectival descriptions in this essay. Write brief explanations in your own words for each of the following expressions, paying special attention to the italicized adjectives:

    a. in my *literal* head (par. 1)

    b. that *antique* afternoon (par. 3)

    c. his *auto mechanic* self (par. 3)

    d. my *spider-and-fly* moment (par. 4)

    e. its *narcotizing* effect (par. 5)

    f. a *seventh-grade shop class* explanation (par. 7)

2. *Colloquial language* (or *colloquialisms*) is language used commonly in conversation but almost never in

formal writing. However, certain informal writing, such as personal narrative, may use colloquial language in order to add a casual "flavor." Identify the use of the following colloquialisms from Young's essay:

  a. would be tough to explain (par. 1)
  b. had no parallel (par. 4)
  c. would've suited me just fine (par. 4)
  d. he'd stuck it to the fly (par. 4)
  e. able to make heads or tails of any of it (par. 4)
  f. something glad was going on (par. 5)
  g. I might've had a notion (par. 5)

3. Throughout the essay, Young uses various words to suggest the unknown nature of the universe. Some of these include *metaphysician* (par. 3), *mystics* (par. 7) and *cosmic* (par. 7). Select two more from the essay and write original sentences of your own for each word.

UNDERSTANDING THE WRITER'S IDEAS

1. How old is Al Young at the time of this narrative? Where is he living? Briefly describe the conditions in which he lives.

2. What incident from his early childhood does he narrate to begin and end this essay?

3. Does this essay contain a directly-stated thesis? What is the main idea of this memoir? What is the "mystery" and the "wordly essence" mentioned in paragraph 2? How do they relate to the theme of the essay?

4. What food that his mother prepared did Young enjoy most? How does he indicate the extent of that enjoyment?

5. What is *java*? Who sang the song "Java Jive"?

6. What does Young like most about the song "Java Jive"? What images did the song provoke in him? How does he describe his Aunt Ethel in relation to that song?

7. What does Young identify as the economic importance of coffee to black people? What contrast does he imply between that importance and the significance of coffee to whites such as the Andrews Sisters? Explain the line, "Around the same time, you see, the Andrews Sisters were drawing checks off something called 'They've Got an Awful Lot of Coffee in Brazil.' "

8. What is the "cosmic drama" mentioned in paragraph 7? Which particular incident in this essay most relates to that "cosmic drama"? How?

9. Why was Young happy when his father called him into the yard? What did his father want? What other feelings did Young have at the same time?

10. What was the incident with the aquaplane pilot? What was Young's attitude toward that incident at the time it took place? What was his attitude toward it at the time he wrote this essay? Why do you think it changed in that way? How does that change reflect the theme of this essay?

11. Why does Young describe the aquaplane pilot (paragraph 9) as "a crisp, airborne Nabisco saltine"? What is the relation between that phrase and the expression "wondering why we called those people crackers" in paragraph 12? Who are "those people"?

UNDERSTANDING THE WRITER'S TECHNIQUES

1. A *memoir* is a narrative composed from past personal experience. On what personal experiences is this memoir composed? What is the significance of the song "Java Jive" in tying together the memoir?

2. What do you think the word *it* refers to in the first sentence of paragraph 3: "Then, finally, it all fell into place"? Why isn't Young more specific in his word choice at this point?

3. How does Young use *chronological order* (the arrangement of events in the order that they happened) in this essay? What is the basic chronological time span here? Briefly outline the chronology of events. Where does he

depart from that chronology? How does he pull the essay back into that chronology?

4. Young makes use of a number of *allusions* (references to literary, biographical, historical, cultural, or sociological events, places, persons, or items—see Glossary), which help set the era of this memoir.

During what era does this narrative take place?

Write explanations for the following allusions and explain how they place the era of the essay:

a. Bond bread (par. 4)

b. Zenith console radio (par. 5)

c. the Ink Spots (par. 5)

d. "Java Jive" (par. 5)

e. Pet Milk (par. 5)

f. the Andrews Sisters (par. 5)

g. blackout nights; blue emergency lightbulbs (par. 11)

h. Ella Mae Morse (par. 11)

5. What is the significance of Young's use of the term "colored peoples" in paragraph 5? Why doesn't he use "blacks" or "Negroes"?

6. Explain the meaning of the one-sentence paragraph 6. How does it act as an important transitional device?

7. In an essay of fully-developed, flowing sentences, why does Young use the short sentences "I stood there. I stood still" in paragraph 7?

8. *Dialect* is a regional or cultural variation on standard language usage. The line of dialogue quoted in paragraph 8 ("Hey, Skippy! C'mere, boy, and gimme some sugar!") is an example of dialectical usage. How does Young translate that line? Why does he give its standard English meaning? Identify other uses of dialect in this essay.

9. Compare the attitudes Young had toward the spider-and-fly "mystery" when he was three with when he wrote this memoir. Which was more *concrete*? Which more

abstract? Explain. As an adult, what meaning does he assign to the web? The spider? The fly?

10. How is the last paragraph an effective conclusion to this essay? Summarize Young's "message" in that conclusion. Why does he use such strong language as the "positively neutral nature of existence"?

EXPLORING THE WRITER'S IDEAS

1. Young shows that he is aware of how a young mind works. For example, he writes: "I knew deep beneath or beyond what little mind I must've had by then that I was glimpsing a mystery of some kind." In general, how does the way a person's mind works—or the way it perceives things—change over the years? What stages of development or change do you consider most important? What changes of perception have you recently experienced?

2. Although Young does not make any direct connection between the song "Java Jive" and his own maturing thoughts, he obviously feels it is important enough to make it the title of his memoir. Why do you think the song is so important to this essay? How has music played a formative role in the development of your ideas? In what ways does music shape the culture? How is the opposite also true?

3. In paragraph 9, Young indicates that what seemed an innocent smile and wave from the aviator may have had much less innocent overtones. He comes to this realization "millions of mind-hours later." Think of some incidents—either personal or public—which seemed innocent enough at the time, but which in hindsight seem much less innocent. How do we come to such realizations? What do we lose and gain by them?

4. What, if any, social and cultural implications does coffee have in today's society? In his description of coffee in paragraph 5, Young implies that the same thing can have vastly different significance for different races or cultures. In general, do you think that assessment is true? Give examples to support your opinion.

5. Compare the nature of Young's "realization" with that of Langston Hughes's in his essay "Salvation" (pages 79–82).

Guided Writing

Write a narrative essay centered around a minor, yet particular childhood incident, which proved of great significance to you because it started you thinking in new ways.

1. Begin your essay with a description of the specific incident.

2. Identify how old you were and where you lived at the time.

3. Indicate in retrospect how you must have perceived the incident at that age. Identify what new way of thinking it began.

4. Mention how your parents or others you were living with affected your perceptions. Tell about something specific which you liked about one of those people.

5. Embed the "message" of the essay in your narration of the incident and others surrounding it. However, be certain you have a specific theme in mind.

6. Use original adjectival descriptions. Also, make your writing less stilted by blending in some colloquialisms.

7. Include allusions throughout the essay which will help identify the era.

8. Relate the incident to a particular song, television show, or movie of the era. Tell what you liked best about that song, show, or film. What images did it provoke for you at the time?

9. Briefly narrate a specific incident other than the main one. Use this incident to begin to show the changes in your perceptions as you grew older.

10. Use the conclusion of your essay to evaluate your changes in attitude as you matured. End with a summary of your present ideas.

More Writing Projects

 1. Narrate the earliest experience you can remember of your childhood.

 2. Select a song that calls up vivid memories for you. Relate a personal experience that you associate with the song.

George Orwell

A HANGING

One of the masters of English prose, George Orwell
(1903–1950) often used narration of personal events to
explore important social issues. Notice here how he involves the reader in a simple yet fascinating and tragic
story, almost as if he were writing fiction. Orwell takes
a brief time span and expands that moment with specific
language. At one point, as you will see, the purpose of the
narrative comes into sharp focus.

Words to Watch

sodden (par. 1): heavy with water
absurdly (par. 2): ridiculously
desolately (par. 3): gloomily; lifelessly; cheerlessly
prodding (par. 3): poking or thrusting at something
Dravidian (par. 4): any member of a group of intermixed races of
    southern India and Burma
pariah (par. 6): outcast; a member of a low caste of southern India
    and Burma
servile (par. 11): slave-like; lacking spirit or independence
reiterated (par. 12): repeated
abominable (par. 13): hateful; disagreeable; unpleasant
timorously (par. 15): fearfully
oscillated (par. 16): moved back and forth between two points
garrulously (par. 20): in a talkative manner
refractory (par. 22): stubborn
amicably (par. 24): friendly; peaceably

It was in Burma, a sodden morning of the rains. A 1
sickly light, like yellow tinfoil, was slanting over the high
walls into the jail yard. We were waiting outside the
condemned cells, a row of sheds fronted with double bars,
like small animal cages. Each cell measured about ten feet
by ten and was quite bare within except for a plank bed and
a pot of drinking water. In some of them brown silent men
were squatting at the inner bars, with their blankets draped
round them. These were the condemned men, due to be
hanged within the next week or two.

One prisoner had been brought out of his cell. He 2
was a Hindu, a puny wisp of a man, with a shaven head and
vague liquid eyes. He had a thick, sprouting moustache,
absurdly too big for his body, rather like the moustache of
a comic man on the films. Six tall Indian warders were
guarding him and getting him ready for the gallows. Two
of them stood by with rifles with fixed bayonets, while the
others handcuffed him, passed a chain through his handcuffs
and fixed it to their belts, and lashed his arms tight to his
sides. They crowded very close about him, with their hands
always on him in a careful, caressing grip, as though all the
while feeling him to make sure he was there. It was like
men handling a fish which is still alive and may jump back
into the water. But he stood quite unresisting, yielding his
arms limply to the ropes, as though he hardly noticed what
was happening.

Eight o'clock struck and a bugle call, desolately thin 3
in the wet air, floated from the distant barracks. The
superintendent of the jail, who was standing apart from the
rest of us, moodily prodding the gravel with his stick, raised
his head at the sound. He was an army doctor, with a grey
toothbrush moustache and a gruff voice. "For God's sake
hurry up, Francis," he said irritably. "The man ought to
have been dead by this time. Aren't you ready yet?"

Francis, the head jailer, a fat Dravidian in a white 4
drill suit and gold spectacles, waved his black hand. "Yes
sir, yes sir," he bubbled. "All iss satisfactorily prepared. The
hangman iss waiting. We shall proceed."

"Well, quick march, then. The prisoners can't get 5
their breakfast till this job's over."

We set out for the gallows. Two warders marched on 6
either side of the prisoner, with their files at the slope; two
others marched close against him, gripping him by arm and
shoulder, as though at once pushing and supporting him.
The rest of us, magistrates and the like, followed behind.
Suddenly, when we had gone ten yards, the procession
stopped short without any order or warning. A dreadful
thing had happened—a dog, come goodness knows whence,
had appeared in the yard. It came bounding among us with
a loud volley of barks, and leapt round us wagging its whole
body, wild with glee at finding so many human beings
together. It was a large woolly dog, half Airedale, half
pariah. For a moment it pranced round us, and then, before
anyone could stop it, it had made a dash for the prisoner,
and jumping up tried to lick his face. Everyone stood aghast,
too taken aback even to grab at the dog.

"Who let that bloody brute in here?" said the super- 7
intendent angrily. "Catch it, someone!"

A warder, detached from the escort, charged clumsily 8
after the dog, but it danced and gambolled just out of his
reach, taking everything as part of the game. A young
Eurasian jailer picked up a handful of gravel and tried to
stone the dog away, but it dodged the stones and came after
us again. Its yaps echoed from the jail walls. The prisoner,
in the grasp of the two warders, looked on incuriously, as
though this was another formality of the hanging. It was
several minutes before someone managed to catch the dog.
Then we put my handkerchief through its collar and moved
off once more, with the dog still straining and whimpering.

It was about forty yards to the gallows. I watched 9
the bare brown back of the prisoner marching in front of
me. He walked clumsily with his bound arms, but quite
steadily, with that bobbing gait of the Indian who never
straightens his knees. At each step his muscles slid neatly
into place, the lock of hair on his scalp danced up and down,
his feet printed themselves on the wet gravel. And once, in

spite of the men who gripped him by each shoulder, he stepped slightly aside to avoid a puddle on the path.

It is curious, but till that moment I had never 10 realised what it means to destroy a healthy, conscious man. When I saw the prisoner step aside to avoid the puddle, I saw the mystery, the unspeakable wrongness, of cutting a life short when it is in full tide. This man was not dying, he was alive just as we were alive. All the organs of his body were working—bowels digesting food, skin renewing itself, nails growing, tissues forming—all toiling away in solemn foolery. His nails would still be growing when he stood on the drop, when he was falling through the air with a tenth of a second to live. His eyes saw the yellow gravel and the grey walls, and his brain still remembered, foresaw, reasoned—reasoned even about puddles. He and we were a party of men walking together, seeing, hearing, feeling, understanding the same world; and in two minutes, with a sudden snap, one of us would be gone—one mind less, one world less.

The gallows stood in a small yard, separate from the 11 main grounds of the prison, and overgrown with tall prickly weeds. It was a brick erection like three sides of a shed, with planking on top, and above that two beams and a crossbar with the rope dangling. The hangman, a grey-haired convict in the white uniform of the prison, was waiting beside his machine. He greeted us with a servile crouch as we entered. At a word from Francis the two warders, gripping the prisoner more closly than ever, half led, half pushed him to the gallows and helped him clumsily up the ladder. Then the hangman climbed up and fixed the rope round the prisoner's neck.

We stood waiting, five yards away. The warders had 12 formed in a rough circle round the gallows. And then, when the noose was fixed, the prisoner began crying out on his god. It was a high, reiterated cry of "Ram! Ram! Ram! Ram!", not urgent and fearful like a prayer or a cry for help, but steady, rhythmical, almost like the tolling of a bell. The dog answered the sound with a whine. The hangman, still standing on the gallows, produced a small cotton bag like a flour bag and drew it down over the prisoner's face. But the sound, muffled by the cloth, still persisted, over and over again: "Ram! Ram! Ram! Ram! Ram!"

The hangman climbed down and stood ready, holding 13 the lever. Minutes seemed to pass. The steady, muffled crying from the prisoner went on and on, "Ram! Ram! Ram!" never faltering for an instant. The superintendent, his head on his chest, was slowly poking the ground with his stick; perhaps he was counting the cries, allowing the prisoner a fixed number—fifty, perhaps, or a hundred. Everyone had changed colour. The Indians had gone grey like bad coffee, and one or two of the bayonets were wavering. We looked at the lashed, hooded man on the drop, and listened to his cries—each cry another second of life; the same thought was in all our minds: oh, kill him quickly, get it over, stop that abominable noise!

Suddenly the superintendent made up his mind. 14 Throwing up his head he made a swift motion with his stick. "Chalo!" he shouted almost fiercely.

There was a clanking noise, and then dead silence. 15 The prisoner had vanished, and the rope was twisting on itself. I let go of the dog, and it galloped immediately to the back of the gallows; but when it got there it stopped short, barked, and then retreated into a corner of the yard, where it stood among the weeds, looking timorously out at us. We went round the gallows to inspect the prisoner's body. He was dangling with his toes pointed straight downwards, very slowly revolving, as dead as a stone.

The superintendent reached out with his stick and 16 poked the bare body; it oscillated, slightly. "*He's* all right," said the superintendent. He backed out from under the gallows, and blew out a deep breath. The moody look had gone out of his face quite suddenly. He glanced at his wrist-watch. "Eight minutes past eight. Well, that's all for this morning, thank God."

The warders unfixed bayonets and marched away. 17 The dog, sobered and conscious of having misbehaved itself, slipped after them. We walked out of the gallows yard, past the condemned cells with their waiting prisoners, into the big central yard of the prison. The convicts, under the command of warders armed with lathis, were already receiving their breakfast. They squatted in long rows, each man holding a tin pannikin, while two warders with buckets marched round ladling out rice; it seemed quite a homely, jolly scene, after the hanging. An enormous relief had come upon us now that the job was done. One felt an impulse to sing, to break into a run, to snigger. All at once everyone began chattering gaily.

The Eurasian boy walking beside me nodded towards 18 the way we had come, with a knowing smile: "Do you know, sir, our friend (he meant the dead man), when he heard his appeal had been dismissed, he pissed on the floor of his cell. From fright.—Kindly take one of my cigarettes, sir. Do you not admire my new silver case, sir? From the boxwallah, two rupees eight annas. Classy European style."

Several people laughed—at what, nobody seemed 19 certain.

Francis was walking by the superintendent, talking 20 garrulously: "Well, sir, all hass passed off with the utmost satisfactoriness. It wass all finished—flick! like that. It iss not always so—oah, no! I have known cases where the doctor wass obliged to go beneath the gallows and pull the prisoner's legs to ensure decease. Most disagreeable!"

"Wriggling about, eh? That's bad," said the super- 21 intendent.

"Ach, sir, it iss worse when they become refractory! 22 One man, I recall, clung to the bars of hiss cage when we went to take him out. You will scarcely credit, sir, that it took six warders to dislodge him, three pulling at each leg. We reasoned with him. 'My dear fellow,' we said, 'think of all the pain and trouble you are causing to us!' But no, he would not listen! Ach, he wass very troublesome!"

I found that I was laughing quite loudly. Everyone 23 was laughing. Even the superintendent grinned in a tolerant way. "You'd better all come out and have a drink," he said quite genially. "I've got a bottle of whisky in the car. We could do with it."

We went through the big double gates of the prison, 24

into the road. "Pulling at his legs!" exclaimed a Burmese magistrate suddenly, and burst into a loud chuckling. We all began laughing again. At that moment Francis's anecdote seemed extraordinarily funny. We all had a drink together, native and European alike, quite amicably. The dead man was a hundred yards away.

BUILDING VOCABULARY

1. It is often possible to figure out the meaning of a difficult word by using context clues—clues in surrounding words and sentences. Without a dictionary, make an "educated guess" on the definitions of the words in italics below. Before you guess, look back to the paragraph for clues. Afterward, check your guess in a dictionary.

    a. *condemned* men (par. 1)
    b. puny *wisp* of a man (par. 2)
    c. Indian *warders* (par. 2)
    d. careful *caressing* grip (par. 2)
    e. stood *aghast* (par. 6)
    f. it danced and *gambolled* (par. 7)
    g. *solemn* foolery (par. 10)
    h. armed with *lathis* (par. 17)
    i. a tin *pannikin* (par. 17)
    j. quite *genially* (par. 23)

2. What are definitions for the words below? Look at words within them, which you may be able to recognize.

    a. moodily
    b. dreadful
    c. Eurasian
    d. incuriously
    e. formality

3. a. Select any five words from the Words to Watch section on page 97 and write a sentence of your own for each.

    b. Select any five words from Exercises 1 and 2 above and write a sentence of your own for each.

UNDERSTANDING THE WRITER'S IDEAS

1. What is the main point that the writer wishes to make in this essay? Which paragraph tells the author's purpose most clearly? Which sentence in that paragraph best states the main idea of the essay?

2. The events in the essay occur in Burma, a country in Asia. Describe in your own words the specific details of the action.

3. Who are the major characters in this essay? Why might you include the dog as a major character?

4. In a narrative essay the writer often tells the events in chronological order. Examine the following events from "A Hanging." Arrange them in the order in which they occurred.

> a. A large wooly dog tries to lick the prisoner's face.
>
> b. A Eurasian boy talks about his silver case.
>
> c. The superintendent signals "Chalo!" to the hangman.
>
> d. One prisoner, a Hindu, is brought from his cell.
>
> e. Francis discusses with the superintendent a prisoner who had to be pulled off the bars of his cage.
>
> f. The prisoner steps aside to avoid a puddle as he marches to the gallows.

5. What is the author's opinion of *capital punishment* (legally killing someone who has disobeyed the laws of society)? How does the incident with the puddle suggest that opinion, even indirectly?

UNDERSTANDING THE WRITER'S TECHNIQUES

1. In the first paragraph of the essay, we see clear images such as "brown silent men were squatting at the inner bars, with their blankets draped around them." The use of color and action make an instant appeal to our sense of sight.

> a. What images in the rest of the essay do you find most vivid?

b. Which sentence gives the best details of sound?

c. What word pictures suggest action and color?

d. Where do you find words that describe a sensation of touch?

2. In order to make their images clearer, writers use *figurative language* (see Glossary). "A Hanging" is especially rich in *similes*, which are comparisons using the word *like* or *as*.

a. What simile does Orwell use in the first paragraph in order to let us see how the light slants over the jail yard walls? How does the simile make the scene clearer?

b. What other simile does Orwell use in the first paragraph?

c. Discuss the similes in the paragraphs listed below. What are the things being compared? Are the similes, in your opinion, original? How do they contribute to the image the author intends to create?

(1) "It was like man handling a fish. . . ." (par. 2)

(2) "A thick sprouting moustache . . . rather like the moustache of a comic man in the films." (par. 2)

(3) "It was a high, reiterated cry . . . like the tolling of a bell." (par. 12)

(4) "The Indians had gone grey like bad coffee. . . ." (par. 13)

(5) "He was dangling with his toes pointed straight downwards, slowly revolving, as dead as a stone." (par. 15)

3. You know that an important feature of narration is the writer's ability to look at a brief span of time and to expand that moment with specific language.

a. How has Orwell limited the events in "A Hanging" to a specific moment in time and place?

b. How does the image "a sodden morning of the rains" in paragraph 1 set the mood for the main event portrayed in the essay? What is the effect of the image "brown silent men"? Why does Orwell describe the prisoner as "a puny wisp of a man, with a shaven head and vague liquid eyes"? (par. 2) Why does the author present him in almost a comic way?

c. What is the effect of the image about the bugle call in paragraph 3? Why does Orwell create the image of the dog trying to lick the prisoner's face (par. 6)? How does it contribute to his main point? In paragraph 12, Orwell tells us that the dog whines. Why does he give that detail? Discuss the value of the images about the dog in paragraphs 15 and 17.

d. Why does Orwell offer the image of the prisoner stepping aside "to avoid a puddle on the path"? How does it advance the point of the essay? What is the effect of the image of the superintendent poking the ground with his stick (par. 13)?

e. What is the importance of the superintendent's words in paragraph 3? What is the value of the Eurasian boy's conversation in paragraph 18? How does the dialogue in paragraphs 20 to 24 contribute to Orwell's main point?

f. Why has Orwell left out information about the crime the prisoner committed? How would you feel about the prisoner if you knew he were, say, a rapist, a murderer, a molester of children, or a heroin supplier?

4. Analyze the point of view in the essay. Is the "I" narrator an observer, a participant, or both? Is he neutral or involved? Support your opinion.

5. In "A Hanging," Orwell skillfully uses several forms of *irony* to support his main ideas. Irony, in general, is the use of language to suggest the opposite of what is said. First, there is *verbal irony*, which involves a contrast between what is said and what is actually meant. Second, there is *irony of situation*, where there is a contrast between what is expected or thought appropriate and what actually happens. Then, there is *dramatic irony*, in which there is a contrast between what a character says and what the reader (or the audience) actually knows or understands.

a. Look at paragraph 2. Why does Orwell describe the prisoner as a *comic* type? Why does he emphasize the prisoner's *smallness*? Why does Orwell write that the prisoner "hardly noticed what was happening"? Why might this be called ironic?

b. When the dog appears in paragraph 6, how is its behavior described? How do the dog's actions contrast with the situation?

c. What is the major irony that Orwell analyzes in paragraph 10?

d. In paragraph 11, how does the fact that one prisoner is being used to execute another prisoner strike you?

e. Why is the Superintendent's remark in paragraph 11—"*He's* all right"—a good example of verbal irony?

f. After the hanging, the men engage in seemingly normal actions. However, Orwell undercuts these actions through the use of irony. Find at least three examples of irony in paragraphs 17 to 24.

EXPLORING THE WRITER'S IDEAS

1. Orwell is clearly against capital punishment. Why might you agree or disagree with him? Are there any crimes for which capital punishment is acceptable to you? If not, what should society do with those convicted of serious crimes?

2. Do you think the method used to perform capital punishment has anything to do with the way we view it? Is death by hanging or firing squad worse than death by gas or by the electric chair? Or are they all the same? Socrates— a Greek philosopher convicted of conspiracy—was forced to drink *hemlock,* a fast acting poison. Can you accept that?

3. Orwell shows a variety of reactions people have to an act of execution. Can you believe the way the people behave here? Why? How do you explain the large crowds that gathered to watch public executions in Europe in the sixteenth and seventeenth centuries?

IDEAS FOR WRITING

Guided Writing

Write a narrative theme of four or five paragraphs in which you tell about a punishment you either saw or received. Use sensory language, selecting your details carefully. At one point in your paper—as Orwell does in paragraph 10—state your opinion or interpretation of the punishment clearly.

1. Use a number of images that name colors, sounds, smells, and actions.

2. Try to write at least three original similes. Think through your comparisons carefully. Make sure they are logical. Avoid overused comparisons like "He was white as a ghost."

3. Set your narrative in time and place. Tell the season of the year and the place in which the event occurred.

4. Fill in details of the setting. Show what the surroundings look like.

5. Name people by name. Show details of their actions. Quote some of their spoken dialogue.

6. Use the first-person point of view.

More Writing Projects

1. Write a narrative essay in which you tell the story of an execution from the point of view of either the executioner or the person condemned to die. Focus on the last moments before the execution.

2. Write an essay in which you narrate an event that turned out differently from what you expected—a blind date, a picnic, a holiday. Try to stress the irony of the situation.

3. Write a narrative that describes a vivid event in which you hid your true feelings about the event, such as a postelection party, the wedding of someone you disliked, a job interview, a visit to the doctor.

4

Illustration

One convenient way for writers to present and to support a point is through *illustration*—that is, by means of several examples to back up an idea. Illustration helps a writer put general or abstract thoughts into specific examples. It also holds a reader's interest: We all respond to concrete instances when we are trying to understand a point. Certainly, you are no stranger to illustration as a way to present information. Every time you try to explain why you believe or feel something to be true, and you give more than one case to back it up, you are using this technique.

Suppose you want to share with a friend your belief that the Los Angeles Dodgers are a great baseball team. First you might point out the pitching staff; then you might bring up the quality hitters; then the fielders; then the management. Your friend would, no doubt, expect you to explain each of those illustrations by giving some details. And so you would name a couple of first-rate pitchers, perhaps describe them and state their won-lost record; you would tell which of the hitters you thought outstanding and point out their runs-batted-in and their hitting averages; you would describe a good fielder or two in action, even telling a story, perhaps, of one really first-rate play you saw when the Dodgers pounded the Reds.

When you present illustrations, it is best to have *several* reasons that lead you to a certain conclusion. A single, isolated example might not convince anyone easily, unless it is a strong, extended example. You have to make decisions, of course, about the number and kinds of details to offer for each example. Sometimes each illustration will itself require a few different examples to make the point. And you have to decide which illustration to give first: No doubt you would save the most important for last.

As you have probably guessed, when you write an essay of illustration you will be using much of what you have already learned so far. Techniques of description and narration will help you support and organize your examples clearly and strongly. In fact, a number of ways to develop essays discussed later on—comparison, cause and effect, process analysis, definition, and classification—lend themselves to development by illustration. The selections you will read in this section show how four writers use illustration to advance their ideas.

Edwin Newman

BAYBUH, BAYBUH . . . .

In "Baybuh, Baybuh . . . ." Edwin Newman, who was for many years one of NBC's most insightful and witty correspondents, illustrates the uses of a term that seems to be everywhere at once as loud as possible. Known for his advocacy of clear and proper language usage in such books as *Strictly Speaking* and *A Civil Tongue*, Newman vividly, and a bit satirically, illustrates the term so that we, too, can feel its presence everywhere.

Words to Watch

indispensable (par. 3):   absolutely necessary
solace (par. 3):   a source of relief or consolation
defiant (par. 4):   bold; without fear
yearning (par. 5):   longing for; desiring
normative (par. 5):   relating to norms or standards

Where'er you walk," wrote Alexander Pope—Han- 1
del later put it to music—"cool gales shall fan the glade, /
Trees, where you sit, shall crowd into a shade; / Where'er
you tread, the blushing flow'rs shall rise, / And all things
flourish where you turn your eyes."

Where'er I walk these days, or sit, or tread, or turn 2
my eyes, these things do not happen. They could hardly be

expected to. What does happen is that I find myself, thanks to the miracle of modern communication, with Baybuh. Someone is walking along the street carrying a portable tape player, the device known as "the box." The odds are that the recording being blasted out involves an apostrophe to Baybuh. A truck goes by, its radio or tape playing on: "Baybuh." A taxi: "Baybuh." A private car, usually with a young person at the wheel, intent on hearing impairment, yours included: "Baybuh." If someone is listening to a radio or tape player on headphones, his or her lips are likely to be moving: "Baybuh." You've gone to buy a pair of shoes; "Baybuh" may well be present. Some airlines pump "Baybuh" at their passengers before takeoffs and landings. Restaurants serve "Baybuh" with the food.

"Baybuh" doesn't really say it. It's more nearly 3 "Baybuh!" The exclamation point is indispensable. It may also be "Oh, Baybuh!" Or "Baybuh, Baybuh!" For emphasis, "Yes, Baybuh!" and "Yeah, Baybuh!" On behalf of a soul in torment, crying out *de profundis* for solace and understanding, "Please, Baybuh!" Or, when a singer is suffering from an extreme case of love, loneliness and lust, "Baybuh, Baybuh, Baybuh!"

There is also "Ooh, Baybuh!" which bespeaks sat- 4 isfaction: Baybuh has shown up and down what it is desired that Baybuh do. This comes about infrequently. Finally, there is the defiant "No, Baybuh!" This is an announcement that the sufferer has decided to suffer no longer and the unequal relationship is over.

Current popular music could not exist without Bay- 5 buh. Indeed, it appears that the world as popular music knows it today is 50 percent peopled by Baybuhs. Maybe it is 100 percent, if the Baybuhs, the situation reversed, take their turns in the depths. I am, I confess, slightly cloudy on this point. Suppose a Baybuh, accustomed to being appealed to, himself or herself becomes a supplicant? Does this carry with it automatic loss of Baybuh status? In other words, can a Baybuh appeal to a Baybuh? Or is the one making the appeal at best a former Baybuh? Is a Baybuh necessarily and only top dog? Perhaps some student of today's music, with a doctoral thesis in preparation on " 'Baybuh' as an

Expression of Complaint and Yearning, and Its Normative Influence on Composers and Performers in the American Folk Idiom of the 80's," could tell us. He or she might also tell us how the gentle "Baby" of days gone by—"Yes, Sir, That's My Baby"—turned into the steamy and urgent "Baybuh" of today.

I am rarely able to pick out much more than the "Baybuh" in what I hear, but at a guess, a typical current composition might go something like this:
6

Need you, Baybuh!
Want you, Baybuh!
Miss you, Baybuh!
Want to hold you, Baybuh!
Don't stay away, Baybuh!
Got to have you, Baybuh!
Need you so bad, Baybuh!
Can't live without you, Baybuh!
Oh, Baybuh!

And finally: 7

Oh, Baybuh!

Release. 8

BUILDING VOCABULARY

1. Newman uses quite a bit of *connotative language* (see Glossary) in order to create a special tone in this essay. In the following excerpts from the essay, replace the italicized words with more *denotative* ones.

a. Handel later *put* it to music (par. 1)
b. The *device* known as "the box" (par. 2)
c. The recording being *blasted out* (par. 2)
d. Some airlines *pump* "Baybuh" at their passengers (par. 2)
e. when a singer is *suffering* from an extreme *case* of love, loneliness and lust (par. 3)
f. I am, I confess, slightly *cloudy* on this point (par. 5)

g. turned into the *steamy and urgent* "Baybuh" of today (par. 5)

h. a typical current composition might *go* something like this (par. 6)

2. Newman deliberately places some very formal, even somewhat archaic, language against the slangy "Baybuh" usage examples. Explain the italicized words in the following expressions:

a. *Where'er* I walk these days, or sit, or *tread* (par. 2)

b. involves an *apostrophe* to Baybuh (par. 2)

c. crying out *de profundis* (par. 3)

d. "Ooh, Baybuh!" which *bespeaks* satisfaction (par. 4)

e. himself or herself becomes a *supplicant* (par. 5)

UNDERSTANDING THE WRITER'S IDEAS

1. Who are Pope and Handel? What type of environment is described in the lines quoted from Pope? How does it compare with the environment Newman perceives "these days"?

2. Who—or what—is "Baybuh"?

3. What does Newman mean when he writes that the driver of a private car is "intent on hearing impairment"? What attitude does he express towards that driver?

4. According to Newman, where are the most likely places to find or be accosted by Baybuh? What examples does he describe of why Baybuh is used? What is the purpose of the expression, "Yes, Baybuh!"? How does it differ from "Yeah, Baybuh!"?

5. In your own words, under what circumstances would one use the following expressions:

a. "Please, Baybuh!"

b. "Baybuh! Baybuh! Baybuh!"

c. "Ooh, Baybuh!"

d. "No, Baybuh!"

6. What is Newman's main point in this essay? Does he ever state it directly? Why or why not?

7. What would you estimate Newman's age to be? How can you tell?

8. What is the meaning of the expression "top dog" (par. 5)? To which generation does it belong—Newman's or Baybuh's?

9. What is the special meaning in this essay of the final word, "Release"? How might that word have a *double entendre* (see page 66) in the context of Newman's writing here?

UNDERSTANDING THE WRITER'S TECHNIQUES

1. Why does Newman begin the essay by quoting lines of poetry from Alexander Pope? What is the effect of his beginning this way? What does it say about Newman's point of view or attitude towards his main subject?

2. What is Newman's intended audience for this essay? Why do you think so? How has his audience influenced his choice of illustrations? Give specific examples.

3. What is Newman's *purpose* in this essay? Does he want to criticize? To instruct? To change opinions? Merely to amuse? How does he attempt to fulfill his purpose? Do you think he is successful?

4. Would you characterize the author's writing as more *subjective* or *objective?* Why has he chosen that strategy? How is it appropriate or not to the theme of the essay?

5. What would you say is the overall *tone* (see page 44) of this essay? What is the particular tone of the expression "thanks to the miracle of modern communication" (par. 2)? Identify other expressions in the essay which have a similar tone.

6. How does Newman arrange the details he chooses as illustrations of Baybuh?

7. What statistics does Newman cite? What opinion does he use them to support? Do you think they are accurate? Do you think Newman believes they are? Why?

8. Identify the song, "Yes, Sir, That's My Baby" to which Newman refers in paragraph 5. What era is it from? How does the use of "Baby" in that title differ from the uses of "Baybuh" that Newman outlines?

9. *Satire* is a humorous treatment of a serious subject, while *sarcasm* adds a bit of a biting, critical edge (see Glossary). How is Newman satirical or sarcastic in paragraph 5?

10. What essay writing techniques besides illustration does Newman use in this essay?

11. How and why does Newman use exaggeration in the final paragraph?

EXPLORING THE WRITER'S IDEAS

1. Look up the word *baby* in the complete *Oxford English Dictionary*. What have been some of the more unusual contexts for its use over the years?

2. Obviously, Newman is suffering from something of a "generation gap." In the past, anthropologists had defined generations as approximately thirty-year cycles; however, some contemporary social scientists feel that new generations seem to "pop up" every few years in terms of attitudes, trends, and so on. How are language use, various tastes, and styles influenced by generational changes? What aspects of the generation one younger than yours do you find distasteful or confusing? Do you feel that members of that generation are as smart or interesting as members of your generation? Give examples.

3. Newman indicates that he can't seem to escape the music of "Baybuh." How do you feel about the ways in which music seems to pervade our daily culture? Do you generally function better in a noisy or a quiet environment? What type of noise (or music) do you find most comforting? Most annoying? What do you do about the annoying kind?

4. Recently, certain sections of parks and beaches have been designated as "No Noise" areas where a person blasting "a box" may be fined fifty dollars and have the radio confiscated. Do you feel this is fair? Why or why not?

IDEAS FOR WRITING

Guided Writing

Choose a word that epitomizes the most up-to-date "hip" language in your social group. Write an illustrative essay that shows the various uses for that word.

1. Begin with a citation from a fiction writer or poet to provide a context for your essay.
2. Continue that context into the second paragraph, in which you give some examples of where the word is most often heard and used.
3. Illustrate various current uses of the word.
4. Describe what makes the word particularly "hip" to use.
5. Subtly blend in your attitude (either positive or negative) about the word's current use.
6. Use some satire or slight sarcasm to create a tone in your essay.
7. Provide an illustration in which you compare current uses of the word to former ones.
8. Describe some confusion you have about the word's use.
9. End with a somewhat exaggerated, longer illustration of how the word might currently be used.

More Writing Projects

1. Write an illustrative essay in which you discuss some annoying aspect of daily life.
2. Write an essay in which you illustrate some feature that you greatly admire of a past generation.
3. Bring to class a collection of photographs and illustrations from various sources that reveal the changes in a style of fashion or physical appearance over the past fifty to one hundred years. Use these examples as the basis of an illustrative essay on changing fashions.

Randall Williams

DADDY TUCKED
THE BLANKET

Randall Williams was a reporter for *The Alabama Journal*
when he wrote this autobiographical essay. He is trying
here to show how the social conditions of the poor have an
ugly effect upon personal relationships. A number of
examples point out how his family reacted to each other
and to the environment created by poverty.

Words to Watch

humiliating (par. 5): lowering the pride or dignity of someone
shiftless (par. 7): incapable; inefficient; lazy
articulate (par. 7): able to speak clearly
teetering (par. 8): wavering; moving unsteadily
deteriorating (par. 12): becoming worse
futility (par. 13): the quality of being useless
abuse (par. 16): mistreatment
psyche (par. 20): the mind
affluent (par. 21): wealthy
grandeur (par. 23): magnificence

About the time I turned 16, my folks began to 1
wonder why I didn't stay home any more. I always had an
excuse for them, but what I didn't say was that I had found
my freedom and I was getting out.

I went through four years of high school in semirural 2 Alabama and became active in clubs and sports; I made a lot of friends and became a regular guy, if you know what I mean. But one thing was irregular about me: I managed those four years without ever having a friend visit at my house.

I was ashamed of where I lived. I had been ashamed 3 for as long as I had been conscious of class.

We had a big family. There were several of us 4 sleeping in one room, but that's not so bad if you get along, and we always did. As you get older, though, it gets worse.

Being poor is a humiliating experience for a young 5 person trying hard to be accepted. Even now—several years removed—it is hard to talk about. And I resent the weakness of these words to make you feel what it was really like.

We lived in a lot of old houses. We moved a lot 6 because we were always looking for something just a little better than what we had. You have to understand that my folks worked harder than most people. My mother was always at home, but for her that was a full-time job—and no fun, either. But my father worked his head off from the time I can remember in construction and shops. It was hard, physical work.

I tell you this to show that we weren't shiftless. No 7 matter how much money Daddy made, we never made much progress up the social ladder. I got out thanks to a college scholarship and because I was a little more articulate than the average.

I have seen my Daddy wrap copper wire through the 8 soles of his boots to keep them together in the wintertime. He couldn't buy new boots because he had used the money for food and shoes for us. We lived like hell, but we went to school well-clothed and with a full stomach.

It really is hell to live in a house that was in bad 9 shape 10 years before you moved in. And a big family puts a lot of wear and tear on a new house, too, so you can imagine how one goes downhill if it is teetering when you move in. But we lived in houses that were sweltering in summer and freezing in winter. I woke up every morning for a year and a half with plaster on my face where it had fallen out of the ceiling during the night.

This wasn't during the Depression; this was in the late 60's and early 70's. 10

When we boys got old enough to learn trades in school, we would try to fix up the old houses we lived in. But have you ever tried to paint a wall that crumbled when the roller went across it? And bright paint emphasized the holes in the wall. You end up more frustrated than when you began, especially when you know that at best you might come up with only enough money to improve one of the six rooms in the house. And we might move out soon after, anyway. 11

The same goes for keeping a house like that clean. If you have a house full of kids and the house is deteriorating, you'll never keep it clean. Daddy used to yell at Mama about that, but she couldn't do anything. I think Daddy knew it inside, but he had to have an outlet for his rage somewhere, and at least yelling isn't as bad as hitting, which they never did to each other. 12

But you have a kitchen which has no counter space and no hot water, and you will have dirty dishes stacked up. That sounds like an excuse, but try it. You'll go mad from the sheer sense of futility. It's the same thing in a house with no closets. You can't keep clothes clean and rooms in order if they have to be stacked up with things. 13

Living in a bad house is generally worse on girls. For one thing, they traditionally help their mother with the housework. We boys could get outside and work in the field or cut wood or even play ball and forget about living conditions. The sky was still pretty. 14

But the girls got the pressure, and as they got older it became worse. Would they accept dates knowing they had to "receive" the young man in a dirty hallway with broken windows, peeling wallpaper and a cracked ceiling? You have to live it to understand it, but it creates a shame which drives the soul of a young person inward. 15

I'm thankful none of us ever blamed our parents for this, because it would have crippled our relationships. As it 16 worked out, only the relationship between our parents was damaged. And I think the harshness which they expressed to each other was just an outlet to get rid of their anger at the trap their lives were in. It ruined their marriage because they had no one to yell at but each other. I knew other families where the kids got the abuse, but we were too much loved for that.

Once I was about 16 and Mama and Daddy had had 17 a particularly violent argument about the washing machine, which had broken down. Daddy was on the back porch— that's where the only water faucet was—trying to fix it and Mamma had a washtub out there washing school clothes for the next day and they were screaming at each other.

Later that night everyone was in bed and I heard 18 Daddy get up from the couch where he was reading. I looked out from my bed across the hall into their room. He was standing right over Mama and she was already asleep. He pulled the blanket up and tucked it around her shoulders and just stood there and tears were dropping off his cheeks and I thought I could faintly hear them splashing against the linoleum rug.

Now they're divorced.   19

I had courses in college where housing was discussed, 20 but the sociologists never put enough emphasis on the impact living in substandard housing has on a person's psyche. Especially children's.

Small children have a hard time understanding 21 poverty. They want the same things children from more affluent families have. They want the same things they see advertised on television, and they don't understand why they can't have them.

Other children can be incredibly cruel. I was in 22 elementary school in Georgia—and this is interesting be-cause it is the only thing I remember about that particular school—when I was about eight or nine.

After Christmas vacation had ended, my teacher 23 made each student describe all his or her Christmas presents. I became more and more uncomfortable as the privilege passed around the room toward me. Other children were reciting the names of the dolls they had been given, the kinds of bicycles and the grandeur of their games and toys. Some had lists which seemed to go on and on for hours.

It took me only a few seconds to tell the class that 24 I had gotten for Christmas a belt and a pair of gloves. And then I was laughed at—because I cried—by a roomful of children and a teacher. I never forgave them, and that night I made my mother cry when I told her about it.

In retrospect, I am grateful for that moment, but I 25 remember wanting to die at the time.

BUILDING VOCABULARY

1.   For each expression in italics in Column A select from Column B the best definition. On a separate sheet of paper, write the correct letter after each number.

Column A	Column B
a. one thing was *irregular* about me	1. absolute
b. *conscious* of class	2. object to
c. I *resent* the weakness	3. way to express anger
d. houses that were *sweltering*	4. are expected to
e. an *outlet for his rage*	5. force
f. the *sheer* sense of futility	6. not correct
g. they *traditionally* help mother	7. very hot
h. the *impact* living in substandard housing has	8. unbelievably
i. *incredibly* cruel	9. aware
j. in *retrospect*	10. looking back

UNDERSTANDING THE WRITER'S IDEAS

1.   Why did the author never have a friend visit his house? How did he explain to his parents the fact that, at sixteen, he did not stay home any more?

2.   Describe some of the situations Williams remembers about the houses in which he lived as a child. Why

was it hard to keep the houses clean? Why was living in such a house so bad for the author's sisters? Why did the family keep moving around?

3. Why did the Williams family never "progress up the social ladder"? Why does he stress the idea that the family was not shiftless?

4. Why, according to the author, was his parent's relationship damaged? Why were they frequently having violent arguments? How does Williams show the love his father had for his mother?

5. Why does the author believe that children can be incredibly cruel?

6. What is the meaning of the last paragraph? For which moment do you think the author is grateful, the moment in school or the moment in which his mother cried? Why would he be grateful for either of those moments?

UNDERSTANDING THE WRITER'S TECHNIQUES

1. What is Williams's main point in this essay? Which sentence expresses the writer's *thesis?*

2. What details does Williams offer to illustrate the fact that he lived in bad houses? Which details are clearest to you?

3. How does Williams illustrate how little money his father had for himself?

4. How does Williams illustrate the way his parents argued? What elements of narration do you find in that example? Where else does the author use narrative as part of an illustration?

5. In which illustrations does the author use description? Where do you find good descriptive details in this essay? On the whole, though, the author has not used descriptive language very much. Why? Where would you have liked to see more concrete detail?

6. One way that the author has for tying together his ideas is by frequently reminding the reader of his thesis. Review your response to question 1 above; then, find words or word groups later on in the essay that repeat the main

point, either through the same words or through words that mean the same or similar things.

7.   This essay is written in a very simple style. How does the author achieve this simplicity? Is it the vocabulary? How would you describe it? Is it the sentence structure? What kinds of sentences does Williams write most of the time? What is the effect of the numerous short paragraphs? What is your reaction to the two paragraphs that have only one sentence in each of them?

8.   Do the author's illustrations support his main point successfully? Why do you think he chose illustration as a way to develop his idea? Which illustration do you find most effective? Why does he tell the story about his experience in school after Christmas one year at the *end* of the essay?

9.   When a writer exaggerates emotions, he is often accused of *sentimentality*. In sentimental writing the author plays with the reader's emotions simply for their own sake. Would you call Williams sentimental? Why? Which images deliberately convey an emotional stance? Do you feel as if he is exaggerating emotions here? Where has he *avoided* sentimentality when he might have played up the scene for its emotional content?

EXPLORING THE WRITER'S IDEAS

1.   Williams says that it is hard to talk about his humiliating past experiences, and then he says, "I resent the weakness of these words to make you feel what it was really like." Do you agree that words are weak in conveying feeling to someone who might not have experienced that feeling? Williams is talking about *humiliation* and how words are not strong enough to make people feel it. What other feeling have you had that might be hard to convey in words? Despite the fact that the author complains about words, he writes, nonetheless, about his experiences. How do you explain that?

2.   Has Williams fairly presented the condition of poverty in America? How does his own situation show some

ways that a family or an individual may overcome certain features of poverty? Would you say that poverty in a rural area is the same as poverty in a large city like Atlanta, or Chicago, or New York?

3. Do you agree with Williams' analysis that his father and mother yelled at each other because they needed an outlet for their anger? Do you think the need for such an outlet can force apart two people who love each other? Is it possible for people to fight constantly and still to love each other? What instances from your own experience can you quote to demonstrate these points? How do you account for the fact that despite poverty and frequent fights, some parents stay together without divorcing?

4. The author suggests that housing plays an important part in the development of a person's psyche. Do you agree? Why? What ingredients would you list for perfect home conditions? Would you include anything other than simple physical conditions like walls that do not crumble or washing machines that work?

5. Williams' father and mother obviously sacrificed many of their own needs and comforts for their children. Do you believe that parents should make such sacrifices? Why or why not?

6. Do you agree that living in a bad house is more difficult for girls than boys? Why?

IDEAS FOR WRITING

Guided Writing

On a separate sheet of paper, fill in the blanks in this sentence and then write an essay of 350 to 500 words in which you use illustration to present your ideas:

> Being ⸺ is a ⸺
> experience for a young person.

1. For the blank spaces select words which reflect important aspects of your own experiences. You do not have to pick negative qualities: You might say, "Being *free* is an *important* experience for a young person." Or, you might

follow one of these other suggestions if you cannot think of one of your own. But be sure to avoid overused words like *good, bad, nice, fantastic,* or *interesting.*

> a. Being *lonely* is a *terrible* experience for a young person.
>
> b. Being *frightened* is an *unforgetable* experience for a young person.
>
> c. Being *loved* is a *vital* experience for a young person.
>
> d. Being *"different"* is a *sad* experience for a young person.

2. Use the sentence you have written as the thesis sentence of your paragraph. Build an introduction around it.

3. Illustrate your thesis with examples drawn from your own experience. Provide at least three illustrations.

4. If your illustrations require narrative, follow the techniques you learned in Chapter 2 about good narration.

5. If you have to use description, make sure you follow the suggestions in Chapter 1 about good description. Use concrete, sensory language to help your reader see your points clearly.

6. Connect the different illustrations in your essay by referring to the main point in your thesis sentence.

More Writing Projects

1. Write an essay of illustration in which you show how certain conditions affected your parents' relationship. You might show the effect of *poverty* on their lives; or you might show the effect of a *city, love, religion, education, superstition, fear, children* on their lives. Feel free to name any condition you choose.

2. Write an essay in which you provide illustrations to show the nature of poverty in your neighborhood, city, or state. You may want to select illustrations from your own experience or observation. Or, you might want to use other sources, like newspaper articles, books, magazines, presentations on radio or television.

Ray Bradbury

TRICKS! TREATS! GANGWAY!

Ray Bradbury (1920–   ) is noted for his science fiction writing—you may have read *Farenheit 451* or have seen the movie—but in this piece he is recalling a special time of year for a boy who grew up in the midwest in the 1920s and 1930s. Illustrations drawn from his childhood show what a grand time Halloween really was in Illinois.

Words to Watch

corrupted (par. 2): spoiled; ruined
induce (par. 2): cause; bring about
climax (par. 6): the highest point of interest or excitement
corn shocks (par. 7): a bunch of corn sheaves drawn together to dry
grisly renderings (par. 8): terrifying examples
crump-backed (par. 8): creased; humpbacked
caldron (par. 10): a large kettle
banshee (par. 10): a female spirit that warns of death
bereavements (par. 10): losses of people through death
serpentines (par. 10): coils
papier-mâché (par. 10): a material made of paper pulp that can be molded into objects when moist
vulnerable (par. 15): open to attack
disemboweled (par. 17): with the bowels or entrails removed

Halloweens I have always considered wilder and 1
richer and more important than even Christmas morn. The
dark and lovely memories leap back at me as I see once
again my ghostly relatives, and the lurks and things that
creaked stairs or sang softly in the hinges when you opened
a door.

For, you see, I have been most fortunate in the 2
selection of my aunts and uncles and midnight-minded
cousins. My grandma gave me her old black-velvet opera
cape to cut into batwings and fold about myself when I was
eight. My aunt gave me some white candy fangs to stick in
my mouth and make delicious and most terrible smiles. A
great-aunt encouraged me in my witchcrafts by painting my
face into a skull and stashing me in closets to induce cardiac
arrest in passing cousins or upstairs boarders. My mother
corrupted me completely by introducing me to Lon Chaney
in *The Hunchback of Notre Dame* when I was three.

In sum, Halloween has always been *the* celebration 3
for me and mine. And those Halloweens in the late 1920s
and early '30s come back to me now at the least scent of
candlewax or aroma of pumpkin pies.

Autumns were a combination of that dread moment 4
when you see whole windows of dime stores full of nickel
pads and yellow pencils meaning School is Here—and also
the bright promise of October, that stirring stuff which lurks
in the blood and makes boys break out in joyful sweats,
planning ahead.

For we *did* plan ahead in the Bradbury houses. We 5
were three families on one single block in Waukegan, Ill.
My grandma and, until he died in 1926, grandpa, lived in
the corner house; my mom and dad, and my brother Skip
and I, in the house next south of that; and around the block
my Uncle Bion, whose library was wise with Edgar Rice
Burroughs and ancient with H. Rider Haggard.

1928 was one of the prime Halloween years. Every- 6
thing that was grandest came to a special climax that
autumn.

My Aunt Neva was 17 and just out of high school, 7
and she had a Model-A Ford. "Okay, kiddo," she said around

about October 20. "It's coming fast. Let's make plans. How do we use the attics? Where do we put the witches? How many corn shocks do we bring in from the farms? Who gets bricked up in the cellar with the Amontillado?"

"Wait, wait, wait!" I yelled—and we made a list. 8 Neva drew pictures and made paintings of the costumes we would all wear to make the holiday truly fascinating and horrible. That was Costume Painting Night. When Neva finished, there were sketches of Grandma as the nice mother in "The Monkey's Paw," paintings of my dad as Edgar Allan Poe, some fine grisly renderings of my brother as crump-backed Quasimodo, and myself playing my own xylophone skeleton as Dr. Death.

After that came, in one flying downpour, Costume 9 Cutting Night, Mask Painting Night, Cider Making Night, Candle Dippling and Taffy Pulling Night, and Phonograph Playing Night, when we picked the spookiest music. Halloween, you see, didn't just stroll into our yards. It had to be seized and shaped and *made* to happen!

My grandparents' home, then, was a caldron to 10 which we might bring hickory sticks that looked like witches' broken arms and leaves from the family graveyard out where the banshee trains ran by at night souling the air with bereavements. To their house, upstairs and down, must be fetched corn shocks from fields just beyond the burying tombs, and pumpkins. And from Woolworth's, orange-black crepe serpentines, and bags of black confetti which you tossed on the wind, yelling, "A witch just sneezed!" and papier-mâché masks that smelled like a sour dog's fur after you had snuffed in and out while running. All of it had to be fetched, carried, touched, held, sniffed, crunched along the way.

October 29 and 30 were almost as great as October 11 31, for those were the late afternoons, the cool, spicy dusks when Neva and Skip and I went out for the Slaughter and final Gathering.

"Watch out, pumpkins!" 12

I stood by the Model A as the sun furnaced the 13 western sky and vanished, leaving spilled-blood and burnt-pumpkin colors behind. "Pumpkins, if they had any brains, would hide tonight!" said I.

"Yeah," said Skip. "Here comes the Smiler with the 14 Knife!" I beamed, feeling my Boy Scout knife in my pocket.

We reached our uncles' farms and went out to dance 15 around the corn shocks and grab great armfuls and wrestle them like dry Indian ghosts back to the rumble seat. Then we went back to get the harvest-moon pumpkins. They burrowed in the cereal grass, but they could not escape the Smiler and his friends. Then home, with the cornstalks waving their arms wildly in the wind behind us, and the pumpkins thudding and running around the floorboards trying to escape. Home toward a town that looked vulnerable under burning clouds, home past real graveyards with real cold people in them, your brother and sister, and you thinking of them suddenly and knowing the true, deep sense of Halloween.

The whole house had to be done over in a few short, 16 wildly laughing hours. All staircases must be eliminated by grabbing leaves out of dining-room tables and covering the steps so you could only scrabble and slip up and then slide, shrieking, down, down, down into night. The cellar must be mystified with sheets hung on lines in a ghostly maze through which giggling and screaming banshees must blunder and flee, children suddenly searching for mothers, and finding spiders. The icebox must be stashed with chicken viscera, beef hearts, ox tongues, tripe, chicken legs and gizzards, so that at the height of the party the participants, trapped in the coal cellar, might pass around the "parts" of the dead witch: "Here's her heart! . . . Here's her finger! . . . Here's her eyeball!"

Then, everything set and placed and ready, you run 17 out late from house to house to make certain-sure that each boy-ghost remembers, that each girl-become-witch will be there tomorrow night. Your gorilla fangs in your mouth, your winged cape flapping, you come home and stand in front of your grandparents' house and look at how great and spooky it has become, because your sappy aunt and your loony brother and you yourself have magicked it over, doused the lights, lit all the disemboweled pumpkins and got it ready like a dark beast to devour the children as they arrive through its open-mouth door tomorrow night.

You sneak up on the porch, tiptoe down the hall, 18 peer into the dim pumpkin-lit parlor and whisper: "Boo."

And that's *it*. 19

Oh, sure, Halloween arrived. Sure, the next night 20 was wild and lovely and fine. Apples swung in doorways to be nibbled by two dozen hungry mice-children. Apples and gargling kids almost drowned in water tubs while ducking for bites.

But the party was almost unimportant, wasn't it? 21 Preparation was 70 percent of the lovely, mad game. As with most holidays, the getting set, the gathering sulfur for the explosion, was sweeter, sadder, lovelier than the stampede itself.

That Halloween of 1928 came like the rusted moon 22 up in the sky—sailing, and then down like that same moon. And it was over. I stood in the middle of my grandma's living room and wept.

On the way home across the lawn to my house, I 23 saw the pile of leaves I had made just that afternoon. I ran and dived in, and vanished. I lay there under the leaves, thinking. This is what it's like to be dead. Under grass, under dirt, under leaves. The wind blew and stirred the grand pile. Way out in farm country, a train ran past, wailing its whistle. The sound cut my soul. I felt the tears start up again. I knew if I stayed I would never get out of the grass and leaves; I would truly be dead. I jumped up, yelling, and ran in the house.

Later, I went to bed. "Darn," I said in the middle of 24 the night.

"Darn what?" asked my brother, awake in bed beside 25 me.

"365 darn days until Halloween again. What if I die, 26 waiting?"

"Why, then," said my brother, after a long silence, 27 "you'll *be* Halloween. Dead people *are* Halloween."

"Hey," said I, "I never *thought* of that." 28

"Think," said my brother.   29

I thought: 365 days from now . . .   30

Gimme a pad, some paper. Neva, rev up that Model   31
A! Skip, hunch your back! Farmyards, grow pumpkins!
Graveyards, shiver your stones! Moon, rise! Wind, hit the
trees, blow up the leaves! Up, now, run! Tricks! Treats!
Gangway!

And a small boy in midnight Illinois, suddenly glad   32
to be alive, felt something on his face. Between the snail-
tracks of his tears . . . a smile.

And then he slept.   33

BUILDING VOCABULARY

1.   Bradbury has often used informal expressions
in this essay. First, explain the meaning of the words in
italics in each group below. Then suggest a word or phrase
that an author who wished to be more formal might have
used instead.

> a. *"Okay, kiddo"* (par. 7)
> b. When we picked the *spookiest* music (par. 9)
> c. Your *sappy* aunt and your *loony* brother and
>   yourself have *magicked* it over (par. 17)
> d. *Gangway!* (par. 31)

2. A number of figurative expressions (see Glossary) spark this essay. In the list of examples of simile,
metaphor, and *personification* below, explain each figure.
(Personification is giving an object, thing, or idea lifelike or
human qualities.) What is being compared to what? What
other figures can you find in the essay?

> a. "Halloween, you see, didn't just stroll into our
> yards. It had to be seized and shaped and made to happen"
> (*personification*) (par. 9)
> b. "My grandparents' home was a caldron (*meta-
> phor*) to which we might bring hickory sticks that looked
> like witches' broken arms" (*simile*) (par. 10)

    c. "Where *banshee* trains *ran* by at night" (*metaphor*) (par. 10)

    d. "papier mâché masks that smelled *like* a *sour dog's fur*" (*simile*) (par. 10)

    e. "The sun *furnaced* the Western sky (*personification*) and vanished, leaving *spilled blood* and *burnt pumpkin colors* behind" (*metaphor*) (par. 13)

UNDERSTANDING THE WRITER'S IDEAS

    1. What part of the essay most clearly states the author's purpose?

    2. What two things did autumn signify to Bradbury?

    3. What were some of the various activities for the Bradburys before October 29?

    4. Why were October 29 and 30 almost as great as October 31? What did Bradbury and Neva and Skip do?

    5. What is the "true, deep sense of Halloween"?

    6. How did the young Bradburys change the house into a Halloween place?

    7. How do the activities before Halloween compare with the activities after it? Which activities did the narrator prefer?

    8. Why does the author say "Darn" in the middle of the night after Halloween? Why is he unhappy?

    9. How does his brother ease Bradbury's unhappiness?

    10. Why does the author smile just before he goes to sleep?

UNDERSTANDING THE WRITER'S TECHNIQUES

    1. How is this essay an example of *illustration?* What examples does Bradbury give to show he has been lucky to have Halloween-minded relatives? How does he illustrate that "1928 was one of the prime Halloween years"?

2. The examples Bradbury offers to show the quality of the 1928 Halloween vary in their length and degree of development. Which examples are developed most fully?

3. In any essay of illustration the writer will often provide a simple listing of examples to demonstrate a point he is trying to make. Paragraph 15 offers a listing of details, but none of the examples is fully developed. Why does Bradbury use this technique here? What other paragraphs offer a listing of details to illustrate a point?

4. Check your responses to the question in Building Vocabulary 2. How do all the figurative expressions contribute to Bradbury's topic? How are most of the metaphors and similes related to the topic and to each other?

5. Underline some sentences that you think have the best sensory details. Where does the author use color? action? sound? smell?

6. Look at the last sentence in paragraph 9: "All of it had to be fetched, curried, touched, held, sniffed, crunched along the way." Why has Bradbury used so many verbs? What is the effect upon the reader?

7. It is clear that the style here is simple, direct, and informal. Why has the writer chosen such a style? How is it related to the topic of the essay? to the character represented in it?

8. What is the meaning of the title? Why do you think the author selected it? How does it reflect the personality of a young boy?

9. To enrich the meaning of an essay, a writer will often use *allusion,* a reference to some other work in literature (see Glossary). The statement made by Aunt Neva, "Who gets bricked up in the cellar with the Amontillado?" is an allusion to a short story by Edgar Allan Poe, "The Cask of Amontillado." What is that brief story about? Why would Bradbury want to allude to Poe in this essay about Halloween? What other references to literature does the writer make (see paragraphs 2 and 8)? Explain them, or ask your instructor to if you are not familiar with them.

10. In what sequence has Bradbury presented the events in this essay? How has he used the order he selects

to create a kind of suspense, a building up from minor events to major ones?

11.   Before he states his purpose in this essay, Bradbury offers a couple of paragraphs of introduction. What information does he deal with in his introduction? How does that information set the stage for the real point of the essay?

EXPLORING THE WRITER'S IDEAS

1.   It is a strong statement to make that Halloween is "wilder and richer and more important than Christmas morn." Does Bradbury support his point well? In your experience, is Halloween so wild, so rich, and so important a holiday? Why? In your family, is there a special holiday for which everyone makes grand preparations? Describe it.

2.   Bradbury's wild view of Halloween was, to a large degree, encouraged by his relatives' reaction to the holiday, too. How do your views about some holiday—like the Fourth of July, Thanksgiving, even Halloween—compare with or differ from the views of your relatives? In what cases do your relatives enrich your appreciation? detract from it?

3.   What is the real significance of Halloween (check the dictionary or encyclopedia)? Why does that holiday still have a hold on the imagination of children today? Bradbury says that passing by a graveyard, he knew from the dead the "true deep sense of Halloween." Do you agree? Is *that* the true sense of Halloween?

4.   Bradbury says in paragraph 20 that the party was less important than the preparation for it. Would you agree, in general, that the *preparation* for an event—such as a holiday, a wedding, a party—is often more important than the event itself? Explain your answer by giving a specific example from your own life.

5.   How are Bradbury's feelings after Halloween is over typical of feelings any young child would have? How is he able to overcome these feelings? Are children generally able to cope with disappointment in the way young Bradbury has?

IDEAS FOR WRITING

Guided Writing

Write an essay of 500 words in which you *illustrate* the value to you of some holiday you celebrate.

    1. Write an introduction that builds up to your thesis, as Bradbury has. State in your thesis sentence just how you feel about the holiday. Is it a wild time, like Bradbury's Halloween, or deeply religious, or just a time of nonstop fun with marvelous meals and parties?

    2. Decide on an effective order for the illustrations you present. If you offer examples to support an idea about one particular holiday (the Christmas of 1982, for example) you might want to use chronology. If you present several examples (drawn over a number of years) to show why one holiday is important to you, you might again use chronology. But you might also want to tell the events according to their importance, saving the most important for last.

    3. Depending upon how many examples you offer, develop your illustrations with enough details. Some of your illustrations will require expanded treatment, others will not. In any case, offer at least three examples to support your point.

    4. Since you are drawing from your own experience, you will want to use sensory language—colors, smells, actions, sounds, images of touch. Try to use figurative expressions as effectively as Bradbury has.

    5. After you present and develop your illustrations, discuss in your conclusion how you feel after the holiday is over.

More Writing Projects

    1. In recent years, Halloween has become a rather dangerous holiday where innocent children often come to harm by thoughtless, mean adults. Write an essay of 350 to 500 words illustrating the dangers of Halloween. Or, write an essay in which you show by means of illustration what

steps your town or community takes to prevent Halloween accidents.

2. Write an essay in which you show how one relative shared in the joys or pains of your childhood experiences. Select as illustration important moments that you can narrate clearly and in concrete, sensory language.

3. Do some research about a local festival, the preparations for it, and the activities involved in its celebration. Or, you might choose to investigate a more remote festival in another part of the country, such as the chili contest in Texas, sausage festivals in Wisconsin, pie-eating contests associated with State Fairs. After you collect your research, write a four or five paragraph essay illustrating different features of this festival.

Lewis Thomas

DEATH IN THE OPEN

Dr. Lewis Thomas is president of the Memorial Sloan-Kettering Cancer Center in New York City. He has written numerous articles about science, medicine, and life structures and cycles geared for the lay reader. His observations often bring fascinating clarity to the cycles of life and death on our planet. The following essay, a brilliant inquiry into the "natural marvel" of death, appears in his book *Lives Of A Cell* (1974), which won the National Book Award for Arts and Letters in 1975.

Words to Watch

voles (par. 1): rodents
impropriety (par. 2): an improper action or remark
progeny (par. 4): descendants or offspring
mutation (par. 4): a sudden genetic change
amebocytes (par. 4): one-celled organisms
stipulated (par. 6): to make a special condition for
incongruity (par. 6): something which is not consistent with its environment
conspicuous (par. 7): very obvious
inexplicably (par. 7): unexplainably
anomalies (par. 10): irregularities
notion (par. 11): an idea
detestable (par. 11): hateful
synchrony (par. 11): simultaneous occurrence

Most of the dead animals you see on highways near 1
the cities are dogs, a few cats. Out in the countryside, the
forms and coloring of the dead are strange; these are the
wild creatures. Seen from a car window they appear as
fragments, evoking memories of woodchucks, badgers, skunks,
voles, snakes, sometimes the mysterious wreckage of a
deer.

It is always a queer shock, part a sudden upwelling 2
of grief, part unaccountable amazement. It is simply as-
tounding to see an animal dead on a highway. The outrage
is more than just the location; it is the impropriety of such
visible death, anywhere. You do not expect to see dead
animals in the open. It is the nature of animals to die alone,
off somewhere, hidden. It is wrong to see them lying out on
the highway; it is wrong to see them anywhere.

Everything in the world dies, but we only know 3
about it as a kind of abstraction. If you stand in a meadow,
at the edge of a hillside, and look around carefully, almost
everything you can catch sight of is in the process of dying,
and most things will be dead long before you are. If it were
not for the constant renewal and replacement going on
before your eyes, the whole place would turn to stone and
sand under your feet.

There are some creatures that do not seem to die at 4
all; they simply vanish totally into their own progeny. Single
cells do this. The cell becomes two, then four, and so on,
and after a while the last trace is gone. It cannot be seen
as death; barring mutation, the descendants are simply the
first cell, living all over again. The cycles of the slime mold
have episodes that seem as conclusive as death, but the
withered slug, with its stalk and fruiting body, is plainly
the transient tissue of a developing animal; the free-swim-
ming amebocytes use this organ collectively in order to
produce more of themselves.

There are said to be a billion billion insects on the 5
earth at any moment, most of them with very short life
expectancies by our standards. Someone has estimated that
there are 25 million assorted insects hanging in the air over
every temperate square mile, in a column extending upward
for thousands of feet, drifting through the layers of the

atmosphere like plankton. They are dying steadily, some by being eaten, some just dropping in their tracks, tons of them around the earth, disintegrating as they die, invisibly.

Who ever sees dead birds, in anything like the huge 6 numbers stipulated by the certainty of the death of all birds? A dead bird is an incongruity, more startling than an unexpected live bird, sure evidence to the human mind that something has gone wrong. Birds do their dying off somewhere, behind things, under things, never on the wing.

Animals seem to have an instinct for performing 7 death alone, hidden. Even the largest, most conspicuous ones find ways to conceal themselves in time. If an elephant missteps and dies in an open place, the herd will not leave him there; the others will pick him up and carry the body from place to place, finally putting it down in some inexplicably suitable location. When elephants encounter the skeleton of an elephant out in the open, they methodically take up each of the bones and distribute them, in a ponderous ceremony, over neighboring acres.

It is a natural marvel. All of the life of the earth 8 dies, all of the time, in the same volume as the new life that dazzles us each morning, each spring. All we see of this is the odd stump, the fly struggling on the porch floor of the summer house in October, the fragment on the highway. I have lived all my life with an embarrassment of squirrels in my backyard, they are all over the place, all year long, and I have never seen, anywhere, a dead squirrel.

I suppose it is just as well. If the earth were otherwise, 9 and all the dying were done in the open, with the dead there to be looked at, we would never have it out of our minds. We can forget about it much of the time, or think of it as an accident to be avoided, somehow. But it does make the process of dying seem more exceptional than it really is, and harder to engage in at the times when we must ourselves engage.

In our way, we conform as best we can to the rest of 10 nature. The obituary pages tell us of the news that we are dying away, while the birth announcements in finer print, off at the side of the page, inform us of our replacements, but we get no grasp from this of the enormity of scale. There are 3 billion of us on the earth, and all 3 billion must be dead, on a schedule, within this lifetime. The vast mortality, involving something over 50 million of us each year, takes place in relative secrecy. We can only really know of the deaths in our households, or among our friends. These, detached in our minds from all the rest, we take to be unnatural events, anomalies, outrages. We speak of our own dead in low voices; struck down, we say, as though visible death can only occur for cause, by disease or violence, avoidably. We send off for flowers, grieve, make ceremonies, scatter bones, unaware of the rest of the 3 billion on the same schedule. All of that immense mass of flesh and bone and consciousness will disappear by absorption into the earth, without recognition by the transient survivors.

Less than a half century from now, our replacements 11 will have more than doubled the numbers. It is hard to see how we can continue to keep the secret, with such multitudes doing the dying. We will have to give up the notion that death is catastrophe, or detestable, or avoidable, or even strange. We will need to learn more about the cycling of life in the rest of the system, and about our connection to the process. Everything that comes alive seems to be in trade for something that dies, cell for cell. There might be some comfort in the recognition of synchrony, in the information that we all go down together, in the best of company.

BUILDING VOCABULARY

1. Thomas uses *adjectives* freely throughout this essay to create vivid descriptions. Adjectives can be fairly obvious in their modification of nouns; for example: a *red* caboose, a *cold* winter, and a *slender* woman. However, Thomas makes imaginative and often unique use of adjectival expressions. Explain the meaning of each of the following:

   a. *queer* shock (par. 2)
   b. *unaccountable* amazement (par. 2)

c. *visible* death (pars. 2, 10)
d. *transient* tissue (par. 4)
e. *ponderous* ceremony (par. 7)
f. *neighboring* acres (par. 7)
g. *natural* marvel (par. 8)
h. *vast* majority (par. 10)
i. *relative* secrecy (par. 10)
j. *transient* survivors (par. 11)

2. An *idiom* is an expression that has a special meaning only when taken as a whole; taken separately, the words may not make sense.

What are the meanings of the following idioms?

a. upswelling of grief (par. 2)
b. catch sight of (par. 3)
c. on the wing (par. 6)
d. in time (par. 7)
e. no grasp on (par. 10)
f. for cause (par. 10)

UNDERSTANDING THE WRITER'S IDEAS

1. Why does Thomas feel that it is strange to see dead animals in the countryside? How are dead animals more varied in the country than in the city? According to Thomas, for what reason is it a shock to see a dead animal on the road?

2. In paragraph 3, Thomas suggests that death is often an "abstraction." What does he mean by this statement? How does he suggest we can make death something more real? In your own words, for what reasons does he suggest we accept the life-death cycle as a more concrete idea?

3. Why, according to Thomas, do single cells seem not to die?

4. What is the meaning of the question at the beginning of paragraph 6? How does it relate to the theme of the essay? To what does the author compare seeing a dead bird? Why does he call it an "incongruity"? How is it "sure evidence . . . that something has gone wrong"?

5. Explain the process of death among elephants as Thomas describes it.

6. Explain the meaning of "the old stump" in paragraph 8. What two examples of "the old stump" does Thomas offer?

7. What example from personal experience does Thomas give to show that dead animals seem "to disappear"?

8. Explain the meaning of the first sentence of paragraph 9. In your own words, tell why Thomas feels the way he does.

9. What is the "secret" in paragraph 11?

10. Thomas says, "In our own way, we conform as best we can to the rest of nature." What does he mean? What supporting examples does he offer? What is the result? What examples does Thomas give of our reactions to the death of other human beings?

11. Why does Thomas say we must change our attitude toward death? How does he suggest that we do so?

UNDERSTANDING THE WRITER'S TECHNIQUES

1. Study the introductory paragraphs. Why does the author offer several examples? Why is "the mysterious wreckage of a deer" an especially effective example?

2. Are there any clear illustrations in paragraph 2? Why or why not? What is the effect? Explain the connection between paragraphs 2 and 3.

3. Paragraphs 4 to 8 use illustrations to support a series of generalizations or topic sentences. Put a checkmark by the topic sentence in these paragraphs and identify the generalization. Then, analyze the illustrations used to support each one. Which examples are the most specific; the most visual; the most personal? Are there any extended examples?

4. How does paragraph 9 serve as a transition to the topic of paragraph 10? Why does Thomas use statistics in paragraph 10? How do they drive his point home?

5. What is Thomas's thesis in this essay? In what way is it reinforced by the concluding paragraph?

6. The author's use of pronouns in this essay is

interesting. First, trace the use of first-person pronouns ("I," "we," "my," "our"). Why does Thomas use such pronouns? Why is their use in paragraph 8 especially effective? Next, consider Thomas's frequent use of the pronoun *it*. (Beginning writers are often instructed to minimize their use of such pronouns as *it*, *this*, and *that* because they are not specific and may leave the reader confused). Explain what the word *it* stands for in paragraphs 2, 4, 8, and 9. Why does Thomas use a word whose meaning may be confusing?

7. Thomas uses *figurative language* (see Glossary) in this essay, particularly *similes* and *metaphors* (see Glossary). Explain in your own words the meanings of the following similes and metaphors:

a. "*the mysterious wreckage* of a deer" (par. 1)
b. "episodes that seem *as conclusive as death*" (par. 4)
c. "drifting through the layers of the atmosphere *like plankton*" (par. 5)

8. We may say that the expression "dropping in their tracks" in paragraph 5 is a kind of pun. (A *pun* is a humorous use of a word or an expression that suggests two meanings.) What is the popular expression using the words *dropping* and *flies* that Thomas' phrase puns on?

9. Thomas makes use of a technique called "repetition with a difference," that is, saying *almost* the same thing for added emphasis. Explain how repetition with a difference adds effectiveness to the sentences in which each of the following expressions is used:

a. "alone, hidden" (par. 7)
b. "each morning, each spring" (par. 8)
c. "unnatural events, anomalies, outrages" (par. 10)
d. "catastrophe, or detestable, or avoidable, or even strange" (par. 11)

10. *Parallelism* is a type of sentence structure within a paragraph that creates a balance in the presentation of ideas and adds emphasis. It often uses a repeating pattern

of subjects and verbs, prepositional phrases, questions, and so on (see Glossary). How does Thomas use parallelism in paragraph 3? paragraph 10? paragraph 11?

EXPLORING THE WRITER'S IDEAS

1. We might say that Thomas's title, "Death in the Open," is a double entendre (that is, has a double meaning; see Glossary). In what two ways may we interpret the phrase "in the open" as it relates to the contents of the essay? How do the two meanings relate to the philosophical points Thomas makes, especially in the two opening paragraphs and in the conclusion? Do you feel it is important to be more "open" about death? Why?

2. In paragraph 10, Thomas writes, "We speak of our own dead in low voices; struck down, we . . ." "Struck down" is used here as a *euphemism* (a word or phrase used to replace others that are upsetting or distasteful; see Glossary). What other euphemisms do we have for death? Euphemisms for dying are often used to explain death to children. Do you think it is right, or necessary, to use such "guarded language" with youngsters? Why? For what other words or expressions do we commonly use euphemisms?

3. At the end of the essay, Thomas suggests that we might be less comfortable with death if we understood it more clearly as a natural, common occurrence. What are your feelings about this philosophy?

4. According to Thomas's views in paragraph 9, because we don't often see dead animals "in the open," we are less prepared when we do encounter death. Do you think this reasoning is correct? Why or why not?

5. In paragraph 7 Thomas explains the process of death among elephants. What is your impression of the elephant herd's behavior at the death of one of its members? Why does Thomas call it "a natural marvel"? Have you ever heard the expression "the elephant dying grounds"? What does it mean?

IDEAS FOR WRITING

Guided Writing

Write an essay in which you illustrate "＿＿＿＿＿＿ in the open." Fill the blank with a word of your choice, a word that reflects some phenomenon, emotion, or idea that has features often hard to understand. You might write about birth in the open, concerts in the open, love in the open, fear in the open, war in the open, for example.

1. Develop an introduction with general examples that are relevant to your topic.

2. Add one or two paragraphs in which you speculate or philosophize on the phenomenon you are writing about.

3. Point out how the topic is most common throughout nature, society, or the world.

4. Give at least three extended examples that illustrate your topic.

5. Use the first-person pronouns "I" and "we" to add emphasis.

6. Illustrate ways in which we are generally unaware of certain features of the topic or tend to hide these features.

7. Try to include at least one statistic in your essay.

8. Use some idiomatic expression in your essay.

9. Conclude your essay with some examples of how and why we can become more "open" about the topic.

More Writing Projects

1. Write an essay in which you use examples to tell of your first experiences with death. You may want to write about the death of a relative, a friend, an acquaintance, a celebrity, or a pet.

2. Visit a place in the countryside (or a park) for one hour. Make a written record as you walk around detailing all evidence of natural death that you come across. Then write an illustrative essay on natural death as you observed it.

3. In your library, explore various burial practices among different races, religions, or ethnic groups and write an essay in which you illustrate several of these practices.

146 ILLUSTRATION

5

Comparison and Contrast

Comparison and contrast is a method of analyzing likenesses and differences between two or more subjects. Writers use comparison and contrast simply because it is often the best way to explain something. An object or an idea is often better understood only when its features stand next to those of another object or idea. We appreciate soccer when we compare it with football; we understand communism when we see it in the light of capitalism.

In *comparison,* the likenesses or similarities appear in a carefully organized manner. In *contrast,* the approach centers on the differences between two items. Often you will employ only comparison or only contrast in an essay, but it is also possible to combine both methods in the same paper.

You frequently make comparisons and contrasts in the course of your daily life. If you have to select an accounting course during registration, you might find out about the instructors for the various sections before making a choice. If you want to buy a new car, you might locate comparative performance ratings for models that interest you most. If you are planning to buy ten packages of hot dogs for a barbecue, you might check prices, product quality, and other details before choosing one brand over another. In all cases, you employ a thought pattern that sorts out likenesses and differences and arrives at a decision based on a comparative analysis of items.

The pattern of comparison and contrast in writing is more carefully organized than the comparative pattern we employ in everyday situations. Yet both circumstances demand common sense. For one thing, any strong pattern of comparison and contrast treats items that are only in the same category or class. It makes little or no sense to compare an accounting teacher with a history teacher, a car with an ant, or a hot dog with a head of lettuce. Second, there always has to be a basis for your comparison; in other words, you compare or contrast two items in order to make a decision or choice about them. And third, you always try to deal with all important aspects of the things being compared before arriving at a final determination. These common-sense characteristics of comparison and contrast apply to our pattern of thought as well as to our pattern of writing.

When you write a comparison and contrast essay, you should begin by identifying clearly the subjects of your comparison and by establishing the basis of your comparison. The thesis sentence performs this function for you ("Professor Smith is a better accounting teacher than Professor Williams because he is more experienced, more structured, and more intelligent"). There are three main ways to present your points of comparison (block, alternating, and combination); each will be dealt with in detail in this chapter. It is necessary to note here, however, that in presenting your material you should maintain a balance in the treatment of the two subjects in your comparison. In other words you do not want to devote most of your essay to subject A, and only a small fraction to subject B. Proper arrangement and balance of items in a comparative essay is a major consideration.

Rachel Carson

A FABLE FOR TOMORROW

Rachel Carson wrote a number of books and articles in the 1950s and 1960s that alerted Americans to dangers facing our natural environment. In this section from *Silent Spring* (1962), look for the ways in which Carson establishes a series of contrasts for her imaginary American town.

Words to Watch

migrants (par. 2): people, animals, or birds that move from one place to another
blight (par. 3): a disease or condition that kills or checks growth
maladies (par. 3): illnesses
moribund (par. 4): dying
pollination (par. 5): the transfer of pollen (male sex cells) from one part of the flower to another
granular (par. 7): consisting of grains
specter (par. 9): a ghost; an object of fear or dread
stark (par. 9): bleak; barren; standing out in sharp outline

There was once a town in the heart of America 1 where all life seemed to live in harmony with its surroundings. The town lay in the midst of a checkerboard of prosperous farms, with fields of grain and hillsides of orchards where, in spring, white clouds of bloom drifted above the green fields. In autumn, oak and maple and birch set up a blaze of color that flamed and flickered across a backdrop of pines. Then foxes barked in the hills and deer silently crossed the fields, half hidden in the mists of the fall mornings.

Along the roads, laurel, viburnum and alder, great 2 ferns and wildflowers delighted the traveler's eye through much of the year. Even in winter the roadsides were places of beauty, where countless birds came to feed on the berries and on the seed heads of the dried weeds rising above the snow. The countryside was, in fact, famous for the abundance and variety of its bird life, and when the flood of migrants was pouring through in spring and fall people traveled from great distances to observe them. Others came to fish the streams, which flowed clear and cold out of the hills and contained shady pools where trout lay. So it had been from the days many years ago when the first settlers raised their houses, sank their wells, and built their barns.

Then a strange blight crept over the area and 3 everything began to change. Some evil spell had settled on the community: mysterious maladies swept the flocks of chickens; the cattle and sheep sickened and died. Everywhere was a shadow of death. The farmers spoke of much illness among their families. In the town the doctors had become more and more puzzled by new kinds of sickness appearing among their patients. There had been several sudden and unexplained deaths not only among adults but even among children, who would be stricken suddenly while at play and die within a few hours.

There was a strange stillness. The birds, for exam- 4 ple—where had they gone? Many people spoke of them, puzzled and disturbed. The feeding stations in the backyards were deserted. The few birds seen anywhere were moribund; they trembled violently and could not fly. It was a spring without voices. On the mornings that had once throbbed with the dawn chorus of robins, catbirds, doves, jays, wrens, and scores of other bird voices there was now no sound; only silence lay over the fields and woods and marsh.

On the farms the hens brooded, but no chicks 5 hatched. The farmers complained that they were unable to raise any pigs—the litters were small and the young survived only a few days. The apple trees were coming into bloom but no bees droned among the blossoms, so there was no pollination and there would be no fruit.

The roadsides, once so attractive, were now lined 6 with browned and withered vegetation as though swept by fire. These, too, were silent, deserted by all living things. Even the streams were now lifeless. Anglers no longer visited them, for all the fish had died.

In the gutters under the eaves and between the 7 shingles of the roofs, a white granular powder still showed a few patches; some weeks before it had fallen like snow upon the roofs and the lawns, the fields and streams.

No witchcraft, no enemy action had silenced the 8 rebirth of new life in this stricken world. The people had done it themselves.

This town does not actually exist, but it might easily 9 have a thousand counterparts in America or elsewhere in the world. I know of no community that has experienced all the misfortunes I describe. Yet every one of these disasters has actually happened somewhere, and many real communities have already suffered a substantial number of them. A grim specter has crept upon us almost unnoticed, and this imagined tragedy may easily become a stark reality we all shall know.

BUILDING VOCABULARY

1. In the second paragraph, find at least five concrete words that relate to trees, birds, and vegetation. How many of these objects could you identify? Look in a dictionary for the meanings of those words you do not know.

2. Try to identify the italicized words through the

context clues (see Glossary) provided by the complete sentence.

    a. half-hidden in the *mists*. (par. 1)
    b. when the first settlers *raised* their houses. (par. 2)
    c. *stricken* suddenly at play. (par. 3)
    d. the hens *brooded,* but no chicks hatched. (par. 5)
    e. *Anglers* no longer visited them, for all the fish had died. (par. 6)

UNDERSTANDING THE WRITER'S IDEAS

1. What is the quality of the world that Carson describes in her opening paragraph? If you had to describe it in just one or two words, which would you use?

2. What are some of the natural objects that Carson describes in her first two paragraphs? Why does she not focus on simply one aspect of nature—like animals, trees, or flowers?

3. How does Carson describe the "evil spell" that settles over the countryside?

4. What does Carson mean when she declares, "It was a spring without voices?" (par. 4) Why does she show that the critical action takes place in the springtime?

5. What do you think is the "white granular powder" that Carson refers to in paragraph 7? Why does she not explain what it is or where it came from?

6. In paragraph 9, the author states her basic point. What is it? Does she offer a solution to the problem that she poses?

UNDERSTANDING THE WRITER'S TECHNIQUES

1. What is the purpose of the description in this essay? Why does the writer use such vivid and precise words?

2. A *fable* is a story with a moral; in other words, a fable is a form of teaching narrative. How does Carson structure her narrative in this essay?

3. Where in this essay does Carson begin to shift from an essentially optimistic tone to a negative one?

4. Does Carson rely on comparison or contrast in this essay?

5. In this selection Carson uses what we call *the block method* of comparison and contrast. The writer presents all information about one subject, and then all information about a second subject, as in the diagram below:

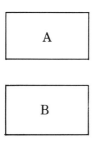

a. How does Carson use this pattern in her essay?

b. Are there actually two subjects in this essay, or two different aspects of one subject? How does chronology relate to the block structure?

c. Are the two major parts of Carson's essay equally weighted? Why or why not?

d. In the second part of the essay, does Carson ever lose sight of the objects introduced in the first part? What new terms does she introduce?

6. How can you explain paragraphs 8 and 9—which do not involve narration, description, or comparison and contrast—in relation to the rest of the essay? What is the nature of Carson's conclusion?

EXPLORING THE WRITER'S IDEAS

1. Today, chemicals are used to destroy crop insects, to color and preserve food, and to purify our water, among other things. Would Carson term this "progress"? Would you? Do you think that there are inadequate safeguards and

controls in the use of chemicals? What recent examples of chemical use have made the news?

2. Why would you agree or disagree that factories and corporations should protect the environment that they use? Should a company, for example, be forced to clean up an entire river that it polluted? What about oil spills?

3. Have there been any problems with the use of chemicals and the environment in your own area? Describe them. How do local citizens feel about these problems?

4. Do you think that it will be possible in the future for Americans "to live in harmony" with their natural surroundings? Why do you believe what you do?

IDEAS FOR WRITING

Guided Writing

Write a fable (an imaginary story with a moral) in which you contrast one aspect of the life of a person, community, or nation with another.

1. Begin with a phrase similar to Carson's "There was once. . . ." so that the reader knows you are writing a narrative fable.

2. Relate your story to an American problem.

3. Use the block method in order to establish your contrast. Write first about one aspect of the topic and then about the other.

4. Use sensory detail in order to make your narrative clear and interesting.

5. Make certain that you establish an effective transition as you move into the contrast.

6. In the second part of your essay, be sure to refer to the same points you raised in the first part.

7. Use the conclusion to establish the "moral" of your fable.

More Writing Projects

1. Write an essay that contrasts the behavior of a person you knew sometime ago with his or her current behavior.

2. Develop a contrastive essay on a place you know well, one that has changed for better or worse. Explain the place as it once was, and as it is now. Use concrete images that appeal to color, action, sound, smell, and touch.

3. Examine the two extremes of the ecology issue today.

4. Using the block method, compare and contrast Carson's fable with the fable you wrote in Guided Writing.

Russell Baker

THE TWO ISMO'S

Russell Baker's witty column "The Sunday Observer" runs each week in *The New York Times* and provides readers with numerous insights into modern life. In this 1982 piece, he treats us to a tongue-in-cheek comparison between two kinds of social behavior in American cities.

Words to Watch

doctrines (par. 1): beliefs that are taught as truths
adherents (par. 1): believers in a particular doctrine
dogma (par. 1): a tenet or code of beliefs
blitz (par. 2): a fast, intensive raid or campaign
recourse (par. 5): a source of aid or assistance
primp (par. 8): to dress in a careful or finicky manner
Ou sont les neiges d'antan? (par. 11): French for *Where are the snows of yesteryear?*

American city life is now torn by two violently 1 opposed doctrines of social conduct. One is machismo. Its adherents pride themselves on being "machos." The opposing dogma is quichismo (pronounced "key shizmo"), and its practitioners call themselves quiche-o's (pronounced "key shows").

A good study of a quichismo victory over machismo 2 in an urban war zone can be found in Philip Lopate's "Quiche

Blitz on Columbus Avenue," included in his recent book, "Bachelorhood." Curiously, however, Mr. Lopate refers to the quichismo doctrine by its French name, *quichisme.*

In doing so he unwittingly reveals that he is himself 3 a quiche-o of the highest order, for no macho would dream of using a French word when discussing philosophy, and even the average quiche-o would avoid a word as difficult to pronounce as *quichisme* for fear of getting it wrong and being sneered at as unquiche-o.

For practitioners of quichismo there is no defense 4 against being sneered at, and they live in dread of it. The machismo adherent, on the other hand, positively enjoys being sneered at since it entitles him to punch the sneerer in the nose, a ritual act ceremonially confirming that he is truly macho.

When a quiche-o is sneered at, his only recourse is 5 to jog until he achieves a higher sense of total fulfillment. This is one reason behind the machismo slogan, "Machos have more fun."

Maybe so, quiche-o's say, but machos don't have 6 French dry cleaning or white bucks. Machos prefer no dry cleaning at all though they sometimes get their clothes pressed if they've slept in them all week and want to impress females during the weekend.

Machos impress females by taking them to bars 7 after opening the top four buttons on their shirts to show off the hair on their chests. Quiche-o women impress males by inviting them to dinner and serving salad from the carry-out gourmet shop, followed by a kiwi fruit. There are no macho women. If there were they would serve pigs' feet and beer because machos believe that real people don't eat salad, kiwi fruit or anything else that comes from gourmet shops.

Quiche-o people buy swedish toothpaste at gourmet 8 drugstores, Italian loafers at gourmet shoe shops, newspapers at gourmet newsstands and dogs at gourmet pet centers. Afterwards they have them wormed by gourmet veterinarians. They also go to the islands for a month or two, especially Bermuda, St. Bart's, Barbados and Trinidad. Machos also go to the islands—Coney and Long—usually for a Sunday afternoon. To primp for these vacations, machos first go to the barber.

No quiche-o has set foot in a barber shop for the last 9 20 years. He goes to a gourmet hairdresser for a styling, then, before jetting off to the islands, goes to the gourmet luggage shop for suitcases covered with the initials of gourmet designers. The macho packs a change of underwear and a drip-dry shirt in a zippered plastic briefcase his uncle brought back from a 1977 convention of T-shirt salesmen.

Quiche-o's are always redecorating. Machos are al- 10 ways repainting the room that has the TV set in it. When a macho's couch and chairs are finally ruined he goes to a department store and buys "a suit of furniture." Quich-o furniture is never ruined, but it goes out of style every two years, and when it does the quiche-o goes to an environ- mental systems boutique and buys a new environment.

No quiche-o would ever take a walk in his undershirt 11 unless it had something amusing printed on it, like *"Ou sont les neiges d'antan?"* No macho would ever appear on the beach in a male bikini. No quiche-o would every wear black U.S. Keds with white soles and laces. No macho would ever walk into a hardware store and ask for a wok spatula.

Machos don't see anything funny about New Jersey. 12 Quiche-o's never laugh at people who drive Volvos, people who pay $5.50 for a hamburger or quiche jokes, unless they're told by another quiche-o. Quiche-o's like a lot of butcher block and stainless steel. Machos like a lot of children.

Machos never bake carrot cake and don't go out with 13 women who do. Quiche-o's are proud of their cholesterol levels and never belch in public and never go out with women who do since they recognize them instantly as unquiche-o and unlikely ever to serve them a salad dinner that concludes with a kiwi fruit.

BUILDING VOCABULARY

1. In this essay Baker uses a number of *geographical* references in paragraph 8. Identify the following locations:

Bermuda, St. Bart's (St. Bartholomew's Island);
Barbados, Trinidad, Coney Island, Long Island

2. Define the following foods or cooking utensils mentioned in the essay:

quiche; kiwi fruit; pig's feet; wok spatula; butcher block; carrot cake

3. Match the words on the left (all from paragraph 4) with correct meanings on the right:

_____ practitioner	a. supporting
_____ sneered at	b. showed contempt
_____ ritual	c. one who engages in some
_____ ceremonially	technique
_____ confirming	d. praying
	e. system of rites
	f. showed great pleasure
	g. ritualistically

UNDERSTANDING THE WRITER'S IDEAS

1. What is quichisme? What is machismo?
2. What does Baker mean when he identifies Philip Lopate as "a quiche-o of the highest order"?
3. How do the two groups respond to sneering?
4. What is the attitude of each group toward clothing? How would you characterize the tasks of each group? Why are there are no macho women?
5. For what reasons do both machos and quiche-o's avoid saying the word "quichisme"?
6. In what ways do macho men and quiche-o men try to impress women? How does each group prepare for vacations?

UNDERSTANDING THE WRITER'S TECHNIQUES

1. What is the thesis statement of this essay? What two things are identified as the subjects for treatment? Is

the essay a *contrast* or a *comparison*? What key words does Baker use to indicate that he is dealing primarily with similarities or differences?

2. Along with the block method (see page 111), comparison and contrast essays can also be organized according to the *alternating method*. When using the alternating method, the writer gives a point-by-point treatment of both subjects A and B. The effect looks like this:

A
B

A
B

A
B

In other words, some discussion of both subjects A and B is presented in each paragraph. Something is said about one and then about the other subject as the writer discusses some specific feature of his topic.

a. How does the author use the alternating method in paragraph 1? How does he achieve *balance* between subjects A and B in the opening paragraph?

b. How is the one-sentence paragraph 3 ("In doing so . . .") a good example of the alternating method?

c. Identify sentences in paragraphs 10 and 11 that reflect Baker's use of the alternating method.

d. For each of paragraphs 3 to 13, identify the primary focus for contrast between each of the subjects.

e. What advantages does the alternating method have over the block method? What disadvantages does the alternating method have?

3. How does Baker use definition (see pages 181 to 182) in the opening paragraph of this essay? How does he use *illustration* (see pages 109 to 110) in the essay?

4. With the alternating method it is very important to use smooth-flowing and interesting *transitions* within and between paragraphs. In this essay, one of Baker's main transition techniques is the use of *repetition with a difference* (see page 144). How does he use this method in paragraphs 7, 8, 10, 11, and 12? What key word does he repeat to make the transition between paragraphs 8 and 9?

5. A satire (see Glossary) is a humorous treatment of a subject in order to expose the subject's vices, follies, or stupidities. Why may this essay be considered a satire on city dwellers? What follies does Baker point up for each of the two groups he is dealing with?

6. As one technique for humor, Baker uses repetition of the word "gourmet" in paragraphs 7 through 9. What does the word mean? How does the repetition achieve the humorous effects Baker wants? What other repetitions do you find here?

7. Baker plays on words as another technique to achieve humor. How does he achieve humorous effects in paragraph 8 by playing on the word "islands"? What word is he playing on within the phrase "a suit of furniture" in paragraph 10? Why does he place the phrase in quotation marks? Why does he use a question in French in paragraph 11?

8. Why does Baker refer to Philip Lopate's book? Might Baker have eliminated paragraphs 2 and 3? Why did he choose to include those paragraphs in the essay?

9. Whom do you think is the intended audience for this essay? Why?

EXPLORING THE WRITER'S IDEAS

1. Baker is implying that people's social behavior reflects the kind of status they want to achieve in society. Often that behavior makes them affected—that is, they pretend to certain tastes and preferences just because fashion dictates them. What affected people have you met? What kind of social behavior would you expect from someone who wanted to be thought of as an intellectual, as upper class, as radical, or as a great lover, for example?

2. In the last decade gourmet shops and boutiques have grown in numbers, and more and more people are interested in purchasing items there. How do you account for the popularity of such places? Why might you choose to purchase something at a gourmet shop or a boutique? Why is Baker poking fun at those people who buy at boutiques and gourmet shops?

3. A recent best-selling humor book was *Real Men Don't Eat Quiche* by Bruce Feirstein. The author's main premise was like Baker's but with a difference. Feirstein believes that not only are quiche-o's and machos at opposite ends of the social scale but also that machos are the much more desirable group to belong to. If you had to choose, would you choose to be macho or quiche-o? Why? Is it necessary to choose between the two, or is it possible to combine features from both groups?

4. Baker as a city dweller understandably focuses his essay on urban personalities. How could you expand the idea of quiche-o's and machos to suburban areas? Rural farm areas? Small towns?

IDEAS FOR WRITING

Guided Writing

Write an essay in which you contrast two types of people in the area where you live.

1. In your first paragraph, write a clear thesis statement that uses key words to indicate the contrast your essay will make.

2. Give the two types of people special names and define those names to help the reader understand your special use of them.

3. Use the alternating method of development in your essay.

4. Base your essay on personal observation of the two types of people.

5. Make sure each paragraph has a special point of contrast around which you organize your examples.

6. Use repetition with a difference as one device to accomplish smooth transitions between subjects in your discussions.

7. Give clear-cut examples of how each group would act in certain situations.

8. Try to cite at least one other writer who has discussed the same subject.

9. If possible, aim for some humorous effects by using satire, repetition, or plays on words.

More Writing Projects

1. Using the alternating method, write an essay in which your generation and your parents' generation did something such as dating, throwing a party, preparing for the future, or some such activity.

2. In one or two paragraphs, compare or contrast two teachers with distinctly different qualities.

Bruno Bettelheim

FAIRY TALES AND MODERN STORIES

Bruno Bettelheim was born in Austria in 1903 and came to the United States in 1939. For many years he has been one of the major child psychologists in the world. In this selection, taken from *The Uses of Enchantment* (1976), Bettelheim compares fairy tales and realistic stories, analyzing the effect that they have on both children and adults. As you read this essay, keep in mind the various stories he is comparing.

Words to Watch

realistic (par. 1): having to do with real things
props (par. 1): supports
elaboration (par. 1): a thing worked out carefully
rankled (par. 1): caused pain or resentment
idyllic (par. 2): pleasing and simple
protracted (par. 2): drawn out
gratifications (par. 2): things that cause satisfaction
sustained (par. 3): maintained; supported; comforted
effected (par. 4): brought to pass; accomplished
consolation (par. 5): comfort
vagaries (par. 5): odd notions; unexpected actions
extricating (par. 5): setting free; getting out of; releasing
prevail (par. 5): to triumph; to gain the advantage
asocial (par. 5): unsocial

The shortcomings of the realistic stories with which 1
many parents have replaced fairy tales is suggested by a
comparison of two such stories—"The Little Engine That
Could" and "The Swiss Family Robinson"—with the fairy
tale of "Rapunzel." "The Little Engine That Could" encour-
ages the child to believe that if he tries hard and does not
give up, he will finally succeed. A young adult has recalled
how much impressed she was at the age of seven when her
mother read her this story. She became convinced that one's
attitude indeed affects one's achievements—that if she would
now approach a task with the conviction that she could
conquer it, she would succeed. A few days later, this child
encountered in first grade a challenging situation: she was
trying to make a house out of paper, gluing various sheets
together. But her house continually collapsed. Frustrated,
she began to seriously doubt whether her idea of building
such a paper house could be realized. But then the story of
"The Little Engine That Could" came to her mind; twenty
years later, she recalled how at that moment she began to
sing to herself the magic formula "I think I can, I think I
can, I think I can . . ." So she continued to work on her paper
house, and it continued to collapse. The project ended in
complete defeat, with this little girl convinced that she had
failed where anybody else could have succeeded, as the Little
Engine had. Since "The Little Engine That Could" was a story
set in the present, using such common props as engines that
pulled trains, this girl had tried to apply its lesson directly in
her daily life, without any fantasy elaboration, and had experienced a defeat that still rankled twenty years later.

Very different was the impact of "The Swiss Family 2
Robinson" on another little girl. The story tells how a
shipwrecked family manages to live an adventurous, idyllic,
constructive, and pleasurable life—a life very different from
this child's own existence. Her father had to be away from
home a great deal, and her mother was mentally ill and
spent protracted periods in institutions. So the girl was
shuttled from her home to that of an aunt, then to that of
a grandmother, and back home again, as the need arose.
During these years, the girl read over and over again the

story of this happy family who lived on a desert island, where no member could be away from the rest of the family. Many years later, she recalled what a warm, cozy feeling she had when, propped up by a few large pillows, she forgot all about her present predicament as she read this story. As soon as she had finished it, she started to read it over again. The happy hours she spent with the Family Robinson in that fantasy land permitted her not to be defeated by the difficulties that reality presented to her. She was able to counteract the impact of harsh reality by imaginary gratifications. But since the story was not a fairy tale, it merely gave her a temporary escape from her problems; it did not hold out any promise to her that her life would take a turn for the better.

Consider the effect that "Rapunzel" had on a third 3 girl. This girl's mother had died in a car accident. The girl's father, deeply upset by what had happened to his wife (he had been driving the car), withdrew entirely into himself and handed the care of his daughter over to a nursemaid, who was little interested in the girl and gave her complete freedom to do as she liked. When the girl was seven, her father remarried, and, as she recalled it, it was around that time that "Rapunzel" became so important to her. Her stepmother was clearly the witch of the story, and she was the girl locked away in the tower. The girl recalled that she felt akin to Rapunzel because the witch had "forcibly" taken possession of her, as her stepmother had forcibly worked her way into the girl's life. The girl felt imprisoned in her new home, in contrast to her life of freedom with the nursemaid. She felt as victimized as Rapunzel, who, in her tower, had so little control over her life. Rapunzel's long hair was the key to the story. The girl wanted her hair to grow long, but her stepmother cut it short; long hair in itself became the symbol of freedom and happiness to her. The story convinced her that a prince (her father) would come someday and rescue her, and this conviction sustained her. If life became too difficult, all she needed was to imagine herself as Rapunzel, her hair grown long, and the prince loving and rescuing her.

"Rapunzel" suggests why fairy tales can offer more 4
to the child than even such a very nice children's story as
"The Swiss Family Robinson." In "The Swiss Family Robinson," there is no witch against whom the child can discharge
her anger in fantasy and on whom she can blame the father's
lack of interest. "The Swiss Family Robinson" offers escape
fantasies, and it did help the girl who read it over and over
to forget temporarily how difficult life was for her. But it
offered no specific hope for the future. "Rapunzel," on the
other hand, offered the girl a chance to see the witch of the
story as so evil that by comparison even the "witch" stepmother at home was not really so bad. "Rapunzel" also
promised the girl that her rescue would be effected by her
own body, when her hair grew long. Most important of all,
it promised that the "prince" was only temporarily blinded—
that he would regain his sight and rescue his princess. This
fantasy continued to sustain the girl, though to a less intense
degree, until she fell in love and married, and then she no
longer needed it. We can understand why at first glance the
stepmother, if she had known the meaning of "Rapunzel" to
her stepdaughter, would have felt that fairy tales are bad
for children. What she would not have known was that
unless the stepdaughter had been able to find that fantasy
satisfaction through "Rapunzel," she would have tried to
break up her father's marriage and that without the hope
for the future which the story gave her she might have gone
badly astray in life.

It seems quite understandable that when children 5
are asked to name their favorite fairy tales, hardly any
modern tales are among their choices. Many of the new tales
have sad endings, which fail to provide the escape and
consolation that the fearsome events in the fairy tale require
if the child is to be strengthened for meeting the vagaries
of his life. Without such encouraging conclusions, the child,
after listening to the story, feels that there is indeed no
hope for extricating himself from his despairs. In the traditional fairy tale, the hero is rewarded and the evil person
meets his well-deserved fate, thus satisfying the child's deep
need for justice to prevail. How else can a child hope that

justice will be done to him, who so often feels unfairly treated? And how else can he convince himself that he must act correctly, when he is so sorely tempted to give in to the asocial proddings of his desires?

BUILDING VOCABULARY

1. *Jargon* is specialized vocabulary that appears in a certain profession or discipline. Bettelheim might be expected to use a certain amount of jargon from psychology. (Fortunately, he keeps it to a minimum.) Try to figure out what Bettelheim means by the following terms:

    a. fantasy elaboration (par. 1)
    b. imaginary gratifications (par. 2)
    c. escape fantasies (par. 4)
    d. fantasy satisfaction (par. 4)
    e. asocial proddings (par. 5)

2. Write sentences in which you use the following words correctly:

    a. *impressed* (par. 1)
    b. *conviction* (par. 1)
    c. *impact* (par. 2)
    d. *predicament* (par. 2)
    e. *victimized* (par. 3)
    f. *astray* (par. 4)
    g. *sorely* (par. 5)

3. Would you say that the level of vocabulary in this essay is concrete or abstract? Why?

UNDERSTANDING THE WRITER'S IDEAS

1. Check in the children's book section of your library to summarize the stories and fairy tales Bettelheim discusses. How many stories is he examining in this essay?

2. What is the most important similarity between *The Little Engine That Could* and *The Swiss Family Robinson?*

3. What is the effect on children of *The Little Engine That Could*? How does it influence the adult whom Bettelheim introduces in paragraph 1?

4. How does Bettelheim summarize the story of *The Swiss Family Robinson*? Does this story, according to the author, have a beneficial effect on adults with problems?

5. Explain why "Rapunzel" was so important to the girl who had lost her mother in the car accident.

6. Why do fairy tales benefit readers more than modern fairy tales and realistic stories do? What do traditional fairy tales provide?

7. What does Bettelheim mean by his last sentence, "And how else can he convince himself that he must act correctly, when he is so sorely tempted to give in to the asocial proddings of his desires?"

UNDERSTANDING THE WRITER'S TECHNIQUES

1. Where does Bettelheim state his main point? How clear is his statement of it? Does he indicate in his thesis sentence his plan of development for the essay?

2. How does Bettelheim order his essay in terms of comparison and contrast? What is interesting about the pattern he chooses?

3. Where does the writer use narration? Why does he use it? How does it support the technique of comparison and contrast?

4. What is the function of paragraph 1? of paragraph 2? of paragraph 3?

5. How does the writer organize paragraph 4?

6. Is the same amount of emphasis given to "Rapunzel" as to the two "realistic" tales? Why or why not?

7. In concluding paragraphs of comparison and contrast papers, it is common to bring the two subjects together for a final observation. Does Bettelheim follow this strategy? How does he organize his subjects in the last paragraph?

8. How does Bettelheim achieve clear transitions from paragraph to paragraph? Discuss some of the words he uses so that his ideas are connected together clearly.

EXPLORING THE WRITER'S IDEAS

1. Bettelheim suggests that certain types of fairy tales help us to cope with problems. Do you agree or disagree? What particular fairy tale do you remember that might help a child deal with his or her problems?

2. Why do most children clearly take delight from traditional fairy tales?

3. Look again at Bettelheim's psychoanalysis of the three children whom he uses as examples in his essay. Do you accept his explanations of their behavior? How might his ideas be criticized by other psychologists?

4. Which fairy tales—traditional or modern—appealed to you as a child? Why were you so fond of them?

5. If exposure to certain types of fairy tales can affect us seriously, then what can we conclude about our exposure to stories on television, film, and other types of media? Is it fair to generalize about television from Bettelheim's argument?

IDEAS FOR WRITING

Guided Writing

Write an essay in which you compare and/or contrast two or three fairy tales or stories that you remember from early childhood. Or, do the same for two films, two television programs, two newspapers, or two subjects from another media form.

1. State the purpose of your comparison as soon as you can.

2. Decide on the best pattern of development (block, alternating, or a combination of both) for your purposes.

3. List the point of comparison or contrast that you plan to cover for each subject.

4. Be certain to support each point with substantial detail. Summarize parts of stories that bear out your point. Quote where you have to.

5. Make certain that, in the closing paragraph, you draw conclusions about all the subjects treated.

More Writing Projects

1. Write an essay in which you compare or contrast two newspapers or magazines. Be prepared to compare and contrast their contents, and also to indicate the type of audience at which they are aimed. Write a comparative paper on your findings.

2. Compare and contrast the style of writing of any two writers in this section.

3. Select two heroes or heroines from popular children's stories or fairy tales; compare and contrast the two characters in regard to personality and behavior.

Roger D. McGrath

THE MYTH OF FRONTIER VIOLENCE

History professor Roger D. McGrath, author of the book *Gunfighters, Highwaymen, and Vigilantes: Violence on the Frontier*, confronts our assumption of the Old West as a lawless and violent society. He does so by a sustained, implied contrast with 1980s American society, a society pervaded by (in McGrath's words) "violence and lawlessness." McGrath's contrast aims at proving that these current conditions are quite unrelated to the actual conditions of the Old West.

Words to Watch

heritage (par. 1): legacy; tradition
prospector (par. 2): a person who explores for mineral deposits, most notably gold and silver
brothel (par. 5): a house of prostitution
bullion (par. 7): bars of uncoined gold or silver
vigilantism (par. 10): actions outside the legal norms, usually by private citizens, to suppress or punish crimes
homicide (par. 13): the crime of one person killing another
sidearms (par. 15): small weapons worn on the side or belt

It is commonly assumed that violence is part of our 1 frontier heritage. But the historical record shows that frontier violence was very different from violence today. Robbery and burglary, two of our most common crimes, were of no great significance in the frontier towns of the Old West, and rape was seemingly nonexistent.

Bodie, one of the principal towns on the trans-Sierra 2 frontier, illustrates the point. Nestled high in the mountains of eastern California, Bodie, which boomed in the late 1870s and early 1880s, ranked among the most notorious frontier towns of the Old West. It was, as one prospector put it, the last of the old-time mining camps.

Like the trans-Sierra frontier in general, Bodie was 3 indisputably violent and lawless, yet most people were not affected. Fistfights and gunfights among willing combatants—gamblers, miners, and the like—were regular events, and stagecoach holdups were not unusual. But the old, the young, the weak, and the female—so often the victims of crime today—were generally not harmed.

Robbery was more often aimed at stagecoaches than 4 at individuals. Highwaymen usually took only the express box and left the passengers alone. There were eleven stagecoach robberies in Bodie between 1878 and 1882, and in only two instances were passengers robbed. (In one instance, the highwaymen later apologized for their conduct.)

There were only ten robberies and three attempted 5 robberies of individuals in Bodie during its boom years, and in nearly every case the circumstances were the same: the victim had spent the evening in a gambling den, saloon, or brothel; he had revealed that he had on his person a significant sum of money; and he was staggering home drunk when the attack occurred.

Bodie's total of twenty-one robberies—eleven of stages 6 and ten of individuals—over a five-year period converts to a rate of eighty-four robberies per 100,000 inhabitants per year. On this scale—the same scale used by the FBI to index crime—New York City's robbery rate in 1980 was 1,140, Miami's was 995, and Los Angeles's was 628. The rate for the United States as a whole was 243. Thus Bodie's robbery rate was significantly below the national average in 1980.

Perhaps the greatest deterrent to crime in Bodie 7
was the fact that so many people were armed. Armed guards
prevented bank robberies and holdups of stagecoaches carrying shipments of bullion, and armed homeowners and
merchants discouraged burglary. Between 1878 and 1882,
there were only thirty-two burglaries—seventeen of homes
and fifteen of businesses—in Bodie. At least a half-dozen
burglaries were thwarted by the presence of armed citizens.
The newspapers regularly advocated shooting burglars on
sight, and several burglars were, in fact, shot at.

Using the FBI scale, Bodie's burglary rate for those 8
five years was 128. Miami's rate in 1980 was 3,282, New
York City's was 2,661, and Los Angeles's was 2,602. The
rate of the United States as a whole was 1,668, thirteen
times that of Bodie.

Bodie's law enforcement institutions were certainly 9
not responsible for these low rates. Rarely were robbers or
burglars arrested, and even less often were they convicted.
Moreover, many law enforcement officers operated on both
sides of the law.

It was the armed citizens themselves who were the 10
most potent—though not the only—deterrent to larcenous
crime. Another was the threat of vigilantism. Highwaymen,
for example, understood that while they could take the
express box from a stagecoach without arousing the citizens,
they risked inciting the entire populace to action if they
robbed the passengers.

There is considerable evidence that women in Bodie 11
were rarely the victims of crime. Between 1878 and 1882
only one woman, a prostitute, was robbed, and there were
no reported cases of rape. (There is no evidence that rapes
occurred but were not reported.)

Finally, juvenile crime, which accounts for a signif- 12
icant portion of the violent crime in the United States today,
was limited in Bodie to pranks and malicious mischief.

If robbery, burglary, crimes against women, and 13
juvenile crime were relatively rare on the trans-Sierra
frontier, homicide was not: thirty-one Bodieites were shot,
stabbed, or beaten to death during the boom years, for a
homicide rate of 116. No U.S. city today comes close to this

rate. In 1980, Miami led the nation with a homicide rate of 32.7; Las Vegas was a distant second at 23.4. A half-dozen cities had rates of zero. The rate for the United States as a whole in that year was a mere 10.2.

Several factors contributed to Bodie's high homicide rate. A majority of the town's residents were young, adventurous, single males who adhered to a code of conduct that frequently required them to fight even if, or perhaps especially if, it could mean death. Courage was admired above all else. Alcohol also played a major role in fostering the settlement of disputes by violence. 14

If the men's code of conduct and their consumption of alcohol made fighting inevitable, their sidearms often made it fatal. While the carrying of guns probably reduced the incidence of robbery and burglary, it undoubtedly increased the number of homicides. 15

For the most part, the citizens of Bodie were not troubled by the great number of killings; nor were they troubled that only one man was ever convicted of murder. They accepted the killings and the lack of convictions because most of those killed had been willing combatants. 16

Thus the violence and lawlessness of the trans-Sierra frontier bear little relation to the violence and lawlessness that pervade American society today. If Bodie is at all representative of frontier towns, there is little justification for blaming contemporary American violence on our frontier heritage. 17

BUILDING VOCABULARY

For each word in italics below, select the correct choice of meaning.

1. seemingly *nonexistent*
a. mischievous   b. important   c. absent
d. everywhere

2. *indisputably* violent
a. debatably   b. certainly   c. necessarily
d. understandably

3. *boom* years

a. destructive   b. immature   c. immoral
d. prosperous

    4. greatest *deterrent* to crime

a. inducement   b. reason   c. benefit
d. preventative

    5. burglaries were *thwarted*

a. hindered   b. abetted   c. desired   d. profitable

    6. regularly *advocated* shooting

a. supported   b. disdained   c. punished
d. practiced

    7. the most *potent*

a. legal   b. evil   c. powerful   d. ominous

    8. *larcenous* crime

a. wicked   b. physical   c. thievish   d. psychotic

    9. *malicious* mischief

a. immature   b. kindly   c. harmful   d. prankish

    10. *fostering* the settlement

a. keeping   b. promoting   c. destroying
d. delaying

    11. made fighting *inevitable*

a. unavoidable   b. fun   c. dangerous   d. wicked

    12. made it *fatal*

a. hopeless   b. annoying   c. senseless   d. deadly

UNDERSTANDING THE WRITER'S IDEAS

1. What is the difference between what people assume about frontier violence and the reality? What does the author say is the commonly accepted assumption about frontier violence?

2. What contrast between Old West violence and today's violence does McGrath make in paragraph 1? What three types of crimes does he specify?

3. What time period of the Old West is covered in McGrath's discussion of the town of Bodie? What was the atmosphere in Bodie during that time? What examples does the author offer to substantiate his generalization about Bodie's atmosphere?

4. According to McGrath, what were the circumstances of the few robberies of individuals that occurred during Bodie's boom years?

5. What is the FBI crime index? According to that index, which U.S. city's robbery rate was highest in 1980? Which city's burglary rate was highest? (Check a dictionary to distinguish between robbery and burglary.) Homicide rate? In general, how did Bodie's crime rate compare to the 1980 highest rates and national averages?

6. What, according to McGrath, was the major factor in Bodie's low crime rate? What role did the newspapers and the police play in reducing the crime rate? What was the result of so many of Bodie's citizens being armed? Which element does McGrath seem to feel was ultimately most important in keeping the crime rate low? Explain. What was the attitude of Bodie's citizens towards killings? Towards a legal system which didn't seem to punish killings? Why?

7. What were the unwritten rules for stagecoach robberies in Bodie?

8. Which crime existed at a much higher rate in Bodie as compared with present-day incidences of crime? For what reasons was this so?

UNDERSTANDING THE WRITER'S TECHNIQUES

1. Would you say that this essay is predominantly a *comparison* or a *contrast?* Why?

2. In many comparison or contrast essays, the precise points of comparison are specifically stated. Does McGrath do so in this essay? What is the implied comparison? What assumptions about the reader's knowledge of the Old West and of modern crime does the implied comparison presume? Do you feel this technique works successfully in this essay? Why?

3. Among the purposes of a comparison or contrast essay are (a) to *explain* something unfamiliar in terms of something already familiar, (b) to *understand* better two things already known by comparing them point for point, or (c) to *evaluate* the relative value of two things.

Which of the above most closely describes McGrath's purpose in this essay? Explain your choice.

4. How does McGrath use statistics to support his main point? Given the context of the comparison, why is the use of statistics especially useful?

5. At two points in the essay, McGrath encloses sentences in parentheses—at the end of paragraph 4 and paragraph 11. Why do you think he uses parentheses in these instances? How do they affect the information contained inside them?

6. Name all the types of crime in Bodie that McGrath mentions. On what basis does he order their presentation in the essay? Which do you think he considers most important? Why?

7. Analyze the way in which McGrath supports his opinion that the "armed citizens" of Bodie were the most significant factor in the low crime rate. How does he use *reiteration* (repeating the same or similar idea) to make this point? How does he use comparison to other factors?

8. A good *closing* for a comparison or contrast essay often will restate the main idea, will offer a solution, or will set a new frame of reference by generalizing from the thesis (see Glossary). Which approach or combination of approaches does McGrath use? How effective is his conclusion? Why? What are the two important points of the conclusion? How are they related to one another? How are they related to the body of the essay? What transition does McGrath use to connect the conclusion to the body of the essay?

EXPLORING THE WRITER'S IDEAS

1. According to McGrath, the arming of citizens in Bodie may have lowered the crime rate and may have elevated the homicide rate as well. What are your opinions about the rights and needs of citizens to own guns? What are some of the positive results of an armed citizenry? What are some of the negative ones? Which, in balance, do you feel outweighs the other?

2. In paragraph 14, McGrath ascribes Bodie's high

homicide rate to "single males who adhered to a code of conduct that frequently required them to fight"—in other words, *macho*. How have macho attitudes been responsible for violence you have witnessed? What "codes of conduct" are predominant in your social circles? By what code of conduct do you live? (Russell Baker pokes fun at the superficial elements of macho in "The Two Ismos" in this chapter, pages 156–158.)

3. What image of violence in the Old West did you have before reading McGrath's essay? From what did that image derive? How has this essay influenced or changed your image?

4. What are your thoughts about violence and crime in the United States these days? How serious do you feel the problem is? What are the main causes of the problem? What solutions can you propose?

IDEAS FOR WRITING

Guided Writing

Write a comparison or contrast essay entitled "The Myth of _____ ." Fill in the blank with an idea or issue about which people commonly hold assumptions that you believe are untrue or incorrect. Draw your idea from past history, modern social values, contemporary politics, or any other area that interests you. You might try a topic such as "The Myth of Renaissance Love," "The Myth of College Dating," or "The Myth of 'Rags to Riches' in America today." To explain this myth, be prepared to compare or contrast the idea or issue with its existence at another time in history.

1. Begin with a clear statement of the assumption as it now exists.

2. Specify two or three different aspects of the assumption.

3. Isolate one particular area or group on which to base your comparative discussion. Briefly explain the area or group.

4. Give a short history of how the assumption relates to the area or group.

5. After some research in your library, use statistical evidence to contrast the assumption with the actuality as you perceive it.

6. In your essay, point out different aspects of the assumption. Choose some logical arrangement by which to order your discussion.

7. Select and discuss one aspect of the assumption that is indeed true.

8. Draw a generalized conclusion from the information presented in your essay. Use your conclusion to reiterate your initial comparative point.

More Writing Projects

1. Use the block or alternating methods—or a combination of the two—to write an essay in which you compare two opinions of a currently important issue in your school or community.

2. Write an essay comparing or contrasting television violence with actual violence. Use examples of specific programs. Discuss effects of each as well.

3. Observe a simple interaction between two people—a surprise meeting, a business transaction, a disagreement—and write a short essay in which you compare the two individuals' reactions, attitudes, body language, expressions, and so on, during the interaction.

6

Definition

Definition is a way of explaining an important word so that the reader knows, as exactly as possible, what you mean by it. You probably have written essays requiring short "dictionary definitions" of words that were not clear to the reader. However, there are terms that require longer definitions because they may be central to the writer's thought. When an entire essay focuses on the meaning of a key word or group of related words, you will need to employ "extended definition" as a method of organization.

Words requiring extended definition tend to be abstract, controversial, or complex. Terms like "freedom," "pornography," and "communism" reflect the need for extended definition. Such words depend on extended definition because they are often confused with some other word or term; because they are easily misunderstood; or because they are of special importance to the writer, who chooses to redefine the term for his or her own purposes. We can, of course, simply offer an extended definition of a word for the sake of definition itself; this is valid. But we usually have strong opinions about complex and controversial words, and, consequently, we try to provide an extended definition for the purpose of illuminating a thesis. The word "abortion" could be defined objectively, with the writer tracing its history, explaining its techniques, and describing its effects on the patient. Yet many writers asked to provide an extended definition of "abortion" would have strong personal opinions about the term. They would want to develop a thesis about it, perhaps covering much of the same ground as the objective account, but taking care that the reader understands the word as they do. It is normal for us to have our own opinions about any word, but in all instances we must make the reader understand fully what we mean by it.

Writers use several techniques to develop extended definitions. One common strategy is to define some general group to which the subject belongs (for instance, the mallard is a member of a larger group of ducks), and to show how the word differs from all other words in that general group. A second technique is to give the etymology of a word—its origin and history in the language—to help the reader. Yet another method of extended definition is to deal with what you do *not* mean by the term—a technique called "negation." Finally, many methods that you already learned can be used profitably in extended definition. You can define a word by narrating an event that reveals its meaning; you can provide specific examples, even a simple listing, to illustrate what you mean by a term; you can compare and contrast related terms; you can describe details that help to establish meaning.

Extended definition involves no single pattern of essay organization, but rather a group of available strategies that you use depending on your purpose and on the word itself. The word selected may be ordinary and relatively concrete, or it may be abstract and complex like "randomness." Often, as in the essays here on "an understanding woman" and on "fun," the definition is never directly stated, but is understood or put together from the information a writer gives. Because so many methods can be applied effectively in an essay of extended definition, you should be able to organize and develop this type of composition easily.

Ellen Goodman

AN UNDERSTANDING WOMAN

In this essay from her 1979 book *At Large,* Ellen Goodman explains a quality that she observes in women. This quality *can* be positive, but it also can contain many potentially dangerous, negative overtones. Note how Goodman uses illustration as well as subtle changes in tone to help create her definition.

Words to Watch

empathy (par. 3):   the capacity for participating in another's feelings or ideas
comprehend (par. 3):   to understand fully
awe (par. 4):   reverent wonder, perhaps slightly fearsome
feats (par. 4):   acts of skill or courage
pat (par. 14):   too exactly suitable
logged (par. 16):   recorded the details of any sustained performance

I know an Understanding Woman. No, not the sort 1
of woman who'll jog along with you a while until she gets tired. I mean a marathon understander.

The Understanding Woman is a good listener and a 2

good human historian. Over the years people have come to her when they were really out of shape and she's paced them over some pretty rough terrain.

She can put pieces together; she can figure out why 3 one person behaves this way and another person behaves that way. She has empathy endurance. And she'll tell you that once you really comprehend someone else's life, it's tough to criticize them.

I've watched the Understanding Woman over the 4 long distance. I've watched with the awe I reserve for feats I can't imagine performing. I am better for an intense short sprint. I fade early. So I've admired the woman's legs, her wind, her stamina.

But lately I've been wondering whether this capacity 5 for understanding is awesome or really kind of awful. If understanding is a good thing, I wonder if she has too much of a good thing. I wonder whether she does the hard work and everyone around her stays flaccid. I wonder if understanding why things happen one way can't become a substitute for making them happen another way.

The last time I saw her I thought about the men in 6 her life. I remembered the husband who said he needed space. And she understood.

I remember the guy who was, from time to time, 7 unfaithful. And she understood.

There was also a man who didn't want to get married 8 and have children because, after all, he had already been there. And now there is a man who has difficulty relating to her son because, after all, he has a boy the same age in another state. It is all very understandable.

She isn't the only marathon woman. Understanding 9 can be a great equalizer. It is as if one person's capacity for hurtful or insensitive behavior could be matched, maybe even topped, by another's capacity for sympathetic comprehension.

But I also suspect that a person can spend so much 10 energy analyzing someone else's needs and track record that they analyze away their own. Psychiatrists always say that understanding is the first step of change, but I guess it can also be a substitute for change. A lot of women end up running in place.

This is not exclusively a "woman's problem." There 11 are a lot of men who go the distance every day. But we're trained for it from the time we get our first sneakers.

If you compare them, the men's magazines all deal 12 with things and the women's magazines all deal with feelings. These magazines are our cheerleaders. They shout encouragement when we leave Hopkinton, and they pass water to us over Heartbreak Hill in Newton.

Women are expected to deal with feelings, even the 13 feeling of being dealt with as a thing. We are, for heaven's sake, coached in the art of understanding why men aren't as understanding.

I have another friend who swears that the Under- 14 standing Woman is getting exactly what she wants; a chance to be superior in sympathy, to be virtuously martyred. But I think that's too pat and too tough. I think she is struggling to do the right thing, even when it gives her a cramp in the side and shin splints.

You don't have to tell me that understanding is a 15 virtue and that what the world needs now is love. Pass me a Coke and turn the other cheek. But sometimes it's paralyzing.

There's a moment, and it's hard to locate it, when 16 you can understand too much and ask for too little. Anyway, it occurs to me that the Understanding Woman has logged too many miles in other people's shoes.

BUILDING VOCABULARY

1. Goodman uses many words that refer to sports or athletics. Make a list of those words and define them.

2. Examine the definitions in the Words to Watch section on page 183. Write an original sentence that uses each word correctly.

UNDERSTANDING THE WRITER'S IDEAS

1. What is the difference between the two types of women—jogger and marathoner—mentioned in paragraph 1? Which is the focus of Goodman's discussion? Which type of woman does she envision herself to be more like? Explain.

2. How does Goodman define "an understanding woman" by her activities and abilities? How is she a "good human historian"?

3. In paragraphs 1–4, Goodman seems to admire "an understanding woman." In what ways does she indicate this respect? How does she change her tone in paragraph 5? Which specific line or expression indicates this change? What is the difference between something *awesome* and something *awful?* Why does Goodman allude to this distinction?

4. According to the author, what is the potential relation between a person who is oblivious to others' feelings and one who is acutely aware of them? What sort of balance is created? What do you feel Goodman's opinion of this balance is? Why?

5. What potentially negative relation does the author discuss between too much understanding and being critical of others? Too much understanding and taking action on things? Too much understanding and personal change? Too much understanding and fulfilling one's personal needs?

6. What is the meaning of the sentence: "A lot of women end up running in place" (par. 10)?

7. According to Goodman, how do men's and women's problems of understanding compare? How does the society's attitudes and instructions to them differ?

8. Explain the meanings of the expressions "What the world needs now is love," "Pass me a Coke," and "turn the other cheek" (par. 15). What is the meaning of *it* in the last sentence of paragraph 15? *What* is paralyzing?

9. What is the "moment" about which Goodman writes in the final paragraph? Compare Goodman's use of a "moment of understanding" to Al Young's use of a similar concept in his essay "Java Jive" on pages 86–90.

10. Would you say, overall, that Goodman is sympathetic to "an understanding woman"? How does she use this essay as a kind of "warning" to women? What other purpose might she have in mind? At what opinion about "understanding women" does Goodman ultimately arrive in this essay?

UNDERSTANDING THE WRITER'S TECHNIQUES

1. Does Goodman ever state a thesis directly in this essay? What is her main idea? How does she present and develop that idea?

2. An *analogy* is a type of figurative comparison that uses examples from one category of ideas or terms in order to explain a difficult idea in another category (see Glossary). In an essay, an analogy may occur in single, isolated instances, or it may be an *extended analogy* that threads through the entire piece of writing. Why does Goodman choose a sports analogy (see page 180) as the organizing device of this essay? How appropriate do you feel it is to the subject? Why?

3. What would you say is Goodman's intended audience for this piece? Be as specific as possible in your response. In what ways does she tailor the essay to this audience?

4. Analyze the organization of paragraphs 5–9:

a. How does paragraph 5 serve as a transition?
b. Why does she repeat the words "I wonder" in paragraph 5?
c. What generalization about too much understanding does she mention at the end of paragraph 5?
d. What category of illustrations of that generalization appears in paragraph 6?
e. What specific illustrations of that category does Goodman offer?
f. What is the use of *repetition* and *repetition with a difference* (see page 144) in these paragraphs?

g. How does the first sentence of paragraph 9 act as a transition within the essay? How does it broaden the scope of the essay? What other later sentence also broadens its scope?

5. To whom does the pronoun *we* refer in paragraph 11? Even if you didn't know the author's name, how would you know the writer's sex based on that paragraph and that pronoun reference?

6. For what purpose does Goodman introduce "another friend" in paragraph 14? How does this friend's attitude about "an understanding woman" differ from the attitude stated or implied up to that point? Do your feel Goodman is *really* writing about friends, or is she using these references in some other way? Explain your answer.

7. Goodman constructs numerous short paragraphs of numerous short (sometimes fragmentary) sentences. Why does she choose this technique? How does it affect the tone of the essay? What does it indicate about her attitude towards the subject?

8. How would you characterize the overall *tone* of this essay? How does that tone change in paragraphs 13–16? What attitudes emerge from those paragraphs? How do these changes in tone help to establish paragraphs 13–16 as the conclusion to this essay? Mention specific words, phrases, and expressions to illustrate the attitudes in this section.

EXPLORING THE WRITER'S IDEAS

1. Based on your understanding of the tone, examples, and development of this essay, do you feel Ellen Goodman is herself "an understanding woman"? Do you think she ever has been one? Explain.

2. It is interesting that Goodman uses a sports analogy to discuss a "woman's problem" which is so historically- and deeply-rooted into our culture. It has only been in the past ten years or so that physical fitness and sports awareness have become a "normal" part of the American

woman's domain. Comment on the relation between this contemporary analogy and this age-old problem.

3. Look ahead to Judy Syfers's essay "I Want a Wife" (pages 351–354). How are these two essays similar in subject matter? Tone and development? Both writers use "friends" as a medium for their discussions. Do you think such a technique is at all rooted in their writing about women's issues? In their being women writers? How so?

4. Conditions for women in society have certainly changed over the past decade. What have been some of the most positive changes? What do you perceive as the most critical problems that remain?

IDEAS FOR WRITING

Guided Writing

Write an extended definition entitled "A Successful Man" in which you lead towards the potentially negative aspects of too much success.

1. Begin with a reference to a successful man you know.

2. Differentiate between two types of successful men, and identify which one you will concentrate on.

3. Early in the essay establish a particular analogy that you can sustain throughout.

4. Offer a definition of a successful man based on his abilities and activities.

5. Tell what you admire about such a man; then indicate your questions about this admiration. Also, question one of the potentially negative results of "success." Give specific illustrations based on your "friend's" most recent experiences.

6. Use repetition, or repetition with a difference, to help set the tone of your essay.

7. Broaden the scope of your essay to include others besides your successful "friend."

8. Highlight some other potentially negative results of too much success.

9. Indicate how the "problem" of success may affect women as well.

10. In your concluding paragraphs, use words and expressions that help indicate your deep-seated feelings about a successful man.

More Writing Projects

1. Write your own definition of "an understanding woman" or "an understanding man." Try to use an extended analogy.

2. Towards the end of the essay, Goodman writes about a relation between feeling virtuous and becoming emotionally paralyzed. Write an extended definition of either the term *virtue* or *paralysis* (for its emotional rather than physical meaning).

Suzanne Britt Jordan

FUN, OH BOY. FUN. YOU COULD DIE FROM IT.

Most of us never really consider exactly what it means to have a good time. Suzanne Britt Jordan, a writer who claims she "tries to have fun, but often fails," offers an extended definition of the word "fun" by pointing out what it is *not*.

Words to Watch

puritan (par. 3): one who practices or preaches a more strict moral code than that which exists
selfless (par. 4): unselfish; having no concern for oneself
fetish (par. 5): something regarded with extravagant trust or respect
licentiousness (par. 9): a lack of moral restraints
consumption (par. 9): to take in or to use up a substance; eating or drinking
epitome (par. 11): an ideal; a typical representation
capacity (par. 12): the ability to hold something
damper (par. 13): something that regulates or that stops something from flowing
reverently (par. 13): respectfully; worshipfully
blaspheme (par. 13): to speak of without respect
weary (par. 14): tired; worn-out
horizon (par. 14): the apparent line where the earth meets the sky
scan (par. 14): to examine something carefully

Fun is hard to have.

Fun is a rare jewel.

Somewhere along the line people got the modern 1
idea that fun was there for the asking, that people deserved 2
fun, that if we didn't have a little fun every day we would 3
turn into (sakes alive!) puritans.

"Was it fun?" became the question that overshad- 4
owed all other questions: good questions like: Was it moral?
Was it kind? Was it honest? Was it beneficial? Was it generous? Was it necessary? And (my favorite) was it selfless?

When the pleasure got to be the main thing, the fun 5
fetish was sure to follow. Everything was supposed to be fun.
If it wasn't fun, then by Jove, we were going to make it fun,
or else.

Think of all the things that got the reputation of be- 6
ing fun. Family outings were supposed to be fun. Sex was
supposed to be fun. Education was supposed to be fun. Work
was supposed to be fun. Walt Disney was supposed to be fun.
Church was supposed to be fun. Staying fit was supposed to
be fun.

Just to make sure that everybody knew how much 7
fun we were having, we put happy faces on flunking test
papers, dirty bumpers, sticky refrigerator doors, bathroom
mirrors.

If a kid, looking at his very happy parents traipsing 8
through that very happy Disney World, said, "This ain't fun,
ma," his ma's heart sank. She wondered where she had
gone wrong. Everybody told her what fun family outings to
Disney World would be. Golly gee, what was the matter?

Fun got to be such a big thing that everybody started 9
to look for more and more thrilling ways to supply it. One way
was to step up the level of danger or licentiousness or alcohol
or drug consumption so that you could be sure that, no matter
what, you would manage to have a little fun.

Television commercials brought a lot of fun and fun- 10
loving folks into the picture. Everything that people in those
commercials did looked like fun: taking Polaroid snapshots,
swilling beer, buying insurance, mopping the floor, bowling,

taking aspirin. We all wished, I'm sure, that we could have half as much fun as those rough-and-ready guys around the locker room, flicking each other with towels and pouring champagne. The more commercials people watched, the more they wondered when the fun would start in their own lives. It was pretty depressing.

Big occasions were supposed to be fun. Christmas, 11 Thanksgiving and Easter were obviously supposed to be fun. Your wedding day was supposed to be fun. Your wedding night was supposed to be a whole lot of fun. Your honeymoon was supposed to be the epitome of fundom. And so we ended up going through every Big Event we ever celebrated, waiting for the fun to start.

It occurred to me, while I was sitting around waiting 12 for the fun to start, that not much is, and that I should tell you just in case you're worried about your fun capacity.

I don't mean to put a damper on things. I just mean 13 we ought to treat fun reverently. It is a mystery. It cannot be caught like a virus. It cannot be trapped like an animal. The god of mirth is paying us back for all those years of thinking fun was everywhere by refusing to come to our party. I don't want to blaspheme fun anymore. When fun comes in on little dancing feet, you probably won't be expecting it. In fact, I bet it comes when you're doing your duty, your job, or your work. It may even come on a Tuesday.

I remember one day, long ago, on which I had an es- 14 pecially good time. Pam Davis and I walked to the College Village drug store one Saturday morning to buy some candy. We were about 12 years old (fun ages). She got her Bit-O-Honey. I got my malted milk balls, chocolate stars, Chunkys, and a small bag of M & M's. We started back to her house. I was going to spend the night. We had the whole day to look forward to. We had plenty of candy. It was a long way to Pam's house but every time we got weary Pam would put her hand over her eyes, scan the horizon like a sailor and say, "Oughta reach home by nightfall," at which point the two of us would laugh until we thought we couldn't stand it another minute. Then after we got calm, she'd say it again. You should have been there. It was the kind of day and friendship and occasion that made me deeply regretful that I had to grow up.

It was fun. 15

BUILDING VOCABULARY

1. *Trite language* refers to words and expressions that have been overused, and, consequently, have lost much of their effectiveness. People do rely on trite language in their conversations, but writers usually avoid overused expressions. However, a good writer will be able to introduce such vocabulary at strategic points. Examples of trite language in Jordan's essay appear below. Explain in your own words what they mean:

   a. "a rare jewel" (par. 2)
   b. "by Jove" (par. 5)
   c. "golly gee" (par. 8)
   d. "his ma's heart sank" (par. 8)

2. For each of the following words drawn from Jordan's essay, write a denotative definition. Then list four connotations (see pages 411–412) each word has for you.

   a. overshadow (par. 4)
   b. flunking (par. 7)
   c. traipsing (par. 8)
   d. swilling (par. 10)
   e. mirth (par. 13)

3. Select five words from the Words to Watch section and use them in sentences of your own.

UNDERSTANDING THE WRITER'S IDEAS

1. What are some of the things Jordan says fun is not?

2. What does Jordan suggest we did to something

if it wasn't already fun? Identify some of the things she says are "supposed" to be fun.

3. In paragraph 7, Jordan lists some common things that certainly aren't any fun. How does she say people made them fun anyway?

4. What are some of the ways people make fun even more thrilling?

5. What does Jordan list as looking like fun on television commercials?

6. Discuss the relationship between big occasions and the experience of fun. Explain the meaning of the statement, "It may even come on a Tuesday."

7. Describe Jordan's attitude concerning how much in life really is fun. According to Jordan, how should we treat fun? Why? Is it something she says can only be experienced at special times?

8. How old was Jordan at the time she remembers having an especially good time with her friend Pam? Describe in your own words why she had such a good time that day. What are some of the candies she remembers buying? Why was it especially funny when Pam would say, "Oughta reach home by nightfall"?

9. For what reason does Jordan feel regretful at the end of the essay? Although she is regretful, do you think she is actually sad? Why?

UNDERSTANDING THE WRITER'S TECHNIQUES

1. Does Jordan ever offer a single-sentence definition of "fun"? Where? Is that sentence sufficient to define the concept? Why?

2. Jordan employs the technique of *negation*—defining a term through showing what it is *not*—so strongly in this essay that the writing verges on *irony*. Irony is using language to suggest the opposite of what is said (see Glossary). Explain the irony in paragraphs 7, 8, and 9.

3. Why does the author continually point out things that are supposed to be fun? What is she trying to tell us about these things?

4. Writers usually avoid vague words such as "everything" or "everybody" in their writing, yet Jordan uses these words frequently in this essay. Explain her purpose in deliberately avoiding concrete terms.

5. What is the *tone* (see Glossary) of this essay? Is it fun? How does Jordan create this tone? Much of the writing in this essay has a very conversational quality to it, as though the author were speaking directly to the reader. Locate five words or phrases that have this quality.

6. Why does Jordan use so many examples and illustrations in this essay? Which paragraphs use multiple illustrations with special effectiveness?

7. There is a definite turning point in this essay where Jordan switches from an ironic to an affirmative point of view in which she begins to explain what fun *can be* rather than what is *is not*. One paragraph in particular serves as the transition between the two attitudes. Which one is it? Which is the first paragraph to be mostly affirmative? What is the result of this switch?

8. Jordan uses specific brand names in the essay. Locate at least four of them. Why do you think she uses these brand names instead of names that simply identify the object?

9. What is the function of narration in the development of this essay? Where does the author *narrate* an imagined incident? Where does she use a real incident? Why does Jordan use narration in this paper?

10. Compare the effects of the two simple, direct statements that begin and end the essay. Why does Jordan not develop a more elaborate introduction and conclusion?

EXPLORING THE WRITER'S IDEAS

1. Jordan begins her essay by stating, "Fun is hard to have." At one point she indicates that "Fun got to be such a big thing that everybody started looking for more and more thrilling ways to supply it" (par. 9). Do you think that fun is hard to have? Why or why not? What relationship does the epidemic use of drugs and alcohol have to our difficulties in having fun today?

2. The author raises the question of how at big events we are sometimes left "waiting for the fun to start" (par. 11). What functions do events or occasions such as holidays, weddings, or birthdays play in our society? Why is there an emphasis placed on having fun at those events? Do you think there should be such an emphasis? Why?

3. This essay appeared as a guest editorial in the *New York Times*. We do not usually think of the *New York Times* as a "fun" newspaper, but rather as one that deals with serious issues of international significance. Jordan's article might be considered popular writing or light reading. Do you feel there is a place in the media—newspapers, magazines, radio, television—for a mixture of "heavy" and "light" attitudes? What well-respected newspapers or magazines that you know include articles on popular topics? What subjects do you think would currently be most appealing to popular audiences?

4. At the end of the essay, Jordan seems to imply that it is easier for children to have fun than it is for grownups. Do you agree? Is the basic experience of fun any different for kids or for adults? Do you feel it was any easier for people to have fun in days past than it is now? Why?

IDEAS FOR WRITING

Guided Writing

Select one of the following highly connotative terms for various types of experiences and write an extended definition about it: love, creativity, alienation, prejudice, fidelity.

1. Prepare for your essay by consulting a good dictionary for the lexical definition of the term. However, instead of beginning with this definition, start with some catchy, interesting opening statements related to the definition.

2. Write a thesis sentence that names the word you will define and that tells the special opinion, attitude, or point of view you have about the word.

3. Attempt to establish the importance of your sub-

ject by considering it in terms of our current understanding of fun.

4. Use the technique of negation (see page 146) by providing various examples and illustrations of what your topic *is not* in order to establish your own viewpoint of what it *is*.

5. Use other strategies—description, narration, comparison and contrast, and so forth—to aid in clearly establishing an extended definition of your topic.

6. At the end of your essay dramatize through narration at least one personal experience that relates the importance of the topic to your life.

More Writing Projects

1. From a book of popular quotations (*Bartlett's Familiar Quotations, The Oxford Dictionary of Quotations*) check under the heading "fun" and select a number of statements about fun by professional writers. Then write an essay in which you expand one of those definitions. Draw upon your own experiences or readings to support the definition you choose to expand.

2. Write an extended definition of "triumph," using the main techniques seen in the Jordan essay.

Gregg Easterbrook

ESCAPE VALVE

A contemporary journalist, Gregg Easterbrook tries here to define a phrase that he has coined to identify a phenomenon of modern life. Take note of the way he develops his definition by means of personal anecdote, history, and causal analysis. As you read, think about whether or not you know anyone guilty of "automatic-out."

Words to Watch

deep-rooted (par. 3): firmly planted
foundations (par. 4): underlying supports
stints (par. 5): fixed share of work to be performed within a given time period
truism (par. 5): statement of a very obvious truth
hierarchies (par. 6): body of people organized or classified according to rank
integrity (par. 7): adherence to a code of behavior: honesty; uprightness
perpetuate (par. 9): prolong the existence of

A man and woman I know moved in together 1 recently. It was, as such occasions are, a moment of sentiment and celebration. It was also a limited engagement. Before moving in, they had already set a fixed date when they would break up.

They explained their reasons to one and all. In a 2
year, the woman planned to change jobs and cities; the man
did not plan to follow. An eventual split is unfortunate, they
said, but also inevitable, so why not plan on it? Yet, far
from being a sad twist of fate, my woman friend's scheduled
departure, I fear, was a liberating force, making possible
whatever short-term romance the couple will enjoy. Without
the escape clause of a pre-set termination of their affair,
they might never have lived together at all.

This situation is not unique. More and more, people 3
are ordering their lives along a principle I call the "automatic-out." In love, friendship, work, and the community,
people increasingly prefer arrangements that automatically
end at some pre-set date. Automatic-out is not a phenomenon
confined to my still-unsettled generation (the late 20's), with
its flair for "flexible" styles of life. It is a force in society as
a whole, as more of us hunger for lives that appear stable
and deep-rooted but lack the complications of commitment.

Automatic-out may have its foundations in the pre- 4
set cycles of academic life. In recent decades, an ever-higher
percentage of the population has been able to attend college
and postgraduate schools. That's a good thing for the cause
of education but perhaps not so good for society's spirit.
Longtime students learn to view institutions as places where
people briefly come to rest, and from which they will be
automatically removed on a date known years in advance.
They also tend to see institutions as a means by which to
take things for themselves, instead of adding things for
others.

So it may be no surprise that professionals—usually 5
the beneficiaries of advanced schooling—seem increasingly
uninterested in staying put. Or, if they remain with one
organization, lean toward fellowships, temporary assignments, and other stints with automatic-outs. For some time,
this has been a troubling truism of Washington. A Brookings
Institution study shows that Government-agency managers
immediately below the rank of Presidential appointees turn
over, on average, every 21 months. Now it is becoming true
of private enterprise as well. According to the Conference

Board, a business research organization, top corporate executives now switch jobs every 4.5 years on average—an all-time high.

The job-switching mania, it is sometimes suggested, 6 stems from a combination of boredom and expectations of promotion. But most switches among Government agencies and corporate hierarchies do not involve dramatic changes of life; they are changes from one job to another fairly similar to it, in a fairly similar organization. The number of top-level positions available doesn't increase just because the switching rate is increasing.

The switch mania is, I think, motivated by the desire 7 for automatic-outs. When you know in advance that you will soon be changing jobs, you are relieved of concern for the overall integrity of your institution—whether the quality of its products, the fairness of its service, the odds of its survival. You have a built-in excuse for selfishness ("I'll be leaving in a year anyway") and can concentrate on advancing yourself, secure in the knowledge that if you fail to improve your organization—or, as in the case of so many business and Government managers, actively damage it—you personally won't suffer. You'll be one step ahead of the crumbling walls.

It seems to be the same way in love. If a romance 8 operates under some pre-set restriction, neither partner feels obliged to sacrifice his interests for joint interests. Why sacrifice for something not expected to last anyway? Thus, the short-term benefits of marriage and living together (companionship, warmth, convenience) remain popular. But long-term obligation to the institution of marriage has fallen into disrepute among many young people. Children and family life are especially in disrepute today, for whenever children are present there is no easy out, emotionally or legally. The weekend romance is especially desirable today, not because "people move around more now" but because distance guarantees an automatic-out. Just step back on the plane Sunday night.

Many troublesome aspects of life perpetuate themselves through downward-drawing spirals. As corporate and 9 public institutions fall deeper into disrepair, as men and women becoming increasingly small-minded and cool to the touch, there seems all the more reason to opt for automatic-outs. Who wants to be committed to the kinds of people and organizations at loose in the world today? This, of course, helps only to accelerate the decay. Many people capable of helping right what's wrong with society seek instead mainly to exempt themselves from responsibility for its condition. Why should I care? I'll be leaving in a year anyway.

BUILDING VOCABULARY

Match each term at the left below with an appropriate definition among those appearing at the right. There are two more definitions than you need.

1. inevitable (par. 2)	a. disgrace
2. stable (par. 3)	b. attractive
3. beneficiaries (par. 5)	c. stimulated to action
4. mania (par. 6)	d. speed up
5. motivated (par. 7)	e. intense, abnormal desire for something
6. disrepute (par. 8)	f. automatic
7. disrepair (par. 9)	g. resistant to change
8. opt (par. 9)	h. free from obligation
9. accelerate (par. 9)	i. choose
10. exempt (par. 9)	j. unavoidable
	k. state of neglect
	l. those who receive advantages

UNDERSTANDING THE WRITER'S IDEAS

1. What arrangement does the couple the author knows make? What reasons do they offer for this arrangement?

2. What is the "automatic-out" principle? Why does the author believe that it appeals to society as a whole and not just to his own generation of men and women in their late twenties?

3. What, according to Easterbrook, are the foundations for automatic-out?

4. What does the Brookings Institution study demonstrate? How does the Conference Board reinforce that study in a business setting?

5. What are the reasons generally offered for what Easterbrook calls "the job-switching mania"? Why are top-level positions not increasing in number? How does Easterbrook explain the switch mania?

6. For what reason does the desire to switch operate for love as well as for jobs? What are the short-term benefits of marriage and living together? Why, according to the author, has the long-term obligation to marriage fallen into disrepute? Why is the weekend romance attractive?

7. How does the automatic-out serve to accelerate the decay of people and institutions today?

UNDERSTANDING THE WRITER'S TECHNIQUE

1. Which sentence of this essay is the thesis sentence? Why does Easterbrook not place it in the opening paragraph?

2. What is your opinion of the introduction in paragraphs 1 and 2? What is the value to the essay of the incident about the author's acquaintances? What rhetorical technique appears?

3. Where does the writer use negation (see page 195)?

4. In paragraph 4 why does he give backgrounds to the concept "automatic-out"?

5. Why does Easterbrook present findings of the Brookings Institution and the Conference Board? How do the findings enhance his point?

6. Where does the writer use causal analysis (see pages 288–290)? Why does he use it?

7. What transitions serve to connect one paragraph to the next? Look especially at the first sentence in paragraphs 3, 4, 5, 6, 7, and 8.

8. In paragraphs 3, 7, and 8 Easterbrook uses

parenthetical expressions. Why does he choose to place information in parentheses?

9. The writer frames a number of questions in the essay. For example, in paragraph 8, he says, "Why sacrifice for something not expected to last anyway?" What is the value of the question? Why doesn't Easterbrook answer it? What other unanswered questions appear?

10. What is your opinion of the conclusion? How does Easterbrook establish a new, broader context for the term "automatic-out"? Why does he choose that context to close the essay?

11. Why do you think that the essay is called "Escape Valve" instead of "Automatic-Out"? What is an escape valve? Used here, of course, the title is metaphorical (see Glossary). What value is there in using the metaphorical title in this case?

12. What is your reaction to the conclusion? Why does Easterbrook end by condemning the automatic-out philosophy? Do you find the last two sentences effective? Why?

EXPLORING THE WRITER'S IDEAS

1. Has Easterbrook defined clearly a recognizable principle in today's society as you view it? Why do you feel as you do? What evidence of the automatic-out do you find among your family, friends, or acquaintances? Have you yourself ever entered into a relationship based upon automatic-out?

2. Easterbrook blames in part the academic institution—our public and private schools and colleges—for our acceptance of the value in short-term commitments. Why might you agree or disagree with him? What other forces or institutions may encourage short-term commitments?

3. Do you agree that the high level of job switching apparent today is related more to the desire for escaping commitments than to "boredom and expectations of promotion"? Defend your answer.

4. Why might you agree or disagree that "marriage

has fallen into disrepute among many young people"? Is automatic-out a real threat to marriage as a basic institution of our culture? Why? (Look ahead to the essay "I Want a Wife" by Judy Syfers for another perspective on marriage.)

5. Answer the question in paragraph 9: "Who wants to be committed to the kinds of people and organizations at loose in the world today?"

6. The writer states that "many people capable of helping right what's wrong with society" try "to exempt themselves from responsibility for its condition." What are some of the things wrong with society today? How might people right those wrongs?

IDEAS FOR WRITING

Guided Writing

Choose a word or term that you think is opposite in meaning to "automatic-out" and write an essay of 500 to 750 words in which you define that term. You may choose a word or term like *commitment, staying in, holding on, hanging in,* or some such expression. You may even want to coin your own phrase.

1. Start with an anecdote about friends or acquaintances and explain it. Your anecdote should demonstrate the word or phrase that you are trying to define.

2. In your thesis statement name the term and give an expanded definition of it in a paragraph or two.

3. Explain the foundations or the history of the situation your term is naming as Easterbrook does in paragraph 4 of his essay.

4. If possible, present data to support your interpretation of the term.

5. Give examples to expand your meanings further. Draw your examples from people at work or from personal relationships with other people.

6. Use an occasional unanswered question to challenge the reader.

7. If you can, use negation to help you define the term.

8. Connect your paragraphs with transitions that relate one idea thoughtfully to the next.

9. In your conclusion, place the term in a broader perspective, one that goes beyond the specific conditions you are explaining.

10. Try to give your essay a metaphorical title.

More Writing Projects

1. Easterbrook uses the term "switch mania" when he writes about jobs. Think about the term and then write a definition of it as it pertains to our culture today.

2. An "escapist" is someone who looks to break loose from unpleasant realities through self-deceiving fantasy or entertainment. In an essay write an extended definition of the word "escapist." Draw upon your own experiences and (or) your readings to support your definition.

Elizabeth Janeway

SOAPS, CYNICISM, AND MIND CONTROL

Elizabeth Janeway is the author of *Man's World, Woman's Place* and *Powers of the Weak*; these, and her forthcoming book, focus acutely on sociological uses of power and manipulation. "Soaps, Cynicism, and Mind Control" appeared in the January 1985 issue of *Ms.* magazine. It explains the dangers of allowing oneself to be too influenced by the media; in so doing, the essay establishes a definition for the abstract notion of *randomness*.

Words to Watch

heightened (par. 1):   made more exciting
catering (par. 1):   supplying what is required or desired
kin (par. 2):   relatives
fidelity (par. 3):   faithfulness to another person
amnesiac (par. 3):   a person who has temporarily lost his or her
     memory
differentiates (par. 4):   discerns separate characteristics of some-
     thing
inevitability (par. 4):   the condition of not being able to be avoided
     or evaded
potentiality (par. 4):   the ability to develop
counsel (par. 6):   to give advice
passivity (par. 8):   attitude of submissiveness or inactivity
subordinates (par. 10):   makes less important
ideology (par. 10):   a system of belief about a subject, often social,
     political, or economic in nature

What does the powerful teaching tool of television have to say to its viewers about desirable attitudes toward life and its problems? And what does the Media Establishment assume that *we* assume about the way this world functions? With these questions, I approached soap operas and evening series—programs that claimed to present ordinary existence, though heightened for drama and catering to everyone's curiosity about how the other half lives.

In between commercial breaks, I noted a deeply disturbing factor in so many of the dramas: the lack of any sense of process, of the eternal truth that events have consequences, and that people can and do influence what happens to them and to others. What I saw instead was a consistent, insistent demonstration of *randomness,* a statement that life is unpredictable and out of control. With rare exceptions what happens on-screen suggests that no one can trust her or his own judgment and (other side of the same coin) that no one, friend, kin, or lover, is really trustworthy.

We may identify with the actors because we all face unpredictable events, but we get no clues to coping with them. No one seems talented at solving the puzzles of life: even J.R. Ewing was shot. Nobody shows us how to decide on the fidelity of kin or associates, no love is certain. Let a wedding date be set and you can be pretty sure the ceremony won't come off. Report a death and expect the corpse to show up in a future segment fleeing a crime, amnesiac, or as survivor of a "fatal" plane crash. Says one of a pair of embracing lovers, "I don't know anything about you." Par for the course. Later in the same segment (of "Another World") a young woman tells a young man she doesn't love him. But wait a minute! She has been hypnotized, it seems, in a program I missed, and here she is on tape declaring she *does* love him to the hypnotist. Not only don't we/they know anything about the others in their lives, they/we don't understand ourselves either. The Guiding Lights we seek are shrouded in fog.

Now drama, and indeed fiction as a whole, has always aimed at surprising its audiences. But those surprises end by showing us something we hadn't known, some truth, about existence. It may be a tragic truth, but tragedy can strengthen us to face the future because it explains and illustrates the processes that lead to defeat instead of victory. And knowledge is power. Even when it tells us some things can't be changed, it differentiates inevitability from potentiality; and moreover, it gives us a chance to plan our own responses: we can't change the weather, but we can take an umbrella when we go out. Our intervention in ongoing existence is shown to be possible. Beginning with childhood fables and fairy tales, such stories bring us useful messages about the workings of the real world and what human beings can do to influence it.

That's not what the TV programs say. The people 5 on the screen are adrift in a world of happenstance, and the messages warn that no action will do any good.

Certainly there's a lot of randomness in the world. 6 Stable unchanging small-town life is fading from the American scene and close ties to extended families are rare. Most of us meet a lot of strangers from unfamiliar backgrounds. Women who have moved into formerly all-male preserves have had to learn or invent patterns of relationships as well as new processes of doing things. These women have begun to take risks and forget old lessons in helplessness. But daily there appears on the screen counsel that the world is unpredictable, that one can't hope to plan or gain control of events. Moreover when we see the rare realistic portrayal of work-life (where competence, daring, and imagination may be rewarded), attention is concentrated on the personal. Intimate relationships are chancy and dangerous, comes the word, but they're the only things that matter.

Randomness, like guilt, is a powerful tool for social 7 control. Survivors of the Holocaust and refugees from Stalin's "Gulag Archipelago" record how personality was deliberately broken down by those in control disrupting their prisoners' normal expectations. Guards separated consequences from action and thus persuaded prisoners that it was hopeless for them to plan a particular behavior, hopeless for them to imagine a future. Survival became a matter of utter chance. Inmates of the camps were thus reduced to subhuman, mindless robots who moved as they were told to.

Today in El Salvador (and who can say how many 8 other places?), terror activates the randomness of danger. No one knows where the death squads will strike next, and therefore people can't take any reasonable action and expect to ensure greater safety. If safety exists at all, it lies in passivity and hiding. *Time* magazine quotes an expert on Central America in a recent issue: "Anybody can be killed with virtual impunity. You do not want to investigate because you might find out, and finding out can itself be fatal."

But it's not only in extreme situations that random- 9 ness can be used to promote self-policing. If the powerful can divide the majority of ordinary folk into disconnected, self-protecting individuals, they need not fear organized resistance. And when television suggests to a woman that even her friends had better not be trusted, it is denying comradeship, sisterhood—and joint action.

I don't suggest that this is a conscious media con- 10 spiracy intended to keep women and other groups in their subordinate places. *It doesn't need to be.* Standard practice and the mythic ideology that enforces it have always played up individual effort as a way of establishing one's value and one's deserts. For instance, the Supreme Court has underlined that message by limiting affirmative action remedies that can be awarded to a group or class. Legal recourse must now be sought by *individuals* rather than on a group basis. When the media repeats this message, it need only appeal to what we've often heard before: success means learning the rules and following them. Don't trust your colleagues. The big world of action is both dangerous and mysterious, you'll never really understand it. Stay out of it, sit still, don't try.

Will we follow that message more than two gener- 11 ations after women won the ballot? Let us refuse the posture of the powerless. People who have begun to feel strong don't have to accept victimization.

BUILDING VOCABULARY

1. While Janeway never really uses *trite language* (see page 194), she does use a number of expressions in fairly common use in daily conversation and media talk or writing. Try to rewrite each of the following expressions in your own words, using less common language; try to create original, interesting expressions.

    a. teaching tool (par. 1)
    b. Media Establishment (par. 1)
    c. how the other half lives (par. 1)
    d. commercial breaks (par. 2)
    e. other side of the same coin (par. 2)
    f. Par for the course (par. 3)
    g. shrouded in fog (par. 3)
    h. a tragic truth (par. 4)
    i. knowledge is power (par. 4)
    j. adrift in a world of happenstance (par. 5)
    k. all-male preserves (par. 6)
    l. a matter of utter chance (par. 7)
    m. with virtual impunity (par. 8)
    n. ordinary folk (par. 9)
    o. a conscious media conspiracy (par. 10)

2. Identify these *allusions* (see page 409) from Janeway's essay:

    a. J.R. Ewing (par. 3)
    b. "Another World" (par. 3)
    c. the Holocaust (par. 7)
    d. Stalin (par. 7)
    e. "Gulag Archipelago" (par. 7)
    f. El Salvador (par. 8)
    g. the death squads (in El Salvador) (par. 8)
    h. *Time* magazine (par. 8)
    i. the Supreme Court (par. 10)
    j. affirmative action (par. 10)

UNDERSTANDING THE WRITER'S IDEAS

1. What are *soap operas* and *evening series*? Give some current examples of each. What does the author say is the intended purpose of these types of programs? How does she say that purpose is altered? Why is it?

2. According to Janeway, how do television dramas present an unrealistic view of life? What attitude toward trust do they convey?

3. Based on your understanding of Janeway's article, who do you think she would say is more capable of dealing with "unpredictable events"—dramatic characters or their viewers? Explain your answer.

4. Explain in your own words the main idea of paragraph 4. What is Janeway's point about the purposes of drama and fiction? What is especially enlightening about tragedy? How do fairy tales and fables fit into this explanation? How do TV programs differ in purpose and effect from the types of drama and fiction that Janeway respects? How is their message significantly different from that of good fiction?

5. What recent changes in American society does Janeway mention in paragraph 6? What is her opinion of those changes? Why are they useful examples to advance the theme of this essay?

6. What does Janeway mean in paragraph 6 by the expression "old lessons in helplessness"? What attitude does she convey in the sentence in which it appears?

7. In the last sentence of paragraph 6, the author uses the expression, "comes the word." From *where* does *the word* come? What is *the word*? In light of her title and theme in this essay, how is that expression particularly appropriate?

8. What, according to the author, is the connection between "randomness" and "mind control"? What does she mean by randomness? What examples of that connection does she provide? For what reason does she choose such examples?

9. What does Janeway suggest is the relation

between a powerful minority and a "majority of ordinary folks"? How do notions of individuality play a role in this relation?

10. What is the author's opinion about the ways in which the media affects the lives of women? Explain your answer with specific references to the article.

11. Ultimately, how do you understand Janeway to define the concept of randomness? Does she define predominantly through indicating its causes, effects, or manifestations?

UNDERSTANDING THE WRITER'S TECHNIQUES

1. How does Janeway use questions in the first paragraph to establish a context for her discussion? Does she ask these questions to search for specific answers or are they rhetorical questions (*rhetorical questions* are meant to stimulate thought rather than specific answers)? Explain.

2. What is defined in this essay? Does Janeway state that definition directly? In brief, what would you say is her thesis in this essay? Why does she use definition as her key organizing technique? How does she use minor definitions to build to her major definition?

3. What is *cynicism* (write a dictionary definition of the term)? How is the first sentence of paragraph 2 an example of cynicism? Find at least three other examples of cynicism in this essay.

4. Comment on Janeway's use of *illustration* (see pages 109–110) in this essay. From where does she draw most of her examples? Which are the most effective? Which least? Why?

5. Explain the author's use of double subject pronouns (*we/they; they/we*) in paragraph 3. What relation between viewer and character does this technique establish? Why does Janeway want to establish such a connection?

6. What is the *double entendre* (see page 66) of the phrase "The Guiding Lights" as it is used in paragraph 3?

7. Why is paragraph 5 so short in comparison to the others in this essay? How does it act as a key turning point in the essay?

8. What is the purpose of italicizing the sentence, *It doesn't need to be* in paragraph 10? What is the effect?

9. For whom is Janeway writing this article? Why do you think so? What "message" is she attempting to convey to that audience? In the last three paragraphs, how does Janeway gear her definition to a feminist perspective? Where does she forecast that perspective earlier in the essay? How do the examples that she chooses in paragraphs 9–11 help create this perspective?

10. Would you characterize the messages and tone of paragraph 10 as more *ironic* (see page 416) or *cynical*? Why?

11. Janeway begins this article by concentrating on TV soaps and dramas, yet by the end, she is dealing with a much wider range of influences. How does she accomplish this broadening of her scope of ideas? Why does she do so? Do you feel she accomplished the transition smoothly and that she maintained *unity* and *coherence* (see Glossary) throughout the essay?

EXPLORING THE WRITER'S IDEAS

1. In this article, Elizabeth Janeway writes about such highly-charged issues as *mind control* and *conscious media conspiracy*. Do you think such things actually exist? If so, to what extent? Do you believe that any sort of media conspiracy currently exists? If so, explain its causes and give examples of its manifestations. What can be done about it? If you don't think it exists, why do you feel so many people are concerned about it these days?

2. Would you say Janeway believes in fate or pre-destination? Why or why not?

3. In paragraph 4, Janeway writes about the powerful effects of drama and fiction, and she gives us examples of what we can learn from them. She includes, also, childhood fables and fairy tales. Give examples of how reading, seeing,

or hearing certain fiction, either as a child or as an adult, has influenced your present way of life. (Bruno Bettelheim, pages 164–168, has some interesting ideas on childhood stories.)

4. Look up the origin of the term *soap opera*. How did the phrase develop?

5. Janeway defines success as "learning the rules and following them." Do you agree with that definition? Why or why not? How might it be possible for someone to achieve success without following the rules?

IDEAS FOR WRITING

Guided Writing

Write a definition of *mind control*. Focus your essay on a medium other than television *or* on a specific aspect of television broadcasting. For example, you may want to focus on newspapers or magazines, *or* on TV news, or advertisements or music videos.

1. Begin your essay with a series of rhetorical questions to set the context for your investigation of the particular medium.

2. State clearly what you feel the underlying purpose of that medium is (as it affects mind control).

3. Give examples of how the medium presents a view of life other than that which is usual or realistic.

4. Give examples—both general and specific—of this unrealistic view of things.

5. Make some statement about what effect this unrealistic view has on us as media consumers.

6. Explain the potential positive uses of this medium.

7. About half-way through your essay, begin a pointed discussion of how the medium you've chosen tends to manipulate our perceptions of the world around us.

8. About two-thirds through the essay, narrow your

point of perspective so that you focus more clearly on one segment of the medium's audience.

9. Include contemporary examples and historical allusions that illustrate both causes and effects of this mind control.

10. End your essay with a strong statement of how people can overcome the "control" of this medium.

More Writing Projects

1. Write an extended definition of any abstract term that is currently popular in the jargon of sociology or pop psychology. Develop your definition with illustrations of both causes and effects.

2. Write about a time when you were influenced by the media to do something you wouldn't have ordinarily considered doing: buying something, talking with others in a certain way, dressing differently, and so on.

7

Classification

Classification is the arrangement of information into groups or categories in order to make clear the relationships among members of the group. Writers need to classify, because it helps them present a mass of material by means of some orderly system. Related bits of information seem clearer when presented together as parts of a group. We are always classifying things in our daily lives: We put all our text books on one shelf or in one corner of the desk; we count on similar items in the supermarket being grouped together so we can buy all our canned vegetables or snacks in a single area; we make categories in our minds of the teachers we like, of the relatives who annoy us, and of the cars that look sleekest on the road. In classifying, we show how things within a large body of information relate to each other; we organize those things into groups so that they make sense to us and to anybody else who is interested in what we are thinking, or saying, or doing.

Classification helps writers explain relationships to their readers. First, a writer will *analyze* a body of material in order to divide some large subject into categories. Called *division* or *analysis*, this first task helps split an idea or an object into parts. Then, some of the parts can serve as categories into which the writer can fit individual pieces that share some common qualities. So, if you wanted to write about sports, for example, you might first break the topic down—*divide* it—into *team sports* and *individual sports* (although there are many other ways you might have made the division). Then you could group together (*classify*) baseball, soccer, and football in the first category; and, perhaps, boxing, wrestling and tennis in the second. Your purpose in dividing or analyzing is to determine the parts of a whole (team sports and individual sports *are* very different).

Division does not always require that classification follow it. Your purpose in classifying, however, is to show how things in a group are similar. (Baseball, soccer, and football have interesting similarities as team sports; boxing, wrestling, and tennis—stressing individual achievement— are related, too.) Yet division and classification do work together. If you emptied the contents of a pocketbook onto a table, you would begin to divide those contents into groups. Through division, you would identify objects relating to finances, objects relating to personal care, objects relating to school work. Once you had the divisions clear, you would place objects in each category: money, checks, and credit cards in the first; cosmetics, a comb, perfume in the second; pens, pencils, a notebook in the third.

When you divide and classify for writing, you have to keep several things in mind. You have to think carefully about the division of the topic so that you limit the overlap from group to group. That is best achieved by creating categories different enough from each other so there is no blending. Since you, the writer, have to establish the groups (and sometimes there are many different ways to set up groups for the same topic), you need to use a principle of classification that is sensible, accurate, and complete. Do not force categories just for the sake of making groups. You have to show how things in a group relate to each other, and this you must do without ignoring their differences and without making them stereotypes. If you stereotype objects in a group (whether the objects are people, things, or ideas), you will be oversimplifying them, taking away their individuality, and forcing them to fit your categories.

Classification resembles outlining. It provides the writer with a plan of organization. Whether the subject is personal, technical, simple, complex, or abstract, the writer can organize material about it into categories, and can move carefully from one category to another in developing an essay.

Judith Viorst

FRIENDS, GOOD FRIENDS— AND SUCH GOOD FRIENDS

In this essay Judith Viorst, who writes for numerous popular magazines, examines types of friends in her life. Her pattern of development is easy to follow, because she tends to stay on one level in the process of classification. As you read this essay, try to keep in mind the similarities and distinctions that Viorst makes among types of friends, as well as the principles of classification that she uses.

Words to Watch

nonchalant (par. 3): showing lack of interest or concern
endodontist (par. 14): a dentist specializing in diseases of dental pulp and root canals.
sibling (par. 16): brother or sister
dormant (par. 19): as if asleep; inactive
self-revelation (par. 22): self-discovery; self-disclosure
calibrated (par. 29): measured; fixed; checked carefully

Women are friends, I once would have said, when 1 they totally love and support and trust each other, and bare to each other the secrets of their souls, and run—no questions asked—to help each other, and tell harsh truths to each other (no, you can't wear that dress unless you lose ten pounds first) when harsh truths must be told.

Women are friends, I once would have said, when they share the same affection for Ingmar Bergman, plus train rides, cats, warm rain, charades, Camus, and hate with equal ardor Newark and Brussels sprouts and Lawrence Welk and camping. 2

In other words, I once would have said that a friend is a friend all the way, but now I believe that's a narrow point of view. For the friendships I have and the friendships I see are conducted at many levels of intensity, serve many different functions, meet different needs and range from those as all-the-way as the friendship of the soul sisters mentioned above to that of the most nonchalant and casual playmates. 3

Consider these varieties of friendship: 4

1. Convenience friends. These are the women with whom, if our paths weren't crossing all the time, we'd have no particular reason to be friends: a next-door neighbor, a woman in our car pool, the mother of one of our children's closest friends or maybe some mommy with whom we serve juice and cookies each week at the Glenwood Co-op Nursery. 5

Convenience friends are convenient indeed. They'll lend us their cups and silverware for a party. They'll drive our kids to soccer when we're sick. They'll take us to pick up our car when we need a lift to the garage. They'll even take our cats when we go on vacation. As we will for them. 6

But we don't, with convenience friends, ever come too close or tell too much; we maintain our public face and emotional distance. "Which means," says Elaine, "that I'll talk about being overweight but not about being depressed. Which means I'll admit being mad but not blind with rage. Which means I might say that we're pinched this month but never that I'm worried sick over money." 7

But which doesn't mean that there isn't sufficient value to be found in these friendships of mutual aid, in convenience friends. 8

2. Special-interest friends. These friendships aren't intimate, and they needn't involve kids or silverware or 9

cats. Their value lies in some interest jointly shared. And so we may have an office friend or a yoga friend or a tennis friend or a friend from the Women's Democratic Club.

"I've got one woman friend," says Joyce, "who likes, 10 as I do, to take psychology courses. Which makes it nice for me—and nice for her. It's fun to go with someone you know and it's fun to discuss what you've learned, driving back from the classes." And for the most part, she says, that's all they discuss.

"I'd say that what we're doing is *doing* together, not 11 being together," Suzanne says of her Tuesday-doubles friends. "It's mainly a tennis relationship, but we play together well. And I guess we all need to have a couple of playmates."

I agree. 12

My playmate is a shopping friend, a woman of 13 marvelous taste, a woman who knows exactly *where* to buy *what,* and furthermore is a woman who always knows beyond a doubt what one ought to be buying. I don't have the time to keep up with what's new in eyeshadow, hemlines and shoes and whether the smock look is in or finished already. But since (oh, shame!) I care a lot about eyeshadow, hemlines and shoes, and since I don't *want* to wear smocks if the smock look is finished, I'm very glad to have a shopping friend.

3. Historical friends. We all have a friend who knew 14 us when . . . maybe way back in Miss Meltzer's second grade, when our family lived in that three-room flat in Brooklyn, when our dad was out of work for seven months, when our brother Allie got in that fight where they had to call the police, when our sister married the endodontist from Yonkers and when, the morning after we lost our virginity, she was the first, the only, friend we told.

The years have gone by and we've gone separate 15 ways and we've little in common now, but we're still an intimate part of each other's past. And so whenever we go to Detroit we always go to visit this friend of our girlhood. Who knows how we looked before our teeth were straightened. Who knows how we talked before our voice got un-Brooklyned. Who knows what we ate before we learned about artichokes. And who, by her presence, puts us in touch with an earlier part of ourself, a part of ourself it's important never to lose.

"What this friend means to me and what I mean to 16 her," says Grace, "is having a sister without sibling rivalry. We know the texture of each other's lives. She remembers my grandmother's cabbage soup. I remember the way her uncle played the piano. There's simply no other friend who remembers those things."

4. Crossroads friends. Like historical friends, our 17 crossroads friends are important for *what was*—for the friendship we shared at a crucial, now past, time of life. A time, perhaps, when we roomed in college together; or worked as eager young singles in the Big City together; or went together, as my friend Elizabeth and I did through pregnancy, birth and that scary first year of new motherhood.

Crossroads friends forge powerful links, links strong 18 enough to endure with not much more contact than once-a-year letters at Christmas. And out of respect for those crossroads years, for those dramas and dreams we once shared, we will always be friends.

5. Cross-generational friends. Historical friends and 19 crossroads friends seem to maintain a special kind of intimacy—dormant but always ready to be revived—and though we may rarely meet, whenever we do connect, it's personal and intense. Another kind of intimacy exists in the friendships that form across generations in what one woman calls her daughter-mother and her mother-daughter relationships.

Evelyn's friend is her mother's age—"but I share so 20 much more than I ever could with my mother"—a woman she talks to of music, of books and of life. "What I get from her is the benefit of her experience. What she gets—and enjoys—from me is a youthful perspective. It's a pleasure for both of us."

I have in my own life a precious friend, a woman of 21 65 who has lived very hard, who is wise, who listens well; who has been where I am and can help me understand it;

and who represents not only an ultimate ideal mother to me but also the person I'd like to be when I grow up.

In our daughter role we tend to do more than our 22 share of self-revelation; in our mother role we tend to receive what's revealed. It's another kind of pleasure—playing wise mother to a questing younger person. It's another very lovely kind of friendship.

6. Part-of-a-couple friends. Some of the women we 23 call our friends we never see alone—we see them as part of a couple at couples' parties. And though we share interests in many things and respect each other's views, we aren't moved to deepen the relationship. Whatever the reason, a lack of time or—and this is more likely—a lack of chemistry, our friendship remains in the context of a group. But the fact that our feeling on seeing each other is always, "I'm *so* glad she's here" and the fact that we spend half the evening talking together says that this too, in its own way, counts as a friendship.

(Other part-of-a-couple friends are the friends that 24 came with the marriage, and some of these are friends we could live without. But sometimes, alas, she married our husband's best friend; and sometimes, alas, she *is* our husband's best friend. And so we find ourself dealing with her, somewhat against our will, in a spirit of what I'll call *reluctant* friendship.)

7. Men who are friends. I wanted to write just of 25 women friends, but the women I've talked to won't let me— they say I must mention man-woman friendships too. For these friendships can be just as close and as dear as those that we form with women. Listen to Lucy's description of one such friendship:

"We've found we have things to talk about that are 26 different from what he talks about with my husband and different from what I talk about with his wife. So sometimes we call on the phone or meet for lunch. There are similar intellectual interests—we always pass on to each other the books that we love—but there's also something tender and caring too."

In a couple of crises, Lucy says, "he offered himself, 27 for talking and for helping. And when someone died in his family he wanted me there. The sexual, flirty part of our friendship is very small, but *some*—just enough to make it fun and different." She thinks—and I agree—that the sexual part, though small is always *some,* is always there when a man and a woman are friends.

It's only in the past few years that I've made friends 28 with men, in the sense of a friendship that's *mine,* not just part of two couples. And achieving with them the ease and the trust I've found with women friends has value indeed. Under the dryer at home last week, putting on mascara and rouge, I comfortably sat and talked with a fellow named Peter. Peter, I finally decided, could handle the shock of me minus mascara under the dryer. Because we care for each other. Because we're friends.

8. There are medium friends, and pretty good friends, 29 and very good friends indeed, and these friendships are defined by their level of intimacy. And what we'll reveal at each of these levels of intimacy is calibrated with care. We might tell a medium friend, for example, that yesterday we had a fight with our husband. And we might tell a pretty good friend that this fight with our husband made us so mad that we slept on the couch. And we might tell a very good friend that the reason we got so mad in that fight that we slept on the couch had something to do with that girl who works in his office. But it's only to our very best friends that we're willing to tell all, to tell what's going on with that girl in his office.

The best of friends, I still believe, totally love and 30 support and trust each other, and bare to each other the secrets of their souls, and run—no questions asked—to help each other, and tell harsh truths to each other when they must be told.

But we needn't agree about everything (only 12- 31 year-old girl friends agree about *everything*) to tolerate each other's point of view. To accept without judgment. To give and to take without ever keeping score. And to *be* there, as

I am for them and as they are for me, to comfort our sorrows, to celebrate our joys.

BUILDING VOCABULARY

1. Find antonyms (words that mean the opposite of given words) for the following entries:

    a. harsh (par. 1)
    b. mutual (par. 8)
    c. crucial (par. 17)
    d. intimacy (par. 29)
    e. tolerate (par. 31)

2. The *derivation* of a word—how it originated and where it came from—can make you more aware of meanings. Your dictionary normally lists abbreviations (for instance, L. for Latin, Fr. for French) for word origins, and sometimes explains fully the way a word came into use. Look up the following words to determine their origins:

    a. psychology (par. 10)
    b. historical (par. 14)
    c. sibling (par. 16)
    d. Christmas (par. 18)
    e. sexual (par. 27)

UNDERSTANDING THE WRITER'S IDEAS

1. What is Viorst's definition of friendship in the first two paragraphs? Does she accept this definition? Why or why not?

2. Name and describe in your own words the types of friends that Viorst mentions in her essay.

3. In what way are "convenience friends" and "special interest friends" alike? How are "historical friends" and "crossroads friends" alike?

4. What does Viorst mean when she writes, "In our daughter role we tend to do more than our share of self-

revelation; in our mother role we tend to receive what's revealed" (par. 22)?

5. How do part-of-a-couple friends who came with the marriage differ from primary part-of-a-couple friends?

6. Does Viorst think that men can be friends for women? Why or why not? What complicates such friendships?

7. For Viorst, who are the best friends?

UNDERSTANDING THE WRITER'S TECHNIQUES

1. Which paragraphs make up the introduction in this essay? How does Viorst organize these paragraphs? **Where does she place her thesis sentence?**

2. How does the thesis sentence reveal the principles of classification (the questions Viorst asks to produce the various categories) that the author employs in the essay?

3. Does Viorst seem to emphasize each of her categories equally? Is she effective in handling each category? Why or why not? Do you think that men belong in the article as a category? For what reasons?

4. Analyze the importance of illustration in this essay. From what sources does Viorst tend to draw her examples?

5. How do definition and comparison and contrast operate in the essay? Cite specific examples of these techniques.

6. The level of language in this essay tends to be informal at times, reflecting patterns that are as close to conversation as to formal writing. Identify some sentences that seem to resemble informal speech. Why does Viorst try to achieve a conversational style?

7. Which main group in the essay is further broken down into categories?

8. Analyze Viorst's conclusion. How many paragraphs are involved? What strategies does she use? How does she achieve balanced sentence structure (parallelism) in her last lines?

EXPLORING THE WRITER'S IDEAS

1. Do you accept all of Viorst's categories of friendship? Which categories seem the most meaningful to you?

2. Try to think of people you know who fit into the various categories established by Viorst. Can you think of people who might exist in more than one category? How do you explain this fact? What are the dangers in trying to stereotype people in terms of categories, roles, backgrounds, or functions?

3. Viorst maintains that you can define friends in terms of functions and needs (see paragraph 3 and paragraphs 29 to 31). Would you agree? Why or why not? What principle or principles do you use to classify friends? In fact, *do* you classify friends? For what reasons?

IDEAS FOR WRITING

Guided Writing

Using the classification method, write an essay on a specific group of individuals—for instance, *types of friends, types of enemies, types of students, types of teachers, types of politicians, types of dates*—and so forth.

1. Establish your subject in the first paragraph. Also indicate to the reader the principle(s) of classification that you plan to use. (For guidelines look again at the second sentence in paragraph 3 of Viorst's essay.)

2. Start the body of the essay with a single short sentence that introduces categories (see paragraph 4). In the body, use numbers and category headings ("Convenience friends" . . . "Special interest friends") to separate groups.

3. Try to achieve a balance in the presentation of information on each category. Define each type and provide appropriate examples.

4. If helpful, use comparison and contrast to indicate from time to time the similarities and differences among groups. Try to avoid too much overlapping of groups, since this is harmful to the classification process.

5. Employ the personal "I" and other conversational techniques to achieve an informal style.

6. Return to your principle(s) of classification and amplify this feature in your conclusion. If you want, make a value judgement, as Viorst does, about which type of person in your classification scheme is the most significant.

More Writing Projects

1. Write an essay classifying the varieties of love.

2. Classify varieties of show business comedians, singers, talk show hosts, star athletes, or the like.

E. B. White

THE THREE NEW YORKS

E. B. White, whose frequently used book *The Elements of Style* is well known to college composition students, here classifies "The Three New Yorks." Although the selection is an excerpt from his book *Here Is New York* (1949), the descriptive illustrations remain remarkably fresh after more than thirty years. Look closely at the way White clearly defines his categories of classification, then skillfully blends them to create a vivid sense of the whole city.

Words to Watch

turbulence (par. 1): wild commotion

locusts (par. 1): migratory grasshoppers that travel in swarms, stripping vegetation as they pass over the land

quest (par. 1): pursuit; search

disposition (par. 1): temperament; way of acting

deportment (par. 1): the way in which a person carries himself or herself

tidal (par. 1): coming in wave-like motions

continuity (par. 1): uninterrupted flow of events

slum (par. 1): a highly congested residential area marked by insanitary buildings, poverty, and social disorder

indignity (par. 1): humiliating treatment

vitality (par. 2): lively and animated character

gloaming (par. 2): a poetic term for *twilight.*

ramparts (par. 2): high broad structures guarding a building

negligently (par. 2): nonchalantly; neglectfully

loiterer (par. 2): a person who hangs around aimlessly

spewing (par. 2): coming in a flood or gush

rover (par. 2): wanderer; roamer

There are roughly three New Yorks. There is, first, 1
the New York of the man or woman who was born here, who
takes the city for granted and accepts its size and its turbulence as natural and inevitable. Second, there is the New
York of the commuter—the city that is devoured by locusts
each day and spat out each night. Third, there is the New
York of the person who was born somewhere else and came
to New York in quest of something. Of these three trembling
cities the greatest is the last—the city of final destination,
the city that is a goal. It is this third city that accounts for
New York's high-strung disposition, its poetical deportment,
its dedication to the arts, and its incomparable achievements. Commuters give the city its tidal restlessness; natives
give it solidity and continuity; but the settlers give it pas-
sion. And whether it is a farmer arriving from Italy to set up
a small grocery store in a slum, or a young girl arriving from
a small town in Mississippi to escape the indignity of being
observed by her neighbors, or a boy arriving from the Corn
Belt with a manuscript in his suitcase and a pain in his
heart, it makes no difference; each embraces New York with
the intense excitement of first love, each absorbs New York
with the fresh eyes of an adventurer, each generates heat
and light to dwarf the Consolidated Edison Company.

The commuter is the queerest bird of all. The suburb 2
he inhabits has no essential vitality of its own and is a mere
roost where he comes at day's end to go to sleep. Except in
rare cases, the man who lives in Mamaroneck or Little Neck
or Teaneck, and works in New York, discovers nothing much
about the city except the time of arrival and departure of
trains and buses, and the path to a quick lunch. He is desk-
bound, and has never, idly roaming in the gloaming, stum-
bled suddenly on Belvedere Tower in the Park, seen the ramparts rise sheer from the water of the pond, and the boys
along the shore fishing for minnows, girls stretched out negligently on the shelves of the rocks; he has never come suddenly on anything at all in New York as a loiterer, because
he has had no time between trains. He has fished in Manhattan's wallet and dug out coins, but has never listened to
Manhattan's breathing, never awakened to its morning,

never dropped off to sleep in its night. About 400,000 men and women come charging onto the Island each week-day morning, out of the mouths of tubes and tunnels. Not many among them have ever spent a drowsy afternoon in the great rustling oaken silence of the reading room of the Public Library, with the book elevator (like an old water wheel) spewing out books onto the trays. They tend their furnaces in Westchester and in Jersey, but have never seen the furnaces of the Bowery, the fires that burn in oil drums on zero winter nights. They may work in the financial district downtown and never see the extravagant plantings of Rockefeller Center—the daffodils and grape hyacinths and birches of the flags trimmed to the wind on a fine morning in spring. Or they may work in a midtown office and may let a whole year swing round without sighting Governor's Island from the sea wall. The commuter dies with tremendous mileage to his credit, but he is no rover. His entrances and exits are more devious than those in a prairie-dog village; and he calmly plays bridge while his train is buried in the mud at the bottom of the East River. The Long Island Rail Road alone carried forty million commuters last year; but many of them were the same fellow retracing his steps.

The terrain of New York is such that a resident sometimes travels farther, in the end, than a commuter. The journey of the composer Irving Berlin from Cherry Street in the lower East Side to an apartment uptown was through an alley and was only three or four miles in length; but it was like going three times around the world.

BUILDING VOCABULARY

1. One very important aspect of vocabulary development is an ability to understand specific place or name references in whatever you are reading. Underline the numerous references in this essay to buildings, people, and areas in and around New York City and be prepared to identify them. If necessary, consult a guidebook, map, or history of New York City for help.

2. White divides the inhabitants of New York into

three categories: commuters, natives, settlers. Write a literal definition for the word that labels each category; then write at least one figurative meaning for each (see Glossary).

3. Write a *synonym* (a word that means the same) for each of these adjectives in the essay:

 a. inevitable (par. 1)
 b. high-strung (par. 1)
 c. essential (par. 2)
 d. drowsy (par. 2)
 e. devious (par. 2)

UNDERSTANDING THE WRITER'S IDEAS

1. What are the three New Yorks?

2. What single-word designation does E. B. White assign to each of the three types of New Yorkers? Match up each of the three New Yorks you identified in the first question with each of the three types of New Yorkers.

3. For what reasons do people born elsewhere come to New York to live? What three illustrations of such people does White describe? What is the young girl's indignity? What is the occupation or hope of the boy from the Corn Belt? Why might he have "a pain in his heart"?

4. What does each type of New Yorker give to the city?

5. What is White's attitude toward the suburbs? What key phrases reveal this attitude?

6. What are some of the things commuters miss about New York by dashing in and out of the city? What does White ironically suggest will be the commuter's final fate?

7. Are we to take literally White's conclusion that "many of them are the same fellow retracing his steps"? Why or why not?

8. Explain the sentence "The terrain of New York is such that a resident sometimes travels farther, in the end, than a commuter." Be aware that White is using language figuratively.

9. The author tells of composer Irving Berlin's jour-

ney through an alley. He is referring to "Tin Pan Alley."
Identify this place.

UNDERSTANDING THE WRITER'S TECHNIQUES

    1.   In this essay what is the thesis? Where is it? Is it developed fully?

    2.   What is the purpose of classification in this essay? What is the basis of the classification White uses? What key words at the beginning of paragraph 1 direct your attention to each category discussed? How do these key words contrast in tone with the descriptions in the first few sentences? What sort of rhythm is established?

    3.   White vividly *personifies* (see Glossary) New York City in paragraph 1. List and explain the effects of these personifications. Where else does he personify?

    4.   Refer to your answer to question 2 in the Building Vocabulary section. Are the literal meanings of those words appropriate to White's three types of New Yorkers? Defend your answer. Figuratively, what does each term make you think of? How do the figurative meanings enhance the essay?

    5.   How does White use *illustration* in this essay? Where does he use it most effectively?

    6.   What is the function of *negation* (see page 142) in the first part of paragraph 2? What is the *implied contrast* in this paragraph?

    7.   How is White's attitude toward New York reflected in the tone of this essay?

    8.   White makes widespread use of *metaphor* (see Glossary) in this essay. How does his use of metaphor affect the *tone* of the essay? State in your own words the meaning of each of the following metaphors:

        a. ". . . the city that is devoured by locusts each day and spat out each night." (par. 1)
        b. "The commuter is the queerest bird of all." (par. 2)
        c. "a mere roost" (par. 2)
        d. "idly roaming in the gloaming" (par. 2)

e. "He has fished in Manhattan's wallet and dug out coins, but he has never listened to Manhattan's breathing." (par. 2)

f. "the great rustling oaken silence" (par. 2)

9. Among all the metaphors, White uses just one *simile* (see Glossary). What is it? What is the effect of placing it where he did?

EXPLORING THE WRITER'S IDEAS

1. At the beginning of the essay, E. B. White states that New York's "turbulence" is considered "natural and inevitable" by its native residents. But such a condition is true for any large city. If you live in a large city, or if you have ever visited one, what are some examples of its turbulence? Do you think it is always a good idea to accept the disorder of the place where you live? How can such acceptance be a positive attitude? How can it be negative? How do you deal with disruptions in your environment?

2. White writes of "a young girl arriving from a small town in Mississippi to escape the indignity of being observed by her neighbors." Tell in your own words what might cause her indignity. How can neighbors bring about such a condition?

3. Some people feel the anonymity of a big city like New York makes it easier just to "be yourself" without having to worry about what others might say. Others feel such anonymity creates a terrible feeling of impersonality. Discuss the advantages and disadvantages of each attitude.

4. Do you agree that the suburbs have "no essential vitality"? Explain your response by referring to suburbs you have visited, have read about, or have inhabited.

5. White claims that those who choose to leave their homes and who come to live in New York give the place a special vitality. Do you know any people who chose to leave their places of birth to live in a large city like New York? Why did they move? How have things gone for them since

they began living in the city? Have you noticed any changes? For what reasons do people leave one place to live in another? When have you moved from place to place? Why?

IDEAS FOR WRITING

Guided Writing

Organize a classification essay around the city or town in which you live.

1.   Begin with a simple direct thesis statement that tells the reader how many categories of classification you will consider.

2.   Briefly outline the different categories. Indicate each with a key organizational word or phrase.

3.   Indicate which category is the most important. Tell why.

4.   Develop this category with at least three vivid illustrations.

5.   Define one of the categories through both negation and an implied contrast to another category.

6.   Use figurative language (metaphors, similes, personification) throughout your essay.

7.   Use specific name or place references.

8.   End your essay with a brief factual narrative that gives the reader a feel for your town or city.

More Writing Projects

1.   Write an essay that classifies three main categories of jobs and the people who work at each.

2.   Write a classification essay on the suburbs, or the country.

3.   Select a cultural group and classify various characteristics common to that group. Be careful to avoid stereotyping.

Noel Perrin

COUNTRY CODES

Noel Perrin, "town-bred" in the East, now lives the country life as a college teacher. In this essay, he classifies the codes for speaking and interacting in the countryside. He relates the sometimes embarrassing ways in which he and others have learned the detailed structures of country codes.

Words to Watch

town-bred (par. 1): raised in the city, not in the country
haycocks (par. 1): small, cone-shaped piles of hay
rural (par. 3): of the countryside, not the city
exposition (par. 4): a detailed explanation
peremptory (par. 5): imperative; domineering
culvert (par. 6): a drain crossing under a road
to scythe (par. 10): to cut grass or grain by a hand implement
motive (par. 14): a reason for doing something
budge (par. 18): to move slightly
fervency (par. 18): intense feeling
stoic (par. 19): someone unaffected by joy, grief, pleasure, or pain
cordwood (par. 22): firewood that has been cut and stacked
B.O. (par. 29): slang for "body odor"

Robert Frost once wrote a poem about a 'townbred' 1
farmer who was getting his hay in with the help of two

hired men, both locals. As they're working, the sky clouds over, and it begins to look like rain. The farmer instructs the two hired men to start making the haycocks especially carefully, so that they'll shed water. About half an hour later (it still isn't raining), one of them abruptly shoves his pitchfork in the ground and walks off. He has quit.

The farmer is utterly baffled. The hired man who 2 stays explains to him that what he said was a major insult.

> 'He thought you meant to find fault with his work,
> That's what the average farmer would have meant.'

This hired man goes on to say that he would have quit, too—if the order had been issued by a regular farmer. But seeing as it was a city fellow, he made allowances.

> 'I know you don't understand our ways.
> You were just talking what was in your mind,
> What was in all our minds, and you weren't hinting.'

Frost called that poem 'The Code.' He published it in 1914.

Sixty-four years later, the country code is still going 3 strong, and it is still making trouble for town-bred people who live in rural areas. Only I think the code is even more complicated than Frost had room to describe in his poem. In fact, there isn't just one country code, there are at least three. What they all have in common is that instead of saying things out plainly, the way you do in the city, you approach them indirectly. You hint.

I am going to call these three the Power Code, the 4 Non-Reciprocity Code, and the Stoic's Code. These are not their recognized names; they don't *have* recognized names. Part of the code is that you never speak of the code, and I am showing my own town-bredness in writing this exposition. (As Frost showed his in writing the poem. He was a city kid in San Francisco before he was a farmer in New Hampshire.)

In Frost's poem, it was the Power Code that the 5 townie violated. Under the rules of the Power Code, you *never* give peremptory orders, and you ordinarily don't even make demands. You make requests. What the code says is that everybody is to be treated as an equal, even when financially or educationally, or whatever, they're not. Treat them as either inferiors or superiors, and you can expect trouble.

Just recently, for example, a young city doctor moved 6 to our town, and began violating the Power Code right and left. Take the way he treated the boss of the town road crew. The house the doctor was renting has a gravel driveway that tends to wash out after storms. It washed out maybe a month after he had moved in. He is said to have called the road commissioner and given him a brisk order. 'I want a culvert installed, and I want it done by this weekend.'

Now in the city that would be a quite sensible 7 approach. You're calling some faceless bureaucrat, and you use standard negotiating technique. You make an outrageous demand; you throw your weight around, if you have any; and you figure on getting part of what you ask for. You're not surprised when the bureaucrat screams, *'This week!* Listen, we got a hunnert and sixty-two jobs aheada you right now. If you're lucky, we'll get to you in October.' You scream back and threaten to call the mayor's office. Then you finally compromise on August.

But it doesn't work that way in the country. The 8 code doesn't encourage throwing your weight around. Our road commissioner had been given an order, and he instantly rejected it. ' 'Tain't the town's job to look after folks' driveways. If you want a culvert, you can buy one down to Write River Junction.'

I happened to hear what the road commissioner told 9 some friends later. The doctor had actually called at a good time. The town had several used culverts lying around— road culverts they had replaced, which were still good enough to go at the end of a driveway. 'If he'd asked decent, we'd have been glad to put one in for him, some day when work was slack.' If he'd used the code, that is.

That's nothing, though, compared with the way the 10 young doctor handled one of our retired farmers. When the doctor decided to live in our town—it meant a fifteen-mile drive to the hospital where he worked—it was because he had gotten interested in country things. He wanted to have a garden, burn wood, learn how to scythe a patch of grass, all those things. During his first spring and summer in town, he probably asked the old farmer a hundred questions. He got free lessons in scything. He consulted on fencing problems. Learned how thick to plant peas.

Then one day the farmer asked *him* a question. 'I 11 understand you know suthin' about arthritis,' the farmer said. 'Well, my wife's is actin' up.' And he went on to ask a question about medication.

The young doctor's answer was quick and smooth. 12 'I'll be glad to see her in office hours,' he said.

Again, normal city practice. You've got to protect 13 yourself against all the people at cocktail parties who want free medical advice. Furthermore, you probably really should examine a patient before you do any prescribing. All the same, what he was saying loud and clear in the country code was, 'My time is worth more than yours; I am more important than you are. So I can ask you free questions, but you must pay for any you ask me.' Not very polite. What he should have done was put down the scythe and say, 'Let's go have a look at her.'

Actually, if he had done that, he probably would 14 have muffed it anyway. Because then he would have come up against the Non-Reciprocity Code, and he didn't understand that, either. The Non-Reciprocity Code says that you never take any favors for granted (or call in your debts, as city politicians say). Instead, you always pretend that each favor done you is a brand-new one. In the case of the young doctor, suppose he *had* stopped his free scythe lesson and gone to examine the farmer's wife. When he was ready to leave, the farmer would have said to him, 'What do I owe you?' And then one of two things would have happened. Old habits would have asserted themselves, and he would have said smoothly, 'That will be twenty-five dollars, please.' Or else, a little cross with the farmer for not recognizing his generous motive (does the old fool think I make *house calls?*), he would have said that it was free, in a sort of huffy, look-what-a-favor-I'm-doing-you voice.

Both answers would have been wrong. The correct response would be to act as if the farmer was doing *you* a favor in letting you not charge. Something like, 'Come on, if you can teach me to scythe, and how to plant peas, I guess there's no harm in my taking a look at your wife.'

One of the funniest instances in which you see the Non-Reciprocity Code operating is after people get their trucks stuck, which during mud season in Vermont is constantly. You're driving along in your pickup, and there's your neighbor with two wheels in the ditch, unable to budge. You stop, get out your logging chain, hook on, and pull him out. 'How much will that be?' he asks, as if his cousin Donald hadn't just pulled you out the week before. In a way it's a ritual question. He would be surprised out of his mind if you thought a minute and said, 'Oh, I guess five dollars would be about right.'

But it's not entirely ritual. He would be surprised. But he would hand over the five dollars. The point of the question is to establish that you don't *have* to pull him out just because he's a friend and will someday pull you out. It's treated as an act of free will, a part of New England independence.

The third code, the Stoic's Code, is sometimes confused with machismo, but really has no connection with it. Country people of both sexes practice it with equal fervency. Basically, it consists of seeing who can go without complaining longest.

I first became aware of the Stoic's Code when I was helping two people put hay bales into a barn loft about fifteen years ago. It was a hot day in late June, with the humidity running at least ninety percent. I function badly in hot weather. Within ten minutes I was pouring sweat—as were my coworkers. The difference was that I kept bitching about it. Finally, after three-quarters of an hour, I flopped down and announced I'd have to cool off before I touched another bale.

To me this just seemed common sense. We had no special deadline to meet in loading that hay. What I really thought was that all three of us should go take a dip in the river.

But the Stoic's Code doesn't stress common sense. It 21 stresses endurance. Maybe that's because to survive at all as a farmer in New England you need endurance. In any case, the other two flicked me one quick scornful look and kept on working. One of them has never really respected me again to this day. The other, like the second hired man in Frost's poem, made allowances for my background and forgave me. We have since become fast friends. I have never dared to ask, but I think he thinks I have made real progress in learning to shut my mouth and keep working.

I could never be a stoic on the true native level, 22 though. Consider the story of Hayden Clark and Rodney Palmer, as Rodney tells it. A good many years ago, before there were any paved roads in town. Hayden ran a garage. (Rodney runs it now.) He also sold cordwood.

One day when there wasn't much doing at the garage, 23 Hayden was sawing cordwood just across the road, where he could keep an eye on the gas pumps. If you saw with a circular saw, and do it right, it takes three men. One person lifts up the logs, one does the actual cutting, and one throws the cut pieces into a pile. The three jobs are called putting on, sawing, and taking off. In all three you are doing dangerous work at very high speed.

On this day a man named Charlie Raynes was 24 putting on, Hayden was sawing, and young Rodney was taking off. Hayden kept the wood coming so fast that Rodney was always a beat behind. He never paused a second to let Rodney catch up, and this torture went on for nearly an hour. No one spoke. (Not that you could hear over a buzz saw, anyway.)

Then finally a customer pulled in for gas. Hayden 25 left the other two sawing, and went over to pump it. Charlie continued to put on, and Rodney sawed in Hayden's place.

Rather than interrupt their rhythm when he came 26 back, Hayden began to take off. Rodney and Charlie exchanged a quick glance, and began putting the wood to Hayden so fast that *he* was off balance the whole time, and not infrequently in some danger of getting an arm cut off.

At this speed and in this way they finished the entire pile. It was Rodney's revenge, and as he told me about it, his eyes gleamed.

It was only a year or two ago that Rodney told me 27 the story. In the very act of telling it, he included me as one who knew the code. But I instantly betrayed it. My city background is too strong. I'm too verbal, too used to crowing over triumphs.

'After you were done sawing, Hayden never said 28 anything about it?' I asked.

'Oh, *no*,' Rodney answered, looking really shocked. 29 'Any more than I'd have said anything to him.'

So, next time you're in a country store and you get a sense 30 that the locals are avoiding you as if you had the worst case of B.O. in the county, you can be pretty sure of the reason. You've probably just said some dreadful thing in code.

BUILDING VOCABULARY

1. Using context clues from the story, explain the figurative meanings of these phrases (see Glossary):

    a. "had room to describe" (par. 3)
    b. "throw your weight around" (par. 7)
    c. "call in your debts" (par. 14)
    d. "surprised out of his mind" (par. 16)
    e. "to cool off" (par. 19)
    f. "flicked me one quick scornful look" (par. 21)

2. Match the words and expressions in Column A with their meanings in Column B.

Column A	Column B
a. utterly baffled (par. 2)	1. complaining
b. muffed it (par. 14)	2. confused
c. take . . . for granted (par. 14)	3. made a mistake
d. bitching (par. 19)	4. to consider as true or already accepted
e. made allowances (par. 21)	5. accepted for special reasons

3. Explain the meanings of the following adjective-noun combinations:

    a. city fellow (par. 2)
    b. brisk order (par. 6)
    c. faceless bureaucrat (par. 7)
    d. outrageous demand (par. 7)
    e. free will (par. 17)
    f. fast friends (par. 21)

UNDERSTANDING THE WRITER'S IDEAS

1. What is a "code"?

2. Perrin opens his essay with a *paraphrase* (a rewording of something that had been written before) and some direct quotations from a Robert Frost poem, "The Code." What is the story line of "The Code"? What is the theme or "message" of the poem? What do Frost and Perrin have in common?

3. How do town-bred people respond to country codes?

4. Name the three country codes that Perrin discusses. Briefly outline the conditions of each code. What is the most important feature of each?

5. What codes does the doctor violate, and how?

6. Describe in your own words the "standard negotiating technique" used in the city. Why doesn't that technique work in the country?

7. What does Perrin say about "rituals"? Explain the meaning of the statement: "In a way it's a ritual question." (par. 16)

8. Name the three jobs involved in cutting cordwood. Describe the actions involved in each activity. In your own words, explain the "torture" mentioned in paragraph 23.

9. How does the author break the code when he talks to Rodney? To what reason does he attribute his error?

10. Explain the meaning of the last sentence of the essay. How is Perrin's use of the expression "in code" different from his use of the word "code" throughout the essay?

UNDERSTANDING THE WRITER'S TECHNIQUES

1. What is the purpose of the Frost poem? What is its connection to the thesis of the essay? Where does Perrin place his thesis?

2. What distinct classifications does the author establish for this essay? How does he *order* his classification (by type, class, chronology, or climactic order?) Why did he choose that order? How does he achieve balance among his groups? What transitional devices does he use to connect his groups?

3. How does Perrin use the young city doctor as an extended example in this essay? What parts of the country code does the doctor illustrate?

4. What are the uses of *narration* in this essay; of *definition*?

5. The author makes frequent use of a variety of punctuation in this essay, including *parentheses, dashes,* and *italics*. In general, what is the use of each of these three types of punctuation? In what ways does Perrin use each in this essay?

6. In his use of dialogue, Perrin attempts to copy the speech patterns of "city-talk" and "country-talk." What are the differences between the city speech patterns of paragraphs 6 and 7 and the country patterns of paragraphs 8 and 9? Where else does he use the two types of speech? Do you think his imitations are effective? Why?

7. What is the *tone* of this essay? Do you think that the author slants his tone toward country life or city life? Explain your response.

8. Why does Perrin set off the concluding paragraph from the rest of the essay? What is the effect on the meaning of the essay?

EXPLORING THE WRITER'S IDEAS

1. Do you agree with the basic premise of this essay: that codes of behavior exist and that those codes are related to geographical regions? Why? What codes have you observed in other places: farms, ranches, towns by the sea, mountain villages, and so on?

2. What conditions other than geographical ones might be responsible for codes of behavior? Consider with the class these as possible sources of behavioral codes: religion, economic status, ethnic background.

3. One of the codes says that country people always make requests and not demands and that "everybody is to be treated as an equal." Do you agree with those premises? Why? Could they—should they—apply to city people as well as country people? Why? Is it possible or desirable at all times to make requests instead of demands? to treat everybody equally?

4. Very often children will use "code languages" to speak, supposedly so that adults or other children won't understand. A common code language is called "pig Latin," in which you drop the first consonant sound and add it to the end of the word joined to the syllable "-ay." For example, the word "bicycle" would become "icycle-bay." The word "China" would become "ina-Chay." What code languages are you familiar with?

IDEAS FOR WRITING

Guided Writing

Write an essay in which you classify three or more codes or categories of acceptable behavior within a group that you know well. Such groups as your family, your team, your fraternity or sorority, your high school "clique," or your parents' social friends would serve as a basis for this classification essay.

1. Begin with an extended reference to something you have read about the social behavior you are describing, and paraphrase or summarize the contents of that reference. Or, as an alternative, provide an anecdote that relates to your thesis.

2. Establish your thesis in a paragraph that comes *after* your paraphrase or your anecdote.

3. Name the typical modes of behavior that you will be classifying.

4. Throughout the essay be sure to remind the reader of your own relationship to the groups you establish.

5. Make use of narratives to illustrate how each category of behavior works. Show how people within the group conform to the code, and how people outside the group can come into conflict with it.

6. Include some "authentic" ways of speaking.

7. Keep the tone of the essay somewhat light and humorous.

8. Try to use figurative language and vivid sensory language throughout the essay.

9. End with an explanation of your difficulty (or ease) in accepting these modes of behavior.

More Writing Projects

1. Different people will approach the same task in different ways. Select a task—such as doing homework, going shopping, planning a vacation, and so on—and write an essay that classifies at least three different approaches to the same task.

2. Write an essay that classifies the different ways in which people express happiness or sadness.

3. Study the students in one of your larger lecture classes. Write a classification essay analyzing their different codes of behavior.

James T. Baker

HOW DO WE FIND THE STUDENT IN A WORLD OF ACADEMIC GYMNASTS AND WORKER ANTS?

As you look around your classrooms, school cafeteria, lecture halls, or gymnasium, perhaps you will recognize representatives of the types of students that James Baker classifies in this witty, wry essay. The author's unique categories are enhanced by his use of description, definition, and colloquial language, which help make his deliberate stereotypes "come alive."

Words to Watch

musings (par. 3): random thoughts
sabbatical (par. 3): a paid leave from a job earned after a certain period of time
malaise (par. 3): uneasiness; feelings of restlessness
impaired (par. 3): made less effective
clones (par. 4): exact biological replicas, asexually produced
recuperate (par. 5): to undergo recovery from an illness
esoteric (par. 7): understood by a limited group with special knowledge
primeval (par. 7): primitive; relating to the earliest ages
mundane (par. 8): ordinary
jaded (par. 20): exhausted; bored by something from overexposure to it

247

Anatole France once wrote that "the whole art of 1 teaching is only the art of awakening the natural curiosity of young minds." I fully agree, except I have to wonder if, by using the word "only," he thought that the art of awakening such natural curiosity was an easy job. For me, it never has been—sometimes exciting, always challenging, but definitely not easy.

Robert M. Hutchins used to say that a good education 2 prepares students to go on educating themselves throughout their lives. A fine definition, to be sure, but it has at times made me doubt that my own students, who seem only too eager to graduate so they can lay down their books forever, are receiving a good education.

But then maybe these are merely the pessimistic 3 musings of someone suffering from battle fatigue. I have almost qualified for my second sabbatical leave, and I am scratching a severe case of the seven-year itch. About the only power my malaise has not impaired is my eye for spotting certain "types" of students. In fact, as the rest of me declines, my eye seems to grow more acute.

Has anyone else noticed that the very same students 4 people college classrooms year after year? Has anyone else found the same bodies, faces, personalities returning semester after semester? Forgive me for violating my students' individual "personhoods," but reality makes it so tempting to see them as types. Doubtless you will recognize at least some of them. They have twins, or perhaps clones, on your campus, too.

There is the eternal Good Time Charlie (or Char- 5 lene), who makes every party on and off the campus, who by November of his freshman year has worked his face into a case of terminal acne, who misses every set of examinations because of "mono," who finally burns himself out physically and mentally by the age of 19 and drops out to go home and recuperate, and who returns at 20 after a long talk with Dad to major in accounting.

There is the Young General Patton, the one who 6 comes to college on an R.O.T.C. scholarship and for a year twirls his rifle at basketball games while loudly sniffing out pinko professors, who at midpoint takes a sudden but predictable, radical swing from far right to far left, who grows a beard and moves in with a girl who refuses to shave her legs, who then makes the just as predictable, radical swing back to the right and ends up preaching fundamentalist sermons on the steps of the student union while the Good Time Charlies and Charlenes jeer.

There is the Egghead, the campus intellectual who 7 shakes up his fellow students—and even a professor or two—with references to esoteric formulas and obscure Bulgarian poets, who is recognized by friend and foe alike as a promising young academic, someday to be a professional scholar, who disappears every summer for six weeks ostensibly to search for primeval human remains in Colorado caves, and who at 37 is shot dead by Arab terrorists while on a mission for the C.I.A.

There is the Performer—the music or theater major, 8 the rock or folk singer—who spends all of his or her time working up an act, who gives barely a nod to mundane subjects like history, sociology, or physics, who dreams only of the day he or she will be on stage full time, praised by critics, cheered by audiences, who ends up either pregnant or responsible for a pregnancy and at 30 is either an insurance salesman or a housewife with a very lush garden.

There is the Jock, of course—the every-afternoon 9 intramural champ, smelling of liniment and Brut, with bulging calves and a blue-eyed twinkle, the subject of untold numbers of female fantasies, the walking personification of he-man-ism—who upon graduation is granted managerial rank by a California bank because of his golden tan and low golf score, who is seen five years later buying the drinks at a San Francisco gay bar.

There is the Academic Gymnast—the guy or gal 10 who sees college as an obstacle course, as so many stumbling blocks in the way of a great career or a perfect marriage—who strains every moment to finish and be done with "this place" forever, who toward the end of the junior year begins to slow down, to grow quieter and less eager to leave, who attends summer school, but never quite finishes those last six hours, who never leaves "this place," and who at 40 is still working at the campus laundry, still here, still a student.

There is the Medal Hound, the student who comes 11 to college not to learn or expand any intellectual horizons but simply to win honors—medals, cups, plates, ribbons, scrolls—who is here because this is the best place to win the most the fastest, who plasticizes and mounts on his wall every certificate of excellence he wins, who at 39 will be a colonel in the U.S. Army and at 55 Secretary of something or other in a conservative Administration in Washington.

There is the Worker Ant, the student (loosely ren- 12 dered) who takes 21 hours a semester and works 49 hours a week at the local car wash, who sleeps only on Sundays and during classes, who will somehow graduate on time and be the owner of his own vending-machine company at 30 and be dead of a heart attack at 40, and who will be remembered for the words chiseled on his tombstone:

All This Was Accomplished Without Ever Having 13 So Much as Darkened The Door Of A Library

There is the Lost Soul, the sad kid who is in college 14 only because teachers, parents, and society at large said so, who hasn't a career in mind or a dream to follow, who hasn't a clue, who heads home every Friday afternoon to spend the weekend cruising the local Dairee-Freeze, who at 50 will have done all his teachers, parents, and society said to do, still without a career in mind or a dream to follow or a clue.

There is also the Saved Soul—the young woman 15 who has received, through the ministry of one Gospel freak or another, a Holy Calling to save the world, or at least some special part of it—who majors in Russian studies so that she can be caught smuggling Bibles into the Soviet Union and be sent to Siberia where she can preach to souls imprisoned by the Agents of Satan in the Gulag Archipelago.

Then, finally, there is the Happy Child, who comes 16 to college to find a husband or wife—and finds one—and there is the Determined Child, who comes to get a degree—and gets one.

Enough said. 17

All of which, I suppose, should make me throw up 18
my hands in despair and say that education, like youth and
love, is wasted on the young. Not quite.

For there does come along, on occasion, that one of 19
a hundred or so who is maybe at first a bit lost, certainly
puzzled; who may well start out a Good Timer, an Egghead,
a Performer, a Jock, a Medal Hound, a Gymnast, a Worker
Ant; who may indeed have trouble settling on a major, who
will be distressed by what sometimes passes for education,
who might even be a temporary dropout; but who has a
vital capacity for growth and is able to fall in love with
learning, who acquires a taste for intellectual pleasure, who
becomes in the finest sense of the word a Student.

This is the one who keeps the most jaded of us going 20
back to class after class, and he or she must be oh-so-
carefully cultivated. He or she must be artfully awakened,
given the tools needed to continue learning for a lifetime,
and let grow at whatever pace and in whatever direction
nature dictates.

For I try always to remember that this student is 21
me, my continuing self, my immortality. This person is my
only hope that my own search for Truth will continue after
me, on and on, forever.

BUILDING VOCABULARY

1. Explain these *colloquialisms* (see Glossary) in
Baker's essay:

    a. "lay down their books forever" (par. 2)
    b. "I am scratching a severe case of the seven-year
       itch" (par. 3)
    c. "some are suffering from battle fatigue" (par. 3)
    d. "worked his face into a case of terminal acne"
       (par. 5)
    e. "burns himself out physically and mentally" (par.
       5)
    f. "loudly sniffing out pinko professors" (par. 6)
    g. "working up an act" (par. 8)

h. "gives barely a nod" (par. 8)
i. "the walking personification of he-man-ism" (par. 9)
j. "to spend the weekend cruising the local Dairee-Freeze" (par. 14)
k. "he or she must be oh-so-carefully cultivated" (par. 20)

2. Identify these references:

a. R.O.T.C. (par. 6)
b. C.I.A. (par. 7)
c. Brut (par. 9)
d. Daree-Freeze (par. 14)
e. Gospel freak (par. 15)
f. Agents of Satan (par. 15)
g. Gulag Archipelago (par. 15)

UNDERSTANDING THE WRITER'S IDEAS

1. In common language, describe the various categories of college students that Baker names.

2. Who is Anatole France? What process is described in the quotation from him? Why does Baker cite it at the beginning of the essay? What is his attitude towards France's idea?

3. For how long has Baker been teaching? What is his attitude towards his work?

4. About what age do you think Baker is? Why? Explain the meaning of the sentence: "In fact, as the rest of me declines, my eye seems to grow more acute" (par. 3).

5. Choose three of Baker's categories and paraphrase each description and meaning in a serious way.

6. What does Baker feel, overall, is the contemporary college student's attitude towards studying and receiving an education? How does it differ from Baker's own attitude towards these things?

7. Although Baker's classification may seem a bit

pessimistic, he refuses to "throw up ... [his] hands in despair" (par. 18). Why?

8. Describe the characteristics that are embodied in the category of *Student*. To whom does Baker compare the "true" Student? Why?

UNDERSTANDING THE WRITER'S TECHNIQUES

1. In this essay Baker deliberately creates, rather than avoids, stereotypes (see Introduction to Chapter 7, page 217). He does so to establish exaggerated representatives of types. Why?

For paragraphs 5–16, prepare a paragraph-by-paragraph outline of the main groups of students classified. For each, include the following information:

    a. type represented by the stereotype
    b. motivation of type for being a student
    c. main activity as a student
    d. condition in which the type ends up

2. What is Baker's thesis in this essay? Does he state it directly or not? What, in your own words, is his purpose?

3. This article was published in "The Chronicle of Higher Education," a weekly newspaper for college and university educators and administrators. How do you think this audience influenced Baker's analysis of types of students? His tone and language?

4. What is Baker's tone in the essay? Give specific examples. In general, how would you characterize his attitude toward the contemporary college student? Why? Does his attitude or tone undergo any shifts in the essay? Explain.

5. Why does Baker use the term "personhoods" in paragraph 4? What attitude, about what subject, does he convey in his use of that word?

6. Why does the author capitalize the names he gives to the various categories of students? Why does he capitalize the word *Truth* in the last sentence?

7. How does Baker use *definition* in this essay? What purpose does it serve?

8. How does Baker use *description* to enhance his analysis in this essay?

9. In this essay, what is the role of *process analysis?* (*Process analysis,* discussed in the next chapter, is telling how something is done or proceeds; see pages 256–257.) Look especially at Baker's descriptions of each type of student. How does process analysis figure into the title of the essay?

10. What is the purpose of the one-sentence paragraph 13? Why does Baker set it aside from paragraph 12, since it is a logical conclusion to that paragraph? Why does he use a two-word sentence as the complete paragraph 17? In what ways do these words signal the beginning of the essay's conclusion?

EXPLORING THE WRITER'S IDEAS

1. Do you think Baker's classifications in this essay are fair? Are they representative of the whole spectrum of students? How closely do they mirror the student population at your school? The article was written in 1982; how well have Baker's classifications held up to the present conditions?

2. Into which category (or categories) would you place yourself? Why?

3. Based on your reaction to and understanding of this article, would you like to have Baker as your professor? Why or why not?

IDEAS FOR WRITING

Guided Writing

Write a classification of at least three "types" in a situation with which you are familiar, other than school—a certain job, social event, sport, or some such situation.

1. Begin your essay with a reference, direct or indirect, to what some well known writer or expert said about this situation.

2. Identify your role in relation to the situation described.

3. Write about your attitude towards the particular situation and why you are less than thrilled about it at present.

4. Make sure you involve the reader as someone who would be familiar with the situation and activities described.

5. Divide your essay into exaggerated or stereotyped categories which you feel represent almost the complete range of types in these situations. In your categorization, be sure to include motivations, activities, and results for each type.

6. Use description to make your categories vivid.

7. Use satire and a bit of gentle cynicism as part of your description.

8. Select a lively title.

9. In the conclusion, identify another type that you consider the "purest" or "most truthful" representative of persons in this situation. Either by comparison with yourself, or by some other means, explain why you like this type best.

More Writing Projects

1. Write your own classification of three college "types." Your essay can be serious or humorous.

2. Look in current magazines for advertisements directed at men or women, or both. Write an essay in which you classify current advertisements according to some logical scheme. Limit your essay to three to five categories.

8

Process Analysis

Process analysis concentrates on *how* something is done, how something works, or how something occurs. If writing aims essentially to explain things, you can see why writers need to use process analysis. Often, the major point that will impress a reader depends on his or her ability to understand the logical steps in some plan of procedure. As a method of paragraph or essay development, process analysis traces all important steps, from beginning to end, in an activity or event. The amount of detail provided for each step in the process will depend on how much the audience knows about the subject.

Whether you are dealing with such subjects as how Columbus discovered America, how a carburetor works, how to deliver a good speech, or how to can fruit at home, you must present all essential information to your audience. Frequently, other methods of essay development help reinforce your analysis of process. (For example, writers often use *definition* to explain terms in a technical process that might not be familiar to readers; and to relate in clear order the steps in a process, an essay might require *narrative* techniques.) These methods will serve your main objective of explaining the process from beginning to end.

Although the purpose of process analysis is to provide your audience with a step-by-step explanation of a procedure, process analysis can also inform readers about the *significance* of the process; that is, it will instruct and inform. A typical problem in explanations of process is that a writer often assumes that readers know more than they do. You can avoid this problem by defining your audience carefully. Certainly, you would use one approach to explain how to make a perfect cheese omelet to newlyweds; and you would use a completely different approach to explain it to students in advanced cooking class. Although both groups might have to follow the same sequence of steps, the kind of information you provide and the range of your explanations would be significantly different. No matter what approach you take to process analysis, remember to present material in a clear and lively manner. In reading about how something is done, or how something works, no reader wants to be bored; make an effort to keep your writing interesting.

Sam Negri

LOAFING MADE EASY

Sam Negri takes a light-hearted look at a topic that seems
funny but is serious business to all those who work hard
constantly. He tells us how to do nothing. A self-proclaimed
expert in the art of loafing, Negri gives a few step-by-step
how to's when it comes to goofing off. Notice how his essay
blends narration, classification, and contrast into the
analysis of process.

Words to Watch

mediocre (par. 3): ordinary
damper (par. 5): fireplace valve to regulate the air flow
lexicon (par. 11): dictionary; word list
debilitating (par. 12): impairing the strength of something
coax (par. 15): to convince by gentle urging or flattery
lush (par. 15): covered with abundant natural growth

The fabled season of the sun is upon us and it is once   1
again time to hook our thumbs in our suspenders and talk
about America's most treasured art form, loafing.

The purest form of loafing is practiced in Arizona,   2
where summertime temperatures will often exceed 110 degrees. If we regard the Arizona loafer as a natural resource,
as I've been doing for the last eight years, we will see that the

art form has applications that go far beyond the business of surviving in hot weather.

When I came to Arizona, I was a mediocre loafer, displaying a definite need for a degree of mental reconditioning. I'd moved here from Connecticut, where people relax by putting aside their copy of Gray's "Anatomy" and picking up a novel by Dostoevsky. In Arizona, this is referred to as insanity. 3

Here is a better method: 4

To begin with, shut the damper on your fireplace, if you have one, and turn on your air-conditioner, if you have one. Otherwise, hang a wet sheet in the window and pray for a breeze. 5

Now you are ready to memorize a handful of important and useful phrases. Try these: "I don't know"; "I don't care"; "no"; and the old standby, "well . . ." 6

These phrases are extremely valuable when your jaws are sagging like deflated bicycle tubes and your mind has turned to wax. 7

For example, it is 106 degrees in the shade and your son comes racing in the house, shouting, "Hey, you seen those long-handled pliers anywhere?" With a minimum of effort you are free to say, "no." 8

His anger may mount and he'll insist: "But you were using them yesterday! Where'd you leave 'em?" 9

If you haven't passed out from the strain of this conversation, you can then reply, "I don't know." 10

"But I need those pliers to fix my skateboard," he will cry. Then you break out the ultimate weapon in the loafer's lexicon. Without any inflection whatsoever, you declare, "Well . . ." 11

You can now get back to some serious loafing, which means that you will try to prove that Benjamin Franklin was correct when he observed: "It is hard for an empty sack to stand upright." In short, empty your mind. Learn to ask questions like these: "Mail come yet?" and "Anything doin'?" The responses to these questions usually involve one word, and often they aren't debilitating. 12

There are a few additional rules to keep in mind for 13 successful loafing.

First, never loaf near a pool or a lake because you 14 might be tempted to go for a swim. Swimming frequently leaves a body feeling refreshed and may lead to a desire to do something.

Second, under no circumstances should you allow 15 anyone to coax you into a camping trip in the mountains. Mountains tend to be lush, green and cool, and next thing you know you'll be wanting to split logs for a fire, go for a hike, or pump up your Coleman stove. Resist. "Patience is a necessary ingredient of genius," said Disraeli. If you want to be a fine loafer you have to make enemies.

Of course, it is impossible to get by in life if you don't 16 do something, even in the summer. Household jobs are the easiest for a loafer to contend with, if he is selective and deliberate.

One satisfying and undemanding job involves a ball 17 of twine. Find a ball of twine that a cat has unraveled so badly that you can't find the end. Get scissors and slowly cut it into small pieces, scrunch it into a smaller ball, and throw it away. Now look at all the extra space you have in your junk drawer.

Another relatively simple and useful job for summer- 18 time loafing centers on light bulbs. Limp through your house or apartment, removing the light bulbs from every lamp. Coat the very bottom of each bulb with petroleum jelly and put it back in the lampsocket. This will clean some of the crud off the contact point and solve the problems with flickering lightbulbs. For variety you can take the bulb that was in a living-room lamp and put it in a bedroom lamp. It helps to sigh and gaze wistfully at the base of the lightbulb as you are performing this function.

Last, if you have a dog, sit in your most comfortable 19 chair and stare at your dog's eyes for five of 10 minutes. Every so often, mutter something incomprehensible. Your dog is certain to understand, and your family will not come near you for the rest of the afternoon.

BUILDING VOCABULARY

1. Though some synonyms can be used inter-
changeably within a given piece of writing, often substituting one word for another will change the *tone* or *shades
of meaning* of a sentence or phrase. Rewrite the following
phrases substituting your own word(s) for those in italics.
Then discuss how your substitution changes the meaning
or tone.

   a. "America's *most treasured* art form" (par. 1)
   b. "the *business* of surviving in hot weather"
      (par. 2)
   c. "a definite need for *mental reconditioning*"
      (par. 3)
   d. "your jaws are sagging like *deflated* bicycle tires"
      (par. 7)
   e. "If you haven't *passed out* from the *strain* of this
      conversation" (par. 10)
   f. "the *ultimate* weapon" (par. 11)
   g. "*gaze wistfully*" (par. 18)
   h. "*mutter* something *incomprehensible*" (par. 19)

2. Identify:

   a. Gray's "Anatomy"
   b. Dostoevsky
   c. Benjamin Franklin
   d. Benjamin Disraeli

UNDERSTANDING THE WRITER'S IDEAS

1. Why is loafing such an important activity in
Arizona?

2. What is the purpose of this essay? Where does
the author announce it?

3. According to the author, how do people in Connecticut relax? Why do people in Arizona consider this
method insanity?

4. What alternative to air conditioning does Negri offer for relaxing in 110° weather?

5. What is the author's attitude toward making conversation while relaxing? What ways does he suggest to avoid undue strain?

6. When loafing seriously, why should you never be near a place to swim? Why should you never let anyone convince you to go camping?

7. Why are household jobs good activities for loafers? What three relatively painless household jobs does Negri describe? Trace the suggested process for performing each.

UNDERSTANDING THE WRITER'S TECHNIQUES

1. Which paragraphs make up the introduction for this essay? How do they serve as an effective beginning?

2. What is the connection between narration and process analysis in paragraphs 6 through 11?

3. Would you say that Negri is ever ironic (see Glossary) in this essay? Is he ever sarcastic? Point to places in the essay that demonstrate irony or sarcasm or both.

4. In any process analysis, it is important to tailor the depth and range of your explanations to your audience. For whom is Negri writing this essay? How does his language and tone reflect his audience?

5. An *aphorism* is a short, often ingenious saying that states a simple truth, usually in one sentence. Negri uses aphorisms by Benjamin Franklin (par. 12) and Benjamin Disraeli (par. 15). What are they? Explain in your own words what you think the original messages of those aphorisms were. Does Negri use them for their original meanings? If not, how does he adapt the aphorisms to the tone of his essay?

6. Explain Negri's use of transitional devices throughout the essay. Compare Negri's use of transitions with E. B. White's use of them in "The Three New Yorks" (pages 187–188).

7. Where does Negri use a one-word sentence? What is your reaction to it? Why does he use it, do you think?

8. How do paragraphs 16 through 19 make use of classification? How do the same paragraphs contribute to the process analysis?

EXPLORING THE WRITER'S IDEAS

1. In paragraph 3, Negri contrasts loafers in Connecticut with loafers in Arizona. What are some of the contrasting ways that people relax in two places you know about? What are some of your favorite ways of goofing off?

2. At the beginning of paragraph 16, Negri writes: "Of course, it is impossible to get by in life if you don't do something." Although the essay is written in a humorous vein, there are certainly many serious implications to the above statement. Discuss what the statement means to you.

3. Negri's point is that loafing is an art and that loafing is good for us. Do you agree? Why? What dangers exist for loafers?

IDEAS FOR WRITING

Guided Writing

Write an essay in which you analyze the best ways to succeed in the art of _____. (Fill in the blank with a word or phrase of your own choice.)

1. Begin by letting the reader know why and how you are intimately familiar with the fine points of this art.

2. State the purpose of your essay at the end of the second paragraph.

3. Contrast a bad way of doing this activity with a good way of doing it.

4. In a tone suited to the activity you are analyzing, describe the best way to avoid letting someone get in the way of your goal. Use narration to illustrate this method.

5. Use an aphorism or two—adapting it to the tone and purpose of your process analysis.

6. Point out two special rules for the reader to keep in mind in order to be successful in this art.

7. Use clear, simple transitions throughout the essay (see Glossary).

8. Somewhere in the essay, use a one-word sentence for a special effect.

9. For your concluding section, consider activities that might be necessary to offset the effects of the art described. Through process analysis, develop examples of the best ways to perform those activities.

More Writing Projects

1. Explain the process you use to *avoid* loafing too much.

2. Give a step-by-step account of what you did the last time you had an unexpected day off from work, school, or other responsibilities.

3. Explain how you keep a balance between working, studying, and relaxing.

Leo Rosten

HOW TO TELL A JOKE

He may not give you the exact words to use, but in an enjoyable essay, which includes use of illustration and definition, humorist Leo Rosten makes the process of telling a joke as clear as can be. Rosten is the author of over thirty books, the latest of which is *Leo Rosten's Giant Book of Laughter,* published in 1985.

Words to Watch

riddle (par. 1): a puzzling question posed as a problem to be solved
battery (par. 13): a number of similar items or devices used together
rapt (par. 13): attentive
undiverted (par. 14): kept on course, unwavering
butcher (par. 15): to destroy randomly
cueing (par. 17): signaling with words or actions
dour (par. 25): sullen; gloomy
exotic (par. 26): strange; very different from the usual
expostulated (par. 30): reasoned earnestly
mauled (par. 37): handled roughly; mangled

I still remember with exceptional vividness the first 1
joke I ever heard, and it still seems a model of technique.
It was a riddle, and my father told it.

"What is it that hangs on a wall, is green, wet and 2
whistles?" he asked me.

I knit my brow and thought and thought. "I give 3
up," I finally said.

"A herring," said my father. 4

"A *herring?*" I said "A herring doesn't hang on the 5
wall!"

"So hang it there." 6

"But a herring isn't green!" 7

"So paint it," my father said. 8

"But a herring isn't wet," I said. 9

"If it's just been painted, it's wet." 10

"But—" and here I summoned all my outrage—*"a* 11
herring does not whistle!"

"Right," my father said. "I just put that in to make 12
it hard."

A joke is a very short, short story, carefully propelled 13
by skillful clues and deliberate and tantalizing miscues.
Most jokes are designed to reach a sudden, surprising
climax—one that triggers the explosion of laughter. Consider
the battery of devices any good storyteller uses to hold you
rapt: a smile, a shrug, a cheerful nod; a coaxing groan, a
soothing murmur; a significant pause, an ironic inflection,
a gasp of simulated or remembered astonishment; an accelerated rhythm toward the story's end. Each of these serves
to cue (and control) the responses of those who listen.

But say you have no talent of the kind that marks 14
a born raconteur: no strong sense of narrative pace, no gift
for comedic emphasis or clever camouflage. What do you do
then? Just follow three simple rules: (1) speak at a brisk
pace; (2) proceed undiverted to the climax; (3) deliver a
clear, exact punch line.

Need further help? Here are six basic tips on how 15
not to butcher your material:

1. Don't preface a humorous story with an exagger- 16
ated promise or an abject apology—"This will have you
rolling in the aisles!" or "I'm not sure I can tell this right."
Oversells and undersells invite resistance.

2. Identify only characters who are going to be 17
essential to the story. If you say, "Herman Plotch, an
undertaker, was walking along," or, "Zelda Glitz, who played
the xylophone," you are cueing your listeners to wait for
the point at which such names and attributes pay off. When
they do not, your punch line will be watered down—or lost—
because an expectation, created by you, was not fulfilled.

In a similar way, don't begin by referring to "this 18
doctor" or "this acrobat." Your listeners automatically will
ask themselves, "Which doctor?" or "Which acrobat?" This
is sure to distract them.

Imagine how the following joke would be ruined by 19
adding "this" and "these" or by introducing characters, or
even characters' names, that have no place in the climax:

Three cross-eyed prisoners stood before a cross-eyed 20
judge. The judge glared at the first prisoner and demanded,
"What's your name?"

"Eli Krantz," answered the second prisoner. 21

"I wasn't talking to you!" the judge snapped. 22

"I didn't *say* anything!" the third prisoner cried. 23

That's a short joke; in longer ones follow the same 24
strategy by sticking to the story line. Don't go off on tangents.
Once you introduce a fact—setting the story in Alaska,
say—your listeners will wait for igloos, huskies, Eskimos,
long winters to appear and to pay off. If they don't, your
friends will be disappointed and even slightly annoyed.

3. As you launch into your joke, show that you enjoy 25
it: smile, chuckle, spread cheer. Don't look dour and self-
conscious, even when you deliver a one-liner: "A diplomat
never forgets a woman's birthday, and never remembers
her age"; "A bore is someone who, upon leaving a room,
makes you feel as though someone *fascinating* just walked
in."

4. Keep your eyes on your listener's eyes; if you are 26
addressing more than one person, look from face to face.
Don't gaze at the ceiling or at the bird cage in the corner.
This causes your listeners to look there too, to see what
exotic object has captured your attention.

5. Use simple verbs: "said," "asked," "cried." Don't 27
use highly colorful or inappropriate verbs. They fight for
attention with your real cues. " 'Hello,' she exploded"; "The
parson hopscotched across the room"—these will cause nervous laughter and not contribute to the joy of the joke's
climax.

6. Above all else: prepare the exact wording and 28
rhythm of your climax. Deliver the final line crisply, cheer-
fully, confidently.

Consider these tips as you read the following abso- 29
lutely dreadful way a good joke can be told:

Listen, last night I heard a story that almost split 30
my *sides*. I only hope that I can get it right. Sally Bernard
and Louella Hansfield, both orchid fanciers, met on Fifth
Avenue, I think, and 52nd, no, 53rd Street. Anyway, Louella
expostulated: "Sally! I haven't seen you since the Dorand
picnic in Central Park!"

"It wasn't in Central Park," Sally retorted. "You 31
remember—it was in *Riverside* Park."

"Oh, right," admitted Louella. "Say you've gained a 32
lot of weight."

"That's because I'm pregnant," confided Sally. 33

"Pregnant!" Louella screamed. "Congratulations!" 34

"Thank you. What's even more wonderful is that 35
Dr. Mittenheim, who is my doctor, just told me—in fact I'm
coming from his office on Madison now. Well, according to
Dr. Mittenheim, there is a very good chance that I'm going
to have—triplets!"

"Oh, Sally!" Louella shrieked. "That's fantastic! But 36
tell me, when. . . ."

I interrupt this heartlessly mauled joke to tell it in 37
a simple way:

Two old friends, Sally and Louella, met in the street 38
one day. "I'm going to have triplets!" Sally said.

"Oh, how nice!" said Louella. 39

"And you know, my doctor tells me that triplets are 40
conceived only once in every three million times!"

"Three *million!* Good gracious, Sally! But tell me, 41
when did you find time to do the housework?"

BUILDING VOCABULARY

1. Rosten uses a number of *figurative expressions* (see Glossary) composed of adjective-noun combinations. Explain the meanings of the following phrases:

   a. tantalizing miscues (par. 13)
   b. cheerful nod (par. 13)
   c. coaxing groan (par. 13)
   d. soothing murmur (par. 13)
   e. significant pause (par. 13)
   f. ironic inflection (par. 13)
   g. simulated astonishment (par. 13)
   h. accelerated rhythm (par. 13)
   i. born raconteur (par. 14)
   j. narrative pace (par. 14)
   k. comedic emphasis (par. 14)
   l. clever camouflage (par. 14)
   m. abject apology (par. 16)
   n. nervous laughter (par. 27)

2. Find other examples of figurative expressions (not composed of adjective-noun combinations) that you consider particularly effective in this essay.

UNDERSTANDING THE WRITER'S IDEAS

1. What does Rosten say is the purpose of most jokes?

2. According to the author, what sorts of methods does a good story-teller use to keep an audience's attention?

3. What are the "three simple rules" of successful joke telling?

4. Explain Rosten's "six basic tips" for good joke-telling, each in a single sentence of your own.

5. What is the point of the joke cited in paragraphs 1–12? How does it still serve as "a model of technique" for Rosten? Who told it to him? When, presumably?

6. Explain what is wrong with the way the joke

cited in paragraphs 30–36 is told. What words clue you to Rosten's feelings about that joke? How is the second version better?

7. Explain in your own words the joke in paragraphs 38–41.

UNDERSTANDING THE WRITER'S TECHNIQUES

1. Explain how Rosten uses paragraphs 1–12 as an introduction for this essay.

2. Where does Rosten use *definition?* What is the relation between definition and the author's purpose in this essay?

3. What is the relation between Rosten's "three simple rules" and "six basic tips"? How are they different? Why are the two categories arranged the way they are in the essay?

4. What principles of *classification* (see Chapter 7) does Rosten use to arrange his "six basic tips"?

5. Rosten makes considerable use of *illustration* (see Chapter 4) in this essay. (a) How does he use illustration to clarify his "six basic tips"? What examples appear in that section? (b) What examples of jokes does he provide? (c) How does he use extended examples at the beginning and end of this essay?

6. What is Rosten's intended audience for this essay? Explain Rosten's relation to his audience. Why does he use the pronoun "you" in various places? What is his purpose: to give instructions or to provide information? How else does Rosten involve the reader in the process explained in this essay?

7. *Diction* refers to the writer's choice of words (see Glossary) and *levels of diction* refers to the relative formality or informality of the language. How would you characterize the level of diction in paragraphs 1–12? What change in the level of diction occurs in paragraph 13? Explain. What is the overall level of diction, or tone, of this essay? How appropriate is it to the essay's audience and purpose?

8. Rosten uses a personal anecdote (an *anecdote* is

a brief story of an interesting incident). Where does he use it, and why is it effective?

9. Discuss how Rosten's advice on the use of verbs (par. 27) differs from what many writing teachers or the introduction to Chapter 2 suggest about verb choice for descriptive passages. Why does he make this suggestion?

10. Discuss the organization of the conclusion to this essay. Which paragraphs make up the conclusion? Explain your answer.

EXPLORING THE WRITER'S IDEAS

1. What are your favorite types of jokes? What are your least favorite? Give examples of each. Do you like physical humor? sight gags? puns? irony? deadpan? black humor? Do you consider the jokes that Rosten includes in this essay to be funny? Why or why not?

2. What do you consider the role of humor in everyday life? Do you usually see the humorous possibilities in serious situations, or do you tend to be more reserved in your viewpoint? In what situations is humor most appropriate? Least? Try to give personal experience examples of each.

3. Who do you consider the funniest comedians? What about their humor—be they stand-up comics, filmmakers, or talk show personalities—most appeals to you?

4. Is it possible for anyone reading this essay to be able to tell a joke? Is joke-telling simply a matter of following rules and tips or are other elements involved? What might they be?

IDEAS FOR WRITING

Guided Writing

Write a process essay with the title "How to _____ ." Fill in the blank with something you know how to do very well, and which involves entertaining people or keeping an audience's attention for a period of time. Such topics as "how to sing a song," "how to make a speech," "how to pantomime," or even "how to tell a joke" (if your way differs significantly from Rosten's) might lend themselves well to development.

1. Begin your essay with a brief personal anecdote.
2. Offer a basic definition of the process.
3. Explain the basic purpose of the process.
4. Identify three basic rules for being successful in the process.
5. Offer additional tips on success—number these tips and include examples which explain how each one works. Cover such important aspects of the process as: how to begin; how to choose appropriate material; how to maintain audience interest; how to end.
6. Include interesting figurative expressions throughout the essay.
7. Near the end of your essay write an extended example of how *not* to do this process.
8. End your essay with a revised, more successful version of your description in question 7 above.

More Writing Projects

1. Tell about a time you recently told a joke and whether you told it successfully or not. Use process analysis to explain your joke-telling from the beginning to the end as a means of evaluating what went right or wrong.
2. Explain how you do a specific process—involving verbal or nonverbal interaction with others—which you don't enjoy.
3. Explain how you get and keep someone's attention: a salesperson, a person you want to meet, a waiter or waitess, for example.

Grace Lichtenstein

COORS BEER

Process analysis often deals with mechanical or technical procedures. In this short selection by Grace Lichtenstein, who is a correspondent for *The New York Times,* the author examines a mechanical process—the brewing of beer. As you read this piece, look for the methods that the author uses to make this technical process interesting and understandable to the general reader.

Words to Watch

palate (par. 1): taste or sense of taste
mystique (par. 2): special, almost mysterious attitudes and feelings
    surrounding a person, place, or thing
Spartan (par. 3): simple and severe
rancid (par. 4): not fresh; having a bad smell
permeate (par. 4): to spread through everything
nondescript (par. 4): lacking any recognizable character or quality
cellulose (par. 5): the main substance in woody parts of plants,
    used in many manufacturing processes

Coors is a light-bodied beer, meaning it is brewed 1
with less malt, fewer hops and more rice than beers with a
tangy taste. Compared with Heineken's or other more full-

bodied foreign beers, Coors does seem almost flavorless and it is this quality that could account for its popularity among young people just starting to get acquainted with the pleasures of beer drinking. A few locals scoff at Coors, calling it "Colorado Kool-Aid." But the fact is that, according to Ernest Pyler, "if you conducted a blindfold test of the four leading beers, the chances of picking our Coors would be minimal." Indeed, one national newspaper conducted an informal test among eight beer drinkers, finding that only three could correctly identify Coors. My own admittedly uneducated palate detects no difference between Coors and Schaefer. In short, the difference between Coors and any other decent beer could be 1,800 miles. Maybe, if Paul Newman suddenly switched to Schaefer, Denverites would pay $15 a case for it.

There is one aspect to the Coors mystique that does 2 have measurable validity. Company officials make much of the fact that Coors has good mountain water and the most expensive brewing process in the country. Several elements are unusual, though not unique.

Thousands of visitors have learned about the process 3 on guided tours through the antiseptic, Spartan plant. (For out-of-towners, the tour is often a pilgrimage—but for local students of the Colorado School of Mines, it's usually more in the line of a quick belt before classes. The tour lasts 30 minutes, at the end of which visitors are invited to quaff to their heart's content in the hospitality lounge. "I've come here 50 times," boasted one student as he polished off a glass at 11:30 one morning in the lounge.) Situated in the center of town, between two high, flat mesas in the foothills of the Rockies, the plant dominates the community just as the somewhat rancid smell of malt seems to permeate the air; one-fourth of the town's families are said to owe their jobs to the factory's operations. Anyone expecting to see in Golden the foaming white waterfall amid mountain pines that is pictured on every yellow can of Coors will be disappointed. The water used in the brewing comes from nondescript wells hidden in concrete blockhouses. The brewery now puts out about 12 million barrels of beer a year, but construction sites throughout the grounds bear witness to the company's hopes for doubling that capacity by 1984.

Like other beers, Coors is produced from barley. 4 Most of the big Midwestern brewers use barley grown in North Dakota and Minnesota. Coors is the single American brewer to use a Moravian strain, grown under company supervision, on farms in Colorado, Idaho, Wyoming and Montana. At the brewery, the barley is turned into malt by being soaked in water—which must be biologically pure and of a known mineral content—for several days, causing it to sprout and producing a chemical change—breaking down starch into sugar. The malt is toasted, a process that halts the sprouting and determines the color and sweetness (the more the roasting, the darker, more bitter the beer). It is ground into flour and brewed, with more pure water, in huge copper-domed kettles until it is the consistency of oatmeal. Rice and refined starch are added to make mash; solids are strained out, leaving an amber liquid malt extract, which is boiled with hops—the dried cones from the hop vine which add to the bitterness, or tang. The hops are strained, yeast is added, turning the sugar to alcohol, and the beer is aged in huge red vats at near-freezing temperatures for almost two months, during which the second fermentation takes place and the liquid becomes carbonated, or bubbly. (Many breweries chemically age their beer to speed up production; Coors people say only naturally aged brew can be called a true "lager.") Next, the beer is filtered through cellulose filters to remove bacteria, and finally is pumped into cans, bottles or kegs for shipping.

The most unusual aspect of the Coors process is that 5 the beer is not pasteurized, as all but a half-dozen of the 90 or so American beers are. In the pasteurization process, bottles or cans of beer are passed through a heating unit and then cooled. This destroys the yeast in the brew which could cause spoilage, if the cans or bottles or barrels are unrefrigerated for any long period. However, pasteurization also changes the flavor of beer. Coors stopped pasteurizing its product 18 years ago because it decided that "heat is an enemy of beer," according to a company spokesman.

Unpasteurized beer must be kept under constant refrigeration. Thus, Coors does not warehouse any of its finished product, as many other brewers do, but ships everything out cold, immediately. In effect, my tour guide, a young management trainee wearing a beer-can tie clip, explained as we wandered through the packaging area, watching workers in surgical masks feed aluminum lids into machines that sealed cans whirling by on conveyor belts, the six-pack you buy in a store contains not only a very fresh beer but also a beer that could be considered draft, since it has been kept cold from vat to home refrigerator.

BUILDING VOCABULARY

1. For the italicized word in each example in Column A below select a definition from Column B.

Column A	Column B
a. locals *scoff* (par. 1)	1. drink heartily
b. *informal* test (par. 1)	2. locations
c. measurable *validity* (par. 2)	3. thickness
d. the *antiseptic* Spartan plant (par. 3)	4. not according to fixed rules
e. to *quaff* to their heart's content (par. 3)	5. a line of certain species
f. flat *mesas* (par. 3)	6. a concentrated form of something
g. construction *sites* (par. 3)	7. soundness
h. a Moravian *strain* (par. 4)	8. make fun of
i. the *consistency* of oatmeal (par. 4)	9. free from infection
j. liquid malt *extract* (par. 4)	10. hills

2. Use five of the italicized words in the first exercise in sentences of your own.

UNDERSTANDING THE WRITER'S IDEAS

1. What is a "light-bodied" beer?

2. What does the author mean when she states, "In short, the difference between Coors and any other decent beer could be 1,800 miles"?

3. What *is* special about Coors beer?

4. Why do college students like to visit the Coors plant?

5. Describe the setting of the Coors brewery. How does it contrast with the picture on the Coors can?

6. Explain in your own words the process by which Coors is produced.

7. Why is the pasteurization process important to the final flavor of any beer?

8. Why can Coors almost be considered a draft beer?

UNDERSTANDING THE WRITER'S TECHNIQUES

1. How do comparison and contrast operate in the first paragraph? Does the author also use definition in this paragraph? Where? For what purpose?

2. What is the function of paragraph 2? What is the purpose of paragraph 3? How does the author develop paragraph 3?

3. Analyze the author's use of transitional devices (see Glossary) between paragraphs 2 and 3.

4. Which paragraphs analyze the process of brewing Coors? Make a list of the steps on a sheet of paper. Is the process clear and complete? Does the author use process analysis simply to inform? Does she also provide commentary? Where?

5. Where does the author introduce personal or subjective elements into this essay? Why, at these points, does she provide personal rather than technical details?

EXPLORING THE WRITER'S IDEAS

1. Suppose that three unidentified brands of beer, cola, or cigarettes were placed before you. Would you be able to identify them by taste? What is the importance of "mystique" (or image) or "brand loyalty" to a product's success?

2. Can you think of other products that have a mystique associated with them? What are they, and what accounts for the mystique?

3. Would the fact that Paul Newman drinks Coors affect people's attitudes toward the brand? Why do manufacturers attempt to have certain celebrities associated with their products? Why should consumers be influenced by these associations?

4. Based on this essay, what are some ways to make a technical analysis of process interesting to the reader?

IDEAS FOR WRITING

Guided Writing

Explain how to make or to assemble a particular item or product. For example, you might want to explain how to prepare a certain dish; how to assemble a piece of equipment; how to produce something in a factory. You might want to follow Lichtenstein's example: Explain how a popular drink is made.

1. Start by introducing the reader to your "perfect product," indicating how it is possible to achieve high-quality results in its preparation.

2. Use as examples of the quality of the product, positive statements made by other individuals. These may be the ideas of friends, relatives, or experts.

3. Explain the "mystique," if there is one, surrounding the product.

4. After arousing reader interest sufficiently, de-

scribe the actual process involved, concentrating on all important details in the sequence.

5. In your last paragraph, try to capture the taste, look, or feel of the final product.

More Writing Projects

1. Consult an encyclopedia or other reference book to learn about the making of some product—steel, automobiles, plywood, and so forth. Then explain this process in your own words.

2. Set up an actual testing situation in your class. Have various members test three types of a particular item, such as chocolate, diet soda, a kitchen cleanser. Then write a report describing the process involved in the testing, as well as the process by which results were obtained.

Ernest Hemingway

CAMPING OUT

In this essay by Ernest Hemingway (1899–1961), the author uses the pattern of process analysis to order his materials on the art of camping. Hemingway wrote this piece for the *Toronto Star* in the early 1920s, before he gained worldwide recognition as a major American writer. In it, we see his lifelong interest in the outdoors and in his desire to do things well.

Words to Watch

relief map (par. 2): a map that shows by lines and colors the various heights and forms of the land

Caucasus (par. 2): a mountain range in southeastern Europe

proprietary (par. 7): held under patent or trademark

rhapsodize (par. 9): to speak enthusiastically

browse bed (par. 9): a portable cot

tyro (par. 11): an amateur; a beginner in learning something

dyspepsia (par. 13): indigestion

mulligan (par. 18): a stew made from odds and ends of meats and vegetables

Thousands of people will go into the bush this 1
summer to cut the high cost of living. A man who gets his
two weeks' salary while he is on vacation should be able to

put those two weeks in fishing and camping and be able to save one week's salary clear. He ought to be able to sleep comfortably every night, to eat well every day and to return to the city rested and in good condition.

But if he goes into the woods with a frying pan, an 2 ignorance of black flies and mosquitoes, and a great and abiding lack of knowledge about cookery the chances are that his return will be very different. He will come back with enough mosquito bites to make the back of his neck look like a relief map of the Caucasus. His digestion will be wrecked after a valiant battle to assimilate half-cooked or charred grub. And he won't have had a decent night's sleep while he has been gone.

He will solemnly raise his right hand and inform 3 you that he has joined the grand army of never-agains. The call of the wild may be all right, but it's a dog's life. He's heard the call of the tame with both ears. Waiter, bring him an order of milk toast.

In the first place he overlooked the insects. Black 4 flies, no-see-ums, deer flies, gnats and mosquitoes were instituted by the devil to force people to live in cities where he could get at them better. If it weren't for them everybody would live in the bush and he would be out of work. It was a rather successful invention.

But there are lots of dopes that will counteract the 5 pests. The simplest perhaps is oil of citronella. Two bits' worth of this purchased at any pharmacist's will be enough to last for two weeks in the worst fly and mosquito-ridden country.

Rub a little on the back of your neck, your forehead 6 and your wrists before you start fishing, and the blacks and skeeters will shun you. The odor of citronella is not offensive to people. It smells like gun oil. But the bugs do hate it.

Oil of pennyroyal and eucalyptol are also much 7 hated by mosquitoes, and with citronella they form the basis for many proprietary preparations. But it is cheaper and better to buy the straight citronella. Put a little on the mosquito netting that covers the front of your pup tent or canoe tent at night, and you won't be bothered.

To be really rested and get any benefit out of a 8
vacation a man must get a good night's sleep every night.
The first requisite for this is to have plenty of cover. It is
twice as cold as you expect it will be in the bush four nights
out of five, and a good plan is to take just double the bedding
that you think you will need. An old quilt that you can
wrap up in is as warm as two blankets.

Nearly all outdoor writers rhapsodize over the 9
browse bed. It is all right for the man who knows how to
make one and has plenty of time. But in a succession of one-
night camps on a canoe trip all you need is level ground for
your tent floor and you will sleep all right if you have plenty
of covers under you. Take twice as much cover as you think
that you will need, and then put two-thirds of it under you.
You will sleep warm and get your rest.

When it is clear weather you don't need to pitch your 10
tent if you are only stopping for the night. Drive four stakes
at the head of your made-up bed and drape your mosquito
bar over that, then you can sleep like a log and laugh at the
mosquitoes.

Outside of insects and bum sleeping the rock that 11
wrecks most camping trips is cooking. The average tyro's
idea of cooking is to fry everything and fry it good and
plenty. Now, a frying pan is a most necessary thing to any
trip, but you also need the old stew kettle and the folding
reflector baker.

A pan of fried trout can't be bettered and they don't 12
cost any more than ever. But there is a good and bad way
of frying them.

The beginner puts his trout and his bacon in and 13
over a brightly burning fire the bacon curls up and dries
into a dry tasteless cinder and the trout is burned outside
while it is still raw inside. He eats them and it is all right
if he is only out for the day and going home to a good meal
at night. But if he is going to face more trout and bacon the
next morning and other equally well-cooked dishes for the
remainder of two weeks he is on the pathway to nervous
dyspepsia.

The proper way is to cook over coals. Have several 14
cans of Crisco or Cotosuet or one of the vegetable shortenings
along that are as good as lard and excellent for all kinds of
shortening. Put the bacon in and when it is about half
cooked lay the trout in the hot grease, dipping them in corn
meal first. Then put the bacon on top of the trout and it will
baste them as it slowly cooks.

The coffee can be boiling at the same time and in a 15
smaller skillet pancakes being made that are satisfying the
other campers while they are waiting for the trout.

With the prepared pancake flours you take a cupful 16
of pancake flour and add a cup of water. Mix the water and
flour and as soon as the lumps are out it is ready for cooking.
Have the skillet hot and keep it well greased. Drop the
batter in and as soon as it is done on one side loosen it in
the skillet and flip it over. Apple butter, syrup or cinnamon
and sugar go well with the cakes.

While the crowd have taken the edge from their 17
appetites with flapjacks the trout have been cooked and they
and the bacon are ready to serve. The trout are crisp outside
and firm and pink inside and the bacon is well done—but
not too done. If there is anything better than that combination the writer has yet to taste it in a lifetime devoted
largely and studiously to eating.

The stew kettle will cook you dried apricots when 18
they have resumed their predried plumpness after a night
of soaking, it will serve to concoct a mulligan in, and it will
cook macaroni. When you are not using it, it should be
boiling water for the dishes.

In the baker, mere man comes into his own, for he 19
can make a pie that to his bush appetite will have it all over
the product that mother used to make, like a tent. Men have
always believed that there was something mysterious and
difficult about making a pie. Here is a great secret. There
is nothing to it. We've been kidded for years. Any man of
average office intelligence can make at least as good a pie
as his wife.

All there is to a pie is a cup and a half of flour, one- 20

half teaspoonful of salt, one-half cup of lard and cold water. That will make pie crust that will bring tears of joy into your camping partner's eyes.

Mix the salt with the flour, work the lard into the flour, make it up into a good workmanlike dough with cold water. Spread some flour on the back of a box or something flat, and pat the dough around a while. Then roll it out with whatever kind of round bottle you prefer. Put a little more lard on the surface of the sheet of dough and then slosh a little flour on and roll it up and then roll it out again with the bottle. 21

Cut out a piece of the rolled out dough big enough to line a pie tin. I like the kind with holes in the bottom. Then put in your dried apples that have soaked all night and been sweetened, or your apricots, or your blueberries, and then take another sheet of the dough and drape it gracefully over the top, soldering it down at the edges with your fingers. Cut a couple of slits in the top dough sheet and prick it a few times with a fork in an artistic manner. 22

Put it in the baker with a good slow fire for forty-five minutes and then take it out and if your pals are Frenchmen they will kiss you. The penalty for knowing how to cook is that the others will make you do all the cooking. 23

It is all right to talk about roughing it in the woods. But the real woodsman is the man who can be really comfortable in the bush. 24

BUILDING VOCABULARY

1. For each word below write your own definition, based on how the word is used in the selection. Check back to the appropriate paragraph in the essay.

     a. abiding (par. 2)
     b. assimilate (par. 2)
     c. valiant (par. 2)
     d. charred (par. 2)
     e. solemnly (par. 3)
     f. requisite (par. 8)

g. succession (par. 9)

h. studiously (par. 17)

i. concoct (par. 18)

j. soldering (par. 22)

UNDERSTANDING THE WRITER'S IDEAS

1. What is Hemingway's main purpose in this essay? Does he simply want to explain how to set up camp and how to cook outdoors?

2. What, according to the writer, are the two possible results of camping out on your vacation?

3. Why is oil of citronella the one insecticide that Hemingway recommends over all others?

4. Is it always necessary to pitch a tent when camping out? What are alternatives to it? How can you sleep warmly and comfortably?

5. Explain the author's process for cooking trout. Also explain his process for baking a pie.

6. Is it enough for Hemingway simply to enjoy "roughing it" while camping out?

UNDERSTANDING THE WRITER'S TECHNIQUES

1. Identify those paragraphs in the essay that involve process analysis, and explain how Hemingway develops his subject in each.

2. What is the main writing pattern in paragraphs 1 and 2? How does this method serve as an organizing principle throughout the essay?

3. How would you characterize the author's style of writing? Is it appropriate to a newspaper audience? Is it more apt for professional fishermen?

4. In what way does Hemingway employ classification in this essay?

5. Analyze the tone of Hemingway's essay.

6. The concluding paragraph is short. Is it effective, nevertheless, and why? How does it reinforce the opening paragraph?

EXPLORING THE WRITER'S IDEAS

1. Camping out was popular in the 1920s, as it is in the 1980s. What are some of the reasons that it remains so attractive today?

2. Hemingway's essay describes many basic strategies for successful camping. He does not rely on "gadgets," or modern inventions to make camping easier. Do such gadgets make camping more fun today than it might have been in the 1920s?

3. The author suggests that there is a right way and a wrong way to do things. Does it matter if you perform a recreational activity right as long as you enjoy doing it? Why?

IDEAS FOR WRITING

Guided Writing

Write a composition on how to do something wrong, and how to do it right—going on vacation, looking for a job, fishing, or whatever.

1. Reexamine the author's first three paragraphs and imitate his method of introducing the right and wrong ways about the subject, and the possible results.

2. Adopt a simple, informal, "chatty" style. Feel free to use a few well-placed cliches and other forms of spoken English. Use several similes.

3. Divide your subject into useful categories. Just as Hemingway treated insects, sleeping, and cooking, try to cover the main aspects of your subject.

4. Explain the process involved for each aspect of your subject. Make certain that you compare and contrast the right and wrong ways of your activity.

5. Write a short, crisp conclusion that reinforces your longer introduction.

More Writing Projects

    1.   Explain how people camp out today.

    2.   Describe how to get to your favorite vacation spot, and what to do when you get there.

    3.   If you have ever camped out, write a process paper explaining one important feature of setting up camp.

9

Cause-and-Effect Analysis

The analysis of cause and effect—often called *causal analysis*—seeks to explain why events occur, or what the outcome or *expected* results of a chain of happenings might be. Basically, cause-and-effect analysis looks for connections between things and reasons behind them. It involves a way of thinking that identifies conditions (the causes) and establishes results or consequences (the effects). In order to discuss an idea intelligently a writer needs to explore causes and effects. The strength of an explanation may lie simply in his or her ability to point out *why* something is so.

Like all the other writing patterns discussed in this text, cause-and-effect analysis reflects a kind of thinking we do every day. If someone were to ask you why you selected the college that you are now attending, you would offer reasons to explain your choice: the cost, the geographic location, the reputation of the institution, and so forth. These would be the *causes* that you have identified. On the other hand, someone might ask you if and why you like the college now that you are there. You could discuss your satisfaction (or lack of it) with the teachers, the course offerings, the opportunity to work part time, the availability of scholarship money and loans, the beauty of the campus, the variety in your social life. Those are the consequences or results—in other words, the *effects*—of your decision. Of course, basic reasoning and common sense are involved in the way that you identify causes and effects.

How do you determine causal relationships? First, you look at the *immediate* causes that gave rise to a situation—that is, you look at the causes most directly related to it, the ones you discover closest at hand. (Here you must be careful not to assume that because one event simply preceded another it also caused it.) But for most events a good analyst looks beyond immediate causes to more fundamental ones. These are the *ultimate* causes of a situation, the basic conditions that stimulated the more obvious ones.

For example, if you looked for causes to explain why your supervisor dismissed you from your job, your first response might be that you and she did not get along well. That could be an *immediate cause*. (Because one of your coworkers left your supervisor's office after a private conference with her just before you were fired, you could *not* assume safely that that coworker necessarily caused your dismissal.) But the immediate cause you uncovered could certainly be influenced by other underlying conditions. Perhaps your attendance record on the job was poor. Perhaps you did not get your work done quickly enough. Or, on the other hand, perhaps you worked so quickly and efficiently that your supervisor saw you as a threat to her own position. One or more of those and others like them might be the *ultimate* causes to explain why you lost the job.

Of course, as in the above example, causes you name for many situations may be thought of only as possibilities. It's often impossible to *prove* causes and effects absolutely. Yet in evaluating the causal relationships you present in an essay, readers expect you to offer evidence. Therefore, you do have to support the causes and effects you present with specific details drawn from personal experiences, from statistics, or from statements by experts, for example. The more details and evidence you offer, the better your paper will be.

When writers use causal analysis as a pattern, they can concentrate either on causes or effects, or they can attempt to balance the two. Moreover, in longer and more complicated papers, a writer can show how one cause produces an effect that, in turn, creates *another* set of causes leading to a second effect. Wherever the pattern takes you, remember to be thorough in presenting all links in your chain of analysis; to consider all possible factors; to avoid oversimplification; and to emphasize all important major and minor causes and effects.

Anne Roiphe

WHY MARRIAGES FAIL

Anne Roiphe is the author of the well-known novel about
relationships, *Up The Sandbox!*, which was later made
into a popular film. In this essay, notice how she presents
a series of interconnected reasons for the currently high
divorce rate.

Words to Watch

obsolete (par. 1): out-of-date; no longer in use
perils (par. 2): dangers
infertility (par. 2): the lack of ability to have children
turbulent (par. 2): very chaotic or uneasy
stupefying (par. 2): bewildering
obese (par. 3): very fat, overweight
entrapment (par. 4): the act of trapping, sometimes by devious
　　　methods
yearning (par. 4): a strong desire
euphoric (par. 7): characterized by a feeling of well-being
proverbial (par. 13): relating to a proverb or accepted truth
infidelity (par. 13): sexual unfaithfulness

These days so many marriages end in divorce that 1
our most sacred vows no longer ring with truth. "Happily
ever after" and "Till death do us part" are expressions that

seem on the way to becoming obsolete. Why has it become so hard for couples to stay together? What goes wrong? What has happened to us that close to one-half of all marriages are destined for the divorce courts? How could we have created a society in which 42 percent of our children will grow up in single-parent homes? If statistics could only measure loneliness, regret, pain, loss of self-confidence and fear of the future, the numbers would be beyond quantifying.

Even though each broken marriage is unique, we 2 can still find the common perils, the common causes for marital despair. Each marriage has crisis points and each marriage tests endurance, the capacity for both intimacy and change. Outside pressures such as job loss, illness, infertility, trouble with a child, care of aging parents and all the other plagues of life hit marriage the way hurricanes blast our shores. Some marriages survive these storms and others don't. Marriages fail, however, not simply because of the outside weather but because the inner climate becomes too hot or too cold, too turbulent or too stupefying.

When we look at how we choose our partners and 3 what expectations exist at the tender beginnings of romance, some of the reasons for disaster become quite clear. We all select with unconscious accuracy a mate who will recreate with us the emotional patterns of our first homes. Dr. Carl A. Whitaker, a marital therapist and emeritus professor of psychiatry at the University of Wisconsin explains, "From early childhood on, each of us carried models for marriage, femininity, masculinity, motherhood, fatherhood and all the other family roles." Each of us falls in love with a mate who has qualities of our parents, who will help us rediscover both the psychological happiness and miseries of our past lives. We may think we have found a man unlike Dad, but then he turns to drink or drugs, or loses his job over and over again or sits silently in front of the T.V. just the way Dad did. A man may choose a woman who doesn't like kids just like his mother or who gambles away the family savings just like his mother. Or he may choose a slender wife who seems unlike his obese mother but then turns out to have other addictions that destroy their mutual happiness.

A man and a woman bring to their marriage bed a blended concoction of conscious and unconscious memories of their parents' lives together. The human way is to compulsively repeat and recreate the patterns of the past. Sigmund Freud so well described the unhappy design that many of us get trapped in: the unmet needs of childhood, the angry feelings left over from frustrations of long ago, the limits of trust and the reoccurrence of old fears. Once an individual senses this entrapment, there may follow a yearning to escape, and the result could be a broken, splintered marriage.

Of course people can overcome the habits and attitudes that developed in childhood. We all have hidden strengths and amazing capacities for growth and creative change. Change, however, requires work—observing your part in a rotten pattern, bringing difficulties out into the open—and work runs counter to the basic myth of marriage: "When I wed this person all my problems will be over. I will have achieved success and I will become the center of life for this other person and this person will be my center, and we will mean everything to each other forever." This myth, which every marriage relies on, is soon exposed. The coming of children, the pulls and tugs of their demands on affection and time, place a considerable strain on that basic myth of meaning everything to each other, of merging together and solving all of life's problems.

Concern and tension about money take each partner away from the other. Obligations to demanding parents or still-depended-upon parents create further strain. Couples today must also deal with all the cultural changes brought on in recent years by the women's movement and the sexual revolution. The altering of roles and the shifting of responsibilities have been extremely trying for many marriages.

These and other realities of life erode the visions of marital bliss the way sandstorms eat at rock and the ocean nibbles away at the dunes. Those euphoric, grand feelings that accompany romantic love are really self-delusions, self-hypnotic dreams that enable us to forge a relationship. Real life, failure at work, disappointments, exhaustion, bad smells, bad colds and hard times all puncture the dream and leave us stranded with our mate, with our childhood patterns pushing us this way and that, with our unfulfilled expectations.

The struggle to survive in marriage requires adapt- 8 ability, flexibility, genuine love and kindness and an imagination strong enough to feel what the other is feeling. Many marriages fall apart because either partner cannot imagine what the other wants or cannot communicate what he or she needs or feels. Anger builds until it erupts into a volcanic burst that buries the marriage in ash.

It is not hard to see, therefore, how essential com- 9 munication is for a good marriage. A man and a woman must be able to tell each other how they feel and why they feel the way they do; otherwise they will impose on each other roles and actions that lead to further unhappiness. In some cases, the communication patterns of childhood—of not talking, of talking too much, of not listening, of distrust and anger, of withdrawal—spill into the marriage and prevent a healthy exchange of thoughts and feelings. The answer is to set up new patterns of communication and intimacy.

At the same time, however, we must see each other 10 as individuals. "To achieve a balance between separateness and closeness is one of the major psychological tasks of all human beings at every stage of life," says Dr. Stuart Bartle, a psychiatrist at the New York University Medical Center.

If we sense from our mate a need for too much 11 intimacy, we tend to push him or her away, fearing that we may lose our identities in the merging of marriage. One partner may suffocate the other partner in a childlike dependency.

A good marriage means growing as a couple but 12 also growing as individuals. This isn't easy. Richard gives up his interest in carpentry because his wife, Helen, is jealous of the time he spends away from her. Karen quits her choir group because her husband dislikes the friends she makes there. Each pair clings to each other and are angry with each other as life closes in on them. This kind of marital balance is easily thrown as one or the other pulls away and divorce follows.

Sometimes people pretend that a new partner will 13 solve the old problems. Most often extramarital sex destroys a marriage because it allows an artificial split between the good and the bad—the good is projected on the new partner and the bad is dumped on the head of the old. Dishonesty, hiding and cheating create walls between men and women. Infidelity is just a symptom of trouble. It is a symbolic complaint, a weapon of revenge, as well as an unraveler of closeness. Infidelity is often that proverbial last straw that sinks the camel to the ground.

All right—marriage has always been difficult. Why 14 then are we seeing so many divorces at this time? Yes, our modern social fabric is thin, and yes the permissiveness of society has created unrealistic expectations and thrown the family into chaos. But divorce is so common because people today are unwilling to exercise the self-discipline that marriage requires. They expect easy joy, like the entertainment on TV, the thrill of a good party.

Marriage takes some kind of sacrifice, not dreadful 15 self-sacrifice of the soul, but some level of compromise. Some of one's fantasies, some of one's legitimate desires have to be given up for the value of the marriage itself. "While all marital partners feel shackled at times, it is they who really choose to make the marital ties into confining chains or supporting bonds, says Dr. Whitaker. Marriage requires sexual, financial and emotional discipline. A man and a woman cannot follow every impulse, cannot allow themselves to stop growing or changing.

Divorce is not an evil act. Sometimes it provides 16 salvation for people who have grown hopelessly apart or were frozen in patterns of pain or mutual unhappiness. Divorce can be, despite its initial devastation, like the first cut of the surgeon's knife, a step toward new health and a good life. On the other hand, if the partners can stay past the breaking up of the romantic myths into the development of real love and intimacy, they have achieved a work as amazing as the greatest cathedrals of the world. Marriages that do not fail but improve, that persist despite imperfections, are not only rare these days but offer a wondrous shelter in which the face of our mutual humanity can safely show itself.

BUILDING VOCABULARY

1. Roiphe loads her essay with some very common expressions to make the discussion more easily understandable to the reader. Below is a list of ten such expressions. Use each in a sentence of your own.

 a. ring with truth (par. 1)
 b. crisis points (par. 2)
 c. tender beginnings (par. 3)
 d. mutual happiness (par. 3)
 e. marriage bed (par. 4)
 f. hidden strengths (par. 5)
 g. marital bliss (par. 7)
 h. healthy exchange (par. 9)
 i. childlike dependency (par. 11)
 j. social fabric (par. 14)

2. Locate and explain five terms that the author draws from psychology.

UNDERSTANDING THE WRITER'S IDEAS

1. What are the "sacred vows" the author mentions in paragraph 1? Identify the source of the expressions "happily ever after" and "till death do us part." What does she mean when she says that these expressions "seem on the way to becoming obsolete"?

2. What is a "single-parent home"?

3. How does Roiphe define "endurance" in a marriage? What does she mean by "outside pressures" in paragraph 2? What are some of these pressures? Does Roiphe feel they are the primary causes for marriages failing? Why?

4. According to the essay, how do we choose husbands and wives? What is the meaning of "our first home" in paragraph 3? According to Roiphe, for what reasons is the way we choose mates a possible cause for marriages failing?

5. What is the "basic myth" of marriage? How does it create a possibly bad marriage?

6. How have the women's movement and the sexual revolution created strains on modern marriages?

7. Explain what the writer means by "Real life, failure at work, disappointments, exhaustion, bad smells, bad colds, and hard times" in paragraph 7? How do they affect marriages?

8. What is the role of communications between husband and wife in a marriage? What are the results of poor communications? What solutions to this problem does Roiphe suggest?

9. What two types of "growth" does Roiphe suggest as necessary to a good marriage? Who are Richard, Helen, and Karen, named in paragraph 12?

10. According to Roiphe, what is the common cause for extramarital sexual affairs? What are her projected results of infidelity?

11. What does Roiphe identify as the primary cause of divorce? What does she propose as a solution to this problem?

12. According to the last paragraph, do you think Roiphe is in favor of each divorces? Why? In this paragraph, she presents both the positive and negative effects of divorce. What are the positive effects? the negative effects?

UNDERSTANDING THE WRITER'S TECHNIQUES

1. How does the title almost predict for the reader that the writer's main technique of development will be cause-and-effect analysis?

2. One strategy for developing an introductory paragraph is to ask a question. What is the purpose of the questions that the author asks in the opening paragraph?

What is the relationship among the questions? How do the questions themselves dictate a cause-effect pattern of development? How do they immediately involve the reader in the topic?

3. In which paragraph does Roiphe list the immediate or common causes of marital failure? Why is this placement effective?

4. The use of clear *topic sentences* for each paragraph can often be an important technique in writing a clear causal analysis because they usually identify main causes for the effect under discussion. Identify the topic sentences for paragraphs 3, 4, and 6. What causes for marriage failure does each identify?

5. What causal chain of behavior does Roiphe build in paragraphs 8 to 13?

6. Why does Roiphe begin paragraph 14 with the words "All right"? Whom is she addressing? How does this address compare with the technique used in her introduction?

7. What two authorities does Roiphe quote in this essay? How are their citations useful? How are they identified? In what ways do their identifications add to their credibility as sources of opinions or information on Roiphe's topic?

8. Where does Roiphe use statistics in this essay? Why is it especially important to the development of the article?

9. Roiphe makes use of *definition* (see pages 181–182) in a number of places in this essay. What are her definitions of the following:

   a. "work" in a marriage (par. 5)
   b. "A good marriage" (par. 12)
   c. "divorce" (par. 16)
   d. "marriages that do not fail but improve" (par. 16)

Locate other places where she uses definition.

10. In some essays, the introduction and conclusion are each simply the first and last paragraphs. In this essay, the writer uses more than one paragraph for each. Which

paragraphs make up her introduction? Which make up the conclusion? Why might she have structured her introduction and conclusion in this way? How does the structure affect the essay?

11. You have learned that two of the most common types of comparisons used by writers to enliven their essays are *similes* and *metaphors*. Look up the definition of these terms in the Glossary to refresh your memory. In addition, writers may use *extended metaphors*. This technique relies upon a number of metaphoric comparisons which revolve around a main idea rather than a single comparison. In each of the following paragraphs identify and explain the comparisons indicated:

> paragraph 2: extended metaphor
>
> paragraph 7: metaphor
>
> paragraph 8: metaphor
>
> paragraph 13: metaphor
>
> paragraph 14: simile
>
> paragraph 15: metaphor
>
> paragraph 16: similes, metaphors

How does Roiphe's frequent use of metaphors and similes affect the tone of the essay?

12. Why does Roiphe end her essay with references to successful marriages? Would you consider that as being off the topic? Why or why not?

EXPLORING THE WRITER'S IDEAS

1. Roiphe discusses quite a few causes for marriages failing. Discuss with the class some additional causes. Why are they also important?

2. Paragraph 6 states that "Couples today must also deal with all the cultural changes brought on in recent years by the women's movement and the sexual revolution." Identify these two social phenomena. Among the people you

know, have these cultural changes affected their marriages? How? If you are not married, and plan to marry, do you feel that the changes will present any foreseeable problems? If you are not married, and do not plan to marry, have they influenced your decision in any ways? What other effects have these two movements had in American society? Do you think these influences have been positive or negative? Why?

3. If you are married or in a close relationship, how did you choose your mate? If you are not married or in a relationship, what qualities would you look for in a mate? Why?

4. In paragraphs 6 and 7, Roiphe mentions "realities of life" that destroy romantic notions of "marital bliss." What other realities can you add to her list?

5. Paragraph 15 discusses the idea of self-sacrifice in marriage. Roiphe writes, "Some of one's fantasies, some of one's legitimate desires have to be given up for the value of the marriage itself." However, some people insist that for a marriage to survive, each partner must maintain complete integrity, that is, must not be forced into major sacrifices of values or life-styles. What is your opinion of these two opposing viewpoints?

6. Both Gregg Easterbrook in "Escape Valve" (pages 199–202) and Judy Syfers in "I Want a Wife" (pages 351–354) provide some insights into marriage that complement Roiphe's. How do their positions compare with hers? How, for example, could the principle of "automatic-out" explain to some degree why marriages fail?

IDEAS FOR WRITING

Guided Writing

Using cause-and-effect analysis, write an essay in which you explain *why marriages succeed.*

1. Limit your topic sufficiently so that you can concentrate your discussion on closely interrelated cause-and-effect patterns.

2. In the introduction, involve your reader with a series of pertinent questions.

3. Identify what many people think are common or immediate causes of successful marriages; then show how other causes are perhaps even more important.

4. In the course of your essay, cite at least one relevant statistic that will add extra importance to your topic.

5. Try to use at least one quotation from a reputable authority. Consult your library for books and articles that deal with marriage. Be sure to include full identification of your source.

6. Use clear topic sentences in each paragraph as you present analysis of the various causes for successful marriages.

7. Make use of metaphors, similes, and extended metaphors.

8. In your essay, offer necessary definitions of terms that are especially important to your topic. Try for at least one definition by negation.

9. Write a conclusion in which you make some commentary upon divorce. Make your comment as an outgrowth of your discussion of a successful marriage.

More Writing Projects

1. In an essay of approximately 750 to 1000 words, explain the reasons why you ever ended a relationship (a marriage, a close friendship, a relationship with a girlfriend or boyfriend). Also discuss how you knew when you had reached the "breaking point." Did you feel you had hung on too long or had given up too soon?

2. Write a long letter to a friend explaining why you think he or she should end or not end a marriage, relationship, or friendship. Be sure to include clear reasons.

3. Write an essay in which you explain the effects of divorce in the lives of the couple involved. Here, do not concern yourself with causes; look only at the results of the failed marriage.

Boyce Rensberger

WHY YOU LIKE SOME FOODS AND HATE OTHERS

In this essay, Boyce Rensberger explores the various reasons for our liking or disliking certain foods. He relates taste preferences to human evolution; and he discusses the ideas proposed about tastes by anthropologists. Pay special attention to the discussions of experiments designed to test people's taste preferences.

Words to Watch

aversion (par. 1): a strong feeling of dislike accompanied by a strong desire to avoid something

insights (par. 2): deep understandings

genetic (par. 3): dealing with hereditary changes in living things

evolution (par. 4): the process of changes through which living beings acquire distinguishing characteristics or traits

foraging (par. 4): wandering in search of food

induced (par. 6): influenced by reasons or persuasion

nausea (par. 12): a stomach illness accompanied by a hatred for food and by an urge to vomit

anesthetized (par. 12): under the influence of a substance which produces a loss of feeling without a loss of consciousness

ingrained (par. 13): deep-seated

assimilated (par. 18): absorbed traditions and values of a culture

viscosity (par. 20): the property of a fluid that prevents it from flowing

staple (par. 21): major or principal element

mainstay (par. 21): chief or main support

putrefaction (par. 22): rotting; decomposition of organic matter

Everybody doesn't like something. Whether the aversion is to sautéed brains or McDonald's hamburgers, to Szechwan spiciness or Middle American blandness, everyone finds at least a few foods or flavors to be objectionable. 1

Yet, as common as taste aversions are, little is reliably known about how they are formed. They are just beginning to be studied by scientists, however, and some insights are developing. 2

There are, for example, genetic differences in people's abilities to taste some substances. Some people cannot taste certain bitter flavors, and hence enjoy foods that others find objectionably bitter. 3

Some authorities have suggested that the widely held strong preference for sweetness, craving for salt and aversion to sour or bitter flavors is innate, a product of evolution during the days when our foraging ancestors lived off the land. Things that taste sweet are usually nutritious and full of energy, while those that are bitter or sour tend more often to be poisonous. As tropical animals, our ancestors lost lots of salt in their sweat and needed to replace it to prevent sodium deficiency in the blood. 4

Our taste preferences and aversions, so this explanation goes, evolved to be generally reliable guides to eating in the wild. It is only after our relatively recent adoption of sedentary ways and synthetic foods that the preference for sweets and salt is getting us into nutritional trouble. 5

Although nutritionists often contend that a preference for very sweet foods is culturally induced or that people actually develop an addiction to sugar, Dr. Gary Beauchamp, a specialist in taste research, says there is no solid evidence to support this. 6

Dr. Beauchamp, of the University of Pennsylvania's Monell Chemical Senses Center, suggests that although people may consciously modify their food choices, the basic preference for sweetness remains. It has only become noticeable now that food technologists "have separated sweetness from the goodness of the natural food" and marketed a number of foods offering little else. 7

Rather than creating a preference for sweetness, 8
Dr. Beauchamp suggests, the food technologists are merely
exploiting an existing preference that, in the past, was no
problem.

Also there is solid evidence that, aside from the 9
aversion to sour and bitter flavors, the sense of taste plays
another role in preventing food poisoning. The evidence was
first seen in animal experiments. If a rat gets sick after
eating some unusual food, it will develop an immediate
aversion to the taste of that food.

In a form of learning quite unlike Pavlovian condi- 10
tioning, the taste aversion develops after a single episode
and the sickness may occur several hours after the food was
eaten. The aversion also persists for a long time. Conditioned
responses usually require many experiences to be learned
and the aversive response must occur immediately after the
stimulus. And they fade quickly.

The phenomenon occurs in many animals and is 11
called "bait shyness" among those who try to poison un-
wanted animals but find that if the animal survives, it
usually learns to avoid the bait.

Dr. John Garcia, a psychologist at the University of 12
California, Los Angeles, has found that laboratory rats can
be made to dislike sugar-flavored water, which they normally strongly prefer, by injecting them with a drug that
induces nausea several hours afterward. Experiments have
also shown that rats learn this taste aversion even if they
are totally anesthetized throughout the period of induced
nausea.

All of this evidence tells scientists that taste aver- 13
sions formed in this way are the effect of a powerful and
deeply ingrained biological capacity. Such powerful and obvious biological traits do not evolve into being and become
widespread unless they confer a distinct advantage to the
survival of the animal. There is now evidence that human
beings share this capacity.

In the only controlled experiment on learned taste 14
aversions in people, Dr. Ilene L. Bernstein, a University of
Washington psychiatrist, found that children could be made

to dislike a novel flavor of ice cream if they became sick after eating it. Children who did not get sick loved it.

Her experiment was aimed at learning why so many 15 cancer patients receiving drug therapy develop aversions to many kinds of food, even foods they once preferred. Cancer drugs often induce severe nausea, and, Dr. Bernstein reasoned, the patients might be victims of the bait-shy response.

She studied children with cancer who had to take 16 nausea-inducing drugs. One group received a new flavor of ice cream, called Mapletoff, before undergoing therapy. Later the children were given a choice of the ice cream and playing with a game. Less than a quarter chose the ice cream. Children who had tried Mapletoff but did not get sick from therapy, preferred Mapletoff to the game almost four to one.

While genetically controlled factors may account for 17 some taste aversions, cultural influences clearly play a more obvious role.

Anthropologists have found that food preferences are 18 among the most stable of cultural traditions. Long after immigrants and their descendants have assimilated most other aspects of their adopted country, including language, they will cling to their native cookery.

When the potato, native to Peru, was introduced in 19 Europe centuries ago, people resisted it as a bizarre-tasting oddity. It was 200 years before they generally adopted the potato into their diets.

While most people dislike foods that are strongly 20 sour and increase their dislikes in proportion to the sourness, at least one group in India says it prefers foods sour, and the sourer the better. This is an economically poor group whose basic foods are sour, and who, for example, eat tamarind fruits as if they were apples. Their culture is apparently their only difference with other Indians.

Cultural preferences apply not only to flavor but to 21 texture and viscosity. One finding has been that people tend to prefer their dietary staple to have a hearty, chewy consistency. To most Americans rice is just another side dish;

they prefer it light and fluffy. But in cultures where rice is the dietary mainstay, it is preferred heavier and more glutinous. When bread was a staple in the United States it was heavy and substantial. But now that it is no longer the staff of life, bread has been turned into fluff.

22　　The role of smell in influencing food aversions and preferences is well known. People with colds often lose their appetites because they cannot smell food. However delicious a dish might appear to the eyes, if the nose perceives any odor like that of putrefaction, the tongue will probably never taste it. What is not so well appreciated is the role of the eyes in modifying food preferences.

23　　Food technologists add orange coloring to their synthetic orange drinks not just to be consistent but because, without the color, the flavor does not taste as orangy. Thus grape-flavored drinks are colored purple, cherry drinks are red, and so on. When lemon drinks and lime drinks came out, however, food synthesizers were faced with a dilemma. Both juices are essentially colorless. How to inform consumers what flavor they were supposed to taste? The decision was to adopt the color of the rind. Thus lime drinks are green and lemon drinks are yellow.

24　　In one experiment, researchers scrambled five flavors and colors and found that if, for example, the lemon-flavored drink was red, taste testers tended to call it strawberry. The test involved drinks flavored with lemon, orange, strawberry, grape and blueberry and colored yellow, orange, red, purple and blue. When the "right" color was combined with the flavor, 72 percent of the testers guessed the correct flavoring. But when the colors were scrambled only 22 percent could name the flavor.

25　　The role of color is not limited to artificial flavors. Experienced wine tasters can also be fooled. In one experiment a white wine was colored to look like a rosé. Tasters concluded that it was sweeter.

26　　Perhaps the ultimate example of the role of experience in influencing food preferences and aversions is that reported by Dr. Howard Schutz, a psychologist at the University of California at Davis. He notes that many people have come to prefer the taste of canned tomato juice over that of fresh tomato juice.

"The taste of tin from the can," Dr. Schutz said, "has 27 been accepted as appropriate in tomato juice. That's what people expect. It's so important that aluminum-can makers have thought about adding the tin flavor to juice packed in their containers."

BUILDING VOCABULARY

1. For each italicized word in Column A, write the correct *antonym* (a word of opposite meaning) from Column B. Look up unfamiliar words in a dictionary.

Column A	Column B
a. to be *objectionable* (par. 1)	1. abundance
b. is *innate* (par. 4)	2. changeable
c. a sodium *deficiency* (par. 4)	3. unsettled
d. *reliable* guides (par. 5)	4. natural
e. *sedentary* ways (par. 5)	5. unoriginal
f. *synthetic* foods (par. 5)	6. acceptable
g. *novel* flavor (par. 14)	7. unsteady
h. most *stable* (par. 18)	8. undependable
i. *bizarre*-tasting (par. 19)	9. unnatural
j. to be *consistent* (par. 23)	10. typical

2. The following words are used in this essay to describe food. Look up their meanings and use each in a sentence of your own.

a. sautéed	f. nutritious
b. Szechwan	g. sodium
c. blandness	h. tamarind fruits
d. bitter	i. glutinous
e. sweetness	j. rind

UNDERSTANDING THE WRITER'S IDEAS

1. In your own words, what condition is the author setting out to analyze in this essay? Where does he state that condition?

2. According to the evolutionary theory of taste preferences, why do we like some foods and hate others? What accounts for our liking of sweets? Our craving for salt? Our dislike of bitter-tasting foods? What two aspects of contemporary life may threaten this evolutionary process?

3. What evidence does Rensberger offer to support the idea that our sense of taste acts as an inborn guard against food poisoning?

4. What is Pavlovian conditioning? What is the phenomenon of "bait shyness"? How do the two processes differ?

5. What is the main reason described to support the theory that taste aversions derive from ingrained biological necessities?

6. Explain in your own words how cancer patients might be victims of the bait-shy response.

7. Although some scientists attempt to explain taste aversions by genetic factors, anthropologists take another viewpoint. What is it? What three examples does Rensberger describe to illustrate this viewpoint?

8. What is the role of the sense of smell in the process of determining tastes we dislike? How is the sense of sight involved in the process?

9. Why do many people no longer like to drink fresh-pressed tomato juice, according to Rensberger's essay? Of what factor influencing food preferences is this taste phenomenon an example?

UNDERSTANDING THE WRITER'S TECHNIQUES

1. Does Rensberger fulfill the purpose stated in the title? Does he give equal treatment to both aspects of the purpose? Explain.

2. Explain the author's use of transitions. List all the transitional words and expressions in paragraphs 1 through 9.

3. Explain Rensberger's use of classification in this selection. How does he classify types of tastes? What major

categories of causes for taste aversions and preferences does he discuss?

4.   Explain the use of cause and effect in paragraphs 13 to 16, paragraphs 17 to 21, and paragraphs 26 to 27. Does each cause have a single effect, or are there chains of inter-related causes?

5.   What specific authorities does Rensberger cite? Why does he quote those authors? What do they add to the essay? Where does he use statistics?

6.   Where is *process analysis* used in this selection? How can the experiments be understood as process analyses? Describe step by step Dr. Ilene Bernstein's process of testing her hypothesis (a *hypothesis* is a tentative assumption made in order to draw out and test its consequences) that cancer patients might be victims of bait-shy response.

7.   Compare your description of process in answer to question 6 with your explanation of the use of cause and effect in answer to question 4. How do process analysis and cause-and-effect analysis reinforce each other in this essay?

8.   What are the tone and purpose of the conclusion to this selection?

9.   What major audience would you say Rensberger is attempting to reach: scientists, administrators of food companies or restaurants, junior high school students, a general educated public? How can you tell?

EXPLORING THE WRITER'S IDEAS

1.   What foods can you think of that are considered tasty by one culture and inedible by another? Why do you think there is such a difference in food preferences among various cultures?

2.   Do you believe our tastes in food are more a result of our genetic makeup or of our cultural conditioning? Explain your opinion.

3.   In an introductory college psychology textbook or some other source, look up the terms *Pavlovian conditioning* and *operant conditioning*. What do they mean? How could conditioning be used to change people's tastes for

foods? In what ways are we conditioned by advertisements to prefer certain products over others? Analyze the process by which your tastes have been conditioned to like a certain product.

4. In paragraph 6, Rensberger says that some nutritionists believe people develop an addiction to sugar. Along with parents and consumer groups they point to the great amounts of sugar found in such foods as breakfast cereals, baby foods, soft drinks, and even in such unlikely items as cold cuts, frozen vegetables, and dairy products.

Check the ingredients of some of the foods you eat most often. Do you find sugar among the list of ingredients? (Ingredients are listed in order of the amounts found in the product, with the most prevalent ingredient listed first and the rest in descending order.) How often and at what point on the list of ingredients does sugar appear? What comment can you make about your own sugar consumption? Do you feel that Americans are a nation of "sugar junkies"? Explain.

5. Compare Rensberger's use of the term *addiction* with the ways Adam Smith (see pages 204–208) uses it in his essay on drugs.

IDEAS FOR WRITING

Guided Writing

Write an essay in which you explain why you hate or love a particular food. Select a specific food like spinach, olives, or mayonnaise. Or choose a group of foods like vegetables, cold cuts, or cereals.

1. Use classification to categorize the main reasons why you hate or love this food.

2. Develop each reason through examples of your positive or negative reactions to that food. Discuss the causes for each of these reactions and relate them to the larger category, which includes those reasons.

3. Devise a possible simple method of experimentation by which your readers could test their aversions or

preferences for this food. Describe the experiment carefully, step by step.

    4.   Explain how you first developed a like or dislike for this food.

    5.   Indicate through specific examples or incidents how each of the following factors influenced your taste or distaste for the type of food: cultural preferences, family tastes, color, smell, looks, texture, experience.

More Writing Projects

    1.   Devise an experiment in which you test people's food aversions or preferences. Begin with a specific hypothesis and try to make the experiment simple enough to try in class. Then write an essay in which you analyze the results for cause and effect.

    2.   Through cause-and-effect analysis, write an essay explaining why you prefer certain types of people as friends and why you avoid other types.

Linda Bird Francke

THE AMBIVALENCE OF ABORTION

In this autobiographical narrative, author Linda Bird Francke tells about her mixed feelings toward the issue of abortion. Although she has strong political convictions on the subject, her ambivalence surfaces when she must confront abortion personally. Notice how she blends descriptive details with personal insights to explain the reasons for her uncertainty.

Words to Watch

dwell (par. 1): keep attention directed on something
heralded (par. 1): announced in a joyous manner
rationalize (par. 2): to justify one's behavior (especially to oneself)
freelance (par. 3): working without long-range contractual agreements
cycled (par. 5): moved through a complete series of operations or steps
common denominator (par. 10): similar traits or themes
rhetoric (par. 13): ways of speaking or writing effectively
fetus (par. 13): an unborn child still in the mother's womb
neurotic (par. 14): emotionally unstable
vaccinated (par. 14): injected with a harmless virus to produce immunity to a disease
inoculated (par. 14): treated with a serum or antibody to prevent disease
uterus (par. 16): the womb; the place within the mother where the fetus develops
sensation (par. 18): feeling
Novocain (par. 18): a drug used to numb the feeling of pain
quivered (par. 18): shook

We were sitting in a bar on Lexington Avenue when 1
I told my husband I was pregnant. It is not a memory I like
to dwell on. Instead of the champagne and hope which had
heralded the impending births of the first, second and third
child, the news of this one was greeted with shocked silence
and Scotch. "Jesus," my husband kept saying to himself,
stirring the ice cubes around and around. "Oh, Jesus."

Oh, how we tried to rationalize it that night as the 2
starting time for the movie came and went. My husband
talked about his plans for a career change in the next year,
to stem the staleness that fourteen years with the same investment-banking firm had brought him. A new baby would
preclude that option.

The timing wasn't right for me either. Having jug- 3
gled pregnancies and child care with what freelance jobs
I could fit in between feedings, I had just taken on a full-time
job. A new baby would put me right back in the nursery just
when our youngest child was finally school age. It was time
for *us,* we tried to rationalize. There just wasn't room in our
lives now for another baby. We both agreed. And agreed.
And agreed.

How very considerate they are at the Women's Ser- 4
vices, known formally as the Center for Reproductive and
Sexual Health. Yes, indeed, I could have an abortion that
very Saturday morning and be out in time to drive to the
country that afternoon. Bring a first morning urine speci-
men, a sanitary belt and napkins, a money order or $125
cash—and a friend.

My friend turned out to be my husband, standing 5
awkwardly and ill at ease as men always do in places that
are exclusively for women, as I checked in at nine A.M. Other
men hovered around just as anxiously, knowing they had to
be there, wishing they weren't. No one spoke to each other.
When I would be cycled out of there four hours later, the
same men would be slumped in their same seats, locked
downcast in their cells of embarrassment.

The Saturday morning women's group was more dis- 6
spirited than the men in the waiting room. There were
around fifteen of us, a mixture of races, ages and back-

grounds. Three didn't speak English at all and a fourth, a pregnant Puerto Rican girl around eighteen, translated for them.

There were six black women and a hodgepodge of 7 whites, among them a T-shirted teenager who kept leaving the room to throw up and a puzzled middle-aged woman from Queens with three grown children.

"What form of birth control were you using?" the 8 volunteer asked each one of us. The answer was inevitably "none." She then went on to describe the various forms of birth control available at the clinic, and offered them to each of us.

The youngest Puerto Rican girl was asked through 9 the interpreter which she'd like to use: the loop, diaphragm, or pill. She shook her head "no" three times. "You don't want to come back here again, do you?" the volunteer pressed. The girl's head was so low her chin rested on her breastbone. "*Sí*," she whispered.

We had been there two hours by that time, filling 10 out endless forms, giving blood and urine, receiving lectures. But unlike any other group of women I've been in, we didn't talk. Our common denominator, the one which usually floods across language and economic barriers into familiarity, today was one of shame. We were losing life that day, not giving it.

The group kept getting cut back to smaller, more 11 workable units, and finally I was put in a small waiting room with just two other women. We changed into paper bathrobes and paper slippers, and we rustled whenever we moved. One of the women in my room was shivering and an aide brought her a blanket.

"What's the matter?" the aide asked her. "I'm 12 scared," the woman said. "How much will it hurt?" The aide smiled. "Oh, nothing worse than a couple of bad cramps," she said. "This afternoon you'll be dancing a jig."

I began to panic. Suddenly the rhetoric, the abortion 13 marches I'd walked in, the telegrams sent to Albany to counteract the Friends of the Fetus, the Zero Population Growth buttons I'd worn, peeled away, and I was all alone with my microscopic baby. There were just the two of us there, and soon, because it was more convenient for me and my husband, there would be one again.

How could it be that I, who am so neurotic about life 14 that I step over bugs rather than on them, who spend hours planting flowers and vegetables in the spring even though we rent out the house and never see them, who make sure the children are vaccinated and inoculated and filled with vitamin C, could so arbitrarily decide that this life shouldn't be?

"It's not a life," my husband had argued, more to 15 convince himself than me. "It's a bunch of cells smaller than my fingernail."

But any woman who has had children knows that 16 certain feeling in her taut, swollen breasts, and the slight but constant ache in her uterus that signals the arrival of a life. Though I would march myself into blisters for a woman's right to exercise the option of motherhood, I discovered there in the waiting room that I was not the modern woman I thought I was.

When my name was called, my body felt so heavy the 17 nurse had to help me into the examining room. I waited for my husband to burst through the door and yell "stop," but of course he didn't. I concentrated on three black spots in the acoustic ceiling until they grew in size to the shape of saucers, while the doctor swabbed my insides with antiseptic. 18

"You're going to feel a burning sensation now," he said, injecting Novocain into the neck of the womb. The pain was swift and severe, and I twisted to get away from him. He was hurting my baby, I reasoned, and the black saucers quivered in the air. "Stop," I cried. "Please stop." He shook his head, busy with his equipment. "It's too late to stop now," he said. "It'll just take a few more seconds."

What good sports we women are. And how obedient. 19 Physically the pain passed even before the hum of the machine signaled that the vacuuming of my uterus was completed, my baby sucked up like ashes after a cocktail party. Ten minutes start to finish. And I was back on the arm of the nurse.

There were twelve beds in the recovery room. Each 20
one had a gaily flowered draw sheet and a soft green or blue
thermal blanket. It was all very feminine. Lying on these
beds for an hour or more were the shocked victims of their
sex, their full wombs now stripped clean, their futures less
encumbered.

It was very quiet in that room. The only voice was 21
that of the nurse, locating the new women who had just
come in so she could monitor their blood pressure, and checking out the recovered women who were free to leave.

Juice was being passed about, and I found myself 22
sipping a Dixie cup of Hawaiian Punch. An older woman
with tightly curled bleached hair was just getting up from
the next bed. "That was no goddamn snap," she said, resting
before putting on her miniskirt and high white boots. Other
women came and went, some walking out as dazed as they
had entered, others with a bounce that signaled they were
going right back to Bloomingdale's.

Finally then, it was time for me to leave. I checked 23
out, making an appointment to return in two weeks for an
IUD insertion. My husband was slumped in the waiting
room, clutching a single yellow rose wrapped in a wet paper
towel and stuffed into a Baggie.

We didn't talk the whole way home, but just held 24
hands very tightly. At home there were more yellow roses
and a tray in bed for me and the children's curiosity to
divert.

It had certainly been a successful operation. I didn't 25
bleed at all for two days just as they had predicted, and then
I bled only moderately for another four days. Within a week
my breasts had subsided and the tenderness vanished, and
my body felt mine again instead of the eggshell it becomes
when it's protecting someone else.

My husband and I are back to planning our summer 26
vacation and his career switch.

And it certainly does make more sense not to be 27
having a baby right now—we say that to each other all the
time. But I have this ghost now. A very little ghost that only
appears when I'm seeing something beautiful, like the full

moon on the ocean last weekend. And the baby waves at me. And I wave at the baby. "Of course, we have room," I cry to the ghost. "Of course, we do."

BUILDING VOCABULARY

1.   Develop definitions of your own for the italicized words by relying on context clues, that is, clues from surrounding words and sentences. Then check your definition against a dictionary definition.

a.   "My husband talked about his plans for a career change in the next year, *to stem* the staleness that fourteen years with the same investment-banking firm had brought him. A new baby would *preclude* that *option*." (par. 2)

b.   "Though I would march myself into blisters for a woman's right to *exercise* the *option* of motherhood, I discovered there in the waiting room that I was not the modern woman I thought I was." (par. 16)

c.   "The pain was *swift* and *severe,* and I twisted to get away from him." (par. 18)

d.   "Lying on these beds for an hour or more were the shocked victims of their sex, their full wombs now stripped clean, their futures less *encumbered*." (par. 20)

e.   "It had certainly been a successful operation. I didn't bleed at all for two days just as they had predicted, and then I bled only *moderately* for another four days." (par. 25)

2.   For each italicized word in Column A, write the correct *synonym* (a word of similar meaning) from Column B. Look up unfamiliar words in a dictionary.

Column A	Column B
a. *impending* birth (par. 1)	1. decreased
b. *hovered* around (par. 5)	2. complying
c. looked *downcast* (par. 5)	3. confused
d. more *dispirited* (par. 6)	4. lingered
e. *puzzled* middle-aged woman (par. 7)	5. about to happen
f. *inevitably* "none" (par. 8)	6. tight
g. *taut* swollen breasts (par. 16)	7. distract

h. how *obedient* (par. 19)
i. curiosity to *divert* (par. 24)
j. had *subsided* (par. 25)

8. dejected
9. unavoidable
10. discouraged

UNDERSTANDING THE WRITER'S IDEAS

1. What is the setting in which Francke breaks the news to her husband that she is pregnant? How does he receive the news?

2. What reasons does the husband give for not wanting another child? Why does Francke feel it is a bad time for herself as well?

3. What is the attitude of the men waiting at the abortion clinic? Explain.

4. Why is there a women's group meeting before Francke actually gets her abortion? Are all the women pretty much alike at this meeting? How so? What is Francke's attitude toward these other women? Give specific examples to support your answer.

5. What common reason do all the women in the group share for being pregnant?

6. In the past, what was the author's viewpoint concerning women's rights to have abortions? What specific examples does she give to illustrate this point of view? Do you assume that she still holds this opinion? Why?

7. What examples does Francke give to illustrate that she supports life? Are they convincing?

8. Explain what the author means by the statement "Though I would march myself into blisters for a woman's right to exercise the option of motherhood, I discovered there in the waiting room that I was not the modern woman I thought I was." (par. 16)

9. When she is in the examining room, what does the author do to deal with her anxieties about the abortion?

10. Explain what the woman means when she says to Francke, " 'That was no goddamn snap.' "

11. How does Francke know the operation has been successful?

UNDERSTANDING THE WRITER'S TECHNIQUES

1. What rhetorical strategy does the word "ambivalence" in the title suggest? How does Francke use that strategy in the very first paragraph? Where does she use it elsewhere in the essay?

2. Does Francke successfully explain the ambivalence named in the title? Why or why not?

3. Which does this analysis concentrate on more—causes, effects, or a combination of the two? What evidence can you offer to support your answer? What specifically is the relationship between cause and effect in paragraphs 6 to 10? Analyze the pattern of cause and effect in paragraphs 19 to 22.

4. What is the use of narration in this essay? What is the narrative *point of view* (see Glossary) in this selection? How is it used to enhance the essay?

5. What would you say is the overall tone of the selection? The author uses repetition in this essay to help set that tone. How does the repetition in "We both agreed. And agreed. And agreed." (par. 3) contribute to it?

6. *Paradox* is a special variety of irony (see Glossary) in which there is a clear contradiction in a situation. A paradox is a statement or attitude which, on the surface, seems unlikely, and yet, on analysis, can indeed be true. For example, it is paradoxical that the author should have such ambivalent feelings about abortion while she is sitting in an abortion clinic. Why is that situation considered paradoxical? What other paradoxes do you find in this essay?

7. What is the function of description in this essay? Select passages in which you feel the descriptions are especially vivid. How is description used by the author to characterize the women mentioned in paragraph 22? Are the women stereotyped in this description? Explain.

8. Only toward the last part of the essay does Francke use any metaphors or similes—some of them quite startling. Identify the metaphors or similes in paragraph 19, paragraph 25, and paragraph 27. Why do you think she saved this figurative language for the end?

9. Analyze the last paragraph. What causes and effects discussed throughout the essay are echoed here? What new ones are suggested? Compare the effect of the statement " 'Of course, we have room' " to the statement in paragraph 3, "There just wasn't room. . . ." How does this repetition affect the conclusion?

10. Writers who write about highly charged emotional issues must take special care to avoid *sentimentality*—the excessive display of emotion (see Glossary). Has Francke been successful in avoiding it everywhere in the essay? How has she used concrete descriptions to avoid being sentimental? Does the conclusion strike you as being excessively emotional or does it strike you simply as a dramatic but effective closing? Explain your responses.

EXPLORING THE WRITER'S IDEAS

1. When this article was originally published in 1976, it appeared under the *pseudonym* (a fictitious name) "Jane Doe." What reason might Linda Francke have had for not using her real name? Why do you think that a few years later she admitted to the authorship of the article? In general, what do you think about a writer publishing his or her work under an assumed name? Explain. What historical examples can you offer for the use of pseudonyms?

2. Francke describes some very intimate personal emotions and experiences in her attempt to explain what causes her ambivalence toward abortion. On the basis of the material presented, do you think she is justified in feeling ambivalent? Do you feel she should have been more definite one way or the other? Why?

3. In her description of the Saturday morning women's group (pars. 6 to 10), Francke shows that the women present were of all types—"a mixture of races, ages, and backgrounds." This suggests, of course, that abortion is a subject affecting all women. Does it, in fact, affect all women equally? Explain your answer.

4. In paragraph 5, the author describes her husband as "standing awkwardly and ill at ease as men always do in

places that are exclusively for women." What sorts of places are exclusively for persons of one sex? Discuss how you felt and acted if you were ever in a place which was really more for persons of the opposite sex.

5. Much controversy about abortion revolves around modern definitions of life and death. Some people argue that life begins at conception; others argue that life begins at birth. With which group do you agree? Why? How has modern science complicated our concepts of life and death?

6. Abortion and antiabortion forces have increased their attacks against each other dramatically in recent years. How does Francke's essay crystallize both sides of the complex, emotionally charged issue?

IDEAS FOR WRITING

Guided Writing

Select an important issue facing society, an issue with which you have had personal experience and about which you have mixed feelings. After you fill in the blank, write an essay titled "Two Sides of _____." In your essay explore the reasons for your ambivalence. You can select from a wide range of social, moral, health, or education topics. For example, you might want to consider ambivalence toward interracial dating or marriages, a compulsory draft, legalization of drugs, cigarette smoking, a liberal arts education—but feel free to select any issue which is especially important to you.

1. Write the essay as a first-person narrative. Begin with an incident when you first clearly realized the ambivalent nature of the issue, and explain why or how this particular incident focused your attention on the subject.

2. Tell about how and for what reasons you came to a decision to take a certain action despite your mixed feelings. What rationalizations did you or others use to help you feel you were doing the right thing?

3. Narrate in detail the sequence of events that followed your decision. Make the narrative come to life with concrete sensory detail. As you tell your story, analyze the various causes and effects of your decision and actions.

4. Discuss how the same event you experienced affects others. Explain how the causes and effects of the action are different or similar for you and for others.

5. Explain how you felt immediately before, during, and after the crucial experience.

6. In your conclusion, express your deepest feelings about the consequences of your decision and experiences. Use similes, metaphors, and an echo of your original attempts to rationalize your ambivalence.

More Writing Projects

1. Write an essay in which you analyze the reasons for your own attitudes toward abortion.

2. Write an essay in which you explain the causes and/or effects of a political standpoint you feel very strongly about.

3. In an essay of analysis, propose the effects on children if elementary schools throughout the country offered compulsory sex education programs.

4. In 1968, Black Panther party leader Eldridge Cleaver ended a speech with the statement, "If you're not part of the solution, you're part of the problem." Analyze what you think Cleaver meant by that statement.

Susan Jacoby

WHEN BRIGHT GIRLS DECIDE THAT MATH IS "A WASTE OF TIME"

In this article, Susan Jacoby explains how cultural expectations and societal stereotyping are overshadowed by women's own decisions to keep themselves away from scientific and technological studies. Notice how she uses narrative and process analysis to reinforce the causes and effects she is exploring here.

Words to Watch

sanguine (par. 3): cheerful, hopeful
vulnerable (par. 6): open to attack or suggestion
syndrome (par. 7): a group of symptoms that characterize a condition
akin to (par. 7): similar to
phobia (par. 7): a group of symptoms that characterize a condition
akin to (par. 7): similar to
phobia (par. 7): an excessive fear of something
constitute (par. 7): to make up; compose
epitomize (par. 8): to be a prime example of
prone (par. 15): disposed to; susceptible
accede to (par. 16): give in to

Susannah, a 16-year-old who has always been an 1
A student in every subject from algebra to English, recently

informed her parents that she intended to drop physics and calculus in her senior year of high school and replace them with a drama seminar and a work-study program. She expects a major in art or history in college, she explained, and "any more science or math will just be a waste of my time."

Her parents were neither concerned by nor opposed 2 to her decision. "Fine, dear," they said. Their daughter is, after all, an outstanding student. What does it matter if, at age 16, she has taken a step that may limit her understanding of both machines and the natural world for the rest of her life?

This kind of decision, in which girls turn away from 3 studies that would given them a sure footing in the world of science and technology, is a self-inflicted female disability that is, regrettably, almost as common today as it was when I was in high school. If Susannah had announced that she had decided to stop taking English in her senior year, her mother and father would have been horrified. I also think they would have been a good deal less sanguine about her decision if she were a boy.

In saying that scientific and mathematical ignorance 4 is a self-inflicted female wound, I do not, obviously, mean that cultural expectations play no role in the process. But the world does not conspire to deprive modern women of access to science as it did in the 1930's, when Rosalyn S. Yalow, the Nobel Prize-winning physicist, graduated from Hunter College and was advised to go to work as a secretary because no graduate school would admit her to its physics department. The current generation of adolescent girls— and their parents, bred on old expectations about women's interests—are active conspirators in limiting their own intellectual development.

It is true that the proportion of young women in 5 science-related graduate and professional schools, most notably medical schools, has increased significantly in the past decade. It is also true that so few women were studying advanced science and mathematics before the early 1970's that the percentage increase in female enrollment does not yet translate into large numbers of women actually working in science.

The real problem is that so many girls eliminate 6 themselves from any serious possibility of studying science as a result of decisions made during the vulnerable period of midadolescence, when they are most likely to be influenced—on both conscious and subconscious levels—by the traditional belief that math and science are "masculine" subjects.

During the teen-age years the well-documented phenomenon of "math anxiety" strikes girls who never had any problem handling numbers during earlier schooling. Some men, too, experience this syndrome—a form of panic, akin to a phobia, at any task involving numbers—but women constitute the overwhelming majority of sufferers. The onset of acute math anxiety during the teen-age years is, as Stalin was fond of saying, "not by accident."

In adolescence girls begin to fear that they will be 8 unattractive to boys if they are typed as "brains." Science and math epitomize unfeminine braininess in a way that, say, foreign languages do not. High-school girls who pursue an advanced interest in science and math (unless they are students at special institutions like the Bronx High School of Science where everyone is a brain) usually find that they are greatly outnumbered by boys in their classes. They are, therefore, introduing on male turf at a time when their sexual confidence, as well as that of the boys, is most fragile.

A 1981 assessment of female achievement in math- 9 ematics, based on research conducted under a National Institute for Education grant, found significant differences in the mathematical achievements of 9th and 12th graders. At age 13 girls were equal to or slightly better than boys in tests involving algebra, problem solving and spatial ability; four years later the boys had outstripped the girls.

It is not mysterious that some very bright high- 10 school girls suddenly decide that math is "too hard" and "a waste of time." In my experience, self-sabotage of mathematical and scientific ability is often a conscious process. I remember deliberately pretending to be puzzled by geometry problems in my sophomore year in high school. A male teacher called me in after class and said, in a baffled tone, "I don't see how you can be having so much trouble when you got straight A's last year in my algebra class."

The decision to avoid advanced biology, chemistry, 11 physics and calculus in high school automatically restricts academic and professional choices that ought to be wide open to anyone beginning college. At all coeducational universities women are overwhelmingly concentrated in the fine arts, social sciences and traditionally female departments like education. Courses leading to degrees in science- and technology-related fields are filled mainly by men.

In my generation, the practical consequences of 12 mathematical and scientific illiteracy are visible in the large number of special programs to help professional women overcome the anxiety they feel when they are promoted into jobs that require them to handle statistics.

The consequences of this syndrome should not, how- 13 ever, be viewed in narrowly professional terms. Competence in science and math does not mean one is going to become a scientist or mathematician any more than competence in writing English means one is going to become a professional writer. Scientific and mathematical illiteracy—which has been cited in several recent critiques by panels studying American education from kindergarten through college— produces an incalculably impoverished vision of human experience.

Scientific illiteracy is not, of course, the exclusive 14 province of women. In certain intellectual circles it has become fashionable to proclaim a willed, aggressive ignorance about science and technology. Some female writers specialize in ominous, uninformed diatribes against genetic research as a plot to remove control of childbearing from women, while some well-known men of letters proudly announce that they understand absolutely nothing about computers, or, for that matter, about electricity. This lack of understanding is nothing in which women or men ought to take pride.

Failure to comprehend either computers or chro- 15

mosomes leads to a terrible sense of helplessness, because the profound impact of science on everyday life is evident even to those who insist they don't, won't, can't understand why the changes are taking place. At this stage of history women are more prone to such feelings of helplessness than men because the culture judges their ignorance less harshly and because women themselves acquiesce in that indulgence.

Since there is ample evidence of such feelings in adolescence, it is up to parents to see that their daughters do not accede to the old stereotypes about "masculine" and "feminine" knowledge. Unless we want our daughters to share our intellectual handicaps, we had better tell them no, they can't stop taking mathematics and science at the ripe old age of 16.

BUILDING VOCABULARY

1. Like Anne Roiphe (pages 291–296), Susan Jacoby uses a number of common expressions, but these are at a higher level of *diction* (the writer's choice of words depending on audience and purpose). Below are some of these expressions, which may contain words that are unfamiliar to you. First, look up any unfamiliar words in your dictionary. Then, write a short explanation of each expression as Jacoby uses it.

  a. sure footing (par. 3)
  b. cultural expectations (par. 4)
  c. overwhelming majority (par. 7)
  d. male turf (par. 8)
  e. spatial ability (par. 9).
  f. the exclusive province (par. 14)
  g. ominous, uninformed diatribes (par. 14)
  h. acquiesce in that indulgence (par. 15)
  i. ample evidence (par. 16)
  j. our intellectual handicaps (par. 16)

2. Explain the connotations (see Glossary) that the following words have for you: "disability" (par. 3), "conspire" (par. 4), adolescent (par. 4), "vulnerable" (par. 6), "acute"

(par. 8). Use each of these words correctly in sentences of your own.

UNDERSTANDING THE WRITER'S IDEAS

1. What condition is Jacoby trying to analyze? Is the main *effect* analyzed in this cause-and-effect analysis? On what primary cause does she blame women's "scientific and mathematical ignorance"? What exactly does she mean by that term? How is society to blame? What is the "process" mentioned in paragraph 4? What point does the example of Rosalyn S. Yalow illustrate?

2. Why does Jacoby think that the greater proportion of women students now in science and medical graduate and professional schools does not really mean that there are many women working in these areas?

3. According to Jacoby, when do most girls decide not to study the sciences? Why does this happen?

4. What is "math anxiety"? Who suffers more from it—boys or girls? Why? What does the author mean by "brains" (par. 8)?

5. Who was Joseph Stalin (par. 7)?

6. What subjects does Jacoby identify as "feminine"? Which are "unfeminine"?

7. According to the research evidence discussed in paragraph 9, how do the math abilities of girls and boys change between ninth and tenth grades? What does Jacoby say is the *cause* for this change? What are the *results*?

8. Explain what Jacoby means by the expression "self-inflicted female wound" (par. 4) and "self-sabotage" (par. 10). How are these expressions similar? How are they different?

9. What is the difference between what men and women study at coeducational universities?

10. What does Jacoby mean by "mathematical and scientific illiteracy" (par. 12)? Do only women suffer from this syndrome? According to Jacoby, why does it lead to "an incalculably impoverished vision of human experience"? What does she mean by this phrase? What examples of scientific illiteracy does Jacoby offer?

11. Why does the author think women feel more helpless than men do about scientific changes?

12. What suggestion does Jacoby offer in her conclusion?

UNDERSTANDING THE WRITER'S TECHNIQUES

1. Which paragraphs make up the introductory section of this essay? What cause-and-effect relation does Jacoby establish and how does she present it? How does Jacoby use narration in her introduction? How does she use illustration?

2. What is the thesis statement of this essay? Why is it placed where it is? Find another statement before it that expresses a similar cause-and-effect relation. How are the two different?

3. Both sentences of paragraph 5 begin with the phrase "It is true," yet the sentences contradict each other. How and why does the author set up this contradiction? What is the effect on Jacoby's analysis of beginning paragraph 6 with the words "the real problem is . . ."?

4. How does she use *process analysis* (see pages 256–257) from paragraph 6 to paragraph 8?

5. Where does the author use definition in this essay?

6. Trace the cause-and-effect developments in paragraphs 7 and 8.

7. In paragraph 9, Jacoby mentions a study conducted under "a National Institute for Education grant." How does the evidence she presents support her position in the essay?

8. What is the effect of the phrase "in my experience" in paragraph 10? What expository technique does she use there?

9. Trace the cause-and-effect patterns in paragraphs 11 through 13. Be sure to show the interrelationship between the causes and the effects (that is, how can the effect of something also be the cause of something else?).

10. How is the first sentence of paragraph 15 ("Failure to comprehend . . .") a good example in itself of cause-and-effect development?

11. Why does Jacoby use quotation marks around the words "masculine" and "feminine" in the phrase " 'masculine' and 'feminine' knowledge" (par. 16)?

12. What is the overall tone of this essay? At three points, Jacoby switches tone and uses irony (see Glossary). Explain the irony in the following sentences:

a. "What does it matter if, at age 16, she had taken a step that may limit her understanding of both machines and the natural world for the rest of her life?" (par. 2)

b. "The onset of acute math anxiety during the teenage years is, as Stalin was fond of saying, 'not by accident'." (par. 7)

c. "Unless we want our daughters to share our intellectual handicaps, we had better tell them no, they can't stop taking mathematics and science at the ripe old age of 16." (par. 16)

Compare the irony in paragraph 16 with that in paragraph 2. How is the impact the same or different?

13. Who do you think is the intended *audience* for this essay? Cite evidence for your answer.

14. Jacoby uses a variety of transitional devices to connect smoothly the ideas expressed in the various paragraphs of this essay. Look especially at paragraphs 1 to 4. How does the writer achieve coherence between paragraphs? What transitional elements do you find in the opening sentences of each of those paragraphs? What other transitions do you find throughout the essay?

EXPLORING THE WRITER'S IDEAS

1. One of the underlying suggestions in this essay is that the society has long considered there to be "masculine" and "feminine" subjects to study. What is your opinion on this issue? Do you feel that any subjects are particularly more suited to men or women? Which? Why? Are there any other school activities that you feel are exclusively masculine or feminine? Why? Are there any jobs that are more suited to men or women?

2. In paragraph 4, Jacoby mentions the "old expectations about women's interests." What do you think these expectations are? What do you consider *new* expectations for women?

3. A *stereotype* is an opinion of a category of people that is unoriginal and often based in strong prejudices. For example, some prejudicial stereotypes include "All immigrants are lazy"; "All Republicans are rich"; "All women are terrible drivers." What other stereotypes do you know? Where do you think they originate?

4. Read the essay by Richard Restak on pages 382–386. How do Restak's ideas compare with Jacoby's? Do you agree more with either one? Why?

5. The general implication of paragraph 8 is that people minimize their skills in order to be socially acceptable. In your experience, where have you seen this principle operating? Do people sometimes pretend to be unable to achieve something? What motivates them, do you think?

6. A recent study shows that among major nations in the world America's students—boys and girls—are the worst mathematics students. How do you account for the poor showing of Americans as mathematicians? How would you remedy this situation?

IDEAS FOR WRITING

Guided Writing

Select a job or profession that is usually male-dominated. Write a cause-and-effect analysis explaining how and why women both have been excluded from this profession *and* (or) have self-selected themselves from the job. (Some examples may include firefighters, physicians, marines, bank executives, carpenters, and so on.)

1. Begin with an anecdote to illustrate the condition that you are analyzing.

2. Present and analyze the partial causes of this condition that arise from society's expectations and norms.

3. State your main point clearly in a thesis statement.

4. Clearly identify what you consider "the real problem."

5. If you believe that women have deliberately excluded themselves, explain when and how the process of self-selection begins for women.

6. Analyze the consequences of this process of self-selection and give examples of the results of it.

7. Provide evidence that supports your analysis.

8. Link paragraphs with appropriate transitions.

9. In your conclusion offer a suggestion to change or improve this situation.

More Writing Projects

1. Margaret Mead, the famous anthropologist, once wrote, "Women in our society complain of the lack of stimulation, of the loneliness, of the dullness of staying at home." Write a causal analysis of this situation.

2. Write an analysis of why boys and men exclude themselves from a certain field of profession—nursing, cooking, grammar-school teaching, and so on.

10

Argumentation and Persuasion

Argumentation in prose is an attempt to convince the reader to have the opinion *you* have on a subject; frequently, it also involves an effort to persuade the reader to act in a particular manner. In many ways, argumentation is a good end point for a course in writing. In a formal argument, you can use, according to your purpose, all the prose strategies and principles of sound composition practiced until now.

You can see how important it is to state your thesis very clearly in argumentation, and to support your main point with convincing minor points. You have to make these points according to reason, and you need to arrange them so they have the greatest effect on your reader. Moreover, as in any prose, writers of argument must offer the reader particulars of details, whether sensory, quoted, statistical, or based upon historical evidence. Finally, techniques of comparison, process analysis, description, narration, cause and effect, definition, all can help strengthen an argument.

Although argumentation reflects all these earlier prose techniques, it is important for you to understand the special characteristics of this method. To begin with, although argumentation as a written form is often emotional, it differs sharply from those little battles and those major disagreements with friends over coffee or in hallways outside class. Perhaps that last shouting match between you and your friend about who would win the World Series is, no doubt, one that you would call an argument: There is a disagreement there for which each of you tries to make your own point of view stick. Yet often these argumentative conversations deteriorate into loss of temper, angry personal comments about your friend's judgment or character, departures from the argument itself, and inability to reason.

In written arguments, writers always should keep clearly in mind the point they wish to make, and should not lose sight of it. They may try to convince readers that some issue requires action ("Colleges and businesses should follow special admissions procedures for minority applicants"). Or, they may try to convince readers that something is true ("wives are taken for granted"). Whatever the point, writers always offer their reasons for their beliefs in a logical way, without losing command of their subject and without attacking anyone personally; they may, though, attack someone's ideas or attitudes.

The main point in an argument—often termed the *major proposition*—is an idea which is debatable or can be disputed. As such it differs from theses in ordinary essays, which state main ideas without necessarily taking sides. The major proposition gives an essay its "argumentative edge." Frequently this argumentative edge appears in the very title of the essay, and it should form the basis of a crisp introductory paragraph laying out the terms of the position that you plan to take.

Once you state clearly and carefully your major proposition at the outset of the essay, you must then proceed to *convince* readers about the position that you have taken. There are basic strategies to succeed in this goal, beginning with the ordered presentation of reasons to defend the major proposition. We term these reasons *minor propositions*—in other words, assertions designed to support your main argument. To support each minor proposition, the writer must offer *evidence* in the form of facts, statistics, testimony from authorities, and personal experience. Here, a variety of writing methods, ranging from comparison and contrast to definition to causal analysis, can serve to develop minor propositions effectively.

In addition to presenting your own argument logically and convincingly, you must also recognize and deal with opposing arguments, a technique called *refutation*. Obviously, there has to be more than one side to any debatable issue, and you have to take this fact into account. For one thing, acknowledgment of the opposition indicates fairness on your part—a willingness to recognize that there *are* two sides to the argument. More significantly, your refutation of rival propositions, both major and minor, makes your own case more convincing. Whether at the outset of your argumentative essay or in the body as you are developing your own minor propositions, you should take care to indicate opposing views and to refute them effectively.

An argumentative essay ultimately is only as strong as the logic that a writer brings to it. Such logical errors as hasty generalizations (main ideas unsupported by sufficient evidence), attacks on the opposition's character, faulty conclusions that do not follow from the facts, faulty analogies, and excessive appeals to emotion damage your argument. In short, any convincing argument requires clear, orderly thinking. By learning how to present ideas logically through the preparation of convincing argumentative essays, you will strengthen your overall reasoning ability. You will also learn how to deal with those arguments, many of which are important, that occur in your daily life.

Howard Scott

VEGETABLE GARDENS ARE FOR THE BIRDS

Howard Scott lets us know in no uncertain terms why he would prefer buying his salad fixings in the supermarket to growing them outside his door. Notice, though, that he seems particularly well-versed in the language, equipment, and procedures of vegetable gardening, and that this knowledge adds credence to his light-hearted argument.

Words to Watch

heresy (par. 1):   an opinion contrary to generally accepted beliefs
optimum (par. 3):   the most favorable (pertaining to conditions)
paraphernalia (par. 5):   apparatus
gluttony (par. 6):   excessive eating or drinking
famine (par. 6):   an extreme scarcity of food
fanaticism (par. 9):   excessively enthusiastic behavior or support
succulent (par. 11):   juicy; full of vitality
bounty (par. 12):   an abundance of things

At the risk of committing heresy, I want to state 1 my biggest summer gripe: I hate vegetable gardens.

Worse, I scorn gardeners and their mulchy Zen. 2

Even more horrendous, I prefer to eat store-bought veggies instead of newly plucked offerings.

Here are my complaints. Growing plants doesn't 3 take much skill. Every gardener pridefully displays a ripe tomato or a giant cucumber as though she's personally carved it out of the earth. "Look at this," she'll say, expecting your face to look as if it were witnessing the Second Coming. The plain fact is that any halfwit can grow things. All it takes is doing dumb repetitive tasks with the plodding consistency of a workhorse.

A garden takes time. Not only is there readying the 4 soil, planting, watering, weeding, debugging, pruning and harvesting, but also there is the research. A gardener is constantly checking into Crockett's about snails, reading up on herbs at the library and phoning fellow planters to arrive at optimum plant dates. So much so, many of us spouses become earth widows(ers).

A garden costs. First there are the tools. Then the 5 seeds and flats. Next comes the renting of the tiller. After that comes mulch, manure and prep medication. Next, water followed by insect spraying. Then the experiments with new irrigation systems and updated equipment. Finally, jars, labels and canning paraphernalia.

A garden creates waste. At harvest time, 15 heads 6 of lettuce must be picked within two weeks' time or they'll rot. So you eat three salads a day and bring bags full to all your friends (most of whom have their own oversupply problems). Needless to say, buying a head or two at the supermarket each week avoids such cycles of gluttony and famine.

Home-grown vegetables aren't as clean as store- 7 bought produce. You risk chomping on worms or slugs, breaking a tooth on a pebble, grinding into dirt and smelling the manure through which the thing prospered. The cellophane wrapping, the official-looking label and the pale, dry coloring of packaged goods eliminate those possibilities.

Garden vegetables don't taste as mellow as shelved 8 stock. The carrots are too crispy, the peppers too tangy, the scallions too potent, the celery too stringy. I prefer my veggies to blend in like a symphony beneath heaping tablespoons of dressing.

A garden ties its owner down. Taking a week's 9 vacation is impossible because, what if—God forbid—it doesn't rain. Even a long weekend is tough. And anybody who lives with a gardener knows the fanaticism of the daily watering.

A gardener's needs tend to expand. This year it's a 10 10 by 12 foot plot. Next year, it's a 15 by 20 space and a compost bin. The year after, it's the larger plot, an experimental patch out front and a shed. The year after, it's a greenhouse.

Gardens make boring conversations. After the ump- 11 teenth walk to see little buds popping up, you run out of things to say. Then, as the summer progresses, it's, "Oh, isn't this salad fresh," and, "I can't get over how succulent these cantaloupes are." On top of all that, you have to listen to shop talk among gardeners. Early on, you might make discreet jokes, but after seeing that nobody's listening you just stand around bored.

Gardens offer the illusion of accomplishment. Seeds 12 are planted, and two months later a lush bounty of vegetables emerges from the ground. Amazing, says the grower. Amazing, nothing. For years, the Government has been paying farmers billions of dollars for not planting their lands. Warehouses are bursting with excess crops. Face it. The success of this nation is based more on perfect climate and fertile soil than any other condition.

A garden induces contentment. Cultivating the earth 13 makes its owner feel at peace with the world. Fine—but, as with cocaine, medication and booze, it reduces ambition to attempt other challenges. And as inwardly satisfying as the routine might be, there are some things growing vegetables can't solve. But try to tell a gardener that.

BUILDING VOCABULARY

1. *Jargon* refers to the special use of words associated with a particular job or activity (see Glossary). Howard

Scott, self-professed hater of gardening as he may be, seems to know quite a bit of vegetable gardening jargon. In paragraph 4, he refers to a number of *processes* such as readying the soil, weeding, and pruning, and in paragraph 5, he refers to various implements, including tiller, mulch, and manure. Read through the essay once again, and list the words that you feel qualify as vegetable gardening jargon.

2. Identify the following *allusions* (see page 409) in this essay: Zen (par. 2); the Second Coming (par. 3); Crockett's (par. 4).

3. Scott uses a number of *colloquial* words and expressions (see Glossary), including

    a. *chomping* on worms or slugs (par. 7)
    b. don't taste as *mellow* (par. 8)
    c. God forbid (par. 9)
    d. Face it. (par. 12)

Explain the meanings of these and any other colloquialisms you select from Scott's essay.

UNDERSTANDING THE WRITER'S IDEAS

1. What does Scott mean by "committing heresy" in paragraph 1? What is his complaint?

2. Explain the meaning of the term "mulchy Zen." (par. 2)

3. What is Scott's *major proposition*—or main point— in this essay?

4. What does Scott think about the skill required for vegetable gardening success?

5. In a note to this essay, Scott wrote that his wife "has become one of those green-thumb fanatics." What does he mean by this judgment? What is the meaning of the term in paragraph 4, "earth widows(ers)?"

6. What is Scott's opinion of store-bought versus home-grown vegetables? Which does he prefer? Why?

7. What does Scott feel about social interactions with people who garden? Explain.

8. In the conclusion, to what does the author compare gardening? How does he compare their effects?

9. Explain the meaning and purpose of the last sentence.

UNDERSTANDING THE WRITER'S TECHNIQUES

1. List the categories of reasons Scott offers to support his "gripe." How does he order them? Which is most and least important?

2. How does Scott use *minor propositions* in this essay? Identify the minor proposition sentences in paragraphs 4–13. How do these sentences contribute to the *unity* and *clarity* (see Glossary) of the essay?

3. For whom do you think Scott intended this article? How does his use of words such as "heresy" and "fanaticism" help identify his intended audience? What other words or phrases help accomplish this?

4. How does the author use *illustration* in this essay?

5. Comment on the use of *process analysis* in paragraph 5.

6. What is the effect of Scott's continual references to *the* or *a* gardener? What relation does he thus set up between himself and gardeners?

7. What is Scott's *tone* in this essay? Identify at least five examples to illustrate this tone.

8. What is Scott's use of *description* in this article? Which descriptions do you find most effective or sensory?

9. Analyze Scott's use of *transitions* between paragraphs. What is his main transitional technique?

10. Does Scott use any *refutation* in this essay? Explain.

11. Is Scott's primary purpose to convince or to persuade in this argument? Explain.

12. What is your opinion of the conclusion of the essay? Is Scott's comparison of gardening to "cocaine, med-

ication, and booze" a fair one? Does his comparison in any way affect the quality of, or your sympathy towards, his argument? Explain.

EXPLORING THE WRITER'S IDEAS

1. This essay includes an implied comparison between city and country ways. What is it? Compare Scott's view of this comparison with Noel Perrin's in his essay "Country Codes" on pages 236–242. With which are you more comfortable? Why?

2. Scott writes about the gardener's "fanaticism of daily watering." Why would a gardener be fanatic about watering? How does a regularly followed hobby lend itself to fanaticism? Is there anything about which you consider yourself fanatical?

3. How specific are you about what you eat? Do you generally try to eat natural or fresh foods, or are you just as happy with store-bought, prepackaged foods? What do you think of the adage: "You are what you eat"?

IDEAS FOR WRITING

Guided Writing

Write an argumentative essay in which you express your "gripe" against some commonly-respected activity.

1. State your gripe directly and openly in the first sentence.

2. State what you feel would be considered the most heretical admission of your distaste for this activity.

3. Outline your main complaints early in the essay.

4. In the body of your essay, write a paragraph for each main reason for your gripe. Begin each paragraph with a clearly-stated minor proposition.

5. Use repetition of key words as a transitional device between paragraphs.

6. Use colloquial language, exaggerated claims, and appropriate jargon to help set the tone of your essay.

7. Keep the tone fairly light and tongue-in-cheek.

8. Use implied refutation in your essay.

9. Use some sensory description.

10. End your essay with an outlandish comparison.

More Writing Projects

1. Tell why you don't like to do something which may be considered somewhat negative, but which lots of others do—for example, smoking in public places, playing loud radios, talking in theaters, and so on.

2. Persuade your reader why a certain type of food preparation is the best.

3. Argue for or against government subsidies to farmers not to grow crops.

Joseph Wood Krutch

THE VANDAL AND THE SPORTSMAN

Joseph Wood Krutch is a renowned author, scholar, and social commentator. Here he argues forcefully—sometimes even righteously—against sports hunting. He uses language for its fullest impact, telling us of "pure evil," "a fathomless abyss," and "wicked ideas." This essay, from *The Best Nature Writing of Joseph Wood Krutch,* is a model of both logical and emotional appeal in argumentative writing.

Words to Watch

impediment (par. 8): obstacle
vitality (par. 3): the quality distinguishing the living from the dead
wantonly (par. 3): without moral restraint
unassailable (par. 5): unquestionable
compassion (par. 6): deep understanding of others' feelings
quail (par. 7): a stout-bodied game bird
delinquency (par. 7): living immorally
cultivate (par. 7): develop

It would not be quite true to say that "some of my 1
best friends are hunters." Nevertheless, I do number among
my respected acquaintances some who not only kill for the

sake of killing but count it among their keenest pleasures. I can think of no better illustration of the fact that men may be separated at some point by a fathomless abyss yet share elsewhere much common ground.

To me it is inconceivable how anyone should think 2 an animal more interesting dead than alive. I can also easily prove to my own satisfaction that killing "for sport" is the perfect type of that pure evil for which metaphysicians have sometimes sought.

Most wicked deeds are done because the doer pro- 3 poses some good to himself. The liar lies to gain some end; the swindler and thief want things which, if honestly got, might be good in themselves. Even the murderer may be removing an impediment to normal desires or gaining possession of something which his victim keeps from him. None of these usually does evil for evil's sake. They are selfish or unscrupulous, but their deeds are not gratuitously evil. The killer for sport has no such comprehensible motive. He prefers death to life, darkness to light. He gets nothing except the satisfaction of saying, "Something which wanted to live is dead. There is that much less vitality, consciousness, and, perhaps, joy in the universe. I am the Spirit that Denies." When a man wantonly destroys one of the works of man we call him Vandal. When he wantonly destroys one of the works of God we call him Sportsman.

The hunter-for-food may be as wicked and as mis- 4 guided as vegetarians sometimes say; but he does not kill for the sake of killing. The rancher and the farmer who exterminate all living things not immediately profitable to them may sometimes be working against their own best interests; but whether they are or are not, the hope to achieve some supposed good by their exterminations. If to do evil not in the hope of gain but for evil's sake involves the deepest guilt by which man can be stained, then killing for killing's sake is a terrifying phenomenon and as strong a proof as we could have of that "reality of evil" with which present-day theologians are again concerned.

Despite all this I know that sportsmen are not 5 necessarily monsters. Even if the logic of my position is unassailable, the fact still remains that men are not logical creatures; that most if not all are blind to much they might be expected to see and are habitually inconsistent; that both the blind spots and the inconsistencies vary from person to person.

To say as we all do: "Any man who would do A 6 would do B," is to state a proposition mercifully proved false almost as often as it is stated. The murderer is not necessarily a liar any more than the liar is necessarily a murderer, and few men feel that if they break one commandment there is little use in keeping the others. Many have been known to say that they considered adultery worse than homicide but not all adulterers are potential murderers and there are even murderers to whom incontinence would be unthinkable. So the sportsman may exhibit any of the virtues—including compassion and respect for life—everywhere except in connection with his "sporting" activities. It may even be often enough true that, as "antisentimentalists" are fond of pointing out, those tenderest toward animals are not necessarily most philanthropic. They no more than sportsmen are always consistent.

When the Winchester gun company makes a prop- 7 aganda movie concluding with a scene in which a "typical American boy" shoots a number of quail and when it then ends with the slogan "Go hunting with your boy and you'll never have to go hunting for him," I may suspect that the gun company is moved by a desire to sell more guns at least as much as by a determination to do what it can toward reducing the incidence of delinquency. I will certainly add also my belief that there are even better ways of diminishing the likelihood that a boy will grow up to do even worse things. Though it seems to me that he is being taught a pure evil I know that he will not necessarily cultivate a taste for all or, for that matter, any one of the innumerable other forms under which evil may be loved.

BUILDING VOCABULARY

1. Match the words or phrases in Column A with a word or phrase in Column B which most closely matches its meaning.

Column A	Column B
a. keenest (par. 1)	1. immeasurable depths
b. fathomless abyss (par. 1)	2. ideas used to damage an opposing cause
c. pure evil (par. 2)	3. understandable reason
d. gratuitously evil (par. 3)	4. dishonest
e. unscrupulous (par. 3)	5. absolute immorality
f. comprehensible motive (par. 3)	6. lack of self-restraint
g. habitually inconsistent (par. 5)	7. most special
h. incontinence (par. 6)	8. with great generosity
i. philanthropic (par. 6)	9. usually changeable
j. propaganda (par. 7)	10. vicious without cause

2. Both "metaphysicians" (par. 2) and "theologians" (par. 4) deal with questions of virtues (par. 6). Look up each word and write a definition.

3. What are the crimes of "adultery" and "homicide" (par. 6)?

UNDERSTANDING THE WRITER'S IDEAS

1. Does Krutch have many close friends who are hunters? How do you know? What does he think of his acquaintances that do enjoy hunting? Explain the sentence that tells you this information.

2. What is Krutch's opinion of hunting as a sport?

3. According to Krutch, what is the major motivation for which people do bad things? What examples does he offer to support his opinion? What does Krutch say is the primary motivation for sports hunters? How does this motivation differ from that of other "evil doers"?

4. For what does the author substitute the phrase "killer for sport" (par. 3)? Why?

5. Explain the difference between a Vandal and a Sportsman in your own words.

6. How are the hunters-for-food different from sports hunters? How are the ranchers and farmers different?

7. Try to explain the meaning of the sentence at the end of paragraph 4 which begins, "If to do evil. . . ."

8. Explain the statement "men are not logical creatures" (par. 5) as it is used by Krutch in this essay.

9. What excuses does the author offer for sports hunters? Do you feel he believes these excuses? Why? In paragraph 6 what does he say about the ethics of sports hunting?

10. What does the phrase "if they break one commandment" refer to?

11. What is the Winchester gun company? What is Krutch's opinion of the film made by that company?

UNDERSTANDING THE WRITER'S TECHNIQUES

1. In your own words, what is Krutch's *major proposition* in this essay? Does he ever state it as a single thesis statement? Why?

2. How does Krutch use logical explanation and appeals to intelligence in this essay? What is he trying to "prove"?

3. A special type of argumentative strategy is *ethical* appeal, in which the writer addresses the moral standards of his or her audience. What is the nature of Krutch's ethical appeal? How is it presented?

4. Throughout this essay Krutch uses very emotionally charged language to describe or explain things. One of the techniques of argumentation is to use such language subtly to influence your readers' opinions. For example, in paragraph 3, Krutch helps the reader to make unconscious connections between a sports hunter and "wicked deeds," a "liar," a "swindler," a "thief," and a "murderer." How and why does he do this?

Read through the essay once again and find as many other examples of emotionally charged language as you can. How do these emotional or nonlogical appeals affect Krutch's intended audience?

5. One of the techniques the author uses is to put quotation marks (" ") around words or groups of words other than for the purpose of quotation or citation. What does the quotation mark indicate about the enclosed words? Find all

the places Krutch uses this technique and explain the meaning of each word or phrase.

6. Krutch also uses exaggeration to influence his readers. *Hyperbole* is a type of very extravagant exaggeration—heightened exaggeration, so to speak. Explain the hyperbole of the last part of paragraph 3, from "the Killer for sport had . . ." to the end. How does this section influence your opinion? Why?

7. A good argumentative essay will in some way deal with the opposition's argument to show that the writer has at least recognized that differing opinions exist. Usually, however, a writer will rebut (disprove) the opposition argument to enhance the correctness of his or her own opinions. Where in this essay does Krutch present the opposition argument? How does he deal with it? How does he feel about the correctness of his own opinions? What one sentence tells us so?

8. What is the tone of this essay? Give at least three examples to support your answer, at lease one of which should come from the introductory paragraph.

9. What is the purpose of the discussion of the film made by the Winchester gun company? How does it connect to the rest of the essay? How does Krutch use extended example in this discussion?

10. Explain the significance of the title.

EXPLORING THE WRITER'S IDEAS

1. In paragraph 3, Krutch compares sports hunters to liars, thieves, even murderers. Do you think they are comparable? Why?

Krutch also says sports hunters enjoy killing and death. Do you agree or disagree? Why?

2. Krutch makes a distinction between hunters-for-food and sports hunters. What do you think are the differences between the two? Do you feel either is more or less justified in his or her activity? Why?

3. The expression in quotations in the first paragraph ("some of my best friends are hunters") is a parody

of an expression often used by people attempting to hide or defend their prejudices. For example, a person might say, "But some of my best friends are Jewish (or black, or Irish, or Chinese, or . . .)" after making an ethnic slur or offensive remark. What is the purpose of Krutch's parody here? What does it tell us about the author?

4. Are there degrees of humaneness in sports hunting? For example, is it more humane to use a rifle, a shotgun, or a bow and arrow? Why?

If you have ever gone sports hunting, describe how you felt when you pulled the trigger or let the arrow fly. Explain what made you feel this way.

5. Research the sports hunting laws in your state. What are they? Do you think they are fair? If possible, find out on what basis some of the laws, quotas, and restrictions were made.

6. Krutch is very forceful and dogmatic in this essay, perhaps even a bit self-righteous at times. For instance, in paragraph 5 he says, ". . . the logic of my position is unassailable." How did the tone of this essay affect you? Were you ever put off by it or did it draw you nearer to the writer's position?

IDEAS FOR WRITING

Guided Writing

Write an argumentative essay in which you support or oppose hunting.

1. Acknowledge your opposition in the first paragraph of the essay. Explain your possible closeness to such individuals, but take a critical attitude toward their position regarding hunting.

2. Tell why it is "inconceivable" to you that anyone would support or oppose hunting.

3. Logically refute the propositions of those who oppose your position. After explaining your opposition's viewpoint, you can *deny* that their point is right or true; or

you can *admit* that what they say seems reasonable, but that they have left out important ideas; or you can try to find a *shortcoming* in the way they reason about the topic.

4. Make your essay strong in *emotional* appeals. Lace your essay generously with emotionally charged terms and comparisons.

5. Introduce *ethical* appeals in support of your argument.

6. Carefully draw distinctions between different types of opponents.

7. End your essay with an extended example from an outside source that substantiates your proposition, that is, that puts your opponents in an unfavorable position.

More Writing Projects

1. Write a letter to the editor in which you argue for or against handgun controls.

2. Write an argumentative essay that responds to the following quotation from the American novelist and screenplay writer Nathaniel West: "In America violence is daily."

Judy Syfers

I WANT A WIFE

Judy Syfers, a wife, and mother of two children, argues in this essay for a wife of her own. Although her argument might seem strange, her position will become apparent once you move into the essay. She presents many points to support her position, so you want to keep in mind those you think are the strongest.

Words to Watch

nurturant (par. 3): someone who feeds and takes care of children as they grow up

hors d'oeuvres (par. 6): food served before the regular courses of the meal

monogamy (par. 8): the habit of having only one mate; the practice of marrying only once during life

I belong to that classification of people known as 1 wives. I am A Wife. And, not altogether incidentally, I am a mother.

Not too long ago a male friend of mine appeared on 2 the scene fresh from a recent divorce. He had one child, who is, of course, with his ex-wife. He is obviously looking for another wife. As I thought about him while I was ironing one evening, it suddenly occurred to me that I, too, would like to have a wife. Why do I want a wife?

I would like to go back to school so that I can become 3 economically independent, support myself, and, if need be, support those dependent upon me. I want a wife who will work and send me to school. And while I am going to school I want a wife to keep track of the children's doctor and dentist appointments. And to keep track of mine, too. I want a wife to make sure my children eat properly and are kept clean. I want a wife who will wash the children's clothes and keep them mended. I want a wife who is a good nurturant attendant to my children, who arranges for their schooling, makes sure that they have an adequate social life with their peers, takes them to the park, the zoo, etc. I want a wife who takes care of the children when they are sick, a wife who arranges to be around when the children need special care, because, of course, I cannot miss classes at school. My wife must arrange to lose time at work and not lose the job. It may mean a small cut in my wife's income from time to time, but I guess I can tolerate that. Needless to say, my wife will arrange and pay for the care of the children while my wife is working.

I want a wife who will take care of *my* physical 4 needs. I want a wife who will keep my house clean. A wife who will pick up after me. I want a wife who will keep my clothes clean, ironed, mended, replaced when need be, and who will see to it that my personal things are kept in their proper place so that I can find what I need the minute I need it. I want a wife who cooks the meals, a wife who is a *good* cook. I want a wife who will plan the menus, do the necessary grocery shopping, prepare the meals, serve them pleasantly, and then do the cleaning up while I do my studying. I want a wife who will care for me when I am sick and sympathize with my pain and loss of time from school. I want a wife to go along when our family takes a vacation so that someone can continue to care for me and my children when I need a rest and change of scene.

I want a wife who will not bother me with rambling 5 complaints about a wife's duties. But I want a wife who will listen to me when I feel the need to explain a rather difficult point I have come across in my course of studies. And I want a wife who will type my papers for me when I have written them.

I want a wife who will take care of the details of my 6 social life. When my wife and I are invited out by my friends, I want a wife who will take care of the babysitting arrangements. When I meet people at school that I like and want to entertain, I want a wife who will have the house clean, will prepare a special meal, serve it to me and my friends, and not interrupt when I talk about the things that interest me and my friends. I want a wife who will have arranged that the children are fed and ready for bed before my guests arrive so that the children do not bother us. I want a wife who takes care of the needs of my guests so that they feel comfortable, who makes sure that they have an ashtray, that they are passed the hors d'oeuvres, that they are offered a second helping of the food, that their wine glasses are replenished when necessary, that their coffee is served to them as they like it.

And I want a wife who knows that sometimes I need 7 a night out by myself.

I want a wife who is sensitive to my sexual needs, 8 a wife who makes love passionately and eagerly when I feel like it, a wife who makes sure that I am satisfied. And, of course, I want a wife who will not demand sexual attention when I am not in the mood for it. I want a wife who assumes the complete responsibility for birth control, because I do not want more children. I want a wife who will remain sexually faithful to me so that I do not have to clutter up my intellectual life with jealousies. And I want a wife who understands that *my* sexual needs may entail more than strict adherence to monogamy. I must, after all, be able to relate to people as fully as possible.

If, by chance, I find another person more suitable as 9 a wife than the wife I already have, I want the liberty to replace my present wife with another one. Naturally, I will expect a fresh, new life; my wife will take the children and be solely-responsible for them so that I am left free.

When I am through with school and have a job, I 10
want my wife to quit working and remain at home so that
my wife can more fully and completely take care of a wife's
duties.

My God, who *wouldn't* want a wife? 11

BUILDING VOCABULARY

1.   After checking a dictionary write definitions of
each of these words:

  a. attendant (par. 3)
  b. adequate (par. 3)
  c. peers (par. 3)
  d. tolerate (par. 3)
  e. rambling (par. 5)
  f. replenished (par. 6)
  g. adherence (par. 8)

2.   Write an original sentence for each word above.

UNDERSTANDING THE WRITER'S IDEAS

1.   What incident made Syfers think about wanting
a wife?

2.   How would a wife help the writer achieve economic independence?

3.   In what ways would a wife take care of the
writer's children? Why would the writer like someone to
assume those responsibilities?

4.   What physical needs would Syfers's "wife" take
care of?

5.   How would a wife deal with the writer's social
life? Her sex life?

UNDERSTANDING THE WRITER'S TECHNIQUES

1.   In formal argumentation, we often call the
writer's main point the *major* or *main proposition*. What is
Syfers's major proposition? Is it simply what she says in

paragraph 2, or is the proposition more complex than that? State it in your own words.

2. What is the value of the question Syfers asks in paragraph 2? Where else does she ask a question? What value does this other question have in its place in the essay? What impact does it have on the reader?

3. The points a writer offers to support the major proposition are called *minor propositions*. What minor propositions does Syfers present to show why she wants a wife? In which instance do they serve as topic sentences within paragraphs? What details does she offer to illustrate those minor propositions?

4. What order has the writer chosen to arrange the minor propositions? Why has she chosen such an order? Do you think she builds from the least to the most important reasons for having a wife? What changes would you urge in the order of the minor propositions?

5. Most of the paragraphs here develop through illustration. Where has Syfers used a *simple listing* of details? Why has she chosen that format?

6. Syfers's style is obviously straightforward, her sentences for the most part simple and often brief. Why has she chosen such a style? What is the effect of the repetition of "I want" at the start of so many sentences? Why has Syfers used several short paragraphs (5, 7, 9, 10,11) in addition to longer ones?

7. What is the author's *tone* (see Glossary)? Point out the uses of *irony* (see Glossary) in the essay. How does irony contribute to Syfers's main intent in this essay? How does the fact that Syfers is a woman contribute to this sense of irony?

EXPLORING THE WRITER'S IDEAS

1. By claiming she wants a wife, Syfers is showing us all the duties and responsibilities of the woman in a contemporary household. Has Syfers represented these duties fairly? Do husbands generally expect their wives to do all these things?

2. To what degree do wives today fit Syfers' description? How could a wife avoid many of the responsibilities spelled out in the essay? How does the "modern husband" figure in the way many couples meet household responsibilities now?

3. Syfers has characterized all the traditional and stereotyped roles usually assigned to wives. What "wifely responsibilities" has she left out?

4. Has Syfers presented a balanced picture of the issues or is her argument one-sided? Support your opinion with specific references to the essay. Could the author have dealt effectively with opposing arguments? Why or why not? What might these opposing arguments be?

5. Answer the question in the last line of the essay.

IDEAS FOR WRITING

Guided Writing

Write an essay of 750 to 1,000 words, which you call, "I Want a Husband."

1. Write the essay from the point of view of a *man*. As Syfers wrote as a woman who wanted a wife, you write this essay as a man who wants a *husband*.

2. Start your essay with a brief personal story as in paragraph 2 in "I Want a Wife."

3. Support your main point with a number of minor points. Expand each minor point with details that explain your premises.

4. Arrange your minor premises carefully so that you build to the most convincing point at the end.

5. Use a simple and straightforward style. Connect your points with transitions; use repetition as one transitional device.

6. Balance your longer paragraphs with occasional shorter ones.

7. End your essay with a crisp, one-sentence question of your own.

More Writing Projects

    1.   Write an essay in which you argue *for* or *against* this issue: "A married woman belongs at home."

    2.   Write an essay in which you argue about whose role you think harder to play effectively in today's society: the role of the mother or the role of the father.

Rachel L. Jones

WHAT'S WRONG WITH BLACK ENGLISH

When she wrote this article, which appeared as a guest
editorial in *Newsweek,* Rachel Jones was a sophomore at
Southern Illinois University. She takes what had often
been an unpopular opinion among her fellow students and
defends it skillfully through a mixture of personal narration, interesting language, and pointed references.

Words to Watch

linguist (par. 1): an expert in languages
peers (par. 2): equals, contemporaries
doggedly (par. 4): with great determination
rabid (par. 5): violent, furious; suffering from rabies
deduced (par. 5): concluded by reasoning
implications (par. 5): underlying meanings or results
articulate (par. 6): able to express oneself readily and effectively
assimilating (par. 9): absorbing into a cultural tradition
ideology (par. 9): system of beliefs

William Labov, a noted linguist, once said about 1
the use of black English, "It is the goal of most black
Americans to acquire full control of the standard language

without giving up their own culture." He also suggested that there are certain advantages to having two ways to express one's feelings. I wonder if the good doctor might also consider the goals of those black Americans who have full control of standard English but who are every now and then troubled by that colorful, grammar-to-the-winds patois that is black English. Case in point—me.

I'm a 21-year-old black born to a family that would 2 probably be considered lower-middle class—which in my mind is a polite way of describing a condition only slightly better than poverty. Let's just say we rarely if ever did the winter-vacation thing in the Caribbean. I've often had to defend my humble beginnings to a most unlikely group of people for an even less likely reason. Because of the way I talk, some of my black peers look at me sideways and ask, "Why do you talk like you're white?"

The first time it happened to me I was nine years 3 old. Cornered in the school bathroom by the class bully and her sidekick, I was offered the opportunity to swallow a few of my teeth unless I satisfactorily explained why I always got good grades, why I talked "proper" or "white." I had no ready answer for her, save the fact that my mother had from the time I was old enough to talk stressed the importance of reading and learning, or that L. Frank Baum and Ray Bradbury were my closest companions. I read all my older brothers' and sisters' literature textbooks more faithfully than they did, and even lightweights like the Bobbsey Twins and Trixie Belden were allowed into my bookish inner circle. I don't remember exactly what I told those girls, but I somehow talked my way out of a beating.

'White pipes'. I was reminded once again of my 4 "white pipes" problem while apartment hunting in Evanston, Ill., last winter. I doggedly made out lists of available places and called all around. I would immediately be invited over—and immediately turned down. The thinly concealed looks of shock when the front door opened clued me in, along with the flustered instances of "just getting off the phone with the girl who was ahead of you and she wants the rooms." When I finally found a place to live, my roommate stirred up old memories when she remarked a few months later, "You know, I was surprised when I first saw you. You sounded white over the phone." Tell me another one, sister.

I should've asked her a question I've wanted an answer to for years: how does one "talk white"? The silly side of me pictures a rabid white foam spewing forth when I speak. I don't use Valley Girl jargon, so that's not what's meant in my case. Actually, I've pretty much deduced what people mean when they say that to me, and the implications are really frightening.

It means that I'm articulate and well-versed. It means that I can talk as freely about John Steinbeck as I can about Rick James. It means that "ain't" and "he be" are not staples of my vocabulary and are only used around family and friends. (It is almost Jekyll and Hyde-ish the way I can slip out of academic abstractions into a long, lean, double-negative-filled dialogue, but I've come to terms with that aspect of my personality.) As a child, I found it hard to believe that's what people meant by "talking proper"; that would've meant that good grades and standard English were equated with white skin, and that went against everything I'd ever been taught. Running into the same type of mentality as an adult has confirmed the depressing reality that for many blacks, standard English is not only unfamiliar, it is socially unacceptable.

James Baldwin once defended black English by saying it had added "vitality to the language," and even went so far as to label it a language in its own right, saying, "Language [i.e., black English] is a political instrument" and a "vivid and crucial key to identity." But did Malcolm X urge blacks to take power in this country "any way y'all can"? Did Martin Luther King Jr. say to blacks, "I has been to the mountaintop, and I done seed the Promised Land"? Toni Morrison, Alice Walker and James Baldwin did not achieve their eloquence, grace and stature by using only black English in their writing. Andrew Young, Tom Bradley and Barbara Jordan did not acquire political power by saying, "Y'all crazy if you ain't gon vote for me." They all have full command of standard English, and I don't think that knowledge takes away from their blackness or commitment to black people.

Soulful. I know from experience that it's important for black people, stripped of culture and heritage, to have something they can point to and say, "This is ours, *we* can comprehend it, *we* alone can speak it with a soulful flourish." I'd be lying if I said that the rhythms of my people caught up in "some serious rap" don't sound natural and right to me sometimes. But how heartwarming is it for those same brothers when they hit the pavement searching for employment? Studies have proven that the use of ethnic dialects decreases power in the marketplace. "I be" is acceptable on the corner, but not with the boss. 8

Am I letting capitalistic, European-oriented thinking fog the issue? Am I selling out blacks to an ideal of assimilating, being as much like white as possible? I have not formed a personal political ideology, but I do know this: it hurts me to hear black children use black English, knowing that they will be at yet another disadvantage in an educational system already full of stumbling blocks. It hurts me to sit in lecture halls and hear fellow black students complain that the professor "be tripping dem out using big words dey can't understand." And what hurts most is to be stripped of my own blackness simply because I know my way around the English language. 9

I would have to disagree with Labov in one respect. My goal is not so much to acquire full control of both standard and black English, but to one day see more black people less dependent on a dialect that excludes them from full participation in the world we live in. I don't think I talk white, I think I talk right. 10

BUILDING VOCABULARY

1. The author uses several examples of black English in the essay. On a sheet of paper write out all the terminology from black English that you can identify. Then write definitions and/or standard spellings for each word or phrase.

2. Use these colloquial expressions from the essay in sentences of your own. Then rewrite the sentences, using "standard" English.

a. "look at me sideways" (par. 2)
b. "to swallow a few of my front teeth" (par. 3)
c. "clued me in" (par. 4)
d. "tell me another one. . . ." (par. 4)
e. "hit the pavement" (par. 8)

3. The author refers to "Valley Girl jargon" (par. 5), otherwise known as Valspeak," a type of language common originally to certain segments of teenage culture in southern California, but now easily recognized across the country. List examples of "Valspeak" and be prepared to explain their meanings.

UNDERSTANDING THE WRITER'S IDEAS

1. What is William Labov's theory of black English? What is Jones's opinion of Labov's theory?

2. What is Jones's background?

3. What is the "unlikely group" Jones mentions in paragraph 2? Why does she call it that?

4. Who are L. Frank Baum and Ray Bradbury? What are the Bobbsey twins, Jekyll and Hyde, and Trixie Belden? What is the author's relation to these characters?

5. What are "white pipes"? How did Jones realize she had "white pipes" when she was apartment hunting in Evanston, Illinois?

6. What, according to Jordan, does it mean to "talk white"? How does it compare with "talking proper"? What is "standard English"?

7. What does the author like about black English? What does she think is not good about it?

8. Explain in your own words the "depressing reality" mentioned in paragraph 6.

9. What is James Baldwin's opinion of black English? How does Jones feel about his opinion? What is her point about the correlation between successful black writers and politicians and the use of black English?

10. What does Jones mean by "capitalistic, European-oriented thinking" (par. 9)? How is it opposed to the use of black English?

11. What is the main point of Jones's conclusion?

UNDERSTANDING THE WRITER'S TECHNIQUES

1. Is the main proposition or thesis in this essay directly stated or implied? Explain your answer.

2. How does the title indicate the author's position in this argument?

3. Why does the author introduce William Labov in her first paragraph? How does she *refute* him in the course of the essay? What other instances of refutation do you find in this written argument?

4. Writers can employ argumentation for a variety of purposes, ranging from persuading people to support a cause to trying to refute a theory. What are Jordan's purposes in this argumentative essay? Cite evidence to support your response.

5. Who is Jordan's audience? Might any part of the audience disagree with her? Who? How does she take such opposition into account in terms of the *tone* of her essay?

6. Why does the author use personal narration in this essay?

7. Explain Jones's use of cause-and-effect analysis in her discussion of black English and job hunting and of black English and education. How does she use causal analysis to logically support her argument?

8. Why does Jones begin paragraph 9 with a series of rhetorical questions? What is the effect? Where else does she use questions, and toward what end?

9. What types of emotional appeals does Jones make to her audience? How effective are these appeals in convincing readers?

10. How does the concluding paragraph logically reinforce or repeat Jones's main proposition?

EXPLORING THE WRITER'S IDEAS

1. In paragraph 8, Jones states, "Studies have proven that the use of ethnic dialects decreases power in the market-place." What does she mean by "ethnic dialects"? In this essay she deals with the black English ethnic dialect. What

other variations on the English language—either ethnic or regional dialects—can you name? How well can you understand other variations? If you were an employer, would a job applicant's use of an ethnic dialect influence your hiring decision? Why or why not?

2. What are your experiences with black English? Do you feel, as James Baldwin does, that it is "a language in its own right"? Why?

3. Compare Jones's attitudes about black cultural identity to those of Al Young in his essay "Java Jive" (pages 86–90).

4. In recent years there has been an ongoing debate—mostly in the cities—over bilingual education. Those in favor of it say that in neighborhoods or regions where a language other than standard English is commonly spoken (such as Spanish or Chinese), schools should teach courses in both languages. Those opposed say that all American students, regardless of their cultural ties, must be taught standard English. Where do you stand on this issue? Cite reasons to support your position.

IDEAS FOR WRITING

Guided Writing

Write an essay using the title "What's Wrong with _____" and fill in the blank with a cultural, political, sociological, or educational issue with which you have had direct involvement.

1. Begin with a reference to an outside authority on the issue. In your first paragraph, question that authority's analysis. Make the entire essay strong in refutation.

2. At the end of the first paragraph or the beginning of the second, establish your own claim as an authority on the issue.

3. Do not state your thesis or proposition directly, but instead use an implied thesis.

4. Narrate an incident or two that establishes your personal involvement and provides evidence for your main proposition.

5. If appropriate, use colloquial, slang, idiomatic, and figurative expressions throughout your essay.

6. Make allusions to well-known people to help illustrate the relative "rightness" or "wrongness" of the issue.

7. Use cause-and-effect analysis and/or comparison and contrast as support for your main proposition.

8. In your conclusion, indicate why the issue is wrong, especially for you. Indicate its effects on you personally and your methods of combating it.

More Writing Projects

1. Write an argument in favor of the use of black English (or any ethnic dialect) as a second language.

2. Write an argument entitled "What's Right with _____" in which you defend a commonly *un*popular issue.

3. Write an essay of persuasion on any topic of great concern to you for which you can use one of the essays in this book as a reference authority.

11

Prose for Further Reading

Lillian Hellman

MEMOIR OF A
NEW ORLEANS
BOARDING HOUSE

Much has come into American life since my childhood that makes things easier and nicer for almost everybody, but much has also been lost, and the shabby substitutes have deprived us of good and modest pleasures. It seems to me, to name a simple few, that we are less for the loss of the climbing sweet pea, the elm tree, and jogging in place could be a violation of the pleasure of walking through woods or just walking downtown.

A major loss in American life to me—perhaps because I knew one of them so well and stayed so often in so many others—is the boarding house, completely replaced now by the ugly, cold motel. The boarding houses ran, depending on the city and its size, all the way from handsome, redeemed mansions with fine food and pleasant service through the not-very-nice houses where people with small incomes, or those passing through, could live, not well but in a less cold atmosphere, and eat better than the junk food of motel coffee shops.

My Aunt Jenny's boarding house in New Orleans was considered upper middle class. There were no lunches served but there were enormous breakfasts, and dinners that very few good French restaurants could now duplicate.

367

Breakfast always included a variety of dishes: whatever fresh fish was in season, creamed finnan haddie if no fish was running well, ham hash or corned beef hash, hot biscuits, scrambled eggs with brains, and always for Sunday breakfast a large dish of tripe.

Two or three times a week my aunt and I, and the upstairs maid, a sad girl named Collie, of no age, no color, who was given shelter and food by my aunt and was, I think, a long way from being all there in the head, would take a streetcar ride down to the French market to buy food for the elaborate dinners. We would return home with snapping turtle meat, chickens that weighed no more than one pound, and in season a basket of crawfish to be made into a most difficult soup called crawfish bisque.

We would also carry back very often, Collie on one handle and I on the other, a large basket of unopened oysters, which always caused my aunt to give a lecture on the contempt she felt for oysters Rockefeller, and to explain her own fine recipe of simply frizzling the oysters in butter, cream and chives.

In season—and that phrase was a piece of nonsense-politesse because Cajuns shot in all seasons—a very old Cajun, who was always accompanied by one of many 6- or 7-year-old boys, would appear at my aunt's kitchen door to sell wild duck, quail, or pheasants. Three for a dollar no matter what birds you bought. The young boy was there for the purpose of plucking and cleaning the birds. He was given 50 cents for his work and as much cake and milk as he wanted. My favorite little boy—I think I was about the same age at the time—took snuff.

My aunt's house had a good reputation, although there were many more fancy boarding houses along St. Charles Avenue. Jenny's house had an almost permanent population. But, of course, sometimes somebody moved away and sometimes people even died although most of them lived to rather a fine age. A few of them had to move after my aunt's retirement, but most of them came back to call on her from time to time, or would write notes complaining that their new places were too stiff, too expensive and not homey.

The word homey understandably amused Jenny, who certainly had not ever meant to make a home for them.

I didn't then and I don't now understand what went on in my Aunt Jenny's head because she was like nobody else I've ever known. She was a very tall, heavy woman, with a pretty, soft face that did not suit her body. She had a high temper that she had learned to control, except sometimes in the early morning. Her sister, Hannah, was not pretty, the face too strong, but she was a soft darling. Hannah had a good job in the city, but she rose at 6 in order to watch over Jenny's possible early morning tempers and to sweep the steps and porch of the house.

The people most likely to bring out Jenny's temper were a Mr. Steffens, a handsome man who was a stockbroker, and his wife, Lucia, who was nothing at all except Mr. Steffens's wife. Mr. Steffens was a flirt, and knew about his own good looks. I never saw very much harm in him but Jenny did and had a tendency not to speak to him at all, and too much tendency to speak in a very sharp voice to Mrs. Steffens for whose indolence she had the greatest contempt. Mrs. Steffens slept a great deal, resting immediately after breakfast, then riding downtown for lunch and shopping, always returning about 3 o'clock for another long nap that took her up to the 6:30 Dubonnet before dinner.

She was a patsy for my aunt's unpleasant questions at breakfast: what bargains had she found in the stores the day before, had she managed to walk by her own feet across Canal Street or had she been escorted or wheeled in some unknown vehicle, or had her doctor given her a new draught for afternoon sleeping that was different from the after-breakfast draught?

Jenny was in a different kind of morning bad humor with Edward, who was a small, thin man, in love, I think, with my mother, who was too innocent to think of his open affection as possibly sexual (and it probably wasn't) but my mother always came to Edward's help when Jenny and others made fun of him because she like him and felt sorry for him.

Edward's last name was Roncourt and somehow it

had been found out that it had once been De Roncourt and that his grandfather had been a count in Northern France. My aunt had questions to ask about what the French aristocracy had been like, knowing full well that Edward had never been to France, and my mother's defense of Edward's stumbling embarrassment both tickled and irritated Jenny. She teased my poor mother about what she called "l'affaire de Roncourt" until my mother once burst into tears and locked her door for the rest of the day. That night, for the first and last time, I saw Hannah lose her temper with Jenny. After that the teasing stopped.

There were also two elderly lady boarders whose names I no longer remember and one elderly gentleman who was their cousin. I think I don't remember them because I don't remember their ever speaking, or maybe I don't remember them because Jenny completely ignored them.

But in looking back, I would not be too certain of my own opinions of any of the guests because I loved and admired Jenny and saw things too much through her eyes and one of the reasons I think I did was that I spent so much time in the kitchen with her where she was in her best humor.

Akira Kurosawa

BABYHOOD

I was in the washtub naked. The place was dimly
lit, and I was soaking in hot water and rocking myself by
holding on to the rims of the tub. At the lowest point the
tub teetered between two sloping boards, the water making
little splashing noises as it rocked. This must have been
very interesting for me. I rocked the tub with all my strength.
Suddenly it overturned. I have a very vivid memory of the
strange feeling of shock and uncertainty at that moment,
of the sensation of that wet and slippery space between the
boards against my bare skin, and of looking up at something
painfully bright overhead.

After reaching an age of awareness, I would occasionally recall this incident. But it seemed a trivial thing,
so I said nothing about it until I became an adult. It must
have been after I had passed twenty years of age that for
some reason I mentioned to my mother that I remembered
these sensations. For a moment she just stared at me in
surprise; then she informed me that this could only have
been something that occurred when we went to my father's
birthplace up north in Akita Prefecture to attend a memorial
service for my grandfather. I had been one year old at the
time.

The dimly lit place where I sat in a tub lodged
between two boards was the room that served as both kitchen

and bath in the house where my father was born. My mother had been about to give me a bath, but first she put me in the tub of hot water and went into the next room to take off her kimono. Suddenly she heard me start wailing at the top of my lungs. She rushed back and found me spilled out of the tub on the floor crying. The painfully bright, shiny thing over head, my mother explained, was probably a hanging oil lamp of the type still used when I was a baby.

This incident with the washtub is my very first memory of myself. Naturally, I do not recall being born. However, my oldest sister, now deceased, used to say, "You were a strange baby." Apparently I emerged from my mother's womb without uttering a sound, but with my hands firmly clasped together. When at last they were able to pry my hands apart, I had bruises on both palms.

I think this story may be a lie. It was probably made up to tease me because I was the youngest child. After all, if I really had been born such a grasping person, by now I would be a millionaire and surely would be riding around in nothing less than a Rolls-Royce.

After the washtub incident of my first year, I can now recall only a few other events from my babyhood, in a form resembling out-of-focus bits of film footage. All of them are things seen from my infant's vantage point on my nurse's shoulders.

One of them is something seen through a wire net. People dressed in white flail at a ball with a stick, run after it as it dances and flies through the air, and pick it up and throw it around. Later I understood that this was the view from behind the net of the baseball field at the gymnastics school where my father was a teacher. So I must say that my liking for baseball today is deep-rooted; apparently I've been watching it since babyhood.

Another memory from babyhood, also a sight viewed from my nurse's back, comes to mind: a fire seen from a great distance. Between us and the fire stretches an expanse of dark water. My home was in the Ōmori district of Tokyo, so this was probably the Ōmori shore of Tokyo Bay, and since the fire appeared very far away, it must have taken place somewhere near Haneda (now the site of one of Tokyo's international airports). I was frightened by this distant fire and cried. Even now I have a strong dislike of fires, and especially when I see the night sky reddened with flames I am overcome by fear.

One last memory of babyhood remains. In this case, too, I am on my nurse's back, and from time to time we enter a small dark room. Years later I would occasionally recall this frequent occurrence and wonder what it was. Then one day all at once, like Sherlock Holmes solving a mystery, I understood: my nurse, with me still on her back, was going to the toilet. What an insult!

Many years later my nurse came to see me. She looked up at this person who had reached nearly six feet and more than 150 pounds and just said, "My dear, how you've grown," as she clasped me around the knees and broke into tears. I had been ready to reproach her for the indignities she had caused me to suffer in the past, but suddenly I was moved by this figure of an old woman I no longer recognized, and all I could do was stare vacantly down at her.

Maya Angelou
"THE FIGHT"

The last inch of space was filled, yet people continued to wedge themselves along the walls of the Store. Uncle Willie had turned the radio up to its last notch so that youngsters on the porch wouldn't miss a word. Women sat on kitchen chairs, dining-room chairs, stools and upturned wooden boxes. Small children and babies perched on every lap available and men leaned on the shelves or on each other.

The apprehensive mood was shot through with shafts of gaiety, as a black sky is streaked with lightning.

"I ain't worried 'bout this fight. Joe's gonna whip that cracker like it's open season."

"He gone whip him till that white boy call him Momma."

At last the talking was finished and the string-along songs about razor blades were over and the fight began.

"A quick jab to the head." In the Store the crowd grunted. "A left to the head and a right and another left." One of the listeners cackled like a hen and was quieted.

"They're in a clench, Louis is trying to fight his way out."

Some bitter comedian on the porch said, "That white man don't mind hugging that niggah now, I betcha."

"The referee is moving in to break them up, but Louis finally pushed the contender away and it's an uppercut to the chin. The contender is hanging on, now he's backing away. Louis catches him with a short left to the jaw."

A tide of murmuring assent poured out the doors and into the yard.

"Another left and another left. Louis is saving that mighty right . . ." The mutter in the Store had grown into a baby roar and it was pierced by the clang of a bell and the announcer's "That's the bell for round three, ladies and gentlemen."

As I pushed my way into the Store I wondered if the announcer gave any thought to the fact that he was addressing as "ladies and gentlemen" all the Negroes around the world who sat sweating and praying, glued to their "master's voice."

There were only a few calls for R. C. Colas, Dr. Peppers, and Hire's root beer. The real festivities would begin after the fight. Then even the old Christian ladies who taught their children and tried themselves to practice turning the other cheek would buy soft drinks, and if the Brown Bomber's victory was a particularly bloody one they would order peanut patties and Baby Ruths also.

Bailey and I lay the coins on top of the cash register. Uncle Willie didn't allow us to ring up sales during a fight. It was too noisy and might shake up the atmosphere. When the gong rang for the next round we pushed through the near-sacred quiet to the herd of children outside.

"He's got Louis against the ropes and now it's a left to the body and a right to the ribs. Another right to the body, it looks like it was low . . . Yes, ladies and gentlemen, the referee is signaling but the contender keeps raining the blows on Louis. It's another to the body, and it looks like Louis is going down."

My race groaned. It was our people falling. It was another lynching, yet another Black man hanging on a tree. One more woman ambushed and raped. A Black boy whipped and maimed. It was hounds on the trail of a man running through slimy swamps. It was a white woman slapping her maid for being forgetful.

The men in the Store stood away from the walls and

at attention. Women greedily clutched the babes on their laps while on the porch the shufflings and smiles, flirtings and pinching of a few minutes before were gone. This might be the end of the world. If Joe lost we were back in slavery and beyond help. It would all be true, the accusations that we were lower types of human beings. Only a little higher than the apes. True that we were stupid and ugly and lazy and dirty and, unlucky and worst of all, that God Himself hated us and ordained us to be hewers of wood and drawers of water, forever and ever, world without end.

We didn't breathe. We didn't hope. We waited.

"He's off the ropes, ladies and gentlemen. He's moving towards the center of the ring." There was no time to be relieved. The worst might still happen.

"And now it looks like Joe is mad. He's caught Carnera with a left hook to the head and a right to the head. It's a left jab to the body and another left to the head. There's a left cross and a right to the head. The contender's right eye is bleeding and he can't seem to keep his block up. Louis is penetrating every block. The referee is moving in, but Louis sends a left to the body and it's the uppercut to the chin and the contender is dropping. He's on the canvas, ladies and gentlemen."

Babies slid to the floor as women stood up and men leaned toward the radio.

"Here's the referee. He's counting. One, two, three, four, five, six, seven . . . Is the contender trying to get up again?"

All the men in the store shouted, "NO."

"—eight, nine, ten." There were a few sounds from the audience, but they seemed to be holding themselves in against tremendous pressure.

"The fight is all over, ladies and gentlemen. Let's get the microphone over to the referee . . . Here he is. He's got the Brown Bomber's hand, he's holding it up . . . Here he is . . ."

Then the voice, husky and familiar, came to wash over us—"The winnah, and still heavyweight champeen of the world . . . Joe Louis."

Champion of the world. A Black boy. Some Black mother's son. He was the strongest man in the world. People drank Coca-Colas like ambrosia and ate candy bars like Christmas. Some of the men went behind the Store and poured white lightning in their soft-drink bottles, and a few of the bigger boys followed them. Those who were not chased away came back blowing their breath in front of themselves like proud smokers.

It would take an hour or more before the people would leave the Store and head for home. Those who lived too far had made arrangements to stay in town. It wouldn't do for a Black man and his family to be caught on a lonely country road on a night when Joe Louis had proved that we were the strongest people in the world.

Garrison Keillor

A RETURN TO BASICS: MEALTIME WITHOUT GUILT

Eating is a perfectly natural activity, we all have natural urges to eat, and we should be able to satisfy those urges simply and naturally without shame and anxiety and numbing self-consciousness either alone or with one other person or two or (if we prefer, and it's strictly a matter of personal preference) with larger groups. It should be a joyous life-affirming experience, not (as I'm afraid it is to so many) *A Problem.*

When I was a boy way out on the open prairie of the American heartland, we were happy eaters and weren't ashamed to have big appetites. Out there in Breughel, N. D., surrounded by an ocean of durum wheat, we got three squares a day, piled our plates and cried "Yes!" to seconds. Tables groaned at picnics, church suppers, Sunday dinners, holiday feasts. Food was a relief against our flat landscape: steamy mountains of fried chicken and pork among foothills of creamed onions, spinach, mashed potatoes with lakes of gravy and great promontories of pie. At least once a week we sat down to table and scaled the Sierras. And what we called "a little lunch" would knock the socks off Pavarotti.

All that has changed in Breughel and everywhere else, thanks to a tiny flock of puritanical food writers who have nagged and bullied and made us a picky people who take small bites and mull the food over in our mouths: Is it excellent? Are we having a truly unique dining experience? No, probably not, for once you pick food apart and hold it up to the light and examine it, you don't feel like eating the stuff. For one thing, it's probably cold.

So church suppers at Breughel Lutheran now are dismal affairs to which people bring elegant casseroles and sip dry wines and talk dry talk and exchange nervous glances. In the fall, the threshing crews sit down at plank tables under the cottonwood trees and eat stir-fried shrimp and pea pods, and each man talks about another meal he had at this absolutely marvelous little out-of-the-way farm that nobody ever heard of before. And Mom's Cafe has changed hands and is now a nouvelle Bulgarian restaurant but nobody goes there, they all know a better one in Bismarck.

Where are the great meals of my youth when we were loose and happy and loved the chow? Gone! Scared off by food authorities, ridiculed, made to seem cheap and coarse and not in good taste. Julia Child, James Beard—both meant to raise our sights, but their effect has been to make eaters nervous that what is set before us may not be good enough and, worse, that we may not realize it and may actually enjoy it. They have also permanently eliminated macaroni and cheese or hamburger-noodle hot dish as anything you'd dare serve to guests or eat in public. A person who truly enjoys macaroni and cheese is forced to eat alone in the dark. A person would rather confess to being from Breughel than admit to any dealings with macaroni and cheese.

I happen to love it, the kind that Kraft makes with the noodles and a packet of powdered cheese in one box. You boil water, cook noodles, drain and dump cheese powder on it. It's no trouble to make, tastes good and reminds me of how simple eating used to be in our home when I was a boy. (My mother, who has studied northern Italian cooking in the Breughel adult education program, now claims to have made Kraft macaroni and cheese "once or twice when I wasn't feeling well," but in fact we had it every Monday night.)

There were no menus at that kitchen table, and

when Dad poured milk, he didn't pour a little bit in your glass and wait for you to swish it around in your mouth and say if it was O.K. My mother taught us to be grateful for the meal, to think of Asian children and to make mealtime a pleasant occasion, not a meeting of critics saying "Yuccchh" and "Ish, beet greens" or "The tuna casserole, while plentiful, is sadly underseasoned."

Maybe it's time all of us got back to basics in the food line, especially those whose appetites have been dulled by too much reading about food, who have been intimidated by cuisine. Here are some helpful guidelines:

1. Eat when you're hungry. Food tastes much better then. Past the age of 30, you don't need much to keep going so you'll need to pass up some meals before you arrive at one you're really up for. You say, "I'm so hungry I could eat bark off trees," and if you are, that meat loaf will have an aura about it and those string beans will be the best you ever ate.

2. Don't ever explain food to your guests, as you bring it to the table: "The soup is burnt" or "The fish fell on the floor so most of the cream sauce got washed off" or "I just saw this recipe for curried chicken in Parade, this is the first time I made it, and then I discovered I was all out of robin's eggs so I had to substitute partridge instead." Don't do that. Simply put the hay down where the goats can get it, say grace and tell a couple of jokes.

3. When you go to a restaurant, don't read the menu. Ask the waiter what's good or look around the room until you see something you like and ask for that. Of if you have a definite meal in mind—say, a cup of soup, a peanut butter sandwich, a dill pickle and lemon gelatin with mayonnaise—say so, and let the restaurant worry about it.

Menu study is a useless exercise; it tells you nothing about the food, and yet people sit and pore over it as if it were the racing form and only one dish can be a winner. Nobody wants to be wrong, nobody wants to order first. "You go ahead," they say. "I'm still thinking." Don't think so hard. Point. Say "Bring me some of that—what those people over there got, the ones with the big smiles and the grease stains." Be happy, say grace, tell a couple of jokes.

4. Don't discuss food while you're eating it. Don't frame judicious compliments for the hosts. Don't compare the food to other foods of its sort, don't inquire about ingredients, don't be reminded of a wonderful meal you had with other people a long time ago—just plain don't talk about it. A sound here and there ("Hooooo-ah!" or "Hah!" or growls and barks) will do for compliments, and any other discussion can wait. Food is a blessing to us, the stuff that sustains our little flame, and we should eat it with gratitude and gusto and talk of many things but not this. Tell jokes.

5. Insofar as possible, given the tangled thread of fate, the requirements of business and the difficulty of worming out of some invitations, avoid eating with people you don't like. If you're with people in front of whom you're afraid to spill food on yourself, you're probably with the wrong bunch. The steam shovel operator can't enjoy food if he is worried about spilling beans from his bucket. Eat with your friends. They're the ones who, if you do spill, won't whip their heads the other way and start up a conversation about tax-increment financing. They'll look right at you and get a good laugh out of it.

In fact, your *true* friends are ones you could toss a little bit of food at—if the situation seemed to call for it. Not as a regular thing, and not a big hunk of something, but a pea or crouton or pinch of tofu thrown at the right moment can be a profound expression of brotherhood and sisterhood. Don't get me wrong: I'm not advocating food fights. I only feel that, at the very happiest meals, the *possibility* has to be there.

Throwing food is a perfectly natural thing. We all have an urge now and then to let fly with a little glistening morsel and plant it on someone's forehead, and I see no reason why mature adults shouldn't feel free to do it—among friends, of course. In Breughel before good taste clamped down on us, we'd often look up and see a pat of butter coming our way, or a single cheesy macaroni, and it lent an intimacy to dining I haven't experienced since.

Richard M. Restak

THE OTHER DIFFERENCE BETWEEN BOYS AND GIRLS

There is no denying it: Boys think differently from girls. Even though recent brain-research evidence is controversial, that conclusion seems inescapable. I know how offensive that will sound to feminists and others committed to overcoming sexual stereotypes. But social equality for men and women really depends on recognizing these differences in brain behavior.

At present, schooling and testing discriminate against both sexes, ignoring differences that have been observed by parents and educators for years. Boys suffer in elementary-school classrooms, which are ideally suited to the way girls think. Girls suffer later, when they must take scholarship tests that are geared for male performance.

Anyone who has spent time with children in a playground or school setting is aware of differences in the way boys and girls respond to similar situations. For example, at a birthday party for five-year-olds it's not usually the girls who pull hair, throw punches or smear each other with food.

Typically, such differences are explained on a cultural basis. Boys are expected to be more aggressive and play rough games, while girls are presumably encouraged to be gentle and nonassertive. After years of exposure to such expectations, the theory goes, men and women wind up with widely varying behavioral and intellectual repertoires. As a corollary, many people believe that if child-rearing practices could be equalized and sexual stereotypes eliminated, most of these differences would eventually disappear. The true state of affairs is not that simple.

Undoubtedly, many differences traditionally believed to exist between the sexes are based on stereotypes. But evidence from recent brain research indicates that some behavioral differences between men and women are based on differences in brain functioning that are biologically inherent and unlikely to be changed by cultural factors alone.

One clue to brain differences between the sexes came from observation of infants. One study found that from shortly after birth, females are more sensitive to certain types of sounds, particularly to a mother's voice. In a laboratory, if the sound of the mother's voice is displaced to another part of the room, female babies react while males usually seem oblivious to the displacement. Female babies are also more easily startled by loud noises.

Tests show girls have increased skin sensitivity, particularly in the fingertips, and are more proficient at fine motor performance. Females are also generally more attentive to social contexts—faces, speech patterns, subtle vocal cues. By five months, a female can distinguish photographs of familiar people, a task rarely performed well by boys of that age. At five and eight months, girls will babble to a mother's face, seemingly recognizing her as a person, while boys fail to distinguish between a face and a dangling toy, babbling equally to both.

Female infants speak sooner, have larger vocabularies and rarely demonstrate speech defects. (Stuttering, for instance, occurs almost exclusively among boys.) Girls exceed boys in language abilities, and this early linguistic bias often prevails throughout life. Girls read sooner, learn foreign languages more easily and, as a result, are more likely to enter occupations involving language mastery.

Boys, in contrast, show an early visual superiority. They are also clumsier, performing poorly at something like arranging a row of beads, but excel at other activities calling on total body coordination. Their attentional mechanisms are also different. A boy will react to an inanimate object as quickly as he will to a person. A male baby will often ignore the mother and babble to a blinking light, fixate on a geometric figure and, at a later point, manipulate it and attempt to take it apart.

A study of preschool children by psychologist Diane McGuinness of Stanford University found boys more curious, especially in regard to exploring their environment. Her studies also confirmed that males are better at manipulating three-dimensional space. When boys and girls are asked to mentally rotate or fold an object, boys overwhelmingly outperform girls. "I folded it in my mind" is a typical male response. Girls are likely to produce elaborate verbal descriptions which, because they are less appropriate to the task, result in frequent errors.

There is evidence that some of these differences in performance are differences in brain organization between boys and girls. Overall, verbal and spatial abilities in boys tend to be "packaged" into different hemispheres: the right hemisphere for nonverbal tasks, the left for verbal tasks. But in girls nonverbal and verbal skills are likely to be found on both sides of the brain. The hemispheres of women's brains may be less specialized for these functions.

These differences in brain organization and specialization are believed by some scientists to provide a partial explanation of why members of one sex or the other are underrepresented in certain professions. Architects, for example, require a highly developed spatial sense, a skill found more frequently among men. Thus, the preponderance of male architects may be partially caused by the more highly developed spatial sense that characterizes the male brain.

Psychological measurements of brain functioning between the sexes also show unmistakable differences. In 11 subtests of the most widely used general intelligence test, only two (digit span and picture arrangement) reveal similar mean scores for males and females. These sex differences are so consistent that the standard battery of this intelligence test now contains a masculinity-femininity index to offset sex-related proficiencies and deficiencies.

Most thought-provoking of all are findings by Eleanor Maccoby and Carol Nagy Jacklin of Stanford University on personality traits and intellectual achievement. They found that intellectual development in girls is fostered among individuals who are assertive and active, and have a sense that they can control, by their own actions, the events that affect their lives. These factors appear to be less important in the intellectual development of boys.

Recent studies even suggest that high levels of intellectual achievement are associated with cross-sex typing: the ability to express traits and interests associated with the opposite sex. Educational psychologist E. P. Torrance of the University of Georgia suggests that sexual stereotypes are a block to creativity, since creativity requires sensitivity— a female trait—as well as autonomy and independence— traits usually associated with males. M. P. Honzik and J. W. Mcfarlane of the University of California at Berkeley support Torrance's speculation with a 20-year follow-up on subjects who demonstrated significant IQ gains. Those with the greatest gains displayed less dependency on traditional sex roles than those whose IQs remained substantially the same.

It's important to remember that we're not talking about one sex being generally superior or inferior to another. In addition, the studies are statistical and don't tell us a lot about individuals. The findings are controversial, but they can help us establish true social equity.

One way of doing this might be to change such practices as nationwide competitive examinations. If boys, for instance, truly excel in right-hemisphere tasks, scholastic aptitude tests should be substantially redesigned to assure that both sexes have an equal chance. Some of the tests now are weighted with items that virtually guarantee superior male performance.

Attitude changes are also needed in our approach to "hyperactive" or "learning disabled" children. The evidence for sex differences here is staggering: More than 90 percent of hyperactives are males. This is not surprising since the male brain is primarily visual, while classroom instruction demands attentive listening. The male brain learns by manipulating its environment, yet the typical student is forced to sit still for long hours in the classroom. There is little opportunity, other than during recess, for gross motor movements or rapid muscular responses. In essence, the classrooms in most of our nation's primary grades are geared to skills that come naturally to girls but develop very slowly in boys. The result shouldn't be surprising: a "learning disabled" child who is also frequently "hyperactive."

We now have the opportunity, based on emerging evidence of sex differences in brain functioning, to restructure elementary grades so that boys find their initial educational contacts less stressful. At more advanced levels of instruction, teaching methods could incorporate verbal and linguistic approaches to physics, engineering and architecture (to mention only three fields where women are conspicuously underrepresented).

The alternative is to do nothing about brain differences. There is something to be said for this approach, too. In the recent past, enhanced social benefit has usually resulted from stressing the similarities between people rather than their differences. We ignore brain-sex differences, however, at the risk of confusing biology with sociology, and wishful thinking with scientific fact.

Judy Klemesrud

SPORTORIAL SPLENDOR

Every so often I wear an Ellesse tennis sweater to work. It is white, with thin navy stripes and red trimming on the V-neck, cuffs and waistband. It has Ellesse written on a black tag on the wrist, so I cover the name by rolling up the cuff. But I can't fool the tennis cognoscenti and other consumers of status sports clothes, who can tell by the familiar trademark—a red and gold sunburst over my heart.

Why do I wear a tennis sweater to work? Perhaps I am fantasizing I am Chris Evert Lloyd, my favorite player. Or maybe I'm trying to let others know that I am "into tennis." Or maybe it's because everyone else is doing it, too—wearing the clothing of sports outside of the arenas.

Your see this sports garb everywhere: Running shoes on business-suited Yuppie women on Wall Street; baseball caps and satin jackets that blare "Islanders" or "Yankees" or "Giants" on people riding trains and buses; velour warm-up suits on women in supermarkets; team jerseys on tots and senior citizens (Georgetown jackets are big, and Mark Gastineau's No. 99 is especially popular around here).

What does it all mean? Offhand, I would say people are wearing these clothes because they love the sports that the clothes represent, which is my reason, or simply because these clothes are comfortable, or are generally more available in stores now.

The experts, of course, have deeper meanings. Fans who wear clothes with a team's name on it are trying to show "social-connectedness," said Ruth P. Rubinstein, an assistant professor of sociology at the Fashion Institute of Technology in Manhattan. "We have lost ties within the family and now we're looking for social-connectedness in society," she added. "These clothes show the world that you're a fan and that you're in some remote way connected to a team."

Running shoes, which I never wear to work because I think they make most women in skirts look dumpy, "are a symbol of women's freedom," Dr. Rubinstein said.

I was especially interested in the real meaning of those ubiquitous warm-up suits, even though I have never owned one. According to the National Sporting Goods Association, sales of these twopiece outfits have almost quintupled from $132.8 million since 1976, and most of my tennis-playing friends own a couple, mostly in purple velour. "They are really comfortable, as opposed to designer jeans, and allow people to move around without restrictions," Dr. Rubinstein explained. "A woman who puts on a warm-up suit is indicating she doesn't need heels and makeup.

"They are also worn for prestige," she added. "People who used to wear ski parkas to the supermarket kept the lift-line tag on the zipper. It's announcing to the world, 'I am a skier.' It requires skill, and it requires money."

Another theory, that the popularity of sports garb is linked to the fact that the population is aging, came from the novelist Alison Lurie, who also wrote "The Language of Clothes," an examination of the meaning of dress. "A lot of these people are way beyond the age of being professional athletes," she said. "This is a way of looking healthy, energetic and fit, which is physically attractive, of course. It is also a way of wearing clothes less standard and boring than their gray flannel and navy 'dress for success' clothes."

Arlene Kaplan Daniels, a professor of sociology at Northwestern University, characterized warm-up suits and designer athletic garb as "symbolic communication."

"What the people who wear them are saying is 'I

am a now, with it, trendy person, I live in a certain apartment, I eat certain kinds of food.' People seize on these items because they're indicators of a certain kind of life." Those are the kind of people I usually can't stand.

But does that mean I'll stop wearing my tennis sweater to work? No, not as long as Chrissie keeps winning, and not as long as I can still wield a racquet.

Nora Ephron

LIVING WITH MY VCR

When all this started, two Christmases ago, I did not have a video-cassette recorder. What I had was a position on video-cassette recorders. I was against them. It seemed to me that the fundamental idea of the VCR—which is that if you go out and miss what's on television, you can always watch it later—flew in the face of almost the only thing I truly believed—which is that the whole point of going out is to miss what's on television. Let's face it: Part of being a grown-up is that every day you have to choose between going out at night or staying home, and it is one of life's unhappy truths that there is not enough time to do both.

Finally, though, I broke down, but not entirely. I did not buy a video-cassette recorder. I rented one. And I didn't rent one for myself—I myself intended to stand firm and hold to my only principle. I rented one for my children. For $29 a month, I would tape "The Wizard of Oz" and "Mary Poppins" and "Born Free," and my children would be able to watch them from time to time. In six months, when my rental contract expired, I would re-evaluate.

For quite a while, I taped for my children. Of course I had to subscribe to Home Box Office and Cinemax in addition to my normal cable service, for $19 more a month— but for the children. I taped "Oliver" and "Annie" and "My

Fair Lady" for the children. And then I stopped taping for the children—who don't watch much television, in any case—and started to tape for myself.

I now tape for myself all the time. I tape when I am out, I tape when I am at home and doing other things, and I tape when I am asleep. At this very moment, as I am typing, I am taping. The entire length of my bedroom bookshelf has been turned over to video cassettes, mostly of movies; they are numbered and indexed and stacked in order in a household where absolutely nothing else is. Occasionally I find myself browsing through publications like Video Review and worrying whether I shouldn't switch to chrome-based videotape or have my heads cleaned or upgrade to a machine that does six or seven things at once and can be set to tape six or seven months in advance. No doubt I will soon find myself shopping at some Video Village for racks and storage systems especially made for what is known as "the serious collector."

How this happened, how I became a compulsive videotaper, is a mystery to me, because my position on video-cassette recorders is very much the same as the one I started with. I am still against them. Now, though, I am against them for different reasons: Now I hate them out of knowledge rather than ignorance. The other technological breakthroughs that have made their way into my life after my initial pigheaded opposition to them—like the electric typewriter and the Cuisinart—have all settled peacefully into my home. I never think about them except when I'm using them, and when I'm using them I take them for granted. They do exactly what I want them to do. I put the slicing disk into the Cuisinart, and damned if the thing doesn't slice things up just the way it's supposed to. But there's no taking a VCR for granted. It squats there, next to the television, ready to rebuke any fool who expects something of it.

A child can operate a VCR, of course. Only a few maneuvers are required to tape something, and only a few more are required to tape something while you are out. You must set the time to the correct time you wish the recording to begin and end. You must punch the channel selector. You must insert a videotape. And, on my set, you must switch the "on" button to "time record." Theoretically, you can then go out and have a high old time, knowing that even if you waste the evening, your video-cassette recorder will not.

Sometimes things work out. Sometimes I return home, rewind the tape, and discover that the machine has recorded exactly what I'd hoped it would. But more often than not, what is on the tape is not at all what I'd intended; in fact, the moments leading up to the revelation of what is actually on my video cassettes are without doubt the most suspenseful of my humdrum existence. As I rewind the tape, I have no idea of what, if anything, will be on it; as I press the "play" button, I have not a clue as to what in particular has gone wrong. All I ever know for certain is that something has.

Usually it's my fault. I admit it. I have mis-set the timer or channel selector or misread the newspaper listing. I have knelt at the foot of my machine and methodically, carefully, painstakingly set it—and set it wrong. This is extremely upsetting to me—I am normally quite competent when it comes to machines—but I can live with it. What is far more disturbing are the times when what has gone wrong is not my fault at all but the fault of outside forces over which I have no control whatsoever. The program listing in the newspaper lists the channel incorrectly. The cable guide inaccurately lists the length of the movie, lopping off the last 10 minutes. The evening's schedule of television programming is thrown off by an athletic event. The educational station is having a fund-raiser.

You would be amazed at how often outside forces affect a video-cassette recorder, and I think I am safe in saying that video-cassette recorders are the only household appliances that outside forces are even relevant to. As a result, my video-cassette library is a raggedy collection of near misses: "The Thin Man" without the opening; "King Kong" without the ending; a football game instead of "Murder, She Wrote"; dozens of PBS auctions and fund-raisers instead of dozens of episodes of "Masterpiece Theater." All told, my success rate at videotaping is even lower than my success rate at buying clothes I turn out to like as much as I did in the store; the machine provides more opportunities per week to make mistakes than anything else in my life.

Every summer and at Christmastime, I re-evaluate my six-month rental contract. I have three options: I can buy the video-cassette recorder, which I would never do because I hate it so much; I can cancel the contract and turn in the machine, which I would never do because I am so addicted to videotaping; or I can go on renting. I go on renting. In two years I have spent enough money renting to buy two video-cassette recorders at the discount electronics place in the neighborhood, but I don't care. Renting is my way of deluding myself that I have some power over my VCR; it's my way of believing that I can still some day reject the machine in an ultimate way (by sending it back)— or else forgive it (by buying it)—for all the times it has rejected me.

In the meantime, I have my pathetic but ever-expanding collection of cassettes. "Why don't you just rent the movies?" a friend said to me recently, after I finished complaining about the fact that my tape of "The Maltese Falcon" now has a segment of "Little House on the Prairie" in the middle of it. Rent them? What a bizarre suggestion. Then I would have to watch them. And I don't watch my videotapes. I don't have time. I would virtually have to watch my videotapes for the next two years just to catch up with what my VCR has recorded so far; and in any event, even if I did have time, the VCR would be taping and would therefore be unavailable for use in viewing.

So I merely accumulate video cassettes. I haven't accumulated anything this mindlessly since my days in college, when I was obsessed with filling my bookshelf, it didn't matter with what; what mattered was that I believed that if I had a lot of books, it would say something about my intelligence and taste. On some level, I suppose I believe that if I have a lot of video cassettes, it will say something—not about my intelligence or taste, but about my intentions. I intend to live long enough to have time to watch my videotapes. Any way you look at it, that means forever.

John Slote

THE SOCIAL SPORT

$\mathbf{A}$ few summers ago, I played for two softball teams. One, called Radio Sports, was made up of athletic, serious guys. We wore uniforms and prepared scouting reports on other teams. But though we won most games by fifteen runs, we were unhappy. I always felt our team competed not only against its opponents but against the game itself. We tried to take ourselves more seriously than the sport would let us.

The members of the other team I played on that summer were staffers on a magazine for which I worked part-time. At four-thirty in the afternoon we would start changing into T-shirts and jeans, and then we would all take the elevator downstairs and make our way to the field. Our team, one of hundreds that played in the parks those afternoons (so promiscuously entwined that someone else's right fielder rubbed shoulders with your shortstop), was a motley bunch. Our beer tasted cold and metallic. The art director, in right field, kept dropping fly balls and getting angry. The catcher's fiancé was good at third, and the pitcher wasn't bad; but, still, we rarely won a game. I didn't know it then, but that mattered to me. I used to leave the park with a nagging feeling in my stomach, a feeling I did not like or understand.

Softball is the game of baseball made less challenging. It is a social sport, since everyone can play it. But when we play the game, we also admit that we can't be everything we want to be—baseball is too good (and difficult) for us. And yet, though easier, softball can be good, too. If the players know how to play their positions, the game can be *played* hard; at the same time, it needn't sacrifice the social appeal that is perhaps its greatest virtue. Somewhere between my magazine team (it didn't even have a name) and Radio Sports, there exists the ideal softball team—a team mature enough to be sociable and innocent enough to play to win.

No position suffers more from the changes that turn baseball into softball than do those of pitcher and catcher. The pitcher's big, difficult hardball delivery becomes an underhand lob with a swollen ball. The catcher no longer has to guard the bases against theft, since in softball there is no base stealing. Thus a team of mixed abilities will stick its less accomplished players at these positions, where—their pride wounded—they wither. No good can come of this. The battery is essential to the team.

At the core of the best softball game is a pitcher who pitches well enough that the other team hits its way to base rather than walks there. It is difficult to strike too many batters out, but a pitcher can at least make batters earn their hits and spare his outfielders the indignity of having to run into the neighboring game's infield to retrieve home runs. And, depending on the amount of arch the rules allow, the pitcher *can* get clever; he can deliver a steeply dropping ball that falls to earth at the back of the strike zone, armpit-level—a pitch that forces the batter to go back on his heels. Or the pitcher can throw to a point just above the batter's front kneecap on the outside corner of the plate, forcing him to lunge forward for the pitch. While in softball a pitcher cannot hope to dominate the game as he can in hardball, he can—by throwing accurately, by fielding his own position aggressively, by racing to cover first, for example, every time the first baseman has to make a play on a hit ball—give his team and the game an edge.

No one wants to be the catcher. It's dirty, dangerous, and uncomfortable back there. But there is much to be made of the catcher's unique relationship with the game. Only he looks out at the whole theater of action. Only he can speed up or slow down the tempo of the game by holding the ball between pitches. Only he can—and must—be responsible for making sure the outfielders are in their correct positions and that everyone knows how many outs there are and where the play is going. He must also watch to see that the pitcher is properly pampered, or harangued, and that he does not fly off the handle if he does not like a call. In short, the catcher takes charge of things. He must also take charge of himself, taking care to protect himself with a cup and to keep his throwing hand in a fist while the pitch is coming to avoid jammed fingers from foul tips. No one else will look out for him.

In my experience, the defensive player who handles the most chances (and handles them most spectacularly) is the shortstop. Thus it is a good thing that there are shortstops in this world, wearing their wristbands and looking sharp, tossing away loose pebbles, and readying themselves to come swooping gracefully in on a ground ball before they fire it to first in a cloud of dust. Elsewhere in the infield, one need not be so fancy; a little brute courage, hustle, and aggressiveness will do.

But for any infielder, the trick is to get in front of the ball, to keep your eyes on it, and to take *control* in whatever way you can. At third you've got time to field the ball off your chest before you make the long, hard, fast throw to first. At second base, since your throw is relatively easy, you can play deep and increase your range; you also have time to drop to your knees to field a ground ball. But at first base the most important thing is to not drop good throws and to not stay glued to the bag: better to let the batter make it to first than to let him take second on an errant throw that might have been stopped had you gotten your body out in front of it.

If for some reason your team does not have a shortstop and *you* end up there, you should try your best to summon all your nerve; you're not only going to have to play like a shortstop, you'll have to look like one, too. While success or failure in the field depends on your ability to move off the balls of your feet, to go far to your left and right, to field the ball cleanly and throw in one artful motion—on a typically weedy, unkempt softball field, it's that dash of vanity your team will count on most.

Things tend to get a bit more complex in the outfield. To play out there, you have to learn to judge the flight of sailing softballs, learn to get a jump on the ball (that is, commit yourself one way or another before you're really ready to) by the sound it makes off the batter's stick, learn to come in hard on ground balls and go back on long flies without getting all twisted up and confused. You have to learn to run evenly on the front of your feet to soften the impact of your steps: trouncing tensely over the outfield ground with your eyes following the ball, you'll suddenly feel the earth quaking beneath you and see your vision go bouncing off to somewhere the ball isn't. In the outfield it is almost always a good idea to take ground balls down on one knee, for there is no one else behind you if the ball hits a cigarette butt and skips your glove. Good outfielders know the earth: they know that a line drive landing on hard, dry ground bounces high overheard. A good outfielder can haul in a fly ball at the same time he is building momentum for his throw. A good outfielder can even fake base runners into thinking he is going to catch a ball that he's really going to take on a bounce.

You can learn to do these things, to glide like a gazelle and coolly snap a ball shut in your mitt while reaching far over your shoulder. But to be an outfielder in a game, you must be a conqueror not only of balls and space but of mind. For having waited inning after inning for some action in the outfield, having reacted time and time again to the swing of the bat only to see an infielder get the play, having been stranded far from anyone for far too long with nothing at all to do, it will inevitably be your first reaction, when at last the ball seems headed out your way, to think: "How ironic, how *awfully* ironic it would be if after all this waiting around doing nothing I missed this ball." Then you are in trouble.

To play the outfield, you must use the waiting time to your advantage. You must think. You must make the play in your mind before it comes up in real life. You must know at every moment exactly what is going on: how many outs there are, where the runners are, where they'll be headed by the time, say, a ground ball through the infield starts toward you. You must fantasize every possibility. If you do, and the moment comes to make a play, *then* it will be time to sit back and let it happen: the ball will come bouncing merrily out to you as little figures dash around the bases like gophers: you will kneel, catch the ball, and come up throwing without a moment's hesitation; and then you will watch as the ball sails through the air to third, where your baseman colleague will casually nail the runner on his way from first.

The ideal softball team plays like a team. It knows how to whip the ball around the horn after an out, knows how to relay the ball in from the outfield, knows who takes whose throw, who covers what bag when. That's what you must work toward: the unity that happens when you hear the sound of one another's voices in the field: when you feel together, solid.

In softball it is the offensive team's task to crack the fielding team's defense. For the team that's up to bat, that means putting the ball in play, forcing the action, and running the bases like a bunch of madpeople. Punch the ball out over the shortstop, make the left fielder throw you out at second. The more the other guys have to throw and catch the ball, the more often your team will cross home plate. (And don't forget to touch the bases; push your inside foot against the inside corner of the bag for turning power.)

Like the pitcher and the catcher on defense, the softball hitter must live with the knowledge that this whole game has been concocted to make his task easy. It is this knowledge, I think, that causes one to lunge and overswing at the plate, that causes one's concentration to collapse just as that big, fat, ridiculous target comes drifting up before one's eyes. Patience, poise, concentration, a continuous view of the ball, a loose and level swing—all this is imperative; as a hitter you must be humble, respect the game, and maintain all the fundamentals. Swing for ground balls before pop-ups, and line drives before long high flies. Let the other team make the difficult play.

The point in softball is to keep steep pressure on the other guys. That's the way to score runs. But the more pressure you put on your opponents, the more pressure you put on the game itself. In some cases this may cause the game to crack. There are some precautions you can take.

When there are no umpires, it is important to approach the contest warily, to fortify it with plenty of rules and regulations and formal agreements. Everyone may be feeling chummy at the game's beginning but how will they be feeling when the score is 2–2 in the last inning and someone tries a squeeze play? Likewise, sooner or later someone is bound to put the foul lines to the test or suddenly claim that sliding is not allowed. Even the most informal game must have their fierce formalities. Standards for what constitutes a ball and strike must be rigidly maintained. There has to be an accepted way of making "out" and "safe" calls at the bases, and there have to be bases. The anchored, canvas type of bag is still the base worth getting. Second best is a rubber slab. After that your choices dwindle. A T-shirt gets tangled up in one's feet. A piece of cardboard blows away, and a mark in the dirt is kind of hard to see.

Softball is a social sport, but what one remembers from a softball game is not only the society but the score, and one's own performance. Thinking back to playing on the magazine team, I can still see myself popping up to third one time in Central Park. Remembering the Radio Sports team, I think of the time I hit a pitch right between the seams for a home run an inning just before the rain came, and then everyone ran for cover.

I think of the night games we played down by the East River, a red boat drifting by left field, and how we once played a team of women professional basketball players: stretching out a single, I slid into the blonde at second and was safe. I remember her legs. I think of the time we played a team sponsored by Meatloaf, the singer, who arrived in his own limousine and pitched. Afterward he stayed out in the field by himself, berating the umpire because he could not bear the score. I had doubled off him twice.

Richard Rodriguez

COMPLEXION

Complexion. My first conscious experience of sexual excitement concerns my complexion. One summer weekend, when I was around seven years old, I was at a public swimming pool with the whole family. I remember sitting on the damp pavement next to the pool and seeing my mother, in the spectators' bleachers, holding my younger sister on her lap. My mother, I noticed, was watching my father as he stood on a diving board, waving to her. I watched her wave back. Then saw her radiant, bashful, astonishing smile. In that second I sensed that my mother and father had a relationship I knew nothing about. A nervous excitement encircled my stomach as I saw my mother's eyes follow my father's figure curving into the water. A second or two later, he emerged. I heard him call out. Smiling, his voice sounded, buoyant, calling me to swim to him. But turning to see him, I caught my mother's eye. I heard her shout over to me. In Spanish she called through the crowd: 'Put a towel on over your shoulders.' In public, she didn't want to say why. I knew.

That incident anticipates the shame and sexual inferiority I was to feel in later years because of my dark complexion. I was to grow up an ugly child. Or one who thought himself ugly. (*Feo.*) One night when I was eleven or twelve years old, I locked myself in the bathroom and carefully regarded my reflection in the mirror over the sink. Without any pleasure I studied my skin. I turned on the faucet. (In my mind I heard the swirling voices of aunts, and even my mother's voice, whispering, whispering incessantly about lemon juice solutions and dark, *feo* children.) With a bar of soap, I fashioned a thick ball of lather. I began soaping my arms. I took my father's straight razor out of the medicine cabinet. Slowly, with steady deliberateness, I put the blade against my flesh, pressed it as close as I could without cutting, and moved it up and down across my skin to see if I could get out, somehow lessen, the dark. All I succeeded in doing, however, was in shaving my arms bare of their hair. For as I noted with disappointment, the dark would not come out. It remained. Trapped. Deep in the cells of my skin.

Throughout adolescence, I felt myself mysteriously marked. Nothing else about my appearance would concern me so much as the fact that my complexion was dark. My mother would say how sorry she was that there was not money enough to get braces to straighten my teeth. But I never bothered about my teeth. In three-way mirrors at department stores, I'd see my profile dramatically defined by a long nose, but it was really only the color of my skin that caught my attention.

I wasn't afraid that I would become a menial laborer because of my skin. Nor did my complexion make me feel especially vulnerable to racial abuse. (I didn't really consider my dark skin to be a racial characteristic. I would have been only too happy to look as Mexican as my light-skinned older brother.) Simply, I judged myself ugly. And, since the women in my family had been the ones who discussed it in such worried tones, I felt my dark skin made me unattractive to women.

Thirteen years old. Fourteen. In a grammar school art class, when the assignment was to draw a self-portrait, I tried and I tried but could not bring myself to shade in the face on the paper to anything like my actual tone. With disgust then I would come face to face with myself in mirrors. With disappointment I located myself in class photographs—

my dark face undefined by the camera which had clearly described the white faces of classmates. Or I'd see my dark wrist against my long-sleeved white shirt.

I grew divorced from my body. Insecure, overweight, listless. On hot summer days when my rubber-soled shoes soaked up the heat from the sidewalk, I kept my head down. Or walked in the shade. My mother didn't need anymore to tell me to watch out for the sun. I denied myself a sensational life. The normal, extraordinary, animal excitement of feeling my body alive—riding shirtless on a bicycle in the warm wind created by furious self-propelled motion—the sensations that first had excited in me a sense of my maleness, I denied. I was too ashamed of my body. I wanted to forget that I had a body because I had a brown body. I was grateful that none of my classmates ever mentioned the fact.

I continued to see the *braceros,* those men I resembled in one way and, in another way, didn't resemble at all. On the watery horizon of a Valley afternoon, I'd see them. And though I feared looking like them, it was with silent envy that I regarded them still. I envied them their physical lives, their freedom to violate the taboo of the sun. Closer to home I would notice the shirtless construction workers, the roofers, the sweating men tarring the street in front of the house. And I'd see the Mexican gardeners. I was unwilling to admit the attraction of their lives. I tried to deny it by looking away. But what was denied became strongly desired.

In high school physical education classes, I withdrew, in the regular company of five or six classmates, to a distant corner of a football field where we smoked and talked. Our company was composed of bodies too short or too tall, all graceless and all—except mine—pale. Our conversation was usually witty. (In fact we were intelligent.) If we referred to the athletic contests around us, it was with sarcasm. With savage scorn I'd refer to the 'animals' playing football or baseball. It would have been important for me to have joined them. Or for me to have taken off my shirt, to have let the sun burn dark on my skin, and to have run barefoot on the warm wet grass. It would have been very important.

Too important. It would have been too telling a gesture—to admit the desire for sensation, the body, my body.

Fifteen, sixteen. I was a teenager shy in the presence of girls. Never dated. Barely could talk to a girl without stammering. In high school I went to several dances, but I never managed to ask a girl to dance. So I stopped going. I cannot remember high school years now with the parade of typical images: bright drive-ins or gliding blue shadows of a Junior Prom. At home most weekend nights, I would pass evenings reading. Like those hidden, precocious adolescents who have no real-life sexual experiences, I read a great deal of romantic fiction. 'You won't find it in your books,' my brother would playfully taunt me as he prepared to go to a party by freezing the crest of the wave in his hair with sticky pomade. Through my reading, however, I developed a fabulous and sophisticated sexual imagination. At seventeen, I may not have known how to engage a girl in small talk, but I had read *Lady Chatterley's Lover*.

It annoyed me to hear my father's teasing: that I would never know what 'real work' is; that my hands were so soft. I think I knew it was his way of admitting pleasure and pride in my academic success. But I didn't smile. My mother said she was glad her children were getting their educations and would not be pushed around like *los pobres*. I heard the remark ironically as a reminder of my separation from *los braceros*. At such times I suspected that education was making me effeminate. The odd thing, however, was that I did not judge my classmates so harshly. Nor did I consider my male teachers in high school effeminate. It was only myself I judged against some shadowy, mythical Mexican laborer—dark like me, yet very different.

George Steiner

THE FUTURE OF READING

It is hardly necessary for me to cite all the evidence of the depressing state of literacy. These figures from the Department of Education are sufficient: 27 million Americans cannot read at all, and a further 35 million read at a level that is less than sufficient to survive in our society.

But my own worry today is less that of the overwhelming problem of elemental literacy than it is of the slightly more luxurious problem of the decline in the skills even of the middle-class reader, of his unwillingness to afford those spaces of silence, those luxuries of domesticity and time and concentration, that surround the image of the classic act of reading. It has been suggested that almost 80 percent of America's *literate*, educated teenagers can no longer read without an attendant noise (music) in the background or a television screen flickering at the corner of their field of perception. We know very little about the cortex and how it deals with simultaneous conflicting input, but every common-sense hunch suggests we should be profoundly alarmed. This breach of concentration, silence, solitude goes to the very heart of our notion of literacy; this new form of part-reading, of part-perception against background distraction, renders impossible certain essential acts of apprehension and concentration, let alone that most important tribute any human being can pay to a poem or a piece of prose he or she really loves, which is to *learn it by heart*. Not by brain, by heart; the expression is vital.

Under these circumstances, the question of what future there is for the arts of reading is a real one. Ahead of us lie technical, psychic, and social transformations probably much more dramatic than those brought about by Gutenberg. The Gutenberg revolution, as we now know it took a long time; its effects are still being debated. The information revolution will touch every facet of composition, publication, distribution, and reading. No one in the book industry can say with any confidence what will happen to the book as we've known it.

It now looks as if the arts of reading will fall into three distinct categories. The first will continue to be the vast, amorphous mass of reading for distraction, for momentary entertainment—the airport book. I suspect that this kind of reading will more and more involve not cheap paperbacks but cable transmissions to home screens. You will select the book you wish, the speed at which you wish it to be presented on the screen, the speed at which you wish the pages to be turned. Some texts will be read to the viewer by a professional reader. Whether or not the text will appear on the screen as it is being read is an open question.

The second kind of reading will be for information— what De Quincey called "the literature of knowledge," to distinguish it from fiction, poetry, and drama, which he called "the literature of power." The means to acquire the literature of knowledge—the micro circuit, the silicon chip, the laser disc—will alter our habits beyond anything we can now conceive. "The Library of Babel," the library of all possible libraries that Borges imagined in his fable, will be literally and concretely accessible for personal and institutional use. We will be able to summon it up on a screen, and here the possibility of a basic change in the structures of attention and understanding is almost incommensurable.

What about reading in the old, private, silent sense? This may become as specialized a skill and avocation as it was in the scriptoria and libraries of monasteries during the so-called Dark Ages. We now know these were in fact key ages, radiant in their patience, radiant in their sense of what had to be copied and preserved. Private libraries may once again become as notable and rare as they were when Erasmus and Montaigne were famous for theirs. The habit of furnishing a room, a large room, possibly, with shelves and filling them with books, not paperbacks but bound books, the attempt to collect the complete editions of an author (itself a very special concept) as well as the first editions, not necessarily the rare books of the Morgan Library but the first editions of a modern author, with the hope of owning everything by a writer—good, bad, or indifferent—whom one loves; the ability—above all, the wish—to attend to a demanding text, to master the grammar, the arts of memory, the tactics of repose and concentration that great books demand—these may once more become the practices of an elite, of a mandarinate of silence.

Such a mandarinate, such an elite of book men and book women, will not have the power, the political reach, or the prestige that it had during the Renaissance and the Enlightenment, and almost to the end of the Victorian age. That power almost inevitably will belong to the aliterate. It will belong to the numerate. It will belong increasingly to those who, while technically almost unable to read a serious book and mostly unwilling to do so, can in preadolescence produce software of great delicacy, logical power, and conceptual depth. The power relations are shifting to them, to men and women who, having freed themselves from the heavy burden of actual alphabetic literacy and its constant referential habits, from the fact that almost all great literature refers to other great literature, are *creators*—nonreaders, but creators of a new kind.

Returning home one night, Erasmus is said to have seen a torn piece of print besmirched in the mud. As he bent to pick it up, he uttered a cry of joy, overcome by the wonder of the book, by the sheer miracle of what lies behind picking up such a message. Today, in a vast traffic jam on a highway or in a Manhattan grid, we can insert a cassette of the *Missa Solemnis* into a tape deck. We can, via paperbacks and soon cable television, demand, command, and compel the world's greatest, most exigent, most tragic or delightful literature to be served up for us, packaged and cellophaned for immediacy. These are great luxuries. But it is not certain that they really help the constant, renewed miracle that is the encounter with a book.

GLOSSARY

Abstract and concrete are ways of describing important qualities of language. Abstract words are not associated with real, material objects that are related directly to the five senses. Such words as "love," "wisdom," "patriotism," and "power" are abstract because they refer to ideas rather than to things. Concrete language, on the other hand, names things that can be perceived by the five senses. Words like "table," "smoke," "lemon," and "halfback" are concrete. Generally you should not be too abstract in writing. It is best to employ concrete words naming things that can be seen, touched, smelled, heard, or tasted in order to support your more abstract ideas.

Allusion is a reference to some literary, biographical, or historical event. It is a "figure of speech" (a fresh, useful comparison) used to illuminate an idea. For instance, if you want to state that a certain national ruler is insane, you might refer to him as a "Nero"—an allusion to the Emperor who burned Rome.

Alternating method in comparison and contrast involves a point-by-point treatment of the two subjects that you have selected to discuss. Assume that you have chosen five points to examine in a comparison of the Volkswagen "Golf" (subject A) and the Honda "Accord" (subject B): cost, comfort, gas mileage, road handling, and frequency of repair. In applying the alternating method, you would begin by discussing cost in relation to A + B; then comfort in relation to A + B, and so on. The alternating method permits you to isolate points for a balanced discussion.

Ambiguity means uncertainty. A writer is ambiguous when using a word, phrase, or sentence that is not clear. Ambiguity usually results in misunderstanding, and should be avoided in essay writing. Always strive for clarity in your compositions.

Analogy is a form of figurative comparison that uses a clear illustration to explain a difficult idea or function. It is unlike a formal comparison in that its subjects of comparison are from different categories or areas. For example, an analogy likening "division of labor" to the activity of bees in a hive makes the first concept more concrete by showing it to the reader through the figurative comparison with the bees.

Antonym is a word that is opposite in meaning to that of another word: "hot" is an antonym of "cold"; "fat" is an antonym of "thin"; "large" is an antonym of "small."

Argumentation is a form of writing in which you offer reasons in favor of or against something. (See Chapter 10, pp. 333–335.)

Block method in comparison and contrast involves the presentation of all information about your first subject (A), followed by all information about the second subject (B). Thus, using the objects of comparison explained in the discussion of the "alternating method" (see entry, p. 409), you would for the block method first present all five points about the Volkswagen. Then you would present all five points about the Honda. When using the block method, remember to present the same points for each subject, and to provide an effective transition in moving from subject A to subject B.

Causal analysis is a form of writing that examines causes and effects of events or conditions as they relate to a specific subject (see Chapter 9, pp. 288–290).

Characterization is the description of people. As a particular type of description in an essay, characterization attempts to capture as vividly as possible the features, qualities, traits, speech, and actions of individuals.

Chronological order is the arrangement of events in the order that they happened. You might use chronological order to trace the history of the Vietnam War, to explain a scientific process, or to present the biography of a close relative or friend. When you order an essay by chronology, you are moving from one step to the next in time.

Classification is a pattern of writing where the author divides a subject into categories and then groups elements in each of those categories according to their relationships to each other (see Chapter 7, pp. 217–218).

Clichés are expressions that were once fresh and vivid, but have become tired and worn from overuse. "I'm so hungry that I could eat a horse" is a typical cliché. People use clichés in conversation, but writers should generally avoid them.

Closings or "conclusions" are endings for your essay. Without a closing, your essay is incomplete, leaving the reader with the feeling that something important has been left out. There are numerous closing possibilities available to writers: summarizing main points in the essay; restating the main idea; using an effective quotation to bring the essay to an end; offering the reader the climax to a series of events; returning to the conclusion and echoing it; offering a solution to a problem; emphasizing the topic's significance; or setting a new frame of reference by generalizing from the main thesis. Whatever type of closing you use, make certain that it ends the essay in a firm and emphatic way.

Coherence is a quality in effective writing that results from the careful ordering of each sentence in a paragraph, and each paragraph in the essay. If an essay is coherent, each part will grow naturally and logically from those parts that come before it. Coherence depends on the writer's ability to organize materials in a logical way, and to order segments so that the reader is carried along easily from start to finish. The main devices used in achieving coherence are *transitions*, which help to connect one thought with another.

Colloquial language is language used in conversation and in certain types of informal writing, but rarely in essays, business writing, or research papers. There is nothing wrong with colloquialisms like "cool," "What's happening?" or "pal" when used in conversational settings. However, they are often unacceptable in essay writing—except when used sparingly for special effects.

Comparison/contrast is a pattern of essay writing treating similarities and differences between two subjects. (See Chapter 5, pp. 147–148.)

Composition is a term used for an essay or for any piece of writing that reveals a careful plan.

Concrete (See Abstract/Concrete)

Connotation/denotation are terms specifying the way a word has meaning. Connotation refers to the "shades of meaning" that a word might have because of various emotional associations it calls up for writers and readers alike. Words like "American," "physician," "mother," "pig," and "San Francisco" have strong connotative overtones to them. With denotation, however, we are concerned not with the suggestive meaning of a word but with its exact, literal meaning. Denotation refers to the "dictionary definition" of a word—its exact meaning. Writers must understand the connotative and denotative value of words, and must control the shades of meaning that many words possess.

Context clues are hints provided about the meaning of a word by another word or words, or by the sentence or sentences coming before or after it. Thus in the sentence, "Mr. Rome, a true *raconteur,* told a story that thrilled the guests," we should be able to guess at the meaning of the italicized word by the context clues coming both before and after it. (A "raconteur" is a person who tells good stories.)

Definition is a method of explaining a word so that the reader knows what you mean by it. (See Chapter 6, pp. 181–182.)

Derivation is how a word originated and where it came from. Knowing the origin of a word can make you more aware of its meaning, and more able to use it effectively in writing. Your dictionary normally lists abbreviations (for example, O.E. for Old English, G. for Greek) for word origins and sometimes explains fully how they came about.

Description is a type of writing that uses details of sight, color, sound, smell, and touch to create a word picture and to explain or illustrate an idea. (See Chapter 2, pp. 40–41.)

Dialogue is the exact duplication in writing of something people say to each other. Dialogue is the reproduction of speech or conversation; it can add concreteness and vividness to an essay, and can also help to reveal character. When using dialogue, writers must be careful to use correct punctuation. Moreover, to use dialogue effectively in essay writing, you must develop an ear for the way other people talk, and an ability to create it accurately.

Diction refers to the writer's choice or use of words. Good diction reflects the topic of the writing. Orwell's diction, for example, is formal, despite colloquial language in the spoken dialogue he quotes. Least Heat Moon's diction (Chapter 2) is more varied, including subtle descriptions in standard diction and conversational sarcasms. Levels of diction refer both to the purpose of the essay and to the writer's audience. Skillful choice of the level of diction keeps the reader intimately involved with the topic.

Division is that aspect of classification (see Chapter 7, pp. 217–218) where the writer divides some large subject into categories. For example, you might divide "fish" into salt water and fresh water fish; or "sports" into team and individual sports. Division helps writers to split large and potentially complicated subjects into parts for orderly presentation and discussion.

Effect is a term used in causal analysis (see Chapter 9, pp. 228–290) to describe the outcome or expected result of a chain of happenings. When dealing with the analysis of effects, writers should determine whether they want to work with immediate or final effects, or both. Thus, a writer analyzing the effects of an accidental nuclear explosion that happened in 1956 might choose to analyze effects immediately after the blast, as well as effects that still linger.

Emphasis suggests the placement of the most important ideas in key positions in the essay. Writers can emphasize ideas simply by placing important ones at the beginning or at the end of the paragraph or essay. But several other techniques help writers to emphasize important ideas: (1) key words and ideas can be stressed by repetition; (2) ideas can be presented in climactic order, by building from lesser ideas at the beginning to the main idea at the end; (3) figurative language (for instance, a vivid simile) can call attention to a main idea; (4) the relative proportion of detail offered to support an idea can emphasize its importance; (5) comparison and contrast of an idea with other ideas can emphasize its importance; and (6) mechanical devices like underlining, capitalizing, or using exclamation points (all of which should be used sparingly) can stress significance.

Essay is the name given to a short prose work on a limited topic. Essays take many forms, ranging from a familiar narrative account of an event in your life, to explanatory, argumentative, or critical investigations of a subject. Normally, in one way or the other, an essay will convey the writer's personal ideas about the subject.

Euphemism is the use of a word or phrase simply because it seems less distasteful or less offensive than another word. For instance, "mortician" is a euphemism for "undertaker"; "sanitation worker" for "garbage collector."

Fable is a narrative with a moral (see Chapter 3, pp. 69–70). The story from which the writer draws the moral can be either true or imaginary. When writing a fable, it is important that a writer clearly presents the moral to be derived from the narrative, as Rachel Carson does in "A Fable for Tomorrow."

Figurative language, as opposed to *literal,* is a special approach to writing that departs from what is typically a concrete, straightforward style. It involves a vivid, imaginative comparison that goes beyond plain or ordinary statements. For instance, instead of saying that "Joan is wonderful," you could write that "Joan is like a summer's rose" (a *simile*); "Joan's hair is wheat, pale and soft and yellow" (a *metaphor*); "Joan is my Helen of Troy" (an *allusion*); or a number of other comparative approaches. Note that Joan is not a rose, her hair is not wheat, nor is she some other person named Helen. Figurative language is not logical; instead, it requires an ability on the part of the writer to create an imaginative comparison in order to make an idea more striking.

Flashback is a narrative technique in which the writer begins at some point in the action and then moves into the past in order to provide necessary background information. Flashback adds variety to the narrative method, enabling writers to approach a story not only in terms of straight chronology, but in terms of a back-and-forth movement. However, it is at best a very difficult technique and should be used with great care.

General/specific words are necessary in writing, although it is wise to keep your vocabulary as specific as possible. General words refer to broad categories and groups, while specific words capture with more force and clarity the nature of a term. The distinction between general and specific language is always a matter of degree. "A woman walked down the street" is more general than "Mrs. Walker walked down Fifth Avenue," while "Mrs. Webster, elegantly dressed in a muslin suit, strolled down Fifth Avenue" is more specific than the first two examples. Our ability to use specific language depends on the extent of our vocabulary. The more words we know, the more specific we can be in choosing words.

Illustration is the use of several examples to support our idea (see Chapter 4, pp. 109–110).

Imagery is clear, vivid description that appeals to our sense of sight, smell, touch, sound, or taste. Much imagery exists for its own sake, adding descriptive flavor to an essay, as when Richard Selzer in "The Discus Thrower" writes, "I unwrap the bandages from the stumps, and begin to cut away the black scabs and the dead, glazed fat with scissors and forceps. A shard of white bone comes loose." However, imagery can also add meaning to an essay. For example, in Francke's essay, the pattern of imagery connected with the setting and procedure of her abortion alerts the reader to the importance of that event in the author's life. Again, when Orwell writes at the start of "A Hanging," "It was in Burma, a sodden morning of the rains. A sickly light, like yellow tinfoil, was slanting over the high walls into the jail yard," we see that the author uses imagery to prepare us for the sombre and terrifying event to follow. Writers can use imagery to contribute to any type of wording, or they can rely on it to structure an entire essay. It is always difficult to invent fresh, vivid description, but it is an effort that writers should make if they wish to improve the quality of their prose.

Introductions are the beginning or openings of essays. Introductions should perform a number of functions. They should alert the reader to the subject, set the limits of the essay, and indicate what the thesis (or main idea) will be. Moreover, they should arouse the reader's interest in the subject, so that the reader will want to continue reading into the essay. There are several devices available to writers that will aid in the development of sound introductions.

1. Simply state the subject and establish the thesis. See the Jade Snow Wong essay (p. 47), and "The Three New Yorks" (p. 229).
2. Open with a clear, vivid description of a setting that will become important as your essay advances. Save your thesis for a later stage, but indicate what your subject is. See the essay by Truman Capote (p. 42).

3. Ask a question or a series of questions, which you might answer in the introduction or in another part of the essay. See the Jordan essay (p. 191).

4. Tell an anecdote (a short, self-contained story of an entertaining nature) that serves to illuminate your subject. See the Jacoby essay (p. 323).

5. Use comparison or contrast to frame your subject and to present the thesis. See the Russell Baker essay (p. 156).

6. Begin by stating your personal attitude toward a controversial issue. See the James Baker essay (p. 247).

These are only some of the devices that appear in the introductions to essays in this text. Writers can also ask questions, give definitions, or provide personal accounts—there are many techniques that can be used to develop introductions. The important thing to remember is that you *need* an introduction to an essay. It can be a single sentence or a much longer paragraph, but it must accomplish its purpose—to introduce readers to the subject, and to engage them so that they want to explore the essay further.

Irony is the use of language to suggest the opposite of what is stated. Writers use irony to reveal unpleasant or troublesome realities that exist in life, or to poke fun at human weaknesses and foolish attitudes. For instance, in "A Hanging," the men who are in charge of the execution engage in laughter and lighthearted conversation after the event. There is irony in the situation and in their speech because we sense that they are actually very tense—almost unnerved—by the hanging; their laughter is the opposite of what their true emotional state actually is. Many situations and conditions lend themselves to ironic treatment.

Jargon is the use of special words associated with a specific area of knowledge or a specific profession. It is similar to "shop talk" that members of a certain trade might know, but not necessarily people outside it. For example, in Bettelheim's essay there are several terms or applications of jargon relating to psychology. Use jargon sparingly in your writing, and be certain to define all spcialized terms that you think your readers might not know.

Journalese is a level of writing associated with prose types normally found in newspapers and popular magazines. A typical newspaper article tends to present information factually or objectively; to use simple language and simple sentence structure; and to rely on relatively short paragraphs. It also stays close to the level of conversational English without becoming chatty or colloquial.

taphor is a type of figurative language in which an item from one category is compared briefly and imaginatively with an item from another area. Writers create metaphors to assign meaning to a word in an original way.

rration is telling a story in order to illustrate an important idea (see Chapter 3, pp. 69–70).

jective/subjective writing refers to the attitude that writers take toward their subject. When writers are objective, they try not to report their own personal feelings about their subject. They attempt to control, if not eliminate, their own attitude toward the topic. Thus in the essay by McGrath (see pp. 172–175), we learn about how violence in the Old West compares with violence today, but we don't learn about the writer's attitudes about such violence. Many essays, on the other hand, reveal the authors' personal attitudes and emotions. In Bradbury's essay (see pp. 127–132), the author's personal excitement over Halloween seems clear. He takes a highly subjective approach to the topic. For some kinds of college writing, such as business or laboratory reports, research papers, or literary analyses, it is best to be as objective as possible. But for many of the essays in composition courses, the subjective touch is fine.

der is the manner in which you arrange information or materials in an essay. The most common ordering techniques are *chronological order* (involving time sequence); *spatial order* (involving the arrangement of descriptive details); *process order* (involving a step-by-step approach to an activity); *deductive order* (in which you offer a thesis and then the evidence to support it); and *inductive order* (in which you present evidence first and build toward the thesis). Some rhetorical patterns such as comparison and contrast, classification, and argumentation require other ordering techniques. Writers should select those ordering principles that permit them to present materials clearly.

radox is a statement that *seems* to be contradictory but actually contains an element of truth. Writers use it in order to call attention to their subject.

Parallelism is a variety of sentence structure in which there is "balance" or coordination in the presentation of elements. "I came, I saw, I conquered" is a good example of parallelism, presenting both pronouns and verbs in a coordinated manner. Parallelism can also be applied to several sentences and to entire paragraphs (see the Syfers's essay, pages 351–354). It can be an effective way to emphasize ideas.

Personification is giving an object, thing, or idea lifelike or human qualities. For instance, Ray Bradbury personifies Halloween when he writes that it "didn't just stroll into our yards" (see p. 129). Like all forms of figurative writing, personification adds freshness to description, and makes idead vivid by setting up striking comparisons.

Point of view is the angle from which a writer tells a story. Many personal or informal essays take the *first-person* (or "I") point of view, as the essays by Welty, Capote, Wong, Moon, Goodman, Hughes, Orwell, Williams, and others reveal. The first-person "I" point of view is natural and fitting for essays when the writer wants to speak in a familiar and intimate way to the reader. On the other hand, the *third-person* point of view ("he," "she," "it," "they") distances the reader somewhat from the writer. The third-person point of view is useful in essays where writers are not talking exclusively about themselves, but about other people, things, and events as in the essays by McGrath, Carson, and White. Occasionally, the second-person ("you") point of view will appear in essays, notably in essays involving process analysis where the writer directs the reader to do something; part of Ernest Hemingway's essay (which also utilizes third-person point of view) uses this strategy. The position that you take as a writer depends largely on the type of essay you write.

Prefix is one or more syllables attached to the front of another word in order to influence its meaning or to create a new word. A knowledge of prefixes and their meanings aids in establishing the meanings of words and in increasing the vocabulary that we use in writing. Common prefixes and their meanings include *bi*-(two), *ex*-(out, out of), *per*-(through), *pre*-(before), re-(back), *tele*-(distant), and *trans*-(across, beyond).

Process analysis is a pattern of writing that explains in a step-by-step way the methods for doing something or reaching a desired end (see Chapter 8, pp. 256–257).

Proposition is the main point in an argumentative essay. It is like a *thesis* except that it usually presents an idea that is debatable or can be disputed.

Refutation is a technique in argumentative writing where you recognize and deal effectively with the arguments of your opponents. Your own argument will be stronger if you can refute—prove false or wrong—all opposing arguments.

Root is the basic part of a word. It sometimes aids us in knowing what the larger word means. Thus if we know that the root *doc*-means "teach" we might be able to figure out a word like "doctrine." *Prefixes* and *suffixes* are attached to roots to create words.

Sarcasm is a sneering or taunting attitude in writing. It is designed to hurt by ridiculing or criticizing. Basically, sarcasm is a heavy-handed form of irony, as when an individual says, "Well, you're exactly on time, aren't you" to someone who is an hour late, and says it with a sharpness in the voice, a sharpness designed to hurt. Writers should try to avoid sarcastic writing and to use more acceptable varieties of irony and satire to criticize their subject.

Satire is the humorous or critical treatment of a subject in order to expose the subject's vices, follies, stupidities, and so forth. Syfers, for instance, satirizes stereotyped notions of wives, hoping to change these attitudes by revealing them as foolish. Satire is a better weapon than sarcasm in the hands of the writer because satire is used to correct, whereas sarcasm merely hurts.

Sentimentality is the excessive display of emotion in writing, whether it is intended or unintended. Because sentimentality can distort the true nature of a situation, writers should use it cautiously, or not at all. They should be especially careful when dealing with certain subjects, for example the death of a loved one, remembrance of a mother or father, a ruined romance, the loss of something valued, that lend themselves to sentimental treatment. Only the best writers—Welty, Thomas, Francke, Hughes, and others in this text—can avoid the sentimental traps rooted in their subjects.

Simile is an imaginative comparison using "like" or "as." When Orwell writes, "A sickly light, like yellow tinfoil, was slanting over the high walls into the jail yard," he uses a vivid simile in order to reinforce the dull description of the scene.

Slang is a level of language that uses racy and colorful expressions associated more often with speech than with writing. Slang expressions like "Gerald's my boss man" or "That chick is groovy" should not be used in essay writing, except when the writer is reproducing dialogue or striving for a special effect. Hughes is one writer in this collection who uses slang effectively to convey his message to the reader.

Suffix is a syllable or syllables appearing at the end of a word and influencing its meaning. As with prefixes and roots, you can build vocabulary and establish meanings by knowing about suffixes. Some typical suffixes are *-able* (capable of), *-al* (relating to), *-ic* (characteristic of), *-ion* (state of), *-er* (one who) appear often in standard writing.

Symbol is something that exists in itself but also stands for something else. Thus the "stumps" in paragraph 20 of Selzer's essay "The Discus Thrower" are not just the patient's amputated legs, but they serve as symbols of the man's helplessness and immobility. As a type of figurative language, the symbol can be a strong feature in an essay, operating to add depth of meaning, and even to unify entire essays.

Synonym is a word that means roughly the same as another word. In practice, few words are exactly alike in meaning. Careful writers use synonyms to vary word choice, without ever moving too far from the shade of meaning intended.

Theme is the central idea in an essay; it is also often termed the *thesis*. Everything in an essay should support the theme in one way or another.

Thesis is the main idea in an essay. The *thesis sentence*, appearing early in the essay, and normally somewhere in the first paragraph, serves to convey the main idea to the reader in a clear way. It is always useful to state your central idea as soon as possible, and before you introduce other supporting ideas.

Title for an essay should be a short, simple indication of the contents of your essay. Titles like "One Writer's Beginnings," "Death in the Open," "The Ambivalence of Abortion," and "The Future of Reading" are the sorts of titles that convey the central subjects of these essays in brief, effective ways. Always provide titles for your essays.

Tone is the writer's attitude toward his or her subject or material. An essay writer's tone may be objective ("Arizona 87"), ironic ("I Want A Wife"), comic ("Salvation"), nostalgic ("Tricks! Treats! Gangway!"), or a reflection of numerous other attitudes. Tone is the "voice" that you give to an essay; every writer should strive to create a "personal voice" or tone that will be distinctive throughout any type of essay under development.

Transition is the linking of one idea to the next in order to achieve essay coherence (See *Coherence*). Transitions are words that connect these ideas. Among the most common techniques to achieve smooth transition are: (1) repeating a key word or phrase; (2) using a pronoun to refer back to a key word or phrase; (3) relying on traditional connectives like "thus," "for example," "moreover," "therefore," "however," "finally," "likewise," "afterwards," and "in conclusion"; (4) using parallel structure (see *Parallelism*); and (5) creating a sentence or an entire paragraph that serves as a bridge from one part of your essay to the next. Transition is best achieved when the writer presents ideas and details carefully and in logical order. Try not to lose the reader by failing to provide for adequate transition from idea to idea.

Unity is that feature in an essay where all material relates to a central concept and contributes to the meaning of the whole. To achieve a unified effect in an essay, the writer must design an introduction and conclusion, maintain a consistent tone and point of view, develop middle paragraphs in a coherent manner, and always stick to the subject, never permitting unimportant elements to enter. Thus, unity involves a successful blending of all elements that go into the creation of a sound essay.

Vulgarisms are words that exist below conventional vocabulary, and which are not accepted in polite conversation. Always avoid vulgarisms in your own writing, unless they serve an illustrative purpose.

Acknowledgments

Maya Angelou, "The Flight," from *I Know Why the Caged Bird Sings* by Maya Angelou. Copyright © 1968 by Maya Angelou. Reprinted by permission of Random House, Inc.

James T. Baker, "How Do We Find the Students in a World of Academic Gymnasts and Worker Ants?" from *The Chronicle of Higher Education.* Copyright © 1982 by The Chronicle of Higher Education. Reprinted with permission.

Russell Baker, "The Two Islands," from *The New York Times,* 1982. Copyright © 1982 by The New York Times Company. Reprinted by permission.

Bruno Bettelheim, "Fairy Tales and Modern Stories," from *The Uses of Enchantment: The Meaning and Importance of Fairy Tales,* by Bruno Bettelheim. Copyright © 1976 by Bruno Bettelheim. Reprinted by permission of Alfred A. Knopf, Inc.

Ray Bradbury, "Tricks! Treats! Gangway!" from *Reader's Digest,* October 1975. Copyright © 1975 by Ray Bradbury. Reprinted by permission of Don Congdon Associates, Inc.

Truman Capote, "Louis Armstrong," from *Observations.* Copyright © 1959 by Richard Avedon and Truman Capote. Reprinted by permission of Simon & Schuster, Inc.

Rachel Carson, "A Fable for Tomorrow," from *Silent Spring* by Rachel Carson. Copyright © 1962 by Rachel Carson. Reprinted by permission of Houghton Mifflin Company.

Norman Cousins, "Why Johnny Can't Write," from *Present Tense: An American Editor's Odyssey.* Copyright © 1967 by McGraw-Hill Book Company. Reprinted with permission.

Gregg Easterbrook, "Escape Valve," from *The New York Times,* December 26, 1981. Copyright © 1981 by The New York Times Company. Reprinted by permission.

Nora Ephron, "Living with My VCR," from *The New York Times,* December 23, 1984. Copyright © 1984 by The New York Times Company. Reprinted by permission.

Linda Bird Francke, "The Ambivalence of Abortion," from *The New York Times,* May 1976. Copyright © 1976 by The New York Times Company. Reprinted by permission.

Ellen Goodman, "An Understanding Woman," from *At Large.* Copyright © 1981 by The Washington Post Company. Reprinted by permission of Summit Books, a division of Simon & Schuster, Inc.

Dan Greenburg, "How I Overhauled My Mechanic's Novel," from *The New York Times Book Review,* October 7, 1984. Copyright © 1984 by The New York Times Company. Reprinted by permission.

Lillian Hellman, "Memoir of a New Orleans Boarding House," from *The New York Times,* May 21, 1980. Copyright © 1980 by The New York Times Company. Reprinted by permission.

Ernest Hemingway, "Camping Out," from *The Toronto Star* and *Star Weekly.* Reproduced with the special permission of Charles Scribner's Sons.

Langston Hughes, "Salvation," from *The Big Sea* by Langston Hughes. Copyright 1940 by Langston Hughes. Copyright renewed © 1968 by Arna Bontemps and George Houston Bass. Reprinted with permission of Hill and Wang, a division of Farrar, Straus, & Giroux, Inc.

Susan Jacoby, "When Bright Girls Decide That Math Is a Waste of Time," from *The New York Times.* Copyright © 1983 by Susan Jacoby. Reprinted by permission of Susan Jacoby.

Elizabeth Janeway, "Soaps, Cynicism, and Mind Control," from *Ms.,* January 1985. Copyright © 1985 by Elizabeth Janeway. Reprinted by permission of Elizabeth Janeway.

Rachel Jones, "What's Wrong with Black English?" from *Newsweek,* December 1982. Copyright © 1982 by Newsweek. Reprinted with permission.

Suzanne Britt Jordan, "Fun, Oh Boy. Fun. You Could Die From It," from *The New York Times,* December 23, 1979. Copyright © 1979 by The New York Times Company. Reprinted by permission.

Garrison Keillor, "A Return to Basics: Mealtime without Guilt," from *The New York Times,* February 2, 1983. Copyright © 1983 by The New York Times Company. Reprinted by permission.

Judy Klemesrud, "Sportorial Splendor," from *The New York Times Sunday Magazine,* March 31, 1985. Copyright © 1985 by The New York Times Company. Reprinted by permission.

Joseph Wood Krutch, "Reverence for Life: The Vandal and the Sportsman," from *The Great Chain of Life* by Joseph Wood Krutch. Copyright © 1956 by Joseph Wood Krutch. Reprinted by permission of Houghton Mifflin Company.

Akira Kurosawa, "Babyhood," from *Something Like an Autobiography,* by Akira Kurosawa, translated by Audie E. Bock. Copy-

Leo Rosten, "How to Tell a Joke." Reprinted with permission from the June 1985 *Reader's Digest*. Copyright © 1985 by The Reader's Digest Assn., Inc.

Howard Scott, "Vegetable Gardens Are for the Birds," from *The New York Times,* May 5, 1985. Copyright © 1985 by The New York Times Company. Reprinted by permission.

Richard Selzer, "The Discus Thrower," from *Confessions of a Knife* by Richard Selzer. Reprinted by permission of Georges Borchardt, Inc. Copyright © 1977 by Richard Selzer.

John Slote, "The Social Sport," from *Esquire,* July 1982: "Sports Clinic." Copyright © 1982 by John Slote. Reprinted by permission of John Slote.

George Steiner, "The Future of Reading." This is excerpted from the R. R. Bowker Memorial Lecture delivered by Dr. George Steiner on April 8, 1985, in New York City, and first published in *Publishers Weekly* under the title "Books in an Age of Post-Literacy." Copyright © 1985 by George Steiner. Reprinted by permission of George Borchardt, Inc.

Judy Syfers, "I Want a Wife," from *The First Ms. Reader.* Copyright © 1970 by Judy Syfers. Reprinted by permission of Judy Syfers.

Lewis Thomas, "Death in the Open," from *The Lives of a Cell* by Lewis Thomas. Copyright © 1973 by the Massachusetts Medical Society. Originally published in the *New England Journal of Medicine.* Reprinted by permission of Viking Penguin, Inc.

Judith Viorst, "Friends, Good Friends—and Such Good Friends." Copyright © 1977 by Judith Viorst. Originally appeared in *Redbook.* Reprinted by permission of Lescher & Lescher, Ltd.

Eudora Welty, "One Writer's Beginnings," from *One Writer's Beginnings.* Copyright © 1983, 1984 by Eudora Welty. Reprinted by permission of Harvard University Press.

E. B. White, "The Three New Yorks," from pages 121–122 in "Here Is New York," in *Essays of E. B. White.* Copyright © 1949 by E. B. White. Reprinted by permission of Harper & Row, Publishers, Inc.

Randall Williams, "Daddy Tucked the Blanket," from *The New York Times,* July 10, 1975. Copyright © 1975 by The New York Times Company. Reprinted by permission.

Elizabeth Wong, "The Struggle to Be an All-American Girl." Originally appeared in the *Los Angeles Times.* Reprinted by permission of Elizabeth Wong.

Jade Snow Wong, "Uncle Kwok," from pages 44–45 in *Fifth Chinese Daughter* by Jade Snow Wong. Copyright 1950 by Jade Snow

Wong. Reprinted by permission of Harper & Row, Publishers, Inc.

Al Young, "Java Jive," copyright © 1984 by Al Young. Reprinted with permission of the author and Creative Arts Book Company.

William Zinsser, "Simplicity," from *On Writing Well*. Copyright © 1976 by William K. Kinsser. Reprinted by permission of the author.